SAP® ERP Financials: Configuration and Design

PRESS

SAP PRESS is a joint initiative of SAP and Galileo Press. The know-how offered by SAP specialists combined with the expertise of the publishing house Galileo Press offers the reader expert books in the field. SAP PRESS features first-hand information and expert advice, and provides useful skills for professional decision-making.

SAP PRESS offers a variety of books on technical and business related topics for the SAP user. For further information, please visit our website: *www.sap-press.com*.

Nancy Muir, Ian Kimbell
Discover SAP
2008, 426 pp., ISBN 978-1-59229-117-5

Manish Patel
Discover SAP ERP Financials
2008, 544 pp., ISBN 978-1-59229-184-7

Aylin Korkmaz
Financial Reporting with SAP
2008 670 pp., ISBN 1-978-59229-179-1

Shivesh Sharma
Optimize Your SAR ERP Financial Implementation
2008, 570 pp., ISBN 978-1-59229-160-1

Naeem Arif, Sheikh Tauseef

SAP® ERP Financials: Configuration and Design

Galileo Press

Bonn · Boston

ISBN 978-1-59229-136-6

1st Edition 2008

Acquisitions Editor   Stephen Soloman
Copy Editor   Ruth Saveedra
Cover Design   Silke Braun
Layout Design   Vera Brauner
Production   Todd Brown
Typesetting   Publishers' Design and Production Services, Inc.
Printed and bound in Canada

Contents at a Glance

Contents

3 Financial Accounting Component (FI) Global Settings 67

7 Asset Accounting 265

cost center } –
profit center }

8 Controlling Component (CO) in SAP ERP 323

11 Period-End Closing 415

12 SAP ERP Financials Reporting 425

Acknowledgments

I would like to acknowledge the support and love of my family which has been ever-present during my life and enabled me to achieve the things I have achieved. Without my parents' parvarish, my wife's support and my own religious faith I doubt I would be where I am today. To my children, you are my inspiration and reason for all I achieve, I hope this book inspires you in your lives ahead.

Naeem Arif

I would like to thank my parents, sisters and brother, Hafeez, my wife, and my children, Rayyan and Zayna for all their prayers and support which made it possible for me to complete this book.

Tauseef Sheikh Muhammad

Thanks go to all the staff at Galileo Press who have been there throughout the project; their support, guidance and availability at the other end of the telephone line has been greatly appreciated.

To the reader: we have taken a lot of time and effort to ensure that the quality of the book you are reading is high. Our goal was to create a book that we were proud of, and we would be pleased to know if while reading this book you feel that you have learned things which were useful to you in the "real world."

This chapter explains the purpose of writing this book and what will be covered. The topics covered in this chapter will take you from some basic concepts all the way through to very advanced configuration topics covered in the next chapters.

1 Overview

1.1 Introduction

In this introduction chapter we explain the approach we use throughout this book and also provide some basic explanations of SAP and how SAP projects work. We end the chapter with some navigation basics that you should all be aware of.

We have taken the approach of applying the configuration to a fictitious organization that we hope has enabled us to bring a real-world holistic explanation of each concept. We include all aspects of the Finance component and explain how the sections integrate together. We also include specific examples, where relevant, from the US and Europe to provide global examples for to show the configuration and application of this important area of most SAP systems.

1.1.1 Key Objectives

The key objective of this book is to serve as a guide that will enable you to configure either a complete SAP ERP Financials solution, or just the parts that are relevant to your business scenario. Significant emphasis has been placed on providing as much real-world process, implementation, and configuration information as possible. As no two SAP ERP Financials implementations are the same, care has been taken to provide industry-proven best practices that can be extended easily to your specific focus.

Note that many references are made throughout this text to your "business partner." If you are a consultant using this book as part of a client implementation, upgrade, or training scenario, your business partner is obvious: the team of stakeholders you are or will be working with as you apply your expertise. If you are an end user, project manager, technical staff member, or line manager assigned to an SAP ERP Financials implementation, your business partner is, to a large extent, similar to that of a consultant's. In this instance, however, you may need to shoulder the dual burden of meeting the overall organizational goals while also making sure that your individual or department business requirements are met. Your "business user" requires you to wear two hats: a business requirements hat and a configuration hat. The goal of this book is to help you make good decisions while alternately wearing both hats, specifically by providing you with a roadmap for the following:

- Developing a plan for the implementation of an SAP ERP Financials solution
- Defining all of the steps necessary to configure the main functional areas (general ledger, accounts payable, accounts receivable, asset accounting, controlling, activation of the new, etc.)
- Highlighting the best practices, design considerations and configuration activities for each of these subcomponents

The focus of this book, and the implementation roadmap contained herein, will largely be on standard SAP functionality. SAP ERP Financials (indeed, the Business Suite as a whole) provides significant flexibility for most businesses and business processes right "out of the box."

1.1.2 Approach

- Each chapter of this book provides sufficient information to enable the reader to complete the configuration tasks that most organizations require. This approach is based on the implementation of SAP ERP Financials within a number of different environments in the United States and Europe. Whereas no book can claim to cover every possible implementation scenario, the representative samples given throughout this book are real-world examples of direct experiences and should satisfy the needs of most readers.

- This book is not designed to explain in detail how every possible scenario works, but to provide guidance on how to deliver a solution to your business partner. We have given relevant examples from our experience with different clients in different countries to give you a real flavour of an SAP implementation. We have also highlighted key questions that you should consider when developing your working solution design.

1.1.3 Versioning

This book covers SAP ERP Central Component (ECC) version 6.0. For implementations or upgrades that may require some degree of backward compatibility, we have provided pointers and explanations of how the configuration and design would work in previous versions of SAP.

1.1.4 Learning Outcomes

This book is designed to be read as a start-to-finish resource for planning and implementing SAP ERP Financials. However, consultants, project managers, or others with some SAP experience can "cherry-pick" the chapters that are relevant to their particular scenario. Regardless of how it is read, anyone using this book can be expected to master the following:

- Determining which configuration activities are relevant based on your organisational requirements for a successful SAP ERP Financials implementation
- Understanding of the impacts of the decisions you make and how to make best use of the system to fulfil your organizations' needs
- The configuration of all aspects of the SAP Financials module, including the main subcomponents (as already listed).

1.1.5 Assumptions

The main assumption being made is that the reader has access to an SAP system within which they can apply and test their learning from this book. SAP education is reliant on the user having time to try out the configuration steps themselves and apply their own business requirements. Simply trying to learn from the pages and screenshots will not be sufficient to complete your implementation. You should therefore get access to a system, most projects or live systems have a sandpit area for you to test things in.

▶ Before we move on to the SAP implementation overview, it would make sense to mention the brief history of SAP.

1.2 Brief history of SAP

SAP stands for Systems, Applications, and Products in Data Processing and was founded in 1972 by five former IBM engineers. SAP has been hugely successful and is globally recognized as a world class Enterprise Resource Planning (ERP) solution. Its success is based on the fact that it provides the user with an integrated Financial Ledger, Sales Ledger, Purchase Ledger, and Management Information system. Historically, computer systems used to integrate by way of complex interfaces.

In terms of revenues, SAP is the world's largest business software company and the third-largest independent software provider. It operates in three geographic regions namely:

▶ EMEA (Europe, Middle East and Africa)

▶ Americas (both North America and Latin America)

▶ Asia Pacific Japan (Japan, Australia and parts of Asia)

In addition, SAP operates a network of 115 subsidiaries, and has Research and Development facilities around the world in Germany, North America, Canada, China, Hungary, India, Israel and Bulgaria. SAP has more than 100,000 successful implementations in over 120 countries with a customer base of more than 41000 companies. There main product is SAP ERP (Enterprise Resource Planning). The name of its predecessor, SAP R/3 reflects its functionality where the "R" stands for real-time and the number "3" relates to a 3-tier client-server architecture (database layer, application layer and presentation layer).

The complex nature of SAP and its presence as a market leader is only realized through a correct implementation route. SAP does not just come out of a box like an installation of Microsoft Office. We spend a little time explaining to the user the SAP Implementation process. Different organizations adopt variations on this approach based on specific needs and requirements.

1.3 SAP Implementation Overview

The following is a brief overview of a typical SAP implementation project that may serve as a useful guide to supplement your own projects methodology and approach. This overview will focus on the following:

▶ A brief description of each phase

▶ A list and brief description of the documentation required during each phase

▶ The deliverables required from each phase

Most organizations adopt an implementation methodology based on SAP's Accelerated SAP (ASAP) model. This model was developed to ensure the successful on-time delivery of projects by providing templates, methods, tools etc that have been built on the successful experiences of thousands of previous SAP implementations. The following sections include an overview of an ASAP implementation; many of the topics discussed are relevant to a variety of different scenarios.

An ASAP project road map generally includes the following phases:

▶ Project preparation

▶ Business blueprint

▶ Realization

▶ Final preparation

▶ Go live and support

Project Preparation

The initial phase of the project is where critical planning and preparation work is done. Each project should have a clearly defined objective and a carefully articulated plan for achieving it. This is common to all projects. The deliverables from this phase should include the following:

▶ **Confirmation of high-level scope**
Identify the modules that needs to be implemented like Financials, Controlling, Materials Management etc.

▶ **Agreement on a technology plan**
Have key IT and functional stakeholders committed to a concrete technology plan (i.e., which SAP versions to use)?

▶ **Project milestones dates**
The key dates will be set for achieving different milestones during the life of the project (e.g., business blueprint, unit testing, integration testing, etc.).

▶ **Definition of the methodology**
Supported by a project organizational structure (with resources assigned to positions) that will best place you to deliver this.

These points should be combined into a project charter that will be referred back to during the project as the overriding principles and guidelines for the project.

Addressing these issues early in the project helps ensure that the project proceeds efficiently and that a solid foundation for a successful SAP implementation is established.

Business Blueprint

As with the construction of a large building, your SAP ERP Financials implementation project should have a clear conceptual design to guide the build stages. The conceptual design is usually arrived at through discussion meetings and workshops with key business stakeholders. The purpose of this collaborative process is to collect valid current business requirements (which we will call the "as-is") and confirm how the SAP solution will deliver these requirements (which we will call the "to-be"). This information is then incorporated into a business blueprint document.

The blueprint stage can be a difficult but important stage to work through as you need to garner acceptance of the "foundations" upon which to build your system from a broad range of stakeholders, some of whom may have limited SAP or technology experience. It can be difficult to translate a highly conceptual design into a concrete implementation strategy for those team members, but it is a critical factor for success in this phase of the project.

Real-World Example: Building a Prototype

Building a prototype for nontechnical or non-SAP users during blueprinting will allow these key stakeholders and business partners to better understand the solution. Translating the highly conceptual design into a functional or semifunctional prototype that gives stakeholders a view of both the as-is and the to-be can have a significant impact on the overall blueprinting and implementation process. It helps the configuration team quickly build the system based on a design that incorporates every stakeholder's input and helps avoid scenarios in which your business partner determines that the solution built and delivered varies significantly from the conceptual design.

In addition to producing the business blueprint document, many other tasks need to be carried out during this phase in order for the project to successfully progress to the next phase. These include:

▶ Capture of the valid current business requirements and process defintion of how things will work in the future (as-is and to-be design)

▶ Capture of all significant reporting requirements, with basic information about the characteristics and key figures involved (list of reporting requirements)

▶ Confirmation of functionality that is not delivered by standard SAP and will require some custom development (list of enhancements)

▶ Construction of a prototype system to demonstrate the functionality of the solution that is being signed off

▶ Confirmation of any interfaces to be built to other systems

▶ Setup of an issues and risk register that identifies overall issues and risks that you will work through during the project lifecycle

▶ Identification of data migration strategy from legacy systems

▶ Mobilization of resources for training and change management

▶ Installation of the development system

Realization

This phase of the project is the busiest, as it centers around actually building the system based on the agreed-upon business blueprint. This phase covers the configuration and development of enhancements right through to the testing phases.

The realization phase is generally the longest phase of the project and includes many of the following deliverables:

▶ Technical building of the system, including configuration, definition of reports, and building of enhancements and interfaces

▶ Implementation of organizational change management and internal communications strategy

▶ Development of test scripts and performance of unit testing and integration testing

▶ Development and delivery of user training and documentation

▶ Definition and configuration of user roles for access to the system

- Detailing field mapping and cleansing activities for data migration
- Building the cutover plan to control activities during the go-live period

Final Preparation (Cut over)

The final preparation phase of the project should mostly focus on the completion of administrator and end-user training and the beginning of the data load exercise. It is often referred to as the cut over period, when we "cut over" to transfer existing data, functions and users from an old system to a new system in a synchronized manner.

The final preparation phase should include the following deliverables:

- Closure of any open issues such as development of reports, training, etc.
- Completion of training
- Migration of static master data
- Communication to the organization of the terms of go-live and post-go-live support
- Development of a disaster recovery scenario
- Receipt of final sign-offs (go or no-go decision)

Go Live and Support

Once the system is live, you may experience a high level of support calls initially, but expect to see this level drop off as the system settles down and the users become accustomed to it.

Depending on the support solution in place, you may find that the original project team handles the first period of support and then gradually transitions the calls to the designated support team.

Summary

This is a very brief overview of the ASAP process for implementation and it is only designed as a guide for inexperienced SAP users. You should always take time to understand the methodology being adopted locally on your project as there can always be variations.

In the final section of the introduction we talk through the basic navigation steps that all readers should be aware of. We include this section in the introduction so as to ensure that all readers have the same basic level of navigation understanding.

1.4 SAP Navigation Basics

This section is included to ensure that all readers are at the same level of understanding with the latest release of SAP ECC 6.0. We recommend that you go through this section to ensure that you are comfortable with the navigation as this is important for the entire book.

1.4.1 Logging on to SAP system

When you log onto SAP, you are not directly logging onto SAP, but on a front-end which is linked to the SAP database. This link is created by a program called SAP GUI (Graphical User Interface). This is the standard program which is used to access all SAP systems. It is possible to have different SAP systems, usually you will have a development system and at least 1 testing system as well as the Production system, which is the real system that live transactions are eventually posted in. We access SAP systems through a Logon Pad as shown in Figure 1.1. The logon pad has all the system addresses in it which all you to connect your SAP system.

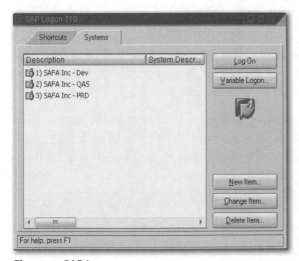

Figure 1.1 SAP Logon

The system settings are stored in a file on your machine called the saplogin.ini file. This file is normally preconfigured centrally and then made available to all the users. Once you have been provided with the SAP Logon, you need a username and password to logon to SAP system. The username and password is unique for each user and you do have an option to change your password using the New Password button available on the screen shown in Figure 1.2.

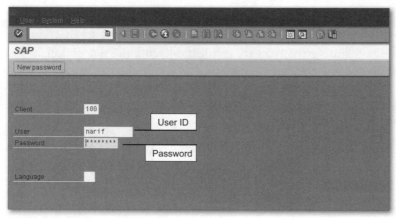

Figure 1.2 Logging on to SAP

When you are logging on to SAP system, you can select the logon language which is supported by that system. Please note that SAP system supports many languages, English must be maintained on all systems with the option to include other languages.

Once you are logged on to the system using your username and password, you can work in several sessions (windows) of an SAP system which could be used for individual processing but the maximum sessions can be 6.

For the reasons of security and licensing, SAP now detects multiple logons from release 4.6 onwards. If the same user logs on more than once, then for each subsequent logon, the system displays a warning message that gives the user three options mentioned below:

▶ Continue with this logon and end any other logons in the system

▶ Continue with this logon without ending any other logons in the system (this will be logged by SAP)

▶ Terminate this logon

1.4.2 Screen structure in SAP system

After logging on successfully, the first screen that appears is known as the SAP Easy Access screen as shown in Figure 1.3 below. This screen is the default initial screen in SAP systems. The left side of the screen contains a tree hierarchy of the menus available to you in the SAP system.

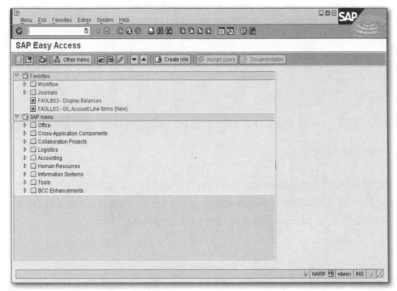

Figure 1.3 SAP Easy Access Screen

A standard SAP screen is shown in Figure 1.4. We will explain some of the key elements of a standard screen in this section.

▶ **Menu bar**

The menu bar is the top line of any main window in the SAP system. The menus shown here depend on which application you are currently working in.

▶ **Command field**

You have an option to start an application by directly entering its transaction code in the command field which is hidden as default.

▶ **Standard toolbar**

The pushbuttons in the standard toolbar are shown on every SAP screen. The push buttons that cannot be used in a specific application are deactivated. You can view the flag with the name or function of the pushbutton if you place the cursor on it for a few second.

▶ **Title bar**

The title bar names the function that you are currently working in.

▶ **Application toolbar**

This shows the pushbuttons available in the application that you are currently working in.

▶ **Checkboxes**

The checkboxes allow you to select several options from a group of fields.

▶ **Radio buttons**

Radio buttons are also options available for selection but remember that you can only select one option in this case.

▶ **Tab**

The tabs allow you to group similar type of fields in different sub-screens to improve clarity.

▶ **Status bar**

The status bar displays information on the current system status, such as warnings and errors. You can also change the display variant to show, for example, the transaction code of the transaction you are currently in.

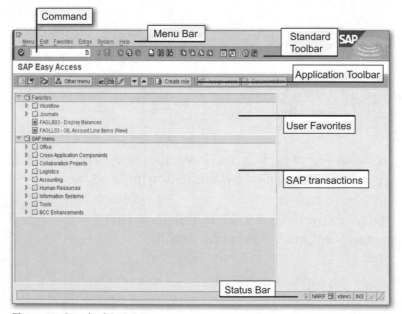

Figure 1.4 Standard SAP Screen

1.4.3 Creating your Favorites List

Once you have logged on, on the left side of screen you have two overview trees at your disposal for selecting functions:

▶ The favorites list

▶ The SAP Menu or role-based user menu

You can use the favorites list for SAP system functions or links to the files on the end users front-end computer or links to Internet content. The favorites list, which is empty as a default, can be changed by each end user according to his own requirements and you can only view your own favorites list. As the structure of the favorites is stored within the SAP system, each user could have different collections of favorites in different systems. You have the flexibility to organize favorites into folders. The Favorites menu gives you the option of adding a function from the SAP or user menu to your own created favorites list by selecting the function and choosing Favorites Ð Add. You can also use the mouse to drag & drop functions into your favorite lists.

1.4.4 Calling Functions in SAP system

There are several options available to you to navigate in SAP systems which are as follows:

▶ Using transaction codes in the command field

▶ Selecting items from menus in the menu bar

▶ Selecting items from the favorites list or from the user or SAP menus

In the command field, you can use many different commands but we have explained a few which we consider are important and used on a regular basis:

▶ From the SAP Easy Access screen, you can call any transaction using its code xxxx without any prefix (where xxxx is referred to as a transaction code).

▶ /n to cancel the current transaction you are working in

▶ /nxxxx to call transaction xxxx directly from another transaction.

▶ /oxxxx to call transaction xxxx in a new session directly from another transaction

▶ /nend to end the logon session with a confirmation dialog box

▶ /nex to end the logon session without a confirmation dialog box

▶ /i to delete the session you are currently using

▶ /o to display an overview of your sessions

1.4.5 Accessing the Customization area

When logging on you are always taken the same initial screens that we have looked at in Figure 1.3. This takes you into the application side, or user side of the system. This is where you process system transactions, maintain master data and run reports. The other side of the system that you need to access as an SAP Consultant will be the configuration side. Customization (commonly referred to as Configuration) is the process by which we make settings in SAP tables to setup the way we want our system to work. This is the main reason why SAP is such a powerful system as you can customize it to meet your own specific business requirements.

SAP provide an Implementation Guide (referred to as the IMG), which structures these activities and make it easier to complete. There are 2 routes through which we can access the IMG as seen in Figure 1.5 and Figure 1.6.

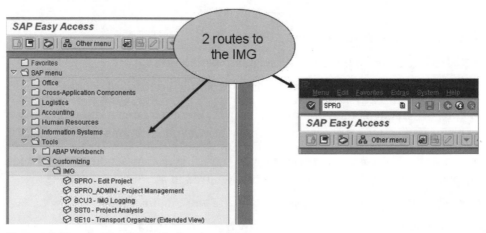

Figure 1.5 Accessing the Customization Area_Routes

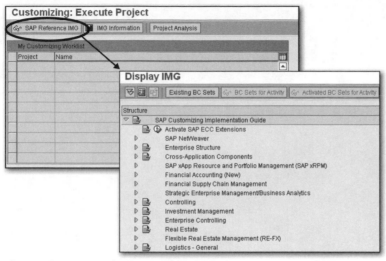

Figure 1.6 Accessing the Customization Area

1.5　Summary

This concludes our introduction to the book as well as some basic concepts in SAP. We believe that these concepts will be very useful for you to get the maximum benefit from the rest of this book. The key learning points of this chapter were:

▶ Key objectives of the book

▶ Brief history of SAP

▶ Overview of SAP implementation

▶ Some basic navigation techniques

In the next chapter we start off our SAP learning with a look at the SAP Enterprise Structure which will set the foundation for configuring the SAP ERP Financials module.

This chapter sets the foundation for configuring the SAP ERP Financials Component. It explains the role of each of the components and gives an understanding of how they interrelate. This chapter should be completed before you configure any of the SAP ERP Financials subcomponents: GL, Accounts Payable (AP), Accounts Receivable (AR), and Asset Accounting (AA).

2   SAP Enterprise Structure

The objective of this chapter is to explain the configuration required to define your SAP enterprise structure. The enterprise structure is the set of key building blocks that need to be put in place to support the rest of your system configuration. Decisions made here regarding system design will be taken forward into the other chapters as these configuration decisions underpin the whole Financials module.

The enterprise structure needs to be defined early in the project to provide a basic structure within which each module team can design, in detail, their own areas. Projects where the enterprise structure is not closed down early can become problematic and can lead to significant implementation issues and cost overruns. It is best to lock down the enterprise structure before undertaking any detailed design to reduce the risk of making detailed design decisions based on a fluid design.

This chapter will cover:

▶ Explanation of the functionality the enterprise structure objects deliver

▶ Explanation of the configuration steps involved in setting up these objects

▶ Details regarding integration between these objects and the rest of the system

The chapter starts by reviewing some of the key discussion areas you should incorporate into your blueprint workshops.

This chapter sets the scene for the remainder of the book, and it should be read first to understand the enterprise structure as a result of SAP ERP Central Component (ECC) 6.0 release.

2.1 Building an Enterprise Structure

Finance enterprise structure is mostly concerned with organizational structures. The key characteristics of your organization that will help in determining your enterprise structure should include:

▶ Legal reporting requirements

▶ Taxation policies

▶ Internal management reporting requirements

▶ Nature of the business operations (e.g., ways of working may differ in different parts of the business)

From a high-level point of view, the following questions should factor heavily into your workshops with your business partners when creating a design for your SAP enterprise structure.

What are your legal entities and business units?

When considering these, you need to determine at what level you want to define your company codes and your cost center and profit center structures. In organizations with many company codes, you also need to consider your needs for your controlling area settings. Specifically, you should decide:

▶ How many company codes you need

▶ What level do you set your controlling areas (discussed in more detail later in this chapter)

▶ What is the relationship between account assignment objects (e.g., cost center and profit center)

What are your internal and external reporting requirements?

Internal reporting requirements are different from external reporting requirements. With ECC 6, SAP ERP offers you a new account assignment object called a segment which can be used to provide an additional reporting dimension. This is discussed in more detail in Chapter 4.

What currencies do you expect to use, and will they differ by companycode?

What currency or currencies will you operate in your solution. In Chapter 4, we discuss the options of maintaining multiple ledgers. If multiple currencies are applicable to your scenario, you should consider the options in Chpater 4.

What decisions have been made in terms of planning and budgeting?'

What level of planning are you expecting to do within your solution, and where do you want to store your budgeting and forecasting figures. This may influence the objects you need to create and the levels of hierarchies.

What interfaces do you currently have, and what do you want to retain?

This is an important decision step early in your scope definition. Maybe you are coming from a scenario with many systems, and a key benefit of your SAP implementation is to migrate to a single system. You will need to consider the specific functionality that you are going to replace in each of these systems and then decide on how they will factor into the overall system design.

2.2   Building a Straw Man

Before you start on a major project like an SAP ERP Financials implementation, it is normally a good idea to have a plan for achieving the main goals and objectives. Many SAP project teams start with a rough outline of how they envision their system design meeting their organizational requirements. Such an outline is usually described as a straw man and it normally functions as a first draft for the system framework or enterprise structure.

Figure 2.1 features a sample straw man that you may use to build your own. It is important to make informed decisions about your enterprise structure objects, or your design will fall apart, as the design may not integrate, especially across modules.

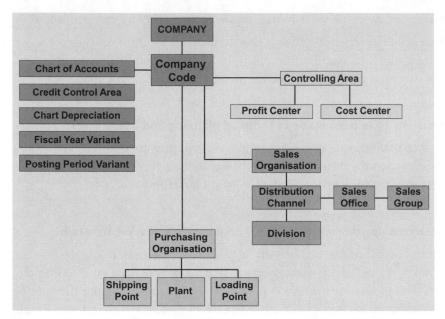

Figure 2.1 Generic Straw Man, Showing the Common Enterprise Structure Objects

If you are at the start of your project and feeling uncomfortable with making such decisions without a good understanding of the objects, setting aside time in your project plan at this point to configure a prototype solution on a small scale to test some of your key business processes may be appropriate This will allow you to check that your understanding of how to use these objects is correct The creation of a prototype is a very worthwhile exercise and will allow you to make better decisions about the way in which you want to use the system and allow you to test some scenarios that you cannot visualize.

Before we look at the configuration of enterprise structure, we first review the purpose of the main objects in order to give the reader some background knowledge. Detailed information on these objects and the configuration and process aspects of each will be covered throughout the book.

2.2.1 Company Code

The company code is a very important mandatory object that needs to be defined. Its purpose is to represent a legal entity and thus enable the production of a complete set of accounts. For some organizations this can be defined at different levels depending on the wider scope of your design. You should consider the following points when making decisions about defining company codes:

▶ Do you have separate legal entities?

▶ Do you operate in different countries and thus produce financial statements in those countries?

▶ Do you have a sizeable organization that you want to report on discrete business units?

Because your decision impacts your internal business processing and reporting, it is important to ensure that the level at which you define your company code offers the most flexibility as well as sufficiently detailed information. It is not necessary to stick to the legal entity requirements, and you may choose to appoint your company code at a lower level to reflect business units or departments. For instance, some organizations may define company code in line with their business units, which consolidate into the same legal entity. If this is your decision, you need to define the process through which you consolidate your figures in order to satisfy your external financial reporting requirements. Alternatively, some organizations will decide to have company code at a higher level and use the SAP ERP Controlling (CO) objects to create their departmental analysis by use of cost or profit centers within a structured hierarchy.

2.2.2 Cost Center

Cost centers are the primary cost collection objects in the Controlling Component (CO). Whereas it is possible to post both income and expenses to a cost center, the recommended approach is to only associate costs with a cost center.

Cost centers are assigned to a single controlling area and a single company code. Cost centers can also be assigned to a profit center (many cost centers can point to the same profit center), which is an important part of your controlling design. Because cost centers represent parts of the organizational structure, by grouping them together into a cost center hierarchy, you can provide analysis of costs to reflect the different parts of the organization.

A more detailed explanation of the use of cost centers is given in Chapter 8, Section 8.4.3.

Profit Center

Profit centers are the primary revenue collection objects in the system. Some organizations do not recognize profit centers and initially expect not to use them at all, as the concept is strange to them. The profit center actually sits opposite the cost center, and whereas a cost center may represent the costs generated by a department, the profit center collects the revenue for that part of the organization. Profit centers are also posted to for all balance sheet postings. As mentioned in the previous section, a cost center can be attributed to a profit center. In this situation, the profit center will also collect the costs from the cost centers to which it is linked and thus can provide some basic revenue versus expenditure analysis.

Profit centers are assigned to a single controlling area and a single company code. They can also be grouped together into a hierarchy to represent the organizational structure and thus provide analysis of income versus expenditure for the different parts of the organization.

A more detailed explanation of the use of profit centers is given in Chapter 8, Section 8.4.5.

2.2.3   Chart of Accounts

The chart of accounts is the set of GL account codes that you to use to provide an analysis of your financial accounts. The chart of accounts can be assigned to one or many company codes and is purely a Financial Accounting Component (FI) object.

2.2.4   Controlling Area

The controlling area is the organizational unit that defines the boundary in which you can allocate costs and revenues to account assignment objects (e.g., cost center, profit center, etc). Controlling areas structure the internal accounting operations of an organization within Controlling.

The controlling area is essentially the internally defined level at which you produce management reporting analysis. International organizations may set their controlling areas by international boundaries, as this often represents boundaries for legal reporting requirements as well. It can also be set at a lower level than that, so organizations may decide to have controlling areas representing discrete business functions. Remember, it is possible to get your departmental reporting analysis from your cost center and profit Center hierarchies.

Company codes are assigned to controlling areas, so a controlling area can have one or many company codes assigned to it. A company code cannot be assigned to more than one controlling area, though.

2.2.5 Business Area

Although Figure 2.1 does not make direct reference to it, it is important to note the role of business areas here. Business areas were used in SAP ERP prior to Profit Center Accounting to provide departmental reporting analysis. Organizations can use business areas to track postings relating to different parts of the business and thus provide additional analysis.

Although the functionality has been largely overtaken by the development of profit centers, internal orders, and profitability analysis, business area functionality remains in the system, and some organizations may use it to satisfy minor business requirements.

Business areas can be used for both balance sheet and profit and loss analysis. An organization cannot assign bank, equity, or tax information to business areas directly, so it is not possible to create legally required financial statements or tax reports using only business areas.

2.2.6 Chart of Depreciation

This is the controlling object in relation to control and depreciation of fixed assets. We discuss this in more detail in Chapter 7.

Having looked at the main enterprise structure objects, we describe the linkage between these objects in the next section as we build the conceptual design of our system.

2.3 Straw Man Design

Having collected together all of the requirements, the production of a straw man design of the enterprise structure is a good idea. This puts together a picture of the decisions made, and the resultant enterprise structure that is produced. You can draw your straw man at whatever level you want. For instance, straw men can be drawn with spider diagrams shooting off the nodes explaining more detailed design. This is entirely at your discretion, in line with the level of competency and detail that you have achieved in the blueprint. Our rule is always: the more detail you can include at this stage, the better.

It is safe to say that the straw man we put together in Figure 2.2 would be a minimal straw man, and if you are unable to get to this level, you should consider spending more time finalizing your design before moving to the next phase of the project.

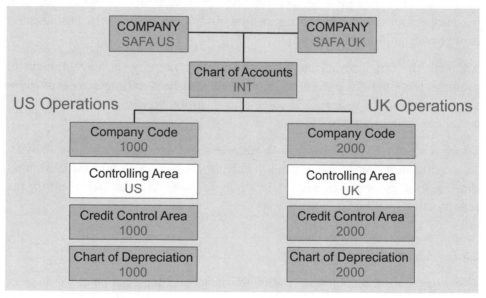

Figure 2.2 Straw Man Showing Conceptual Design for SAFA Inc.

Now that we have a straw man design in place, we can move onto the build phase of this design, that is, configuration.

2.4   Configuration of Enterprise Structure

In the following discussions throughout the book, we will try to explain the steps needed to complete the configuration activity. The reader should be able to link the text and the screenshots to what they are seeing on their own SAP screens. If you have discrepancies, this could be due to version differences (we are following an SAP ERP ECC 6 script), or maybe you have made related configuration settings that caused the difference.

Structure configuration is split into two parts. First, we define all of the components of the enterprise structure which are found together in the same area of the IMG, as shown in Figure 2.3.

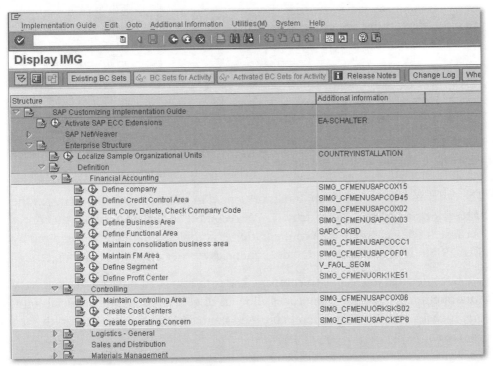

Figure 2.3 Enterprise Structure Definition

Then we make the correct assignments of these components in the accompanying area of the IMG as shown in Figure 2.4.

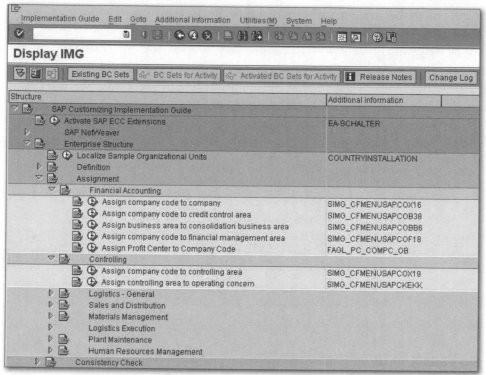

Figure 2.4 Enterprise Structure Assignment

The order in which the information is presented in this section is important, as the IMG is organized by type of activity. We recommend that you follow this order because it will ensure that the configuration is completed in the order required by SAP ERP to take into account the dependencies between the different objects.

We have decided to create two company codes to represent our London and New York operations. Two company codes allow us to generate separate financial statements easily and to assign different business controls (e.g., tax procedures) to each operation.

2.4.1 Define Company

Above the company code, we will first create a company, which is usually a consolidation entity. Users do not actually need to see this and thus will not know what this is, but it will be used for consolidation purposes.

The company is simply a place holder, and you need to give it a name. For our solution, we will create two companies as shown in Figure 2.5. It may be possible to create a single company ID and consolidate both the U.S. and UK company codes. We have chosen not to do this. If in the future SAFA Inc. makes acquisitions in the United States or Europe, then we may want to consolidate operations by geographical location. If we quickly consolidate now, we may restrict our options in the future.

The Company ID is created by following the menu path **IMG • Enterprise Structure • Definition • Financial Accounting • Define Company** or with Transaction code OX15.

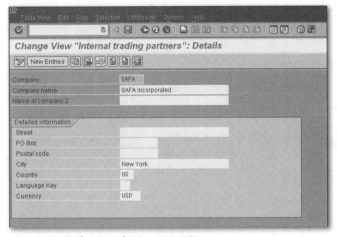

Figure 2.5 Definition of a Company ID

We need two company IDs, for the U.S. and UK operations. Both are merely place-holders against which to record information.

2.4.2 Define Fiscal Year Variant

The fiscal year variant is the object within which we define the period control, that is, the dates of the accounting period. The settings made here control how the document posting date relates to accounting periods. It also controls the period number (see also material periods in the Materials Management component). SAP ERP allows up to 16 posting periods, which reflect the 12 months of the year, as well as 4 special periods that you may use for adjustments where needed.

Organizations can adopt different principles, for instance, a calendar year. The U.S. federal government uses an October to September year, and the UK tax year runs from April to March. You can configure your own variant if your requirements are not available.

This configuration activity is located outside the enterprise structure area, and you will need to look elsewhere in the IMG. In SAP ERP ECC 6.0, you will find the configuration steps in the menu path **IMG • Financial Accounting (new) • Financial Accounting Global Settings • Ledgers • Fiscal Year and Posting Periods • Maintain Fiscal Year Variant**, or use Transaction code OB29.

For SAFA, Inc. we are going to implement an April (Period 1) to March (Period 12) fiscal year variant. Click on **New Entries** (Figure 2.6) to define a new variant, or copy the SAP ERP standard variant K4.

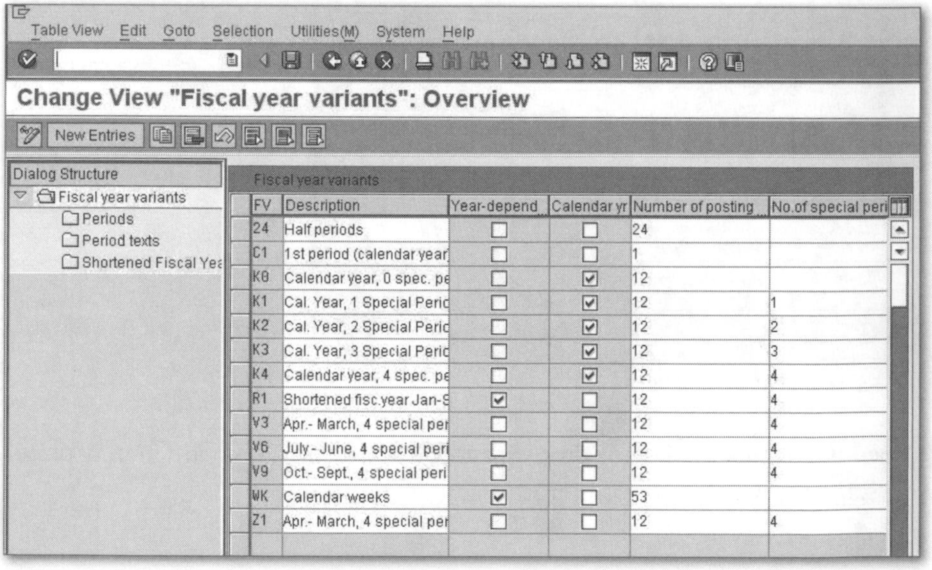

Figure 2.6 Define Fiscal Year Variant

Fiscal year variant Z1 has 12 posting periods, but the 4 special periods may not make sense to you at first. These are additional periods you can make adjustments in when you don't want to go back and make adjustments in closed periods.

You need to define your periods so that we know to what they relate. In an April to March financial year, April is period 1, as shown in Figure 2.7.

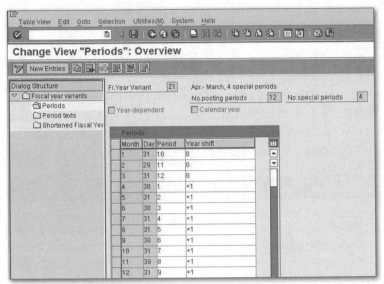

Figure 2.7 Definition of Periods within a Fiscal Year Variant

We assign the fiscal year variant after we have created the company code.

2.4.3 Define Posting Period Variant

The posting period variant is used to control which accounting period is open for posting. This way you can ensure that closed periods remain balanced and reconciled. During your period end processing, you may need to close down subledgers separately and add controls to your posting period variant to represent subledgers.

The posting period variant controls which ledgers are open and closed at any given time, in terms of your ability to posted to them. Finance departments operate a period-end or month-end process to record the financial performance in that period. After completion of this exercise, the old periods are usually closed down to prevent postings being made to them.

The close (locking) of periods process is not usually done as a complete close at a point in time. Instead, the subledgers are closed down one at a time. For instance, sales is usually the first subledger be closed down, so any new sales are posted into the new period only. The next to be closed down would be purchasing, to give a little extra time for invoices to be processed in the old period before it is closed down. A more detailed discussion of the closure of posting periods in the period end cycle is covered in Chapter 11.

The configuration activity for creating the posting period variant is found in the menu path **Financial Accounting (new) • Ledgers • Fiscal Year and Posting Periods • Posting Periods • Define Variants for Open Posting Periods**, or use Transaction code OBBO. The usual approach is to create a variant with the same value as your company code, so in our example we should create two variants for each company code: 1000 (for the United States) and 2000 (for the UK).

Posting Period Variant Per Company Code

Consider our example with SAFA, Inc., where we have people working in the United States and in the UK. There is an approximately 5–6-hour time difference between the two organizations. Having a single variant would mean that both need to close their books at the same time, when the reality is that they are working different hours and thus would want to close at different times.

Once in the screen, click on **New Entries** and enter a value to represent your posting period variant for your company code (Figure 2.8).

Change View "Posting Periods: Specify Time Intervals": Overview

Var.	A	From acct	To account	From per.1	Year	To period	Year	From per.2	Year	To period	Year	AuG
1000	+			1	2007	2	2007	13	2000	16	2010	
1000	A		ZZZZZZZZZZ	1	2007	2	2007	13	2007	16	2008	
1000	D		ZZZZZZZZZZ	1	2007	2	2007	13	2007	16	2008	
1000	K		ZZZZZZZZZZ	1	2007	2	2007	13	2007	16	2008	
1000	M		ZZZZZZZZZZ	1	2007	2	2007	13	2007	16	2008	
1000	S		ZZZZZZZZZZ	1	2007	2	2007	13	2007	16	2008	

Figure 2.8 Define Posting Period Variant

The control of subledgers happens via the account type (second column in Figure 2.8). The top line (Account Type = +) is the overall control. Below it you find lines for different subledgers:

- A = assets
- D = vendors
- K = customers
- M = materials
- S = GL

The values in the other columns cover which periods are open. In this example, period 1 2000 and period 12 2010 are open. The respective special periods (13 to 16) are also open. This of course is not a real example, as in a live situation you would normally only have a single period open. If you create lines for your posting period variant for the different account types, it will be possible for you to close the subledgers individually.

You will see on each line that is possible to make posting period restrictions by account number, so, for instance, in the GL, you can decide to close down certain GL accounts before others. This should all be part of your period end closing process, which we discuss in Chapter 11.

Next assign your variants to your company code via the menu path (see Figure 2.9) **Financial Accounting (new) • Ledgers • Fiscal Year and Posting Periods • Posting Periods • Assign Variants to Company Code**, or use Transaction code OBBP.

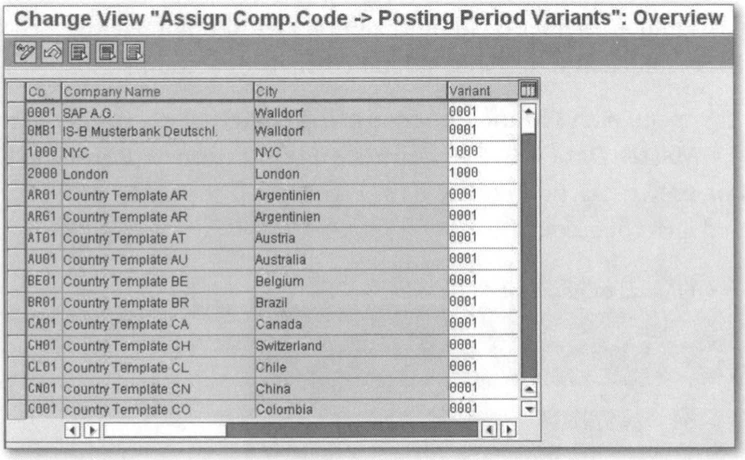
Change View "Assign Comp.Code -> Posting Period Variants": Overview

Co.	Company Name	City	Variant
0001	SAP A.G.	Walldorf	0001
0MB1	IS-B Musterbank Deutschl.	Walldorf	0001
1000	NYC	NYC	1000
2000	London	London	1000
AR01	Country Template AR	Argentinien	0001
ARG1	Country Template AR	Argentinien	0001
AT01	Country Template AT	Austria	0001
AU01	Country Template AU	Australia	0001
BE01	Country Template BE	Belgium	0001
BR01	Country Template BR	Brazil	0001
CA01	Country Template CA	Canada	0001
CH01	Country Template CH	Switzerland	0001
CL01	Country Template CL	Chile	0001
CN01	Country Template CN	China	0001
CO01	Country Template CO	Colombia	0001

Figure 2.9 Assignment of Posting Period Variant to Company Code

We have now defined the posting period and fiscal year variants, which combine to control postings in SAP ERP Financials. Next we look at the chart of accounts, which provides master data controls.

2.4.4 Define Chart of Accounts

The chart of accounts is the structured list of the GL accounts that you want to use to report ledger postings. You should define the chart of accounts based on your reporting requirements to provide you with the appropriate level of financial information needed to manage your business.

GL accounts are defined at the chart of accounts level and then extended into the company codes in which they are used. In our example, we will create each GL account and then extend it into both company codes. We will adopt a single chart of accounts across both companies, as both company codes have the same reporting requirements. Adopting a single chart of accounts will not restrict our ability to satisfy the legal requirements of U.S. and UK law in terms of financial statement reporting and taxation policy (see also Chapter 13).

This configuration step outlines the chart of accounts control information, such as the length of the code. Usually organizations adopt a numeric structure for their GL codes, and there is flexibility in the code length based on the size of your code list. The SAP implementation is sometimes a good time to review your coding structure and decide on the correct combination of GL accounts, cost centers, profit centers, and other account assignment elements. In our example, we adopt a five-digit GL account code, which is sufficient to provide a detailed chart of accounts.

To do this, follow the menu path **Financial Accounting (new)—General Ledger Accounting (new) • Master Data • G/L Accounts • Preparations • Edit Chart of Accounts List**, or use Transaction code OB13. Figure 2.10 shows an example of a system-delivered chart of accounts.

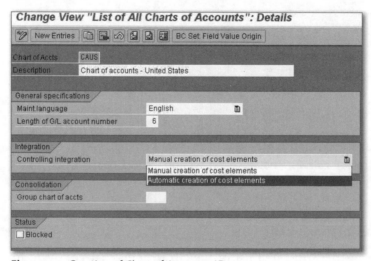

Figure 2.10 Creation of Chart of Accounts ID

We will create our chart of accounts with the standard CAUS Chart settings delivered with the system. In figure 2.10 we show the standard settings for CAUS. If you click on **New Entries**, you can create a chart of accounts called 1000—SAFA, Inc Chart of Accounts. The remainder of the settings are as CAUS, except that we will use a five-digit account code length. This is shown in Figure 2.11

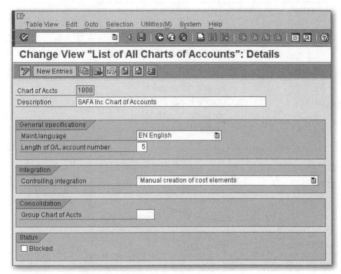

Figure 2.11 SAFA Inc. Chart of Accounts

Having defined your chart of accounts, you need to assign it to the appropriate company codes, which can only be done after you have defined company codes (which is discussed later in this chapter).

2.4.5 Structure of the Chart of Accounts

At this point it is important to have some idea of the structure and conventions of your chart of accounts or GL code list. This is a crucial part of the design, as analysis of the ledger postings is key to understanding financial performance. Existing organizations that are implementing SAP as a replacement system to their current accounting package will have some form of code structure in place and should use it as the starting point.

When identifying groups of codes that are needed, break them down to a lower level and keep going down levels until you reach the actual code level. For example, our coding structure has three levels, and the lowest level is the actual account codes.

Let's look at the code structure for the top two levels in the chart of accounts we are using for SAFA Inc. (Figure 2.12).

Level 1	Level 2		
Balance Sheet			
	10000	14999	Fixed Assets
	15000	19999	Current Assets
	20000	24999	Current Liabilities
	25000	29999	Long Term Liabilities
	30000	39999	Capital & Reserves
Profit & Loss			
	40000	49999	Sales
	50000	59999	Cost of Sales
	60000	69999	Overheads
	70000	79999	Below the line adjustments

Figure 2.12 Top Two Levels in the SAFA Inc. Chart of Accounts

If you are creating a chart of accounts for the first time in SAP ERP, this broad guide maybe useful to adopt. Initially, we define groups within which the respective GL accounts provide us with the level of analysis we need to run our business.

It is important here to separate the roles of the GL account and the account assignment objects (cost center, profit center, internal order, etc.). Remember that a GL account is there to record the type of income or expenditure, whereas an account assignment object is there to provide departmental or business unit analysis.

Numeric or Alphanumeric Chart of Accounts

The use of an alphanumeric policy is not a recommended coding convention, as it causes *masking issues*. Masking issues occur when SAP ERP cannot recognize ranges of codes. If you use a mix of alpha and numeric, SAP ERP cannot allow you to define configuration in ranges. For example, defining the splitting characteristics needs to be done for every account; you cannot enter a range. The same applies for the default cost element settings, where you must enter each value individually into the default settings table.

2.4.6 Define Credit Control Area

The credit control area is used to control the processing of transactions with customers. It is a way of defining an overall credit limit for a defined group of customers. In credit control area, you define the total value of credit that can be given to customers. Most organizations operate a simple view and define one credit control area per company code. A prerequisite is to create the fiscal year variant (see Section 2.4.2).

The credit control area represents a basic control for restricting your *credit exposure*. The limit you set at this level influences all of the customers that fall within this credit control area. For this reason, many organizations choose not to impose strict controls here and instead impose credit control based on individual customers' needs (see Chapter 6, Section 6.8).

In our scenario, we will use some simple settings to support our credit control activities (Figure 2.13). We will create a separate credit control area for each company code, as the U.S. and UK companies adopt different policies in line with their domestic procedures. We define our credit control areas in the menu path **IMG • Enterprise Structure • Definition • Financial accounting • Define Credit Control Area** or by using Transaction code OX15. The settings are described in Table 2.1.

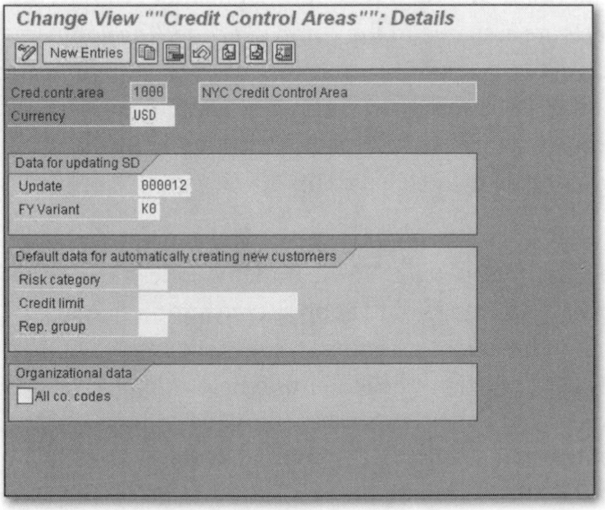

Figure 2.13 Basic Settings for Defining a Credit Control Area

Field	Description
Update	This controls which items are included in the calculation of open items, that is, credit exposure. 000012 is used by many organizations that want to include the value of open sales orders in their credit exposure calculation. This is the setting that we chose for both our U.S. and UK operations.
FY Variant	Here you must enter your fiscal year variant.
Default data for automatically creating new customers	These settings are applied as a default to all new customers when they are created. They are discussed in more detail in Chapter 6, Section 6.8.2 Automatic Credit Control.

Table 2.1 Settings for defining Credit Control Area

The same settings are made for both our credit control areas.

Both of these are now assigned to their respective company codes, but we cannot do that until we have actually created the company codes, so let's go onto this step next.

2.4.7 Define Company Code

Setting a company code is an important step in terms of the remainder of the configuration, as a lot of other objects are assigned to the company code. The company code is an organizational unit used in accounting, and it is used to structure the business organization from a financial accounting perspective. Complete balance sheets and profit and loss reports (financial statements) are produced at the company code level, so it is usually defined at the legal entity level.

For SAFA Inc., we have decided to create two company codes, and for each, we will need to assign the correct address details. The company code has a four-digit alphanumeric naming convention. You should adopt a convention that makes sense for your organization. If you have many company codes, you may want to define criteria that will make it easy to identify each entity. Before long, users of the system will become accustomed to the names of your company codes, so adopt something sensible and appropriate, but don't spend too much time on it. SAFA Inc. uses company codes 1000 and 2000; options such as US01 and UK01 or some other alphanumeric combination could have beenused as well. Configuration is completed by following the menu path **IMG • Enterprise Structure • Definition • Financial Accounting • Edit, Copy, Delete, Check Company Code** or by using Transaction code OX02.

SAP ERP delivers several country-specific templates for you to copy if you feel unsure of the settings to be made. When you copy an SAP ERP-delivered template, the system will ask if you want to copy dependent objects. This prompt allows you to ensure that all of the associated entries are copied over; if you are sure you will not need them, ignore this prompt. Be aware that when you copy all dependent objects, the system will copy over everything in the appropriate language of the template country.

Create your own company code by clicking on **New Entries**.

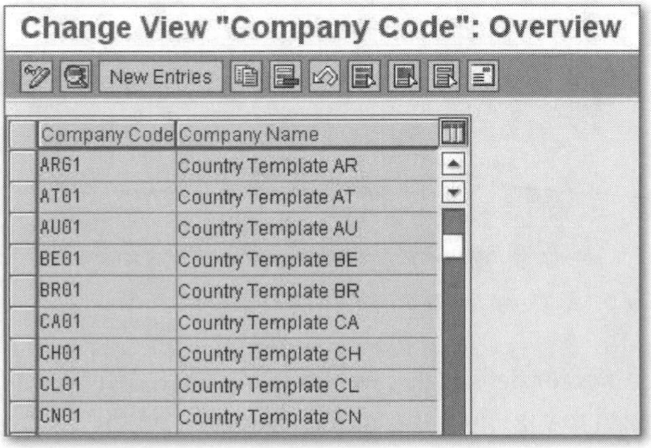

Figure 2.14 SAP ERP-Delivered Company Code Country Templates

The configuration screen for a new company code is very simple, as the company code is merely a placeholder, an ID against which configuration can be made. For our scenario, we have decided to create two company codes, representing the U.S. and UK operations. Two company codes allow for flexibility in managing the differences between the countries' legal requirements. For instance, tax configuration is very different for both company codes.

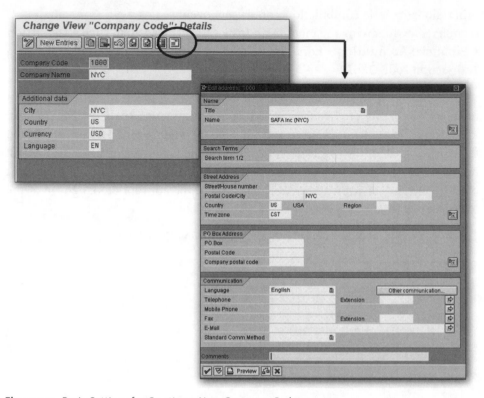

Figure 2.15 Basic Settings for Creating a New Company Code

Figure 2.15 shows the basic settings for defining a new company code. After creating a company code, we also need to configure the address information for it. The address information that is entered can be used for creating output (e.g., customer statements) that you may want to send out to third parties.

A second company code was created for our London-based company, with the appropriate address attached to it as shown in Figure 2.15

At this point it is necessary to assign the company code to a company ID (Figure 2.16), which can be done by following the menu path **IMG • SPRO • Enterprise Structure • Assignment • Financial Accounting • Assign Company Code to Company**.

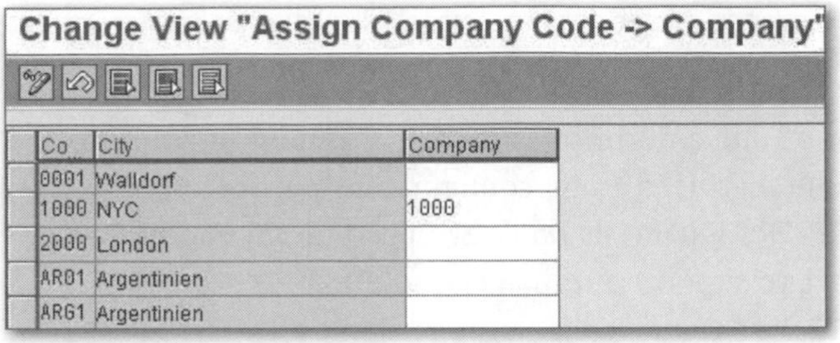
Change View "Assign Company Code -> Company"

Co.	City	Company
0001	Walldorf	
1000	NYC	1000
2000	London	
AR01	Argentinien	
ARG1	Argentinien	

Figure 2.16 Assignment of Company Code to Company ID

The same settings need to be made for our other company code.

2.4.8 Assign Company Code to a Fiscal Year Variant

You now need to assign your fiscal year variant to the company codes for which it is relevant. In our example, both company codes work off the same fiscal year variant. The same fiscal year variant can be assigned to more than one company code. Follow the menu path **Financial Accounting (new) • Financial Accounting Global Settings • Ledgers • Fiscal Year and Posting Periods • Assign Company Code to a Fiscal Year Variant** or use Transaction code OB37.

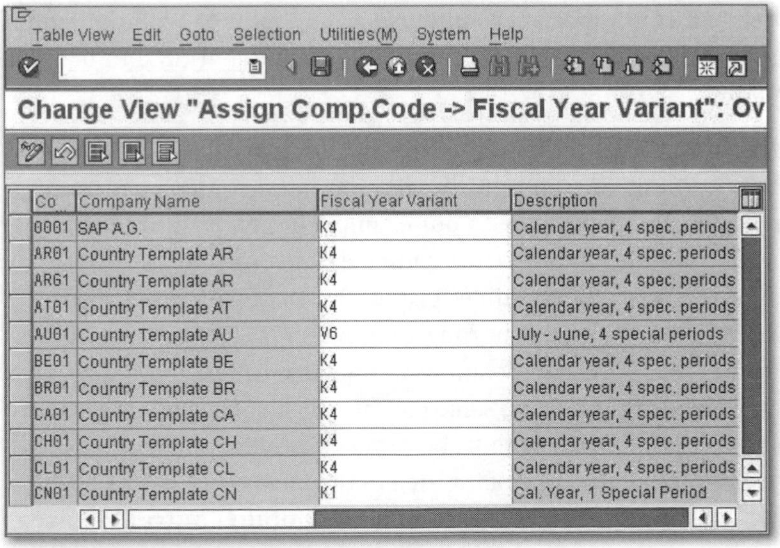

Co	Company Name	Fiscal Year Variant	Description
0001	SAP A.G.	K4	Calendar year, 4 spec. periods
AR01	Country Template AR	K4	Calendar year, 4 spec. periods
ARG1	Country Template AR	K4	Calendar year, 4 spec. periods
AT01	Country Template AT	K4	Calendar year, 4 spec. periods
AU01	Country Template AU	V6	July - June, 4 special periods
BE01	Country Template BE	K4	Calendar year, 4 spec. periods
BR01	Country Template BR	K4	Calendar year, 4 spec. periods
CA01	Country Template CA	K4	Calendar year, 4 spec. periods
CH01	Country Template CH	K4	Calendar year, 4 spec. periods
CL01	Country Template CL	K4	Calendar year, 4 spec. periods
CN01	Country Template CN	K1	Cal. Year, 1 Special Period

Figure 2.17 Assign Company Code to Fiscal Year Variant

Figure 2.17 shows the assignment of variants to company codes, in our scenario, we assign the same fiscal year variant (Z1) to both company codes.

We have configured most of our enterprise structure. We now move onto the controlling area components that need to be configured as part of this exercise. Although the book is a SAP ERP Financials book, we need to have some components of Controlling in place to support our financial solution.

2.4.9 Define Controlling Area

This book is concerned with the configuration of the Financial Accounting Component (FI). The controlling area is the object that sits entirely within the Controlling Component (CO). We need to include it in our discussions, as it is seen as an important integration point, and understanding it's usage is important to our overall system design. Our discussions will be limited to what is necessary to complete our objectives. A more detailed understanding of Controlling Component (CO) topics should be sought elsewhere.

The controlling area is the object that defines the rules and controls for our account assignment objects. Whereas company code can be thought of as satisfying the external or legal entities requirement, the controlling area can satisfy our internal reporting requirement. It is important to understand the roles of both the Financial Accounting Component (FI) and the Controlling Component (CO) to be clear on information flow.

Options here would be to have a controlling area per company code, per country, or per "global business unit" (i.e., internally set). The safest route is per country, which usually reflects a company code, so our example has two controlling areas, representing the UK and the United States. Other designs may be necessary for much more complicated organizational designs, with complex internal reporting requirements combined with legal reporting requirements. For instance, if you have a number of different business operations in the same country, you may have equivalent company codes set up in the same country. In such a scenario, you may define all of these company codes within the same controlling area. This is covered in Chapter 8. We define the controlling area in the menu path **IMG • SPRO • Enterprise Structure • Definition • Controlling • Maintain Controlling Area**.

When you enter this transaction, select **Maintain Controlling Area**, which will show you a list of existing controlling areas that are predelivered by SAP ERP. You can copy one of these or click on **New Entries**. By copying, you will create an exact replica but with a new label that you define.

The common approach is to create a new entry, as the configuration is fairly simple to complete. You need to provide a four-digit code for your controlling area, which can be the same as the label you use to identify your company code, or it can be something completely different.

In our example, we used the same labels for our controlling area as for the company codes, as this is easier for users than creating different conventions for each object. Our configuration settings and assignments are shown in Figure 2.18.

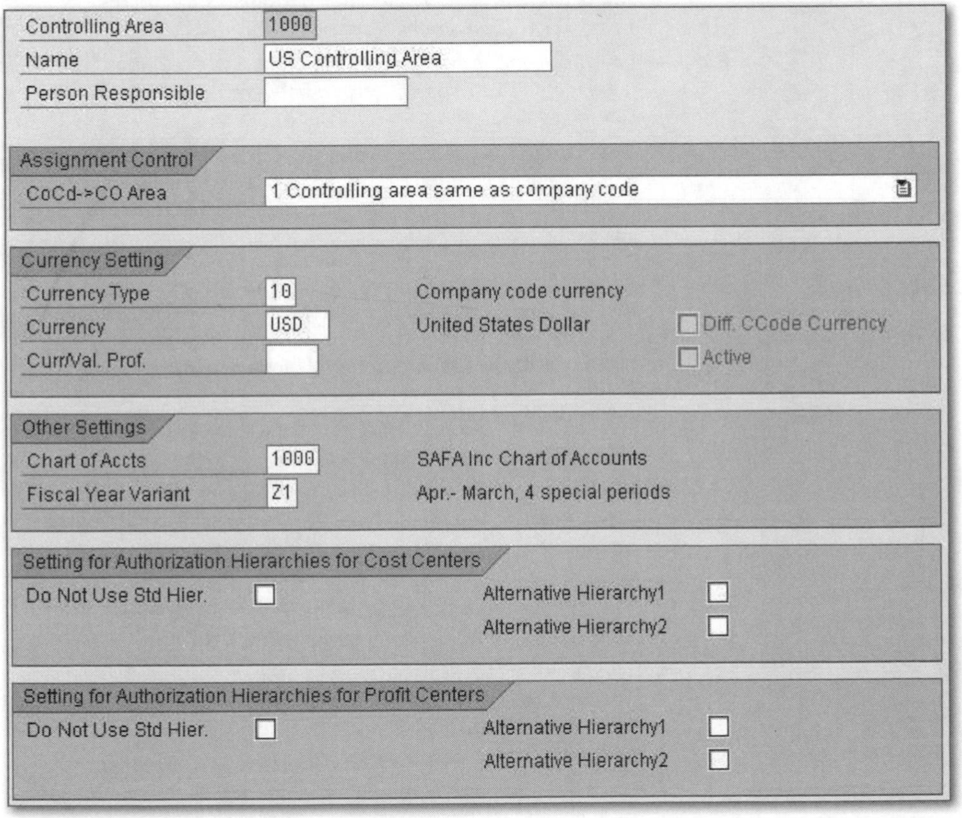

Figure 2.18 Maintain Controlling Area Basic Settings

The settings in Table 2.2 are made for the controlling area.

Field	Description
Controlling Area	Enter the four-digit alphanumeric value to represent your controlling area.
Name	Enter the description of your controlling area.
Person Responsible	Enter the name of the person who is overall in charge of this controlling area. This information is not used anywhere else, so you can simply enter Director of Finance or something more appropriate.
Assignment Control	Enter the relationship between the controlling area and the company code. There are two options in this case: ▶ Controlling area same as company code: Use this option when there is a one-to-one relationship between company code and controlling area. ▶ Cross-company code accounting:Use this option when two or more company codes are assigned to one controlling area. This will allow cross-company cost accounting within this controlling area.
Currency Type	You define the currency that would be used throughout your controlling area in this field. If in the previous field you selected option 1, the system will default the company code currency in this field, but if you selected option 2, you have the following six choices: ▶ Company code currency (10): You can use this currency only when all of the company codes use the same currency. ▶ Any currency (20): You can select any currency in this field, as this gives the maximum flexibility when choosing a controlling area currency. ▶ Group currency (30): You maintain this currency at the client level and can use it to reconcile the Financial Accounting Component (FI) and the Controlling Component (CO). ▶ Hard currency (40): This currency is used in countries where the inflation rate is very high and makes sense where the assigned company codes are from the same country. ▶ Index-based currency (50): This currency is used to support external reporting requirements in countries where inflation is very high and unstable. ▶ Global currency (60): You can use this currency if you have defined global companies in your configuration. You also need to ensure that all of the companies assigned to your controlling area belong to the same company and use the same currency.

Table 2.2 Basic Settings

Field	Description
Currency	In this field, you define the default currency for your controlling area. The selection made in the previous step will influence the choices that are available to you in this field.
Chart of Accts	In this field, you enter the chart of accounts to be utilized by your controlling area. The important point to note here is that all of the company codes assigned to your controlling area must use the same chart of accounts that has been assigned to the controlling area.
Fiscal Year Variant	In this field, you select the fiscal year variant. Just like chart of accounts, this variant must be the same for the assigned company codes and the controlling area.

Table 2.2 Basic Settings (cont.)

Note that each controlling area is only created once but needs to be maintained in different areas. In our scenario, we need to maintain the general controlling and profit center views of the controlling area, which we will do later in this chapter.

Having created the controlling area, we now look at the subcomponents within Controlling Component (CO).

2.4.10   Define Cost Center Group

Cost center hierarchy can be defined to reflect the organizational structure. This allows you to report at each of the levels that are maintained within your hierarchy. Before you can create a cost center or complete you configuration for the controlling area, you need to create a cost center group. (We discuss hierarchies in more detail in Chapter 8, Section 8.4.3.) All we need to do here is create a place holder; we can maintain the full hierarchy later.

This is done on the application side of SAP ERP. Follow the menu path **SAP Easy Access Menu • Accounting • Controlling • Cost Center Accounting • Master Data • Cost Center Group • Create** or use Transaction code KSH1. This step is required for the next configuration activity.

Figure 2.19 shows the basic screen for defining a Cost Center Hierarchy.

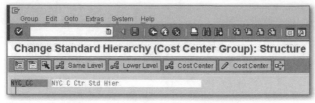

Figure 2.19 Define a Cost Center Group (Hierarchy)

2.4.11 Activate Controlling Area Components

This configuration activity enables activation of components of the Controlling Component (CO). Controlling is a vast component with a number of subcomponents within it; not all of them are relevant to this discussion When you create a Financial Accounting Component (FI) posting, the system automatically creates a document for each subcomponent of the Controlling Component (CO) that you are implementing. In a traditional Financial Accounting Component (FI) implementation, you may activate cost centers (Overhead Cost Controlling component) and profit centers (Profit Center Accounting). With the new GL, we do not need to activate Profit Center Accounting, as explained in more detail in Chapter 4. Activation occurs at the menu path**IMG • SPRO • Controlling • General Controlling • Organization • Maintain Controlling Area** or by using Transaction code OKKP.

Two controlling areas need the following settings:

1. From the initial screen, double-click on **Controlling Area** to maintain the settings shown in Figure 2.20.

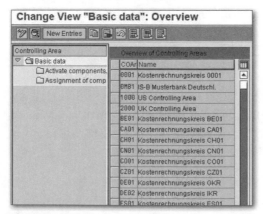

Figure 2.20 Controlling Area Basic Data

2. The components shown in Figure 2.21 need to be maintained. It is important to note here that we are using profit centers but not activating Profit Center Accounting to use document splitting. This is explained further in Chapter 4.

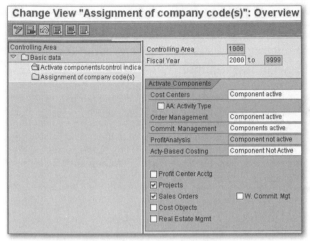

Figure 2.21 Activate Controlling Components

3. Next, double-click on **Assignment of company code(s)** (Figure 2.22) to assign the appropriate company code to the controlling crea. In our scenario we have a single company code per controlling area.

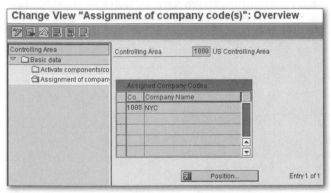

Figure 2.22 Assignment of Company Code to Controlling

Next we look at the creation of the default profit centers.

2.4.12 Create Default Profit Center

Because you are using profit centers, but not switching on Profit Center Accounting, SAP ERP allows you to create this element from within new GL, the use of which is explained in more detail in Chapter 8. As a minimum, we need to create a default profit center and assign it to each company code. This has been referred to by different names including dummy profit center. You may adopt the convention that is most appropriate for your organization.

> **Default Controlling Area**
>
> When you are working with controlling areas, SAP ERP defaults the last controlling area that you used as the value for every screen going forward. If you want to change controlling areas, you need to use Transaction code OKKS to set the controlling area. Use this to switch between controlling areas for all transactions in this book.

First we need to define the standard profit center hierarchy based on which all profit centers will be created (Figure 2.23). At this stage you may not know what your final hierarchy will look like, so you may want to just create the name as a place-holder.

This is also done within the application side of the system in the menu path **SAP Easy Access Menu** • **Accounting** • **Financial Accounting** • **General Ledger** • **Master Records** • **Profit Center** • **Standard Hierarchy** • **Create** or with Transaction code KCH1.

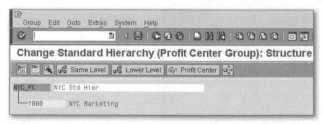

Figure 2.23 Create the Standard Hierarchy for Profit Centers

We can now create our default profit center, which is also done in the application side of the system by the menu path **SAP Easy Access Menu** • **Accounting** • **Financial Accounting** • **General Ledger** • **Master Records** • **Profit Center** • **Create** or by using

Transaction code KE51.

We needed to create the standard hierarchy and the default profit center first because they need to be assigned to the controlling area settings. Follow the menu path **SPRO • Enterprise Controlling • Profit Center Accounting • Basic Settings • Controlling Area Settings • Maintain Controlling Area Settings** or use Transaction code OKE5.

We need to make the settings shown in Table 2.3 for our controlling area.

Field	Description
Dummy profit center	The dummy profit center is the default profit center for the entire controlling area, and it captures all of the postings for which a valid profit center has not been assigned. It also serves as the default profit center for the cost center master record point of view. This field is grayed out, and you cannot make an assignment of dummy profit center through this screen. We will have to create the dummy profit center from another screen (explained below), and the assignment will be made when we are finished with the master data creation.
Standard hierarchy	Enter the name of the standard hierarchy for Profit Center Accounting the same as you did for Cost Center Accounting.
Elimination of internal business	Activate this field if you want to eliminate the internal business activities among different account assignment objects assigned to the same profit center. As a result of this, no Profit Center Accounting document will be created.
Profit center local currency type	Choose the currency type in which you want to maintain all Profit Center Accounting–related transactions. You have an option of selecting from controlling area currency, group currency, and profit center currency.
Profit Center local currency	You are required to fill this field if you chose the profit center currency in the previous screen. If you selected the controlling area currency or group currency, leave this field blank.
Store transaction currency	You should activate this field if you want to store the transaction currency in Profit Center Accounting. This will result in increased volumes, but it might be necessary if the transaction currency is different from the controlling area or profit center currency.
Valuation view	In Profit Center Accounting, you use this field to represent different ways of viewing business transactions within a company. In our structure, there will not be any internal goods movement between different profit centers, so we will not go into more detail on different valuation views.
Control indicator	The system shows the current year as the default setting, and this setting will be enough from the current year onward.

Table 2.3 Maintaining PCA Controlling Area

We have completed the enterprise structure configuration of the controlling elements. Further configuration of the Controlling Component (CO) is covered in Chapter 8.

2.4.13 Check Company Code Global Parameters

The last thing to do is to check the global parameters of the company code. From this screen we need to ensure that all of the objects we have configured have been assigned to the correct company code. This is relevant for both company codes in our scenario. Figure 2.24 shows the settings made for company code 1000. Note that all of the items you configured are correctly assigned to company code 1000.

This configuration screen is a great place to see all of the relevant information for your company code. To get there, follow the menu path **IMG • SPRO • Financial Accounting (new) • Financial Accounting Global Settings (new) • Global Parameters for Company Code • Enter Global Parameters** or use Transaction code OBY6.

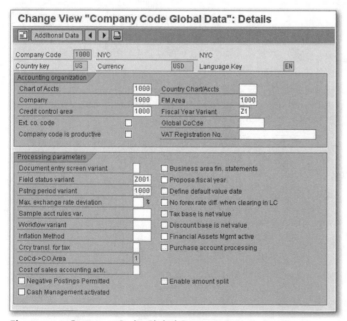

Figure 2.24 Company Code Global Parameters

From this screen you should be able to check that all of the assignments that were made to the company code are correct for each company code.

In addition you can make the settings shown in Table 2.4.

Field	Description
Propose fiscal year	This option proposes a fiscal year for the user when entering a transaction in the system. This is useful for systems where the fiscal year is the same as the calendar year. If you have a calendar-year-independent fiscal year, it is not recommended that you use this option.
Tax base is net value	This indicator proposes the calculation of the base amount of tax for sales-related transactions. This is usually subject to the statutory rules of your country, and you should consider these before selecting this option. This option is usually relevant for the U.S. jurisdiction tax.

Table 2.4 Additional Setting Options

Other options on this screen become relevant based on functionality, which is outside the scope of our discussion.

2.5 Summary

The enterprise structure configuration is a very important step in your overall configuration and is sometimes referred to as the *baseline configuration*. Baseline configuration refers to those configuration items that should not be easily changed once configured, as they form the cornerstones of your overall design. For this reason, it is important to have a good understanding of the roles of each of the objects discussed in this chapter so that you can make good decisions about how to use them within your solutions.

Having completed this chapter, you should now be in a position to:

▸ Understand the role of the components of the enterprise structure in order to decide how to use them

▸ Translate your business requirements into SAP components

▸ Configure a solution to best fit your business requirements

In the next chapter, we begin looking at the configuration settings needed order to configure the Financial Accounting Component (FI) global settings.

This chapter looks at the global settings for all of the Financial Accounting Component (FI) subcomponents. These settings should be in place when you look at the specific configuration of each of the subcomponents, so we are dealing with this early in the book. Please note that global does not imply any geographical location and should not be confused with that.

3　Financial Accounting Component (FI) Global Settings

The objective of this chapter is to show you how to input the global settings for the Financial Accounting Component (FI), mainly in terms of posting controls. It is important to have a plan of action for these settings at the start of the configuration activity, but you may need to come back and review them as you work in the other areas.

This chapter on global settings includes the following areas:

▶ Posting field status groups

▶ GL account groups

▶ Document types and number ranges

▶ Posting keys

▶ Document change rules

▶ Cross-company code postings

▶ Sales and purchase tax

We start by looking at the theory behind the document concept in SAP, as this is the basis for a lot of the material we cover in this chapter. Once this understanding is in place, we will look at the related configuration activities.

By the end of the chapter, you will understand all of the key steps necessary to configure the Financial Accounting Component (FI) global settings. As with every other chapter, you need to refer back to your design (blueprint) for guidance on what your business requirements are and then build a solution to deliver that design. This is an important point, and although we do not mention this at the start of every chapter, it is assumed that the reader will keep this in mind in all of the chapters that follow.

3.1 What Is a Document in SAP?

The SAP document principle is simple: every transaction you process in the system will create a document. This document will act as record of the activity, and if the activity involves transactional value, a financial posting is also created. For example, if you do a goods receipt transaction, you will create a document that shows the movement of goods in inventory (materials management), and this will create a financial document to represent the changes in the value of stock. These documents are linked to one another because they have a relationship, and SAP has a complete audit trail.

Each document you process has a header section and a line item section. SAP configuration focuses on each of these areas separately, and we will look at them separately.

3.1.1 Document Header

Figure 3.1 shows the standard journal entry screen (Transaction FV50). If this is your first time using an SAP system, you should take a while to get accustomed to the layout and look at the **Details** tab. If you are upgrading from an older version of SAP, you may have seen this screen before.

The key pieces of information that we have here are:

▸ **Document type and document number**
The key field in the document header is the **Document Type**, as this defines the type of journal and controls the document number that is assigned to the journal. These should be your main focus, and we discuss them in detail later in this chapter

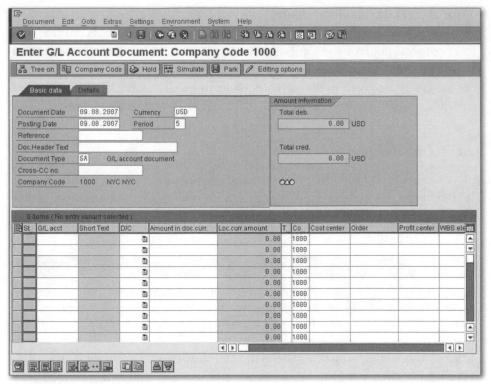

Figure 3.1 Standard Journal Entry Screen

▶ **Posting date and document date**

Another important field in the document header is the **Posting Date**. The posting date is often defaulted into the screen as the current date, because it represents the date on which the transaction enters the system. There is also the **Document Date** field, which can be different from the posting date. A common way of working here is to use the document date as the day on which you enter the journal and the posting date as the day on which you want the journal to hit the ledger.

▶ **Currency**

For foreign currency transactions, you need to confirm the currency as part of the header information by entering the foreign currency in the **Currency** field. This will be most likely the case for accounts payable, who receive invoices from suppliers overseas.

► **Doc Header Text and Reference**

The **Doc Header Text** and **Reference** fields are important fields from a business process point of view, as both are used to label the journals you post. Note that there may already be some convention in place in your legacy system as to what labels are given to journals, and keep in mind the availability of the line item text fields to record information in as well, as we'll discuss next.

3.1.2 Line Items

Below the header information, you enter the line item information for this journal. The line items contain the financial transactions that you want to process, in line with the rules of double-entry bookkeeping. SAP allows you to enter a maximum of 999 lines in a journal.

> **Entering Large Journals**
>
> You may often need to enter journals that have more than 999 lines, for instance, incoming interfaces. For these you need to define a routine in your interface program that splits the interface into more than one document.

In this section of the journal, you need to enter the financial information including debits and credits, amounts, GL accounts, and account assignment objects (cost centers and profit centers).

> **What Is an Account Assignment Object?**
>
> Account assignment objects are used to provide organizational analysis to postings. For an expense item, the GL account defines the type of expense, and the account assignment object (cost center or internal order) assigns the expense to a department.
>
> We discuss account assignments in Chapter 9 (see Section 9.2.1)

The entering of line items is controlled by the controls that you put in place for your master data objects. For instance, GL accounts require a cost center or a profit center, depending on how you define the cost element category. We introduce the importance of master data in the next section but discuss specific master data objects in their respective chapters.

3.1.3 Master Data

For any system you work with, the quality of the information coming out of the system is dependent on the quality of data being put into the system.

Careful attention needs to be given to the process of data capture (the entry of financial information to the system, e.g., through journals) to ensure that the correct information is being recorded to provide the required financial output for analysis. When you define your master data objects, consider all your requirements for data capture and reporting to ensure that your master data objects fit their purpose.

Now that we have overviewed the layout of a document, we can look at the configuration settings.

3.2   Configuration of Global Settings

All of the configuration steps that we cover in this chapter are effective across all Financial Accounting Component (FI) subcomponents. The order in which we cover these steps is the order you should follow, as it ensures that you complete all dependent activities first.

In Chapter 2 we defined our enterprise structure. Those configuration steps created placeholders in which our future configuration can be completed. We start with activities related to the chart of accounts. In Chapter 2, Section 2.4.4, we defined the chart of accounts. We now go a level below this and define the related configuration.

Every GL account has two components: a chart of accounts and a company code. Think of the roles of these two components as being the header and the detail, respectively. The chart of accounts component is the header of the record, holding the basic information such as the account number and name. The company code component holds the more detailed information. The detail can be specific to each company code, as you will see as we move through this chapter. We discuss the specifics of GL accounts master records in Chapter 4.

Looking back at Figure 2.1 in Chapter 2, you can see that more than one company code can be assigned to a chart of accounts. In your organization, you can have a single chart of accounts for all your company codes, or you can have specific charts defined for individual company codes. This depends on your overall solution requirements, and you should consider the points made in Chapter 4, Section 4.3.6, about the use of multiple ledgers for providing for country-specific statutory reporting requirements.

Next, we address the retained earnings account, which is a system default that needs to be in place before you can create any GL accounts.

3.2.1 Define the Retained Earnings Account

As part of year-end processing, GL will carry forward the balance of the profit and loss GL accounts to the retained earnings account. This is a normal procedure in accounting, and the retained earnings appear on the balance sheet as the profit and loss brought forward from previous fiscal years. You may have more than one retained earnings account and define which GL accounts are connected to each retained earnings account, but the usual practice is to have a single account.

All income and expenditure GL accounts need to be assigned to the correct retained earnings account. If you only have one, this happens by default. When you run the year-end balance carry-forward step, the GL account balance is transferred to the corresponding retained earnings account. Let's now look at the steps required to configure the retained earnings account.

The menu path to configure a retained earnings account is **IMG • Financial Accounting (new) • General Ledger Accounting (new) • Master Data • G/L accounts • Preparations • Define Retained Earnings Account**, or you can use Transaction code OB53.

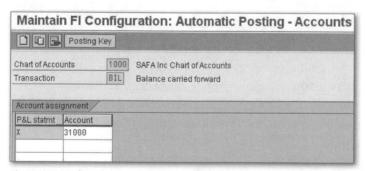

Figure 3.2 Define the Retained Earnings Account

Figure 3.2 shows the configuration settings that need to be made for this activity.

This is our first example of a configuration activity that defines some automatic account determination, that is, the system automatically defines the GL account to which this transaction will post. Whenever we reference account determination, we use our own template chart of accounts, which is included in the appendix as a guide for you to follow.

Although we made an entry here, we did not say anywhere that we had created this GL account, and that is correct because this configuration allows you to define an account here, even though the account may not exist in the system.

Having made the entries, you can now start creating GL accounts. The GL master record is made up of several tabs that hold different sets of information. If you define more than one retained earnings account, an option will appear as shown in Figure 3.3.

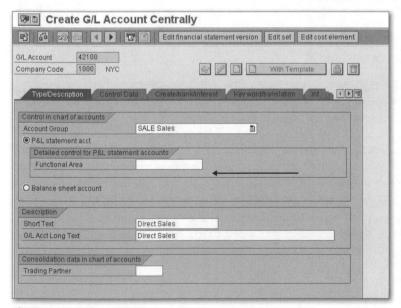

Figure 3.3 Creating a GL Account

For SAFA Inc., there is no such option, as we have only created a single retained earnings account. We will continue looking at the configuration of items that influence the chart of accounts by examining field status groups.

3.2.2 Field Status Groups

Field status group configuration controls which fields are available to be populated when you make a posting to a GL account. Some fields are minimum system requirements, for example, amount, posting key, and GL account, and these cannot be changed.

You can define field status variants for a company code; therefore, it is possible to have different field statuses for the same GL account for each company code in which it exists.

Note
The field status is not the only place where you can configure controls. Additional controls are available in the Controlling Component (CO) when you define your cost elements (see Chapter 8, Section 8.4.2).

Whatever controls you do define need to be in line with system requirements, as illustrated in the box below.

Field Status Controls for Stock Postings
For most solutions involving the implementation of the Materials Management (MM) component, you need to carefully consider the fields required to ensure that stock postings will work correctly. For example, the stock GL account is usually a balance sheet code and as such requires a profit center assignment. Typically, this is done by deriving a profit center from the material master that is involved in the stock transaction.
In this simple example, you can see that the field status for the GL account for stock transactions must include a profit center, but what about the consumption of stock? If stock is issued to a direct cost (or cost of sales) GL code, the cost should be assigned to the department that incurs the expense. It therefore needs a cost center (or internal order) assignment. Your consumption of stock codes will have a different field status than the balance sheet stock account, and you need to understand this when designing your field status groups.
In the appendix we provide some example field status groups that you may want to consider when putting your own design together.

Configuring field status groups is very important to the accuracy of financial data as well as for the production of financial reports. It also is very important because this is a clear integration point across the entire system. During your implementation, you will often need to integrate with other components, and this is a prime example. You should first design your own field status groups based on your requirements and then share this solution outside your team to determine if the solution meets the requirements of the other components.

Creating Field Status Groups

To create (and configure) field status groups, follow the menu path **IMG • Financial Accounting (new) • General Ledger Accounting (new) • Ledgers • Fields • Define Field Status Variants**, or use Transaction code OBC4.

The field status group is so called because it groups together different fields, as shown in Figure 3.6, below. You create individual field status groups within an object called the *field status variant*, where each group corresponds to a specific posting rule you want to apply.

Because we are only creating a single chart of accounts, we only need to create a single field status variant. When we create a GL account, we assign a field status group to that account, and this controls the fields that are available when posting to that GL account. The first step is to create the field status variant as shown in Figure 3.4, by clicking on **New Entries**.

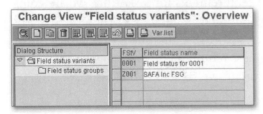

Figure 3.4 Define Field Status Variant

It is possible to copy your variant from the SAP standard variant 0001 that is supplied with the system. We have chosen not to copy, as we want to define specific groups. SAP standard variant 0001 contains many groups for our simple scenario. There are too many groups for the limited chart of accounts that we want to create. It is always recommended that you look at the standard groups in the system and see what controls SAP proposes for each type of posting.

Table 3.1 identifies some general rules that you should validate against your system requirements.

Type of Posting	Primary Object	Possible Account Assignment Object
Balance sheet	GL account	Profit center
Income	GL account Revenue element	Profit center Profitability analysis Revenue project
Expenditure	GL account Cost element	Cost center Internal order Capital project
Internal settlements or internal allocations and assessments	Secondary cost element	Cost center Profit center Internal order

Table 3.1 Common Account Assignment Objects

> **Note**
>
> You will understand the roles of the each of the objects listed in Table 3.1 better after you read Chapter 8, where we discuss the Controlling Component (CO). However, Table 3.1 outlines the options you see when looking at the field status settings.

Having considered the business process requirements for SAFA Inc., we are going to create several field status groups, as outlined in Table 3.2. These field status groups will put in place sufficient controls to ensure the financial accuracy of the data in the system in line with our business requirements. To create a field status group, double-click on the field status variant we created earlier, as shown in Figure 3.4, and then select **New Entries**.

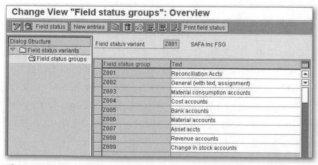

Figure 3.5 Field Status Groups within a Field Status Variant

Table 3.2 shows the purpose of each of these groups. You should create your own groups in line with your specific business requirements.

Field Status Group	Description	Purpose
Z001	Fixed assets	A separate fixed asset group is useful for balance sheet fixed assets accounts. Depending on the complexity of your processes, if you have assets under construction, you may want to include a number of different fields.
Z002	General balance	This is the general group, which is the default setting for any balance sheet GL account. This does not have any cost assignment objects because balance sheet postings do not post to cost centers.
Z003	Cash and bank accounts	This group is for use by the cash and bank GL accounts. Here we include the open item management as well as setting line item display as mandatory.
Z004	Material accounts	This is a balance sheet group that is relevant for GL accounts where there is a posting from the materials management ledger. An example of a specific field that is included here is the quantity field.
Z005	Reconciliation accounts	Posting to system reconciliation accounts happens in the background. The system derives all of the necessary information, so it is best to create this group with all fields optional. Line item display is usually switched off for these accounts.
Z006	Revenue accounts	To record revenue income, we need to assign a billing account assignment object; that is, a profit center and Work breakdown structure (WBS) are the main objects. This group has these set up as optional.
Z007	Cost accounts	This group of accounts has the cost objects activated, so, for example, you can post to a cost center to allocate costs. This group doesn't require a billing account assignment, so profit center can be hidden.
Z008	General income expenditure	It is useful to have a general group that allows both income and expenditure transactions, because some GL accounts may receive both. An example of such an account may be a gains and losses account from foreign currency revaluation.
Z009	Miscellaneous account	A miscellaneous group is created that has all of the fields you may want to use as optional. It does not simply have all fields as optional.

Table 3.2 SAFA Inc. Field Status Groups

Configuring Field Status Groups within a Variant

Field status groups contain the actual field status controls you should configure to suit your business requirements. When you first enter the **Maintain Field Status Group: Overview** screen (by double-clicking on a group), all of the fields are optional and appear blue. You then double-click on one of the groups in the **Select Group** area of the screen to configure the group, as shown in Figure 3.6.

> **Note**
>
> It is common for some groups to be completely suppressed. For instance, the Real Estate Management group is not always required, and once its fields are suppressed, the group changes color and appears to be grayed out.

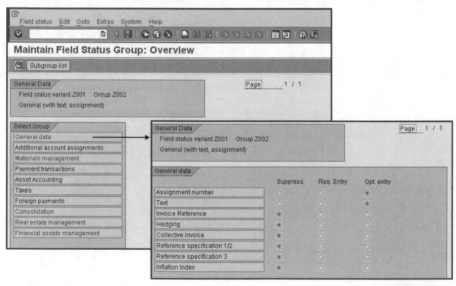

Figure 3.6 Customizing Field Status Groups

You should work your way through the groups and make settings that suit your solution and the specific business posting rule you are creating. We have provided some guidance in the appendices, based on the field status groups that created for SAFA Inc.

Cost elements and revenue elements provide basic controls for the system, which require you to enter cost or revenue objects when posting to these accounts. This is explained in more detail in the Chapter 8.

> **Note**
>
> Posting controls are also configurable within document types and number ranges, which we look at later in this chapter.

The last step is assigning the field status variant to the company codes, which is a separate configuration step, by going to **Financial Accounting (new) • General Ledger Accounting (new) • Ledgers • Fields • Assign Company Codes to Field Status Variants or using Transaction code OBC5.** The results of this are shown in Figure 3.7.

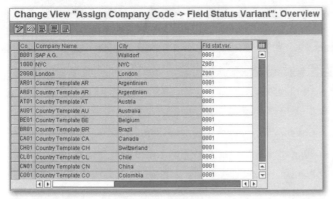

Figure 3.7 Assignment of Company Code and Field Status Variant

Next we look at the controls over the creation of GL master records.

3.2.3   GL Account Groups

When you create a GL account, before you go into the system you should first decide whether it is a balance sheet or profit and loss account. Next, you need to think about the account type. At this point you are actually deciding what the account group should be. The GL account group has two main purposes:

► It defines the fields status when creating a GL account, that is, the fields that must be completed when creating a new GL account.

► It controls the numbering convention within which the GL account can be created.

GL account groups are defined at the chart of accounts level, so you should create a set of account groups per chart of accounts. Looking at our chart of accounts, we should group together our GL accounts by type. For instance, we did something similar when we looked at our level 1 and level 2 structure in Chapter 2 (see Figure 2.12). You should therefore define GL account groups for different types of accounts in line with your level 2 chart of accounts structure. To access the account group configuration screen, use the menu path **Financial Accounting (new) • General Ledger Accounting (new) • Master Data • G/L accounts • Preparations • Define Account Group** or Transaction code OBD4.

For SAFA Inc., we have provided detailed analysis of the GL account groups we will create in the appendices (see Table 3.3). To create a new account group, click on **New Entries** and define the account group name, description, and account range as shown in Figure 3.8.

Chart of Accounts	Account Group	Description	From	To
1000	FASS	Fixed assets	10000	14999
1000	CASS	Current assets	15000	15999
1000	CLIB	Current liabilities	20000	24999
1000	LIAB	Long-term liabilities	25000	29999
1000	CAPT	Capital and reserves	30000	39999
1000	SALE	Sales	40000	49999
1000	COGS	Cost of sales	50000	59999
1000	OHDS	Overheads	60000	69999
1000	BTLI	Below the line items	70000	79999
1000	MISC	Miscellaneous	1	99999

Table 3.3 SAFA Inc. GL Account Group

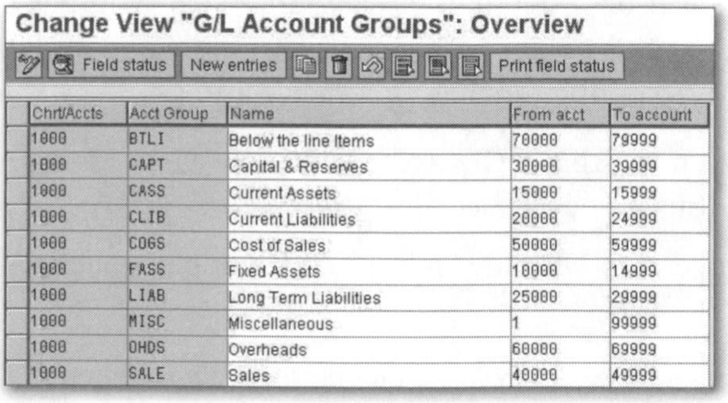
Change View "G/L Account Groups": Overview

ChrtAccts	Acct Group	Name	From acct	To account
1000	BTLI	Below the line Items	70000	79999
1000	CAPT	Capital & Reserves	30000	39999
1000	CASS	Current Assets	15000	15999
1000	CLIB	Current Liabilities	20000	24999
1000	COGS	Cost of Sales	50000	59999
1000	FASS	Fixed Assets	10000	14999
1000	LIAB	Long Term Liabilities	25000	29999
1000	MISC	Miscellaneous	1	99999
1000	OHDS	Overheads	60000	69999
1000	SALE	Sales	40000	49999

Figure 3.8 Example GL Account Groups for SAFA Inc.

Defining account groups ensures that you are putting the correct level of controls in place for data capture. For instance, transactions involving cash receipts require some clearing steps. Therefore, these accounts need to be configured for "open item management." This is not relevant for all accounts, however, so only this range of GL accounts needs to have this setting, and you configure it through GL account groups.

Let's look at a simple example of a fixed-asset GL account group to understand the fields that are involved as shown in Figure 3.9. Each screen relates to an area of the GL master record, and the settings you make here will effect the creation of a GL account in that account group.

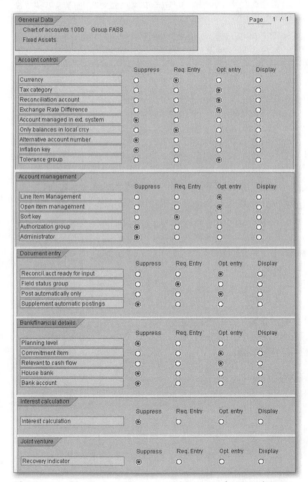

Figure 3.9 GL Account Group: Field Status for Fixed Asset

We have provided detailed examples of GL account groups that we created for SAFA Inc., and you may want to review these and the SAP standard groups provided to understand the types of settings you can make. In Table 3.4 we highlight some key fields that you should consider. You should review the use of all of these fields and then determine which are relevant to your business requirements.

Field	Use
Currency	This setting lets you specify the base currency for this GL account. You should always enter the company code currency here, for example, USD. All transactions that are entered against this GL account will be stored in the currency you specify. If you enter a transaction in another currency, the value will be translated and recorded in the specified currency, and a translation record will be kept.
	Currency is located in the company code view of the GL master record and therefore can be specific to each company code. In our scenario, GL accounts in company code 1000 have USD as the default currency, and company code 2000 has GBP as the default currency.
Tax category	This setting controls which tax categories can be referenced when posting against this GL account. You need to select a tax code when you enter a vendor or customer invoice, and this setting indicates for which types of accounts this is valid. Tax configuration settings are discussed in more detail at the end of this chapter. The following options are available to you:
	- indicates that only input tax postings are allowed to this account.
	+ indicates that only output tax postings are allowed to this account.
	* indicates that both input and output tax postings are allowed to this account.
	< indicates input tax on a tax account. This is for tax-control accounts (i.e., the balance sheet payables and receivables account).
	• indicates output tax on a tax account. This is for tax control accounts (i.e., the balance sheet payables and receivables account).
Reconciliation account	This field is used if the GL account is a system reconciliation account that is needed for postings between subledgers. Here you select the category based on from which subledger you are postings, that is,
	A: Fixed assets
	D: Customers
	K: Vendors
Exchange Rate Difference	If your business processes define foreign currency transactions, you would define configuration settings for the calculation and posting of gains and losses from exchange rate differences. Here you assign the valuation keys you are using.

Table 3.4 Key Fields Available in GL Account Groups

Field	Use
Account managed in ext. system	This option is selected if your GL account is managed elsewhere. If you are implementing a global solution, where different SAP systems are linked together (usually through application link enables technology), your master data objects may be managed through a different SAP system.
Only balances in local crcy	This setting forces all transactions to be recorded in the local currency. If you don't select this and post a foreign currency transaction to this GL account, the transaction will be recorded in the foreign currency and a translation will be done according to the current values in the currency translation tables.
Alternative account number	This field is used to provide a country chart of accounts view in addition to your own chart of accounts. It is possible to run reports on alternative account numbers by defining a financial statement version for the alternative account number. It is also possible to enter here the legacy account number and thus report on this as well.
Tolerance group	Tolerance groups are posting controls that control the value that can be posted and the amounts that are acceptable clearing differences. These are defined at a company code level (see Section 3.2.12).
Line Item Management	Selecting this option ensures that all line items posted against this GL account are maintained at the line item level. If you do not select this option, you will only be able to see balances posted to this account and not the actual line items that make up the balance. Normally, you would not select this option for system reconciliation accounts where numerous postings are made automatically.
Open item management	Open item management is the process of clearing items against one another. Items that are not cleared are referred to as *open items*, whereas items that are cleared are called *cleared items*. You will use open item management for a lot of your reconciliation work. You would select this for some balance sheet accounts, such as bank or cash clearing accounts and the goods receipt and invoice receipt account (see Chapter 9, Section 9.1 for more information on the goods receipt and invoice receipt GL account).
Sort key	When you post a line item in the system, a field called **Assignment** is populated. When you then run a report on this GL account (for instance, a GL account line item report), the system by default sorts by the values specified in the **Assignment** field. You use the **Sort key** field to select what the sort criteria will be for these reports by defining what value is populated in the **Assignment** field.

Table 3.4 Key Fields Available in GL Account Groups (cont.)

Field	Use
Authorization group	You can use this field to restrict access to this GL account. However, you will still need to work with your security and authorizations team to make this happen within the user roles; just entering a value here will not suffice.
Accounting Clerk or Administrator	This option can be used as a reporting tool by assigning this GL account to a clerk who may be responsible for reconciling this account as part of monthly accounting procedures. You can then run a report on the system to see which accounts have uncleared items by accounting clerk. This field has had a name change in recent versions; it was previously called Administrator.
Reconcil. acct ready for input	If you select this option and also specify a category in the **Reconciliation Account** field (as discussed earlier), the account is labeled as a system reconciliation account and cannot be posted to manually. This is a control setting to ensure that the subledger reconciliation accounts are not posted to directly and thus provide and true account of the subledger postings.
Field status group	Enter the field status group according to the earlier discussion (see 3.2.2). The selection you make here determines what fields must be entered when posting against this GL account.
Post automatically only	This option is not required for reconciliation accounts but is for other accounts to which you don't want to post manually. In our example, we will select this option for our stock account, as we do not want any manual postings made to it (and it is not a reconciliation account).
Supplement automatic postings	This option allows you to manually update the account assignment objects (cost center, internal order, etc.) for line items that are automatically generated by the system. This setting is not usually required.
Planning level	This field is used to provide the cash management position in the treasury component. We are not implementing this for our example.
Relevant to cash flow	This option is used to label a GL account for inclusion on cash flow analysis within the treasury component.
House bank	Use this setting to assign the relevant house bank to the GL account. This is valid for cash and bank GL accounts.
Bank account	Here you select the bank account ID for the selected house bank.
Interest calculation	This ID determines the interval at which the interest calculation should be run.

Table 3.4 Key Fields Available in GL Account Groups (cont.)

Let's now consider examples of business requirements that may influence your decision-making process with respect to the available GL account group fields:

- Cash accounts need to have **Open item management** set as optional.

- Line item display should be mandatory on all GL accounts other than reconciliation accounts.

- All balances should be recorded in the local currency, and any foreign currencies values that are posted will be automatically recorded.

- Sort key should be mandatory for all account groups because this is going to be a system-wide default.

- House bank information is only needed for cash and bank GL accounts.

- Fixed asset accounting requires GL accounts to be marked as reconciliation accounts (see Chapter 7).

We have now completed all of the relevant configuration to enable you to create GL accounts. We now move onto configuration relating to other areas of the documents, starting with document types.

3.2.4 Document Types

The *document type* is what you use to differentiate between all of the different documents created as a result of postings being entered into the system. The document type behaves as an identifier, but it also has some controls, such as assigning a specific number range to the document type, so that there is a sequential numbering convention behind each document you create. Number range configuration is discussed in more detail in the next section.

SAP systems are delivered with standard document types that most organizations tend to use. It is recommended that you use the same convention for your own document types, but some solutions require the creation of additional custom document types.

Default and Custom Document Types

The default document type for journals is SA. This is the default setting for all journals that you enter into the system with an out-of-the-box SAP installation. In the sections that follow, we do explain how to create your own document types and the related configuration. If you decide to customize document types and make another document type your default journal document type, then you need to perform the steps outlined in the following sections.

A common reason to create custom document types is to distinguish postings that come from interfaces and to assign separate controls for these interface document types. Document types are assigned a two-digit alphanumeric code to identify them. When defining a range of custom document types, you need to be clear of the business need.

> **Note**
>
> It is uncommon to create hundreds of custom document types. We have, however, worked with clients who have created a large number by defining one document type per interface to deal with numerous interfaces. Multiple document types might also need to be created to distinguish between different types of accounting journals.

Key Document Types

For readers who are new to SAP, we have listed some key document types in Table 3.5 based on SAP standard settings. You should copy from these when creating custom document types. As much as possible, try to use these document types in their current form, as this will make your future support of the system easier when you look for system upgrades.

Subcomponent	Use	Document Types
Asset Accounting	Asset posting	AA
	Depreciation	AF
General Ledger	Journal	SA
Accounts Receivable	Customer invoice	DR
	Customer payment	DZ
	Internal transfer from billing	RV
	Payment clearing	ZV
Accounts Payable	Vendor invoice	KR
	Vendor payment	KZ
	Goods issue	WA
	Goods receipt	WE

Table 3.5 Table of Common Document Types

Creating Finance Document Types

With SAP ERP ECC 6.0 and the new GL, you can have document types in either the entry view or the ledger view.

All Financial Accounting Component (FI) document types are created in the menu path **Financial Accounting (new) • Financial Accounting Global Settings (new) • Document • Document Types • Define Document Types for Entry View** or by using Transaction code OBA7. When you enter this screen, you will see the list of document types as shown in Figure 3.10.

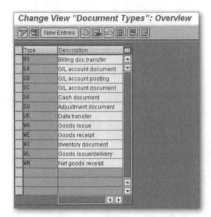

Figure 3.10 Standard Delivered SAP Document Types

Double-click on any line to display the detailed configuration settings for that document type, as shown in Figure 3.11.

Figure 3.11 Detailed Configuration Settings for a Document Type

Table 3.6 explains the purpose of the fields on this configuration screen.

Field	Usage
Account Types	This setting lets you select the account types that use a document type. Certain document types are restricted, however, for example, Document type KR, vendor invoice, will not allow a customer item to be posted on it. A: Assets D: Customers K: Vendors M: Materials S: General Ledger
Reversal Document Type	Within an SAP system, you can reverse original transactions automatically by performing a document reversal transaction. Using the reversal document type configuration setting, you define what document type this reversal will be. The default SAP system setting is for document type SA to reverse as SB. You may want your reversal to remain the same document type. If so, leave this field blank.
Authorization Group	You can use this field within your SAP access and controls design to control who can access or use this document type.
Net Document Type	For vendor invoice-related document types, you can use this field to allow only a single customer or vendor.
Multiple Companies	This setting lets you restrict the document types that can be used for cross-company code postings.
Enter Trading Partner	This setting allows you to manually enter the trading partner on the document, overriding the default value (which would otherwise be derived from the vendor master record).
Reference Number	This setting allows you to make the **Reference** field on the document header mandatory. This is useful in different documents, for instance, on AP invoices, where your process should make it mandatory for the supplier's invoice number to be entered into the **Reference** field. This also makes it possible to configure the duplicate invoice check, which we will discuss in detail later.
Document Header Text	This setting is used to make the document header text field mandatory. You might be inclined to make this field mandatory on all documents, but keep in mind what information will be input here and how useful users will find it. Configuring this for all postings may create additional overhead, without much benefit.

Table 3.6 Configuration Settings for Document Type Configuration

Field	Usage
Batch Input Only	This setting will prevent manual postings being made with this document type. If you use this document type for an interface, you will be able to prevent users from entering their own transactions using this document type.
Exchange Rate for Foreign Currency Documents	If you leave this unselected, transactions in foreign currencies (compared to the company code currency) will be according to the average rate, or M rate, stored in the exchange rate table. This option lets you select the exchange rate type when entering your transaction.

Table 3.6 Configuration Settings for Document Type Configuration (cont.)

Power User Tip

You can search for documents easily in the system by the **Reference** field (via Transaction FB02). Thus, if you can come up with a good convention here, you can use the combination of document type, posting date, and **Reference** field to locate your documents easily.

You need to assign a number range against each document type, and this is the next activity that we look at. Without a number range, you cannot use a document type. It is possible to share number ranges between different document types.

Caution

If you have splitting activated, you need to configure your document type for splitting. This is discussed in detail in Chapter 4.

3.2.5 Document Number Ranges

Each SAP document carries a document number that provides a reference for you to recall the document at a later stage. SAP documents are commonly criticized for having long numbers that are difficult to remember or understand. For this reason, it is normal to do some analysis and evaluation of the volume of transactions that you are likely to process through the system. The SAP system will probably generate more documents than most legacy systems that you may be operating. If you are upgrading from an old version of an SAP system, you have an idea of the volume of data you will generate in your SAP system.

Internal and External Numbering

The normal procedure is to assign a number range, within which the system automatically allocates the next sequential number to the document being saved. There are some instances where you may want to assign the document number based on external criteria. Two common examples are:

▸ For incoming interfaces, your sending system may send a document number that you want to adopt, to keep both the SAP document number and the sending system's document numbers in synch with each other.

▸ In the case of the internal billing interface from the Sales & Distribution component (SD) to Accounts Receivable (AR) (see Chapter 6, Figure 6.1), you may want to have the same billing document number as the equivalent AR document that is produced. This can be done by aligning the billing document number range and the AR document number range. Then set the AR document number range as being externally defined, and the system will accept the document number that is sent from the billing document.

It is worth doing some analysis on the volume of transactions you process in your current system to determine the size of the number range you are likely to need when you implement your SAP system.

Caution
Remember, the document number is there for storing and recording your transactions, so it is likely that some audit requirements need to be satisfied. Do not try to save space by using too few number ranges or go to the opposite extreme and give out too many.

Configuring Number Ranges

Number range configuration can be accessed via the same screen as document types by clicking on the **Number Range Information** button as shown in Figure 3.11, above.

Typically, you copy the number ranges from the SAP-delivered base company code. This ensures that all standard document types have number ranges created for them. Alternatively, you can create your own number ranges via the menu path **Financial Accounting (new)** • **Financial Accounting Global Settings (new)** • **Document** • **Document Types** • **Define Document Types for Entry View** or by using Transaction code OBA7.

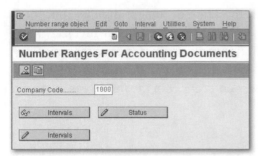

Figure 3.12 Creating Document Number Ranges

The pencil icon with the word **Intervals** indicates change mode, whereas the glasses icon with the word **Intervals** indicates display mode. To create new number ranges, you need to be in change mode, so click on the appropriate button. This brings up the screen shown in Figure 3.13.

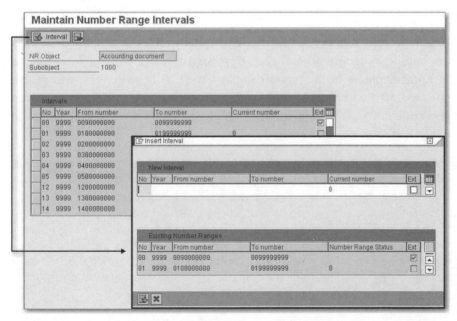

Figure 3.13 Create New Number Range Interval

You add new intervals by clicking on the Insert Interval button (the button with the insert icon plus the word **Interval**) and then entering the range you want to create. Number ranges can be year specific or year independent. If you create them to be year specific, the range will reset itself at the beginning of each year. In this instance, you would have journals with the same document number, but identifiable by their fiscal year. This is not the best idea for customer invoices, however, so you may want to assign a large range and have year-independent number ranges. In this scenario, when you move to the next year, the next sequential number will be used. To do this, you must enter 9999 in the fiscal year as shown in Figure 3.13.

Externally Assigned Number Ranges

We have already mentioned that it is possible to have an externally assigned number range, where the document number is assigned by the user. This is sometimes used in interfaces where an external system passes a file to your SAP system, which already carries a document number that you want to use in the SAP system. For this document type, you assign a number range that is externally defined. You may want to have the same document number in both systems for reconciliation or clearing purposes.

It is possible to copy number ranges across company codes. It is also possible to copy the number range from fiscal year. Copying is only possible if there are no existing number ranges in the target company code. Otherwise, you will get an error message. Start with the SAP standard number ranges that you can copy from company code 0001. Then add number ranges that correspond to the custom document types that you have created.

> **Power User Tip**
>
> When you look at the document types and their corresponding numbers, it is often confusing, as the document type name is usually two alpha characters and the number range name is usually two numeric characters. In our solution designs, we always make the number range name the same as the document type, so we assign a number range SA to document type SA. This makes it very easy to see the linkage. To do this, we usually have to delete some standard number ranges, so you should maintain a spreadsheet to link the number ranges with the document types.

The last point to make in this section is in relation to the document number range table. This table, which you configure, stores the number ranges as discussed, but in addition there is a field called **Current Number**. This is the current number used within this number range. If you transport this table, the value in this current number will also be transported, and if you transport this to a client where postings have already been made, this current number value will be reset in line with the value in the source system (usually zero). Although it is possible to transport this table, it is usually labeled as a manual transport task, that is, you should manually create your number ranges in each new client.

We'll now briefly look at the theory behind interledger postings to prepare for the discussions remaining in this chapter.

3.2.6 Purpose of Subledger Reconciliation Accounts

The Financial Accounting Component (FI) covers a number of different processes, which we have referred to as subledgers. The reason for this is that the principles of one ledger, for example, a purchase ledger will always be different from another ledger, for example, the fixed assets ledger. The strength of SAP ERP Financials is that these subledgers talk to each other very well, and the result is a seamless link for SAP ERP Financials users.

Let's look at an example of a interledger posting.

Entering a Vendor Invoice

When entering a vendor invoice, you will make the following postings:

▶ Cr (31): Vendor

▶ Dr (40): GL expense

The actual posting that takes place will be:

▶ In AP:

  ▶ Cr (31): vendor

  ▶ Dr (40): vendor reconciliation account

▶ In the GL:

  ▶ Cr (50): Vendor reconciliation account

  ▶ Dr (40): GL expense

Note
You do not actually see the two lines being posted to the reconciliation account.

Let's now look in more detail at the configuration of document posting keys.

3.2.7 Document Posting Keys

When making a double-entry posting, there needs to be a balance of the total debits and credits. SAP software uses posting keys to indicate whether the line item being posted is a debit or a credit. It also allows you to have separate posting keys for a type of transaction. Table 3.7 shows the main posting keys that you'll likely encounter.

Transaction Type	Debit	Credit
Vendor items	21	31
GL	40	50
Customer items	01	11

Table 3.7 Common Posting Keys

To complete the configuration, follow themenu path **IMG • Financial Accounting (new) • Financial Accounting Global Settings (new) • Document • Define Posting Keys** or use Transaction code OB41

SAP configuration allows you to define different posting keys per transaction type; that is, a credit for a journal has a different posting key than a credit for a vendor invoice. In addition to providing debit and credit control, you can also define controls over field status similar to the field status group controls discussed previously.

Control is obtained by restricting the types of accounts that can use a particular posting key, so in Figure 3.14, you can see that the posting key is defined for a particular type of account. You can make all of these fields optional and have control purely in the field status groups behind the GL account. This is an acceptable practice. Alternatively, you may want to assign some specific control based on the posting key. Because the posting key can be linked to a type of account (e.g., vendor invoice, customer payment, etc.), you may be able to enforce additional controls on your posting through this configuration activity.

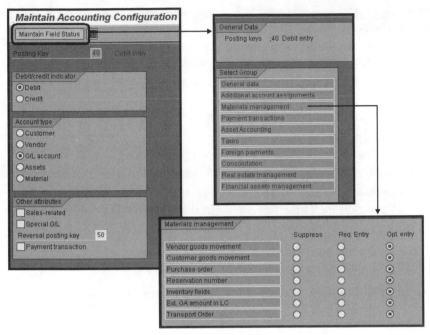

Figure 3.14 Basic Configuration of Posting Keys

In Table 3.8 we explain the purpose of the fields on the posting key header screen.

Field	Usage
Debit or Credit indicator	Select the correct option for this posting key.
Account type	Select the account type for this posting key.
Sales related	This indicates that the posting key is related to invoicing a customer.
Special GL	Here you can indicate if the posting key is used for a special GL transaction (e.g., down payments).
Reversal Posting Key	Enter the reversal posting key. If you reverse this document using Transaction FB08, the system will automatically determine the reversal posting key from this table.
Payment transaction	Indicate if the posting key is used for any type of payment transaction.

Table 3.8 Posting Key Configuration

> **Caution**
>
> It is important not to edit the SAP standard posting keys without knowledge of the consequences of your actions. You may remove a field in the posting key field status that is needed in the field status variants, so both actions should be aligned.

If you edit the field status of a posting key, that change will affect that line of any document that you post using that posting key. A common requirement is to make better use of the **Reason Code** field on payment transactions. Standard SAP posting key configuration has this field suppressed. This might be used for payment processing as well as journal entry, for example. In both cases, a reason code is entered to provide additional information about the nature of the transaction. For instance, if a customer only makes a partial payment, on this line you may want to record the reason for this partial payment. Alternatively, you may use this on lines where you have manually allowed customer discounted payment terms.

Let's now look at additional features of the document entry process.

3.2.8 Updating Layout for Document Entry Screen

When entering a document, you may be unhappy with the fields on display because there are too many to look at. Since the introduction of the new SAP Enjoy screens (from 4.5 onwards), the user layouts are much easier to use. In previous versions, you needed to create a fast entry screen in which you would select only those fields that you wanted to use. Now, you can configure the document entry screen layout to meet your requirements. Note that the changes made here influence all Financial Accounting Component (FI) document entry screens, including transactions vendor and customer document entry.

The document entry screen is configured as follows:

1. Select the **Change Screen Layout** button as shown in Figure 3.15.
2. On the next screen (see Figure 3.16), create a variant, which is either specific to yourself (in which case give it a name) or can be activated as the standard setting for all users (in which case leave the variant name as blank).
3. On the next screen, select the fields you want to activate and that are to become invisible. Once you have made your selection, you need to save and click on the **Transport** button.

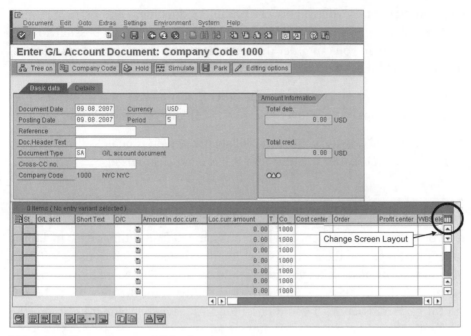

Figure 3.15 Change Document Entry Screen Layout

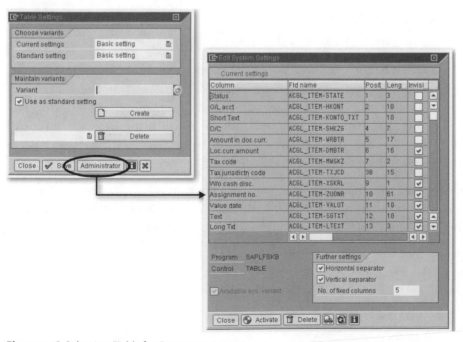

Figure 3.16 Selecting Fields for Document Layout

Having completed this, you will now return to the document entry screen (Figure 3.15). You will now only see the fields that you have selected. It is possible to drag some of the fields so you can order them to suit your needs. The only fixed fields are the **G/L acct**, **Short Text**, **D/C**, and **Amount**.

Once you have arranged your fields in the order that suits you, you should re-enter the table settings option (as shown in Figure 3.16) and save and activate again.

This is a very useful activity; your users will greatly benefit from it, as they will find the screen much more user friendly after it has been customized.

3.2.9   GL Document Display and Layouts (Default Settings)

When you open up a document entry screen, some default settings exist including the document type and the posting keys. You may have decided to use a different document type or posting key for specific transactions. For example, you may be using custom document types for journals and thus want the defaults to be different for each transaction. If you do nothing and leave the standard settings, the system will default the following document types:

▶ Journals: SA

▶ Vendor invoices: KR

▶ Customer invoices: DR

If you want to define your own document types, you can do so by SAP transaction code. Let's say we want to define our own document type and posting key as the system default. We can define our default document type and posting key by following the menu path **IMG • Financial Accounting (new) • Financial Accounting Global Settings (new) • General Ledger Accounting (new) • Business Transactions • GL Account Posting**.

These settings can be made by company code, which is independent of the chart of accounts. In the example of default posting keys, these are set by account type. Figure 3.17 shows the default settings for GL account posting.

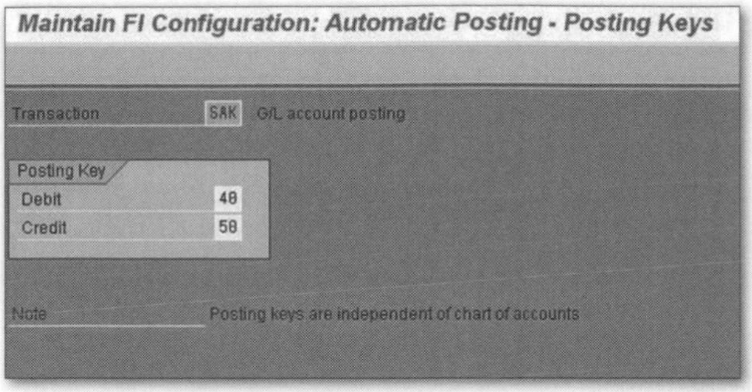

Figure 3.17 Defining Default Posting Keys for Enjoy Transactions

It is also possible to change defaults for other transactions as well. You can make changes for other common transactions in the menu path **IMG • Financial Accounting (new) • Financial Accounting Global Settings (new) • Accounts Receivable and Accounts Payable • Business Transactions • Incoming Invoices / Credit Memos • Make and Check document settings • Define default values** or by using Transaction code OBU1.

This is shown in Figure 3.18.

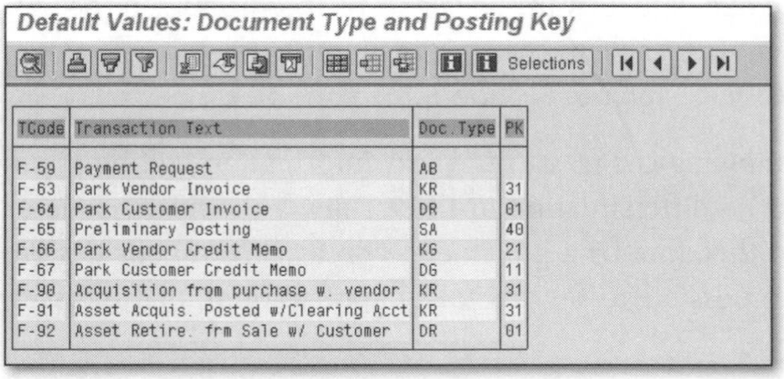
Default Values: Document Type and Posting Key

TCode	Transaction Text	Doc.Type	PK
F-59	Payment Request	AB	
F-63	Park Vendor Invoice	KR	31
F-64	Park Customer Invoice	DR	01
F-65	Preliminary Posting	SA	40
F-66	Park Vendor Credit Memo	KG	21
F-67	Park Customer Credit Memo	DG	11
F-90	Acquisition from purchase w. vendor	KR	31
F-91	Asset Acquis. Posted w/Clearing Acct	KR	31
F-92	Asset Retire. frm Sale w/ Customer	DR	01

Figure 3.18 Default Settings for Other Financial Accounting Component (FI) Transactions

Defining default settings here is only required if you are deviating from the SAP standard document types and posting keys. If you are using the standard settings, then this step is not relevant.

Next we look at document change rules that are applicable to all Financial Accounting Component (FI) documents.

3.2.10 Document Change Rules

When a transaction is entered into the system, a document is created that records the information relating to it. This document is both the record of the transaction and an audit trail to provide information about who made the transaction and when it occurred. If you need to make corrections to a completed document, this needs to be done as a separate correction transaction. It is important to understand that it is not possible to make changes to the financial information contained in the original transaction you entered into the system, but changes are only possible to the supplementary information as explain below. If you enter a journal into the system and it is wrong, you must create a correcting journal or a reversal journal to deal with it. You cannot simply correct it through this functionality.

What you are allowed to change in a journal is some of the textual information. For instance, you may feel after entering the transaction that there is insufficient information to explain its purpose, or you may want to add a note that can be understood by someone else who may come across the journal.

Other fields that you may want to change exist on the vendor or customer invoice. Payment terms and baseline date can be changed to manipulate the invoice due date (i.e., bring the invoice due date forward or take it further back). On the customer invoice, you may want to be able to change the dunning-related fields (e.g., dunning block) as discussed in Chapter 6, Section 6.8.

The rules you define for allowing changes to the text information will be applicable system wide; there is no differentiation of these rules by company code or any other object. It should therefore be a policy decision as part of your design. Figure 3.19 shows that it is possible to set this for type of account, that is, asset, customer, vendor, and so on.

There are two configuration screens to work with here: one for the header information and one for the line items. Both are found in the same area, **IMG • Financial Accounting (new) • Financial Accounting Global Settings (new) • Document • Rules for Changing Documents**, or use Transaction code OB32 (header) or Transaction code OB32A (line items).

For a rule applied for the document line items, the logic is the same for line items. You must first select the field for which you want to apply this rule.

This configuration activity is shown in figure 3.19.

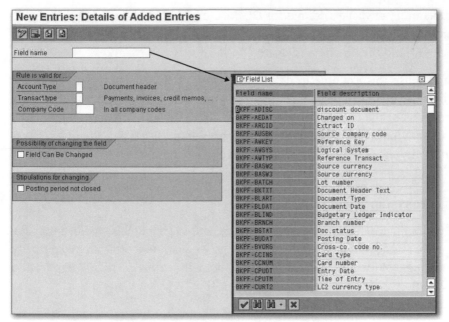

Figure 3.19 Example of a Document Change Rule

You define the rule by account type, so the rule we have created is applicable for GL documents. You can also define the rule by company code, so if there are country specific rules, these are be imposed. Figure 3.20 shows the complete document change rule.

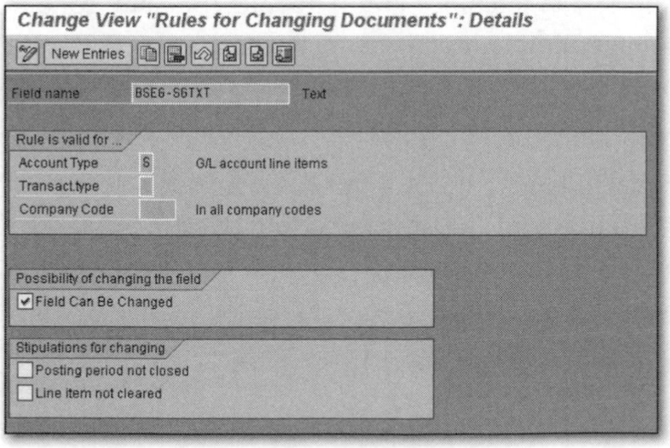

Figure 3.20 Example of a Document Change Rule

In our example, we have said that for GL documents, line item text is changeable only after the document has been posted. This can be changed, even if the period is not closed and the line item is cleared.

You should use this example to define your own rules. You may want to define rules for what fields can be changed. For example, on vendor line items, you may want to prevent the changing of the Payment Terms field. This means you must retain the payment terms that were entered on the invoice when the invoice was created, and you cannot change them to anyone's benefit.

3.2.11 Cross–Company Code Settings

For SAFA Inc., we defined two company codes, and to enable this we need to make appropriate configuration settings. Specifically, we want to enable cross–company code postings. With the changes brought about by new GL, this configuration activity is discussed in Chapter 4, Section 4.3.4.

3.2.12 Employee Tolerances

Despite having done a lot of configuration, you will still be unable to post any documents yet. Before we can make a posting in the system, we need to set up posting tolerances. These tolerances must exist in the system as controls to define the value of documents you can post.

SAP requires you to define at least one tolerance group in your company code to allow postings to take place. Some solution designs use postings tolerance controls to restrict the value of transactions that can be posted by users in the system, so different groups of users will be restricted accordingly.

Two activities need to be completed here. For both, follow the menu path **IMG • Financial Accounting (new) • Financial Accounting Global Settings (new) • Document • Tolerance Groups • Define Tolerance Groups for Employees** or use Transaction code 0BA4.

First we define our tolerance groups as shown in Figure 3.21.

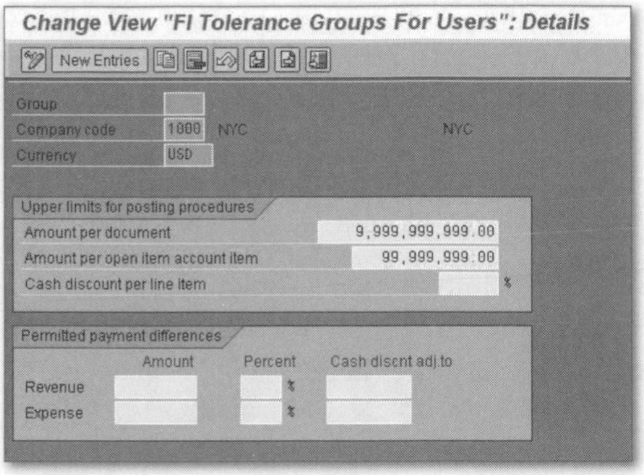

Figure 3.21 General Financial Accounting Component (FI) Tolerance Group

You need to define at least one tolerance group, but notice in Figure 3.20 that we have not given it a name. We will discuss this when we look at assigning users to the tolerance group (see below).

You define the tolerance group for your company code currency, so for company code 1000, we define USD. We then define the upper limits for posting documents, which applies to all Financial Accounting Component (FI) documents. Because we are creating a single group for all users, we defined a global setting to enable all users to make postings, but you may design something that restricts different groups of people by what amounts they can enter and what discounts they can give.

The permitted payment differences restrict the amount of discount you can give to a customer in terms of payment difference. In this example, we have left these fields blank because we will configure this elsewhere (see Chapter 9, Section 9.1.3). The configuration activity that we complete in Chapter 9 is a global setting that controls what payment differences can be posted generally for a customer. In this screen, we can restrict by tolerance group and therefore by user (as we link users to tolerance groups) which are the permitted payment differences (as defined above in figure 3.21). Thus, if you need to control this by user, you should make your settings in this activity.

Once you have decided on your tolerance groups, the next step is to assign them to users. To complete this activity, follow the menu path **Financial Accounting (new) • Financial Accounting Global Settings (new) • Document • Tolerance Groups • Define Tolerance Groups for Employees** or use Transaction code 0B57

In our scenario, we have created a default group that we want to assign to all users. As we did not give this group a name (see Figure 3.21), then when we come to the assignment of Tolerance group screen (Figure 3.22) all users are automatically assigned to this "blank tolerance group." If though your design creates individual Tolerance Groups for different groups of people then you need to assign them specially here.

To be clear, any user ID that is not entered into the table shown in Figure 3.22, will be assigned to our default tolerance group. For specific assignments over and above this default group, we must enter the user IDs here.

Figure 3.22 Assignment of Users to Tolerance Groups

In our example above, the three users specified are assigned to these specific groups, and all other user IDs are assigned to the default tolerance group. Organizations that process large numbers of transactions from customers tend to adopt different tolerance groups to control the ability to give customer discounts, and you should consider this if it relevant to your scenario.

3.2.13 Change Message Control for Posting to GL Accounts

SAP allows you to change the status of system messages from error to warning or even turn them off completely. Before you do this, you need to be aware of that this action could cause a corruption in the integrity of the system. However, some messages are frequently altered in implementations, and this section gives a prime example. To know what message needs to be changed, you need to find out the message number. This is given in the pop-up box, so if your message comes only at the bottom of the screen, you must double-click on for the message to pop-up.

Figure 3.23 shows an example of a system message.

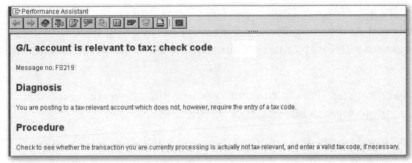

Figure 3.23 Example of a Message for which We Want to Configure Settings

In Figure 3.23, we can see that the message number is **FS 219**, where **FS** is the application area and **219** is the actual message within that application area. You need both pieces of information to make changes.

Application areas are ways of grouping together messages depending on the part of the system. Figure 3.24 gives examples of application areas that are available in the system.

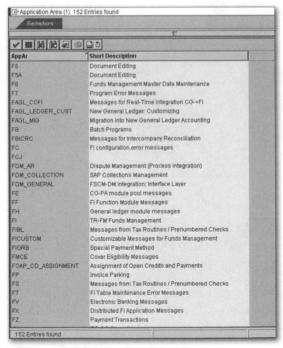

Figure 3.24 Message Class Application Areas

To access the **Change Message Control for Document Processing** screen, follow the path **Financial Accounting (new) • Financial Accounting Global Settings (new) • Document • Default values • Change Message Control for Document Processing**.

In this configuration step, you first need to confirm the application area that is relevant for your message. In our situation we select **FS**.

Next click on **New Entries** and enter the message number and then make the entries you want. The options are usually error, warning, information, or switch off, and you should make your settings appropriate to your overall system design. The system controls the available options here, so it is not always possible to make every message an error message. Figure 3.25 shows the settings that need to be made for this configuration activity.

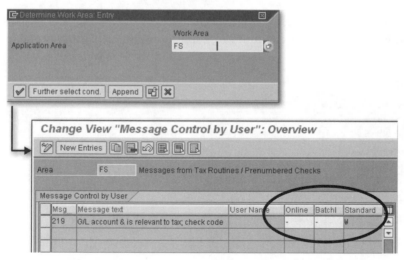

Figure 3.25 Change Message Status

There are online messages (which are called when a user is using the system) and batch messages (which are called when a background program is running a transaction. You should consider using these settings for batch processing.

There is a field here for entering a user name. If this is populated, the message settings you make will be valid for this user only; if you leave it blank, this setting is valid for all system users.

3.2.14 Financial Statement Versions

When I first started working with SAP, in the late 1990's, a lot of emphasis was placed on the creation of a financial statement version (referred to as an FS version), which would serve as a trial balance. As part of the period-end process, you would run the FS version to produce a list of balances for each GL account. The advancements in reporting functionality in SAP ERP Financials result in a reduced need to produce FS versions, as we can obtain data from other sources.

There still remains the need to produce trial balance style information. In earlier versions of SAP ERP Financials, most financial reports came out of the GL, and customized reports were only available from ABAP reporting. FS versions were created in configuration, so changes to the report required configuration activity. The tools available to us now, Report Painter and SAP NetWeaver BI in particular, are a lot more flexible and do not require configuration to make changes to them. As a result, the use of the FS version is less common.

We will briefly explain how an FS version is set up, even though we don't anticipate you needing this activity. This configuration is done in the menu path **Financial Accounting (new) • General Ledger Accounting (new) • Master Data • GL Accounts • Define Financial Statement Versions** or by using Transaction code OB58.

You can see from Figure 3.26 that a number of predefined financial statement versions are delivered, which are valid for the appropriate SAP-delivered SAP charts.

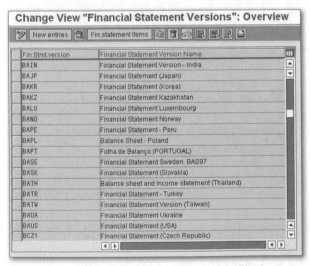

Figure 3.26 SAP-Delivered Financial Statement Versions

You can create your own FS version and define your own structure by clicking on the **New Entries** button as shown in Figure 3.26.

Each FS version must have a header portion where you specify the basic information, such as its name, the language, and the chart of accounts it relates to. If you are manually defining your FS version, you should not select the item keys auto option; if you do select this, the system will automatically assign the GL accounts based on the GL account number. Because we are not adopting a group chart of accounts in our scenario, we do not need to select this. The last option on this page is only relevant if you have a number of functional areas. This option allows you to assign a functional area to the GL accounts.

You now should click on **Fin. Statement items**, which will take you to the structure of the FS version, as shown in Figure 3.27.

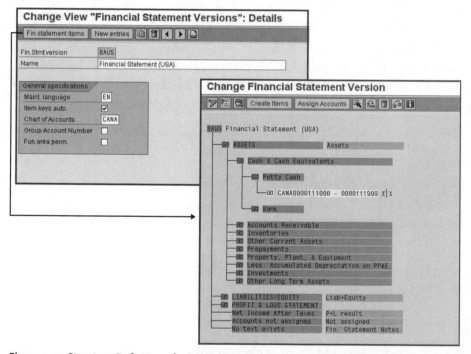

Figure 3.27 Structure Definition of a BAUS (Financial Statement USA) Financial Statement Version

Here you will see some basic groups defined by SAP that need to be assigned against for your FS version to work correctly. You can assign all your accounts to the correct group, and the system will give a trial balance style report.

We have completed our review of the area of configuration that we label financial accounting global settings. We hope you understand how these settings influence all modules within SAP ERP Financials. We end this chapter by looking at sales and purchase tax.

3.3 Sales and Purchase Tax

The configuration of tax in SAP ERP Financials is fairly straight forward, and complications normally result from misunderstanding the statutory rules for the country in which you trade. This section goes into a lot of detail to explain the configuration screens, although this level of understanding is not necessary for most implementation as you can adopt the standard settings available. It is important that you study the taxation rules for the country in which you operate. If you are implementing in the United States, the laws are more complex, and you should be aware of what is required. This chapter is not designed to provide a detailed analysis of tax laws but to provide sufficient information for the reader to be able to adopt the SAP-delivered standard procedures. We also show how you can create additional tax codes that may be required.

> **Note**
>
> Taxation is very specific to the country in which you are operating. For instance, U.S. tax laws are state specific, whereas tax laws in Europe are country specific. This chapter is very important to your overall SAP ERP Financials solution, so we strongly recommend that you clearly understand your specific legal tax requirements before reading this section. It does not matter if you are not a tax expert, as the SAP system comes preconfigured with settings for most countries, and it will be easy to adopt these preconfigured settings to your specific situation.
>
> The adoption of SAP-delivered tax procedures is the usual starting position, as there is enough there to satisfy most requirements.

Basic Definition

A tax is a charge made against a person or property or activity. Most countries have many forms of tax. In this section we are dealing with sales and purchase taxes. Bear in mind that taxes are ultimately collected by companies so that they can be passed onto the tax authorities. Because of this, accounting principles require us to post any tax amounts received from customers as current liabilities and tax already paid to vendors as current assets. We post these values to balance sheet GL accounts.

When invoices are processed, the account determination in the background makes postings to the correct GL accounts as defined in the configuration. The user defines in the invoice the appropriate tax code for this transaction, thereby controlling the posting to GL.

Taxes are defined as being either input (purchase) or output (sales) taxes. This definition comes from the direction in which the tax is being paid. In the United States, the tax procedures are much more complicated than those of some other countries because there are variations based on state law. For this reason the TAXUS procedure is adopted as it stands without much detailed discussion.

Tax configuration in SAP ERP Financials is done at the country level to meet legal requirements. SAP ERP Financials comes preconfigured with tax procedures for a number of countries. As a result, most implementations utilize the standard SAP procedures. It is important to note that in many global SAP ERP Financials projects, you will need to use different tax procedures to comply with each country's legal requirements. For instance, for SAFA Inc., we will use TAXUS (for our U.S. company) and TAXGB (for our UK company). In the following pages we explain how tax codes are configured within a tax procedure.

> **Note**
>
> There are additional settings not covered in this chapter that you will need to check if you are implementing in Argentina, Brazil, India, South Korea, Spain, or Slovakia.

Building Your Design for Tax Calculations

Tax codes are used as part of invoice processing, and the assumption is that you select the tax code to put some control into both your calculation and your recording of the tax collected or paid. The posting of tax should be an automatic step within the invoice, so you select the tax code, and the system calculates the percentage payable and the correct GL account to which to post it. With the implementation of document splitting, the system now determines the correct profit center assignment for tax as well, which is explained in detail in Chapter 4, Section 4.3.5.

Most organizations have a tax officer or a nominated person in the finance team who understands the legal requirements as well as the GL postings. We recommend creating a table (see Table 3.9) and agreeing on this level of information before you start configuring.

Tax Code	Description	Percentage	GL Account
E1	AP sales tax, 6% state, 1% county 1%, city accrued	6.00	15180
I1	AP sales tax, 6% state, 1% county, 1% city distributed	6.00	15181
O1	AR sales tax, 6% state, 1% county, 1% city	6.00	20180
O0	AP sales tax, 6% state, 1% county, 1% city distributed	0.00	20181

Table 3.9 Tax Code Configuration List

In Table 3.9 we have listed all of the required tax codes for our tax solution, and this table will become the control for configuration settings.

Tax calculation configuration is completed in the menu path **Financial Accounting (new) • Financial Accounting Global Settings (new) • Tax on sales/purchases**. The first activity to do is the assignment of nontaxable tax codes to your company code.

Assign Nontaxable Transactions to Company Code

You need to assign the tax codes that should be used for tax exempt transactions. To configure this, follow the menu path **Financial Accounting (new) • Financial Accounting Global Settings (new) • Tax on sales/purchases • Posting • Assign tax codes for non-taxable transactions** or use Transaction code OBLC. Figure 3.28 shows how to make this assignment.

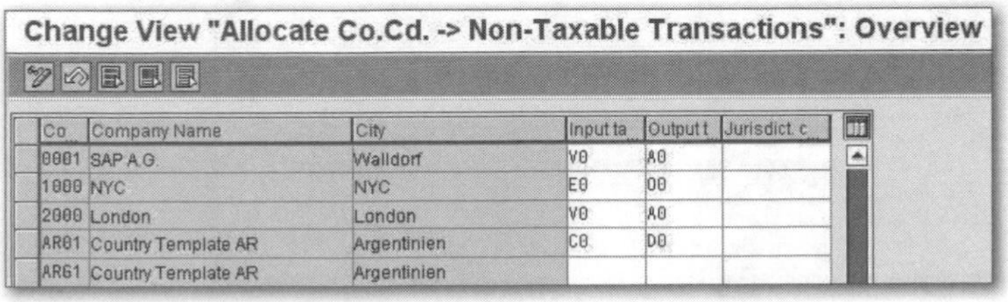

Figure 3.28 Assign Nontaxable Codes

This step must be completed, as it is a system requirement. You may have other tax codes that are also nontaxable, which you cannot assign here because the system only allows you to make a single pair of entries. You will still be able to use these other tax codes as well, so this step won't restrict your ability to use them.

We will now move through the steps, explaining how the configuration works and looking at examples from different countries to explain the differences in tax laws.

3.3.1 Basic Settings

Tax Calculation Procedures

SAP ERP Financials comes preloaded with tax calculation procedures for each country. In addition, tax codes are defined for each country that are relevant to that country's tax laws and regulations. It is always worth looking on OSS to find any new releases for your country. In addition, many tax authorities are familiar with SAP and have SAP-specific advice to give you.

Financial Accounting (new) • **Financial Accounting Global Settings (new)** • **Tax on sales/purchases** • **Basic settings** • **Check calculation procedure** or Transaction code OBYZ.

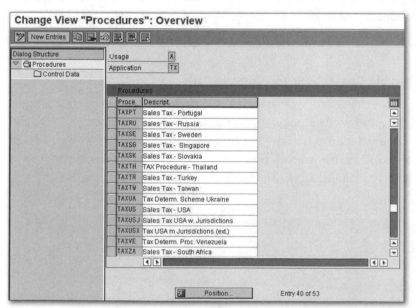

Figure 3.29 Standard Tax Procedures

Figure 3.29 shows the list of procedures that are standard in a system. Look to see which are relevant for your situation. There is more than one procedure for the United States.

It is also important to remember that you should not change these standard tax calculation procedures. If you have a specific requirement resulting from a recent change in the taxation legislation in your country, it is advisable to first contact SAP to see if they are issuing any updates (these are called hotpacks) for taxes. SAP remains in contact with local taxation offices globally and will probably be aware of an impending change that you should review and adopt.

Although we are telling you to configure access sequences (see below), it is important to understand their makeup. The calculation procedure is made up of three components.

Access Sequences

Access sequences define the fields that the system will validate and that are relevant for your country's tax procedure. This can be seen in Figure 3.30

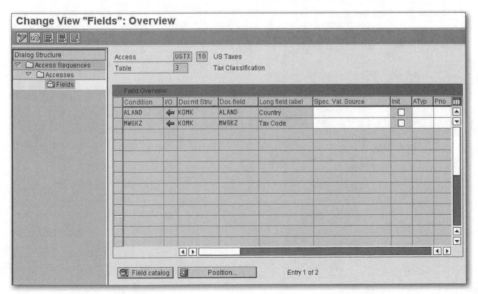

Figure 3.30 U.S. Tax Access Sequence

Tax Condition Types

MWST is the name of the tax condition type that has control over all tax calculations. All of the conditions in this tax condition table reference MWST, except for Brazil and the United States, which have their own condition type.

Behind a condition type is a configuration screen that defines how the tax condition works, but it does not require any percentages or link to GL to control postings. Figure 3.31 shows the universal configuration, meaning this condition can be used under different legal conditions.

You can see in Figure 3.31 that the condition is defined as a tax condition and calculated on a percentage basis (setting made in section **Control Data 1**).

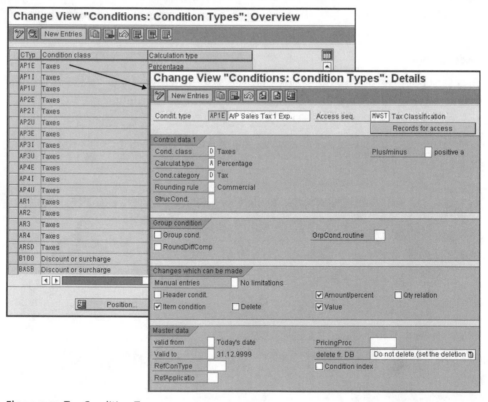

Figure 3.31 Tax Condition Type

Countries other than Brazil and the United States tend to use condition types MWAS (output tax) and MWVS (input tax). Both of these conditions have similar settings to those in Figure 3.31.

Tax Procedures

The country tax procedure brings together the condition types and the access sequence. Usually, you will not need to change the tax access procedure, and this is not a standard requirement.

Now we have completed the three components, the next activity would be to assign the procedure to the company code.

Assign Procedure to Company Code

Each country has a calculation procedure assigned to it. Because U.S. tax laws are more complicated, three separate calculation procedures are delivered with the system. You should consult SAP and your local tax rules to confirm which calculation procedures are most appropriate for your organization.

You make this assignment by following the menu path **Financial Accounting (new) • Financial Accounting Global Settings (new) • Tax on sales/purchases • Basic settings • Assign country to calculation procedure** or using Transaction code OBBG. This can be seen in Figure 3.32.

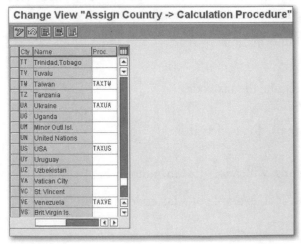

Figure 3.32 Assign Country to Tax Calculation Procedure

This completes our review of the basic settings for taxes. Next we look at the configuration of tax codes that control the posting of tax amounts to the ledger.

3.3.2 Posting

This section of the IMG covers the configuration steps that define the actual calculation percentages and the ways in which these values post to the GL. When we create an invoice, the system calculates the tax amount and posts it to the ledger, as shown in the following table.

Debit	Customer recon	129
Credit	Sales	100
Credit	Tax	29

Against the customer, we select a tax code, which then calculates the tax amount and posts it to the GL account that we assign to the that tax code. Follow the menu path **IMG • SPRO • Financial Accounting • Financial Accounting Global Settings • Tax on Sales/Purchases • Calculation • Define Tax Codes for Sales and Purchases** or use Transaction code FTXP to make this configuration.

Tax procedures are country specific, so within a country you should only adopt a single convention for your tax codes. This means we can use a code, for instance, A0, for both our company codes and have different meanings associated with them, but only because they are in different countries.

The tax code has three pieces of information:

▶ **Description**
This is the name we use to describe the tax code.

▶ **Percentage rates**
This is the percentages that are used for calculation.

▶ **Tax accounts**
These are the GL accounts against which we post the amount.

These become clearer as we look at an example of a tax code in Figure 3.33.

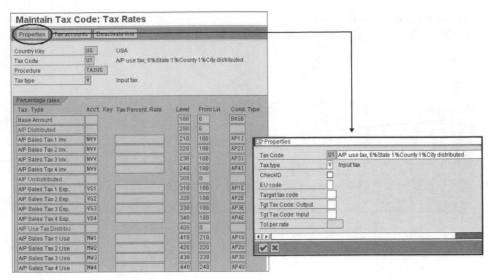

Figure 3.33 Example of Tax Code U1

Under **Properties** you can see the tax code's basic properties, description, and type. You can also see the check box that controls whether an error message is generated or not. The properties are normally the first thing you define in a new code.

Within the main area of the screen, you need to select the tax type and the percentage that this tax code relates to, as shown in Table 3.10.

Field	Description
Select Tax Type	Because this is a vendor-related tax code, it must be an input tax, so the values entered go against this line.
Tax Percent Rate	This is the rate applicable to this tax code, correct to three decimal places.

Tax codes in the UK are much simpler to explain and understand, as they tend to have a single percentage rate. Figure 3.34 shows how we assign the percentage.

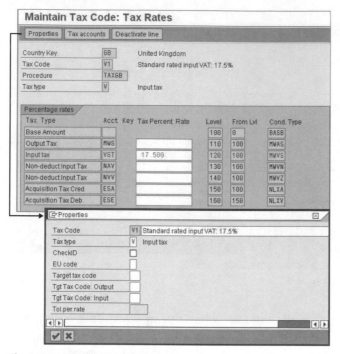

Figure 3.34 Example Tax Code V1

Because this example is of input tax, we defined our 17.5% value against the VST line. We could spend a lot of time explaining the different state taxes that are applicable in the United States, but for the purposes of our discussion, we will only explain how the percentage rate is defined against a tax code. Consult your country-specific settings to confirm the percentage rates you would use.

Assign a GL account to each tax code to receive postings. Click on the **Tax Accounts** button on the top menu bar to define this. It is possible to have different tax types within a single tax code. For instance, in some European countries you have a 50% exempt portion, which means tax types activate in the tax code. For this, you have two GL accounts to define in the tax accounts setting, which you can assign to the same or different GL accounts.

Figure 3.35 shows this example which is a real-life example from a European country requirement.

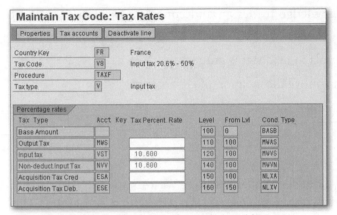

Figure 3.35 Example Tax Code with Nondeductable Portion

Custom Tax Codes

If you do want to create a custom tax code, you need to go into the FTXP screen and select your country and then enter the tax code you want to create. When you press Enter, the system displays a message saying, **Tax code is not defined** and opens the **Properties** box for you to create your tax code.

Having adopted this, you may see the need to create some custom tax codes to provide a detailed analysis of transactions. These codes should all be based on the standard codes within your procedure, so you should make copies of them.

We have looked at some different examples in different countries to explain the configuration of tax codes. We recommend trying to adopt the standard tax procedure relevant for your country as far as possible. This will ensure that there are sufficient links to the tax codes you need to define.

We close by again making the point that sales and purchase tax is a very specialized area. For the correct configuration, you need to consult both your local statutory laws and the SAP-delivered standard tax procedures and tax codes. There is usually sufficient information in the system to satisfy most organizations' requirements.

3.4   Summary

The objective of this chapter was to put into place the configuration settings that are relevant across all areas of finance. Having completed this chapter, the reader should have sufficient knowledge to design and configure a solution to meet requirements including:

▶ Document posting controls in field status groups

▶ GL account groups that control the creation of GL accounts

▶ Document types and number ranges

▶ Document change rules

▶ Sales and purchase tax

Now that we have configured the global settings, we can start looking at the detailed configuration specific to the subledgers. We start with a look at the GL in Chapter 4.

The new GL is a much awaited release from SAP. It is designed to improve data accuracy, enabling faster period close. This chapter gives a detailed explanation of the options available to you as you design your solution, as well as the configuration steps necessary to implement it.

4   New General Ledger

The objective of this chapter is to explain the functionality of the GL. With the release of SAP ERP Central Component (ECC) 6.0, SAP has made huge changes to the workings of the GL. Most organizations that implement SAP ERP ECC use the new GL, as it has significantly improved functionality. It is also possible to implement SAP ERP ECC 6.0 and retain the use of the classic GL, although there are significant shortcomings to doing so. We cover both of these scenarios throughout this chapter.

This chapter covers the new GL functionality, including:

▸ The differences in functionality between the classic and new GL

▸ Configuration of the new GL

▸ Introduction of a new account assignment object segment

▸ The new functionality included with document splitting

▸ Use of multiple ledgers

There is so much new information about the new GL that a single chapter cannot cover all of the complexities and available functionality that may be relevant for your specific needs. We have written this chapter to explain the concepts, and to demonstrate a standard new GL implementation. Most of the discussion and examples should be applicable for most implementations.

Additional information is available in Chapter 10, on data migration and reporting, which supports the implementation of the new GL.

4.1 Overview of the GL

The purpose of the GL in any SAP system is to provide the financial ledger that is used to produce the financial analysis. The ledger records all financial postings that may be generated from within the GL or from other ledgers. Because the GL receives all transactions that have a financial impact, it is often referred to as the heart of SAP (see Figure 4.1).

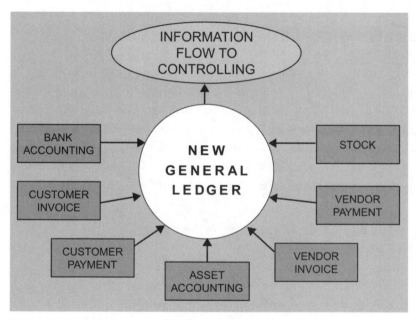

Figure 4.1 The GL Is the Heart of SAP

4.1.1 The New GL

With the introduction of SAP ERP ECC, there is a major difference in the functionality in the GL. The changes are so significant (see Figure 4.2) that it is referred to as the new GL. There are changes in basic principles, in that the makeup of the GL is now completely different.

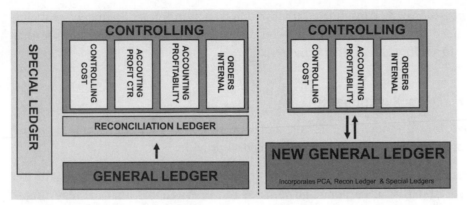

Figure 4.2 Differences in Classic and new GL

As SAP developed over time, additional components were developed as the need arose; for example, Profit Center Accounting and the special ledger were added on to provide additional reporting analysis. The move to SAP ERP ECC represents an improvement of the GL to incorporate the functionality that was previously outside it. Note that the menus now contain both classic and new GL nodes, so you can use it either way.

The changes have been brought about as a result of both internal and external pressure. Internally, customers have demanded improvements to reduce the amount of work involved in period end and increase the visibility of transaction processing. Externally, there has been a lot pressure as a result of the work done by the Sarbanes-Oxley requirements for more accurate financial reporting. In addition to this, customers had many concerns about the time it took to close the books at period end.

The shortcomings in functionality in previous releases that are addressed in the new GL include:

▶ Multinational organizations that need to provide consolidated financial reporting in line with different statutory requirements (i.e., United States vs. EU, etc.)

▶ Requirements to report multiple accounting methods such as U.S. GAAP Generally Accepted Accounting Principles) and IFRS (International Financial Reporting Standards)

▶ Requirements to provide departmental, product-category, or some other segment performance analysis

Desire to provide consolidated information, faster and more accurately, reducing the need to spend time at period-end reconciling control accounts and use that time for more value-adding activities

4.1.2 New Functionality

What does the new GL offer us, and why should organizations migrate to it? According to SAP, the new GL is designed to provide:

Streamlined functionality that makes it significantly easier to comply with the latest standards for corporate governance and international financial reporting—while adding flexibility and supporting a fast close.

Specifically, the new functionality includes the following:

▶ **Extended Data Structure**
This allows you to activate additional fields (e.g., segment) in the new GL table.

▶ **Document splitting**
This allows real-time allocation of an account assignment object to all your balance sheet postings; this is particularly relevant when you have postings from subledgers.

▶ **Parallel ledgers**
This provides the ability to produce different sets of financial statements.

▶ **Improved management reporting**
Profit centers are now part of the GL, which allows you to produce departmental or management accounts directly from the GL.

▶ **Segment reporting**
A segment is a new account assignment object that can be used to produce segment reports to provide an additional dimension. It helps in running analyses for objects at a level lower than company code. This is in line with the IFRS/IAS segment reporting requirements.

▶ **Fast close**
A reduction in the amount of time needed to complete the period-end cycle enables a fast close to be completed.

These points are explained in more detail later in the chapter. The net effect of implementing the new GL should always be a reduction in costs for the organization.

4.1.3 New Tables

The new GL continues to interface with standard tables from other modules, so integration there is not affected. However, three new tables have been created to support the new functionality:

▶ **New Totals Table**
Because we have incorporated additional fields, there is a requirement for a new table, FAGLTFLEX. This table can be customized to some extent to include additional fields and to change totals criteria. Some organizations may feel the need to create their own table due to the volume and complexity of data. Before you take this step you should consult SAP Note 820495. Any new tables you create will not be supported by standard reporting, so you should try to use the standard tables where possible.

▶ **Ledger-specific lines table**
Whereas FAGLTFLEX stores totals, the tables FAGLFLEXA and FAGLF-LEXP store specific line items for both actual and planned postings. These tables should be used for reporting purposes, because the lines contain the splitting information that is not held in SAP standard tables (BSEG, BSIS, BSAS, etc.)

▶ **Year-end closing in selected parallel ledgers**
This table holds postings that occur at year-end closing when performing valuation steps. This table is a standard part of the GL but is only posted to as part of a year-end closing.

4.1.4 Document Splitting

Document splitting is a process by which we ensure that all postings are assigned to the correct account assignment group at the point of document entry. Traditionally, some transactions generate postings that do not carry the correct account assignment object. For instance, when raising an invoice, the debtor's posting that goes to the customer reconciliation account does not carry the correct account assignment object. As part of the period-end process, a transfer of balances from Profit Center Accounting (Transaction code 1KEK) would need to be done to provide correct assignment of these debtor's balances. With document splitting, this happens in real time and at the point of the document being saved; then splitting occurs.

In every document that is impacted by splitting, you create an entry view, which is the data you enter, and a GL view, which shows the effect of splitting.

The benefit to the business is that you can produce real-time financial statements because all your balance sheet items are now allocated to the correct account assignment object. This helps reduce the amount of time needed to process period end and is a huge contributor to fast close.

Table 4.1 is an example of a customer invoice that explains the power of document splitting better.

Classic GL Customer Invoice			
Debit	Customer	1160	
Credit	Sales	100	P Ctr 1
Credit	Sales	900	P Ctr 2
Credit	Tax	160	

New GL Customer Invoice			
Debit	Customer	129	P Ctr 1
Credit	Sales	100	P Ctr 1
Credit	Tax	29	P Ctr 1
Debit	Customer	1031	P Ctr 2
Credit	Sales	900	P Ctr 2
Credit	Tax	131	P Ctr 2

Table 4.1 Invoices Showing Document Splitting

Splitting is applicable to a number of different postings. In the customer invoice example, the tax amount would also be split according to the rules you have in place. Splitting is often applicable, but as a rule of thumb you should accept that any transaction that is posted to the GL from a subledger, via reconciliation accounts, is now split in real time to allocate the correct account assignment object to each line.

The subcategories of document splitting include:

▸ **Passive splitting**
During clearing of a payment, for example, the account assignment objects of the payment lines are inherited (derived). This is automatic and nonconfigurable.

▸ **Active splitting**
This is the splitting of vendor balances, based on rules specify in the configuration tables.

▸ **Zero-balancing**
Activating the zero balance flag within your splitting method, allows you to enable fully balanced documents (by account assignment object, e.g., profit center) within the GL view of your document.

4.1.5 Ongoing Use of Classic GL

You can still use the functionality and processes of the classic GL, just as you did in previous versions of SAP ERP ECC. The main difference is that you do not need to activate Document Splitting. If you decide that you do not want to use document splitting, it is possible to retain the same functionality as was present in SAP ERP ECC 4.7.

In such a scenario you would need to complete all of the configuration settings discussed in Chapter 3 to configure the classic GL for use. You would also need to take steps to configure the Controlling Component (CO) fully. The enterprise structure configuration would also need to be different, as the configuration steps are described for a scenario in which we activate the new GL. We cover details of the differences of configuration needed for the Controlling Component (CO) in a classic GL scenario in Chapter 8.

4.2 Building Your New GL Blueprint

When designing your GL blueprint, you should be aware of the following key issues and use them to determine your overall design.

New GL or Classic?

The most common concerns related to implementing the new GL are the additional database space required and the overhead of managing different views. As most organizations will recognize the benefits of reduced period-end cycle time (fast close) and real-time financial reporting, the trade-off is usually acceptable. There is no real additional overhead in terms of maintenance, and you can always buy a bigger server if you are worried about this.

Remember, it is possible to implement the classic GL in an SAP ERP ECC system. Taking the time to effectively prototype your proposed design will enable you to make an informed decision about whether it is something you want to implement or not.

What Object To Split On

You should be clear about on which account assignment object you want to split.

Which Account Assignment Objects To Incorporate into Your Model?

You may already be familiar with the concepts of cost center, profit center, and business area. SAP ERP ECC brings you an additional object, the segment, which can be used to provide an additional dimension to your reporting. Segments can be defined below company code and above profit center. You can assign a segment against your profit center master record, which enables you to link together a number of profit centers within a segment.

> **Note**
>
> It is important to mention that a segment is derived through a user exit (BAdi FAGL_DERIVE_SEGMENT).

The use of a segment should be looked at in conjunction with the GL migration exercise to understand which profit centers should have segment assignments. This is discussed in more detail in Chapter 10.

How Document Splitting Fit in with Other Add-Ons

Note that you need to consult with SAP about the integration between SAP ERP ECC and other new add-ons or subcomponents. SAP Note 1070629 includes notes on this and related topics.

In our SAFA, Inc. scenario we will activate Document Splitting and configure it to split on profit centers. This requirement is fairly common for most organizations, as profit centers are commonly used to provide divisional or departmental analysis. Splitting on profit centers enables you to produce complete financial statements by profit centers. This provides you with balance sheet–level reporting by profit center, including breakdown of debtors, creditors, stock, and cash. Fixed assets can also be analyzed by profit center.

In addition to this, you may want to activate segments that will provide you with analysis above profit centers. Reporting can be done at the segment level.

4.3 Configuration Steps to Activate the New GL

When you enter the SPRO, you will see that there are now some changes to the descriptions of certain tasks. SAP allows you to maintain both sets of menu paths in the SPRO, so that you can configure both the classic and new GL. If you want to remove classic Financial Accounting Component (FI) menu paths, you can run the program RFAGL_SWAP_SPRO_OLD. Once the SPRO is updated, you can still use the traditional transaction codes to access screens if you need to. In upgrade scenarios, this should form part of your migration activity, as this will also make available several new nodes that are not there initially.

When you install the SAP ERP ECC software the new GL is active as the default setting. If you intend to use the classic GL, you will need to deactivate the new GL. The steps needed to accomplish this are included in the next section

4.3.1 Activation of New GL Accounting

If you are switching the new GL on within an existing system, or setting up a fresh system, you should first ensure that this flag is set by following the menu path **SPRO • Financial Accounting (new) • Financial Accounting Global Settings • Activate New General Ledger Accounting** or using Transaction code FAGL_ACTIVATION. The systen produces a message to confirm the status of the client as seen in Figure 4.3.

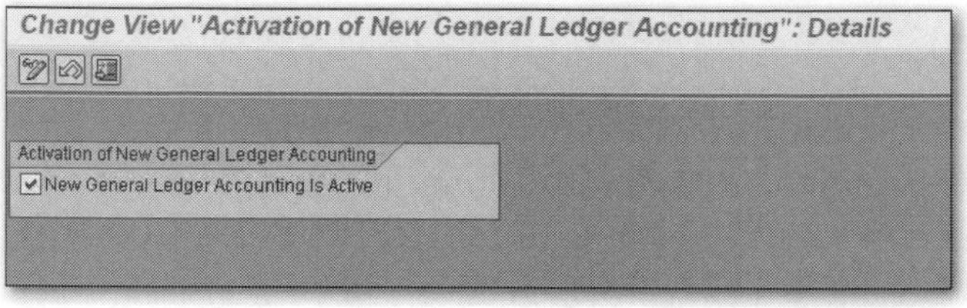

Figure 4.3 Activation of the New GL

This activation flag is client-dependent, and this transaction needs to be run in each client that you have. This process should therefore form part of your manual configuration activity list.

4.3.2 Define Ledgers for GL Accounting

The first step is to define a leading ledger, which will be our main ledger. In addition, we can define additional ledgers based on specific reporting requirements that we may have. All ledgers are based on a new totals table, FAGLFLEXT, which replaces GLT0 in holding financial data. The additional ledgers you add will behave as they did in the old special ledger, that is, they are there alongside your leading ledger Only the leading ledger integrates with the Controlling Component (CO). As we move through the chapter, your understanding of ledgers will improve with the multiple ledger

Your Company Code settings drive the general settings of the ledgers, for example, the base currency, fiscal year variant, and posting period variant. Your non-leading ledgers can be created to provide parallel accounting. You can assign different general settings (currency, fiscal year) to your non-leading ledgers.

This activity is completed in two stages; first you need to define all your ledgers by following the menu path **SPRO • Financial Accounting (new) • Financial Accounting Global Settings (new) • Ledgers • Ledger • Define Ledgers for General Ledger Accounting** (see Figure 4.4).

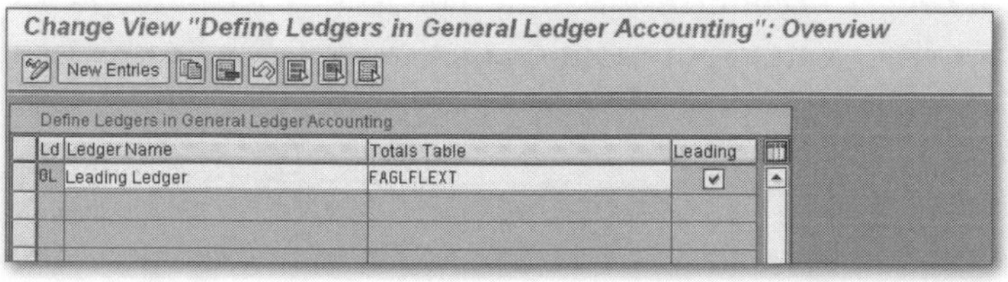

Figure 4.4 Define Ledgers for G/L Accounting

If you have created additional ledgers, you need to also define and activate non-leading ledgers as appropriate in the following location: **SPRO • Financial Accounting (new) • Financial Accounting Global Settings (new) • Ledgers • Ledger • Define and Assign non-leading ledgers**. We look at the benefits and configuration of additional ledgers in Section 4.3.6. If you have defined additional ledgers, you need to define a ledger group (see Section 4.3.5).

FAGLFLEXT contains additional fields not found in GLT0, including many fields from Profit Center Accounting.. Experienced SAP users may recognize some of the fields listed in Table 4.2, which are all found in FAGLFLEXT.

Field Description	Field Name
Account Number	RACCT
Cost Center	RCNTR
Profit Center	PRCTR
Functional Area	RFAREA
Segment	SEGMENT

Table 4.2 Additional Fields Available for Activation

It is possible to extend FAGLFLEXT to include either existing SAP fields or entirely new customer fields.

Define Currency of Leading Ledger

As in classic GL, different currency types can be assigned to the ledger. . Most implementations only know and use the company code currency, but as mentioned in Chapter 2, it is possible to have a controlling area currency as well, which provides you with a different set of analyses based on your overall organizational design.

The standard procedure is to define additional currencies against non-leading ledgers so that they produce separate financial reports. It is possible to assign additional currencies for each company code (see Figure 4.5) by following the menu path **SPRO • Financial Accounting (new) • Financial Accounting Global Settings (new) • Ledgers • Ledger • Define Currencies of Leading Ledger**.

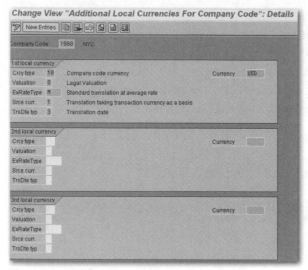

Figure 4.5 Define Currencies for Company Code

The additional currencies available include:

▶ Group currency

▶ Hard currency

▶ Index-based currency

▶ Global company currency

Wherever you define additional currencies, you need to define the valuation status and exchange rate type. For our example, we have only assigned a single currency for each company code, as SAFA, Inc. produces financial statements for each company separately. The Controlling Component (CO) offers extensive consolidation functionality that you should consider if you have detailed consolidation requirements.

Assign Scenarios and Customer Fields to Ledgers

SAP ERP ECC comes with several scenarios that define the way in which fields are updated within the ledgers. The concept of document splitting is flexible enough to cater to your specific business requirements. You can design your solution with a number of fields being populated to provide data for many reporting requirements. The number of fields you select should be as needed by your overall solution, so it is not necessary to select more fields than are necessary.

In this SPRO activity you should assign your scenarios, customer fields, and versions to the appropriate ledgers. Due to the complex integration, it is not possible to define your own scenarios.

Table 4.3 gives some examples of common scenarios that you can activate. You can assign up to six scenarios to your leading ledger. You can design your ledgers to collect different sets of information by assigning scenarios and customer fields to them. These are selected as shown in Figure 4.6.

Scenario	Description
FIN_CCA *Cost Center Update*	Updates the sender and receiver cost centers
FIN_GSBER *Business Area Update*	Updates the sender and receiver business area fields
FIN_PCA *Profit Centre Update*	Updates profit center and partner profit center fields
FIN_SEGM *Segmentation*	Updates segment, partner segment, and profit center fields

Table 4.3 List of Common Scenarios

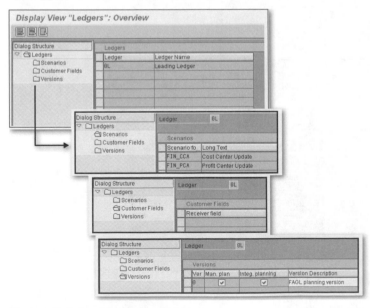

Figure 4.6 Define Scenarios and Versions

In our scenario we have chosen to only activate FIN_CCA and FIN_PCA. You may consider additional objects for your solution based on your specific requirements. A segment is a reporting dimension you can use that provides "divisional" analysis.

We have not seen the need to define additional fields to the FAGLFLEXT table, as there are sufficient fields for our reporting needs. The third component of this activity was the creation of a single planning version. It is possible to create additional versions based on your planning and budgeting requirements.

You should only activate fields that are relevant to your scenario. Activating scenarios for fields that you are not using will cause problems with your internal interfaces as SAP tries to send information to fields that may not exist. Each scenario is triggered based on internal interfaces. For the scenarios we have selected, you can see the fields it is triggered on in the menu path **SPRO • Financial Accounting (new) • Financial Accounting Global Settings (new) • Ledgers • Fields • Display Scenarios for General Ledger Accounting**.

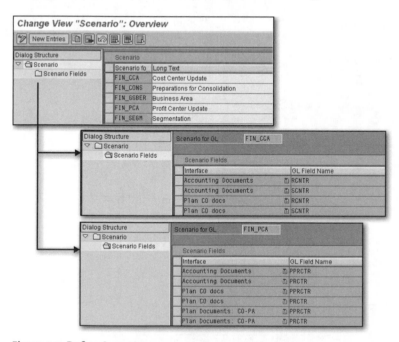

Figure 4.7 Define Scenarios

Define Ledger Group

All of the ledgers you define need to be brought together within a ledger group. This allows you to apply control settings to the ledger group, which applies to all of the ledgers within it. Within the ledger group, you define the leading ledger as the representative ledger of that ledger group. Figure 4.8 shows the configuration screen for this activity.

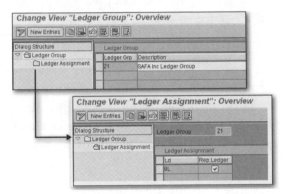

Figure 4.8 Define Ledger Group

These steps complete the configuration of your ledgers. Next we move on to the configuration settings needed to enable the internal interfaces to the GL from subcomponents.

4.3.3 Segment

We mentioned at the blueprint stage of this chapter that it is possible to make use of a segment as an additional account assignment object in your solution.

Quote from IAS 14

Reporting is required for a business or geographical segment when the majority of its revenues stems from sales to external customers and segment revenues account for at least 10% of total internal and external revenues of all segments, segment income accounts for at least 10% of all segment income, or segment assets account for at least 10% of the assets of all segments. A segment can be reported separately even if it does not meet these size requirements. If the segments subject to reporting requirements account for less than 75% of total consolidated revenues or enterprise revenues, then other segments must be reported on separately, irrespective of the 10% limit, until at least this 75% is reached.

It may seem good to create as many reporting dimensions as possible, but you should consider which you need and which are value adding. If you create additional account assignment objects, you need to maintain them. In large multinational organizations, with many company codes, you can use a segment to bring a dimension together within a controlling area. In this chapter we have mentioned the options where you can select a segment as a splitting object or to split on a segment. Because the segment is a new object in SAP ERP ECC, we include this section to explain the configuration steps needed to complete the configuration.

Define Segment

In your enterprise structure you need to define the segments you want to use. There are no restrictions on their use, and you should define them in line with your organization's reporting requirements. For SAFA Inc., we have determined the need to report performance based on our four product portfolios, as shown in Figure 4.9.

Segments are created as part of the enterprise structure are of the IMG, under the menu path **SPRO • Enterprise Structure • Definition • Financial Accounting • Define Segment**

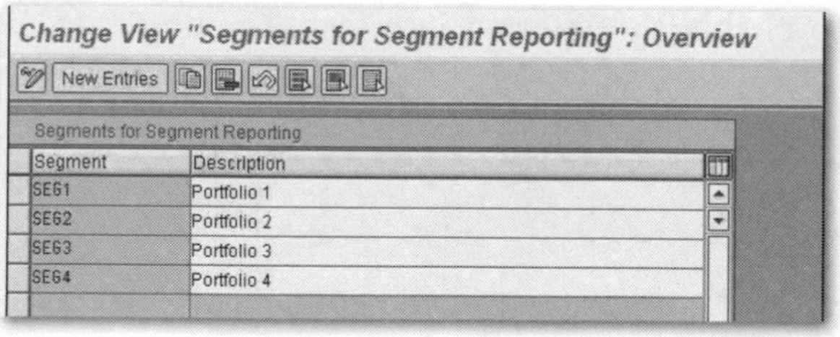

Figure 4.9 Definition of Segments

Maintain Scenarios

To use segments for splitting, you need to activate scenarios related to segments (FIN_SEGM). This point was raised above in Section 4.3.2.

Assign Segments to Profit Centers (see Chapter 8)

The segments you define should be assigned to the appropriate profit center (see Figure 4.10). When you maintain your profit center (Transaction KE52), you assign the relevant profit center. This needs to be included in your data migration mapping exercise so that when new profit centers are created, the correct Segment is assigned to them.

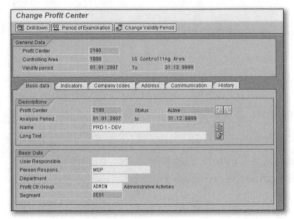

Figure 4.10 Assignment of Profit Center to a Segment

This covers the master data aspect. We will now look at the transactional settings needed to use segments.

Maintain Field Status Variants and Posting Keys

We have the master data defined, so now we need to ensure that **Segment** is an available field in the field status of both GL accounts (see Chapter 3, Section 3.2.2) and posting keys (see Chapter 3, Section 3.2.7). An example is shown in Figure 4.11.

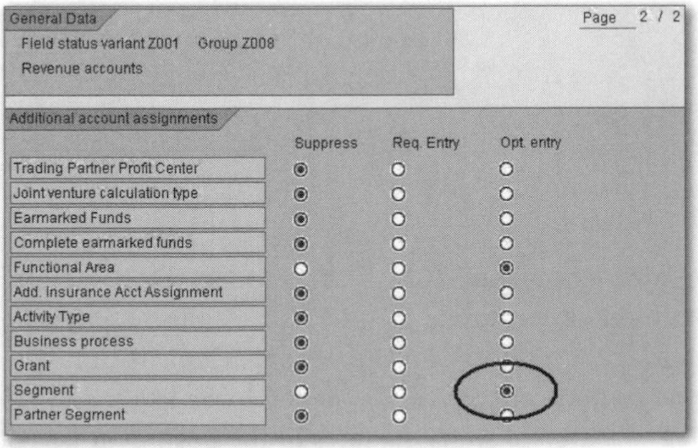

Figure 4.11 Enable Segment Field in Field Status Groups

You do not directly post to the segment, but it is derived when you post to the profit center, so you should be able to see the field being populated.

4.3.4 Integrating the GL with Subcomponents

This area of configuration concerns how we integrate subcomponents with the new GL. These settings influence the document splitting functions, so it is important to understand them before we look at document splitting. The GL continues to be the heart of the system, receiving all postings and providing management information (see Figure 4.1, above).

At all of the touch points with the GL, document splitting is not triggered, which ensures that the correct account assignments are determined. With the classic GL, you needed to configure Table 3keh to ensure that a profit center was assigned to each line item posting to the GL. The limitation here was a time delay in the transfer of information to Profit Center Accounting. Because splitting happens in real time, we have real-time assignment of account assignment objects.

Payables and Receivables Integration

The classic GL integrated with customer and vendor transactions perfectly, which was a major selling point of SAP. What do we get in addition when we implement the new GL? We get real-time integration. To explain this, let's look at the simple example of a vendor invoice:

PK	Account	Amt	Cost Ctr	Profit Ctr
Credit	Vendor	100		
Debit	Expense GL 1	50	C Ctr 1	P Ctr 1
Debit	Expense GL 2	50	C Ctr 2	P Ctr 2

This is referred to as the entry view of the document.

The classic GL posts the vendor amount of 100 to the vendor reconciliation account. As part of month end, the procedure is then to transfer the vendor balances to Profit Center Accounting, at which point the vendor reconciliation balance is allocated to the correct profit center. With the new GL, we use the same invoice as above. Upon saving, the system splits the lines of the document based on the rules you have defined. In our example, we have allocated the cost center and profit center scenarios, so we should see the following result of splitting:

PK	Account	Amt	Cost Ctr	Profit Ctr
Credit	Vendor reconciliation	50		P Ctr 1
Credit	Vendor reconciliation	50		P Ctr 2
Debit	Expense GL 1	50	C Ctr 1	P Ctr 1
Debit	Expense GL 2	50	C Ctr 2	P Ctr 2
Debit	Expense GL 2	50	C Ctr 2	P Ctr 2

This is seen within the GL view of the document.

We discuss the settings needed for splitting line items later in this chapter. We first need to define integration at a higher level. At a ledger level, we define the integration between the Financial Accounting Component (FI) and the Controlling Component (CO) by following the menu path **SPRO • Financial Accounting (new) • Financial Accounting Global Settings (new) • Real-time Integration of Controlling with Financial Accounting**. The first thing we need to do is create a variant for Financial Accounting Component (FI) to Controlling Component (CO) integration.

Define Variants for Real-Time Integration

In the classic GL, there is realtime integration between the Financial Accounting Component (FI) and the Controlling Component (CO). With standard configuration, you can enable document flow from the Financial Accounting Component (FI) to the Controlling Component (CO). In this situation, though, the following transactions would remain in the Controlling Component (CO) only:

▸ Periodic allocations (assessments, distributions)

▸ Settlements (from orders or projects)

With the new GL, Controlling Component (CO) postings now update in the opposite direction (see Figure 4.12), so each the Controlling Component (CO) document you create will generate a follow on Financial Accounting Component (FI) document. This is a improvement over the previous situation, where you needed to run Transaction code KALC, which would produce summary adjustment postings for each cost element. Transaction code KALC had the limitation that it was unable to reconcile segment account assignment objects.

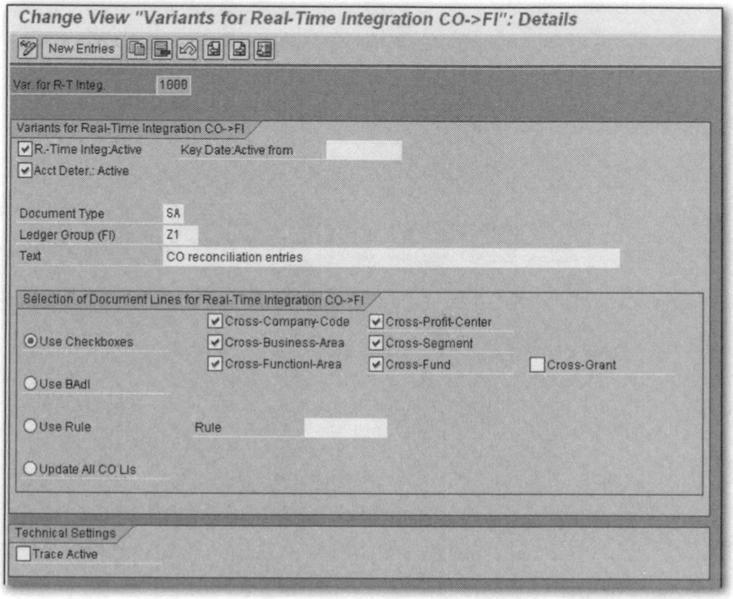

Figure 4.12 Define Variant for Financial Accounting Component (FI) to Controlling Component (CO) Integration

In this configuration step, you define a variant to control your Financial Accounting Component (FI) to Controlling Component (CO) integration postings. This variant has an activation date, so if you are upgrading in stages, you can define additional variants depending on which components are active.

You need to define a document type that will receive the Financial Accounting Component (FI) and Controlling Component (CO) postings. You should decide if you require a separate document type for this posting, as this will allow you to quickly identify these Controlling Component (CO) transfers. The variant is specific to a ledger group, so if your SAP system has multiple ledger groups, you can define these rules per ledger group.

The selection of document lines for Financial Accounting Component (FI) to Controlling Component (CO) integration can be done by specific rules. In our scenario we chose the checkboxes as indicated. It is possible to select all Controlling Component (CO) line items, and this will take over all Controlling Component (CO) documents without any restriction. You may want to consider this if you are using a very restricted amount of controlling. (See Define Rules for Real-Time Integration.)

It is also possible to transfer secondary cost element line items. This may seem an attractive option for organizations that use many secondary cost elements. To enable this, you need to create an account assignment rule (discussed later in this section).

The Financial Accounting Component (FI) to Controlling Component (CO) integration can be logged with a trace by selecting **Trace Active** for your variant. This provides you with the following information:

▸ Document number of the original Controlling Component (CO) document

▸ Document number of the target document

▸ Transfer information (success, failure, and reason for transfer)

▸ All line item information including posting objects and partner objects

Activating traces would create significant overhead in terms of additional data being created and stored in the system, so you should consider it carefully. If you have not activated trace in your variant, you can switch it on and off at any time via Transaction FAGLCOFITRACEADMIN.

Having defined the variant, we now need to assign the variant to the company code in which it is being used (see Figure 4.13).

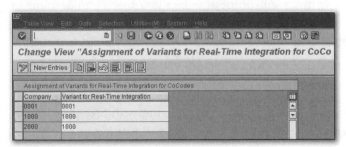

Figure 4.13 Assign Variant for Controlling Component (CO) Integration

Define Rules for Selecting Controlling Component (CO) Line Items

In this configuration activity you define the rules to determine which Controlling Component (CO) line items are selected for transfer to the Financial Accounting Component (FI). If you do nothing at this stage, the system will automatically transfer all Controlling Component (CO) items to the Financial Accounting Component (FI), so you should only go into this screen if you want to create a specific rule for excluding items. For our solution design, we do not need to make any changes to this rule because we want all our Controlling Component (CO) postings to post to the Financial Accounting Component (FI).

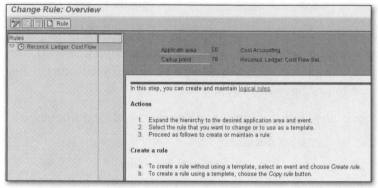

Figure 4.14 Defining Custom Rules for CO Line Items

Define Account Determination for Real-Time Integration

Here we need to define the account determination that is posted to when Financial Accounting Component (FI) to Controlling Component (CO) integration occurs. This account determination is a similar configuration to set up of MM account determination which is discussed in Chapter 9. Your choices are:

▶ Account determination without substitution, where you specify an account to which all Financial Accounting Component (FI) to Controlling Component (CO) reconciliation postings go

▶ Account determination with substitution, where you use substitution rules to determine the account

The first option is the recommended route, as it is in line with SAP practices of assigning a single reconciliation account for all interledger postings.

This configuration is completed using the menu path **SPRO • Financial Accounting (new) • Financial Accounting Global Settings (new) • Ledgers • Real-Time Integration of Controlling with Financial Accounting • Account Determination for Real Time Integration • Define Account Determination for Real-Time Integration**.

The recommended approach is to assign a single reconciliation GL account for all postings. It may make sense to assign a debtors' and creditors' account to receive the debits and credits separately —just bear in mind how you will reconcile the two accounts, because they will continue to accumulate balances over time. The account determination key being triggered is CO1.

Click on the **Change Account Determination** button, which opens up the rules for your account determination, as shown in Figure 4.15. Here you select the rules you want to impose. If you want to allocate a single GL account for all postings, you don't need to make any selections. Just save the rules.

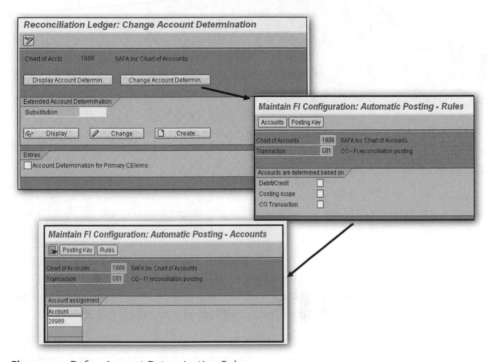

Figure 4.15 Define Account Determination Rules

On the **Accounts** screen you need to assign the GL account you want to act as the reconciliation account. If you have selected **Posting Key** as a rule, this screen will contain additional entries for which you need to define GL accounts.

The GL account you define here can be set up as open item managed (**Open item management** checkbox) to enable reconciliation to take place (Figure 4.16).

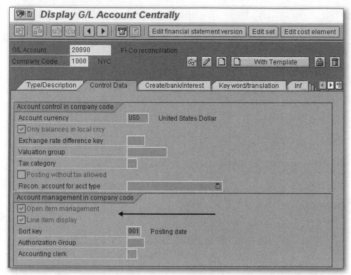

Figure 4.16 Define G/L Account Settings for Control Account

Intercompany Clearings

If, like our SAFA Inc. scenario, you have defined multiple company codes, you should set up intercompany clearing rules to enable intercompany postings to take place.

This is configured through the same menu path: **SPRO • Financial Accounting (new) • Financial Accounting Global Settings (new) • Ledgers • Real-Time Integration of Controlling with Financial Accounting • Account Determination for Real Time Integration • Define Intercompany Clearing Accounts**.

A common use of intercompany postings is to recharge costs incurred on behalf of another trading unit. For instance, you may receive services from an external vendor that benefit both company codes. In this situation, the vendor has invoiced company code 1000 for all of their costs. We now do a journal to move the costs from company code 1000 to 2000. The journal reads as follows:

PK	Account	Amt	Cost Ctr	Company Cd
Credit	Expense GL 1	100	C Ctr 1	1000
Debit	Expense GL 1	100	C Ctr 2	2000

The actual posting goes through the system via an intercompany journal, and this creates the following lines:

PK	Account	Amt	Cost Ctr	Company Cd
Credit	Expense GL 1	100	C Ctr 1	1000
Debit	Intercompany clearing	100	C Ctr 1	
Credit	Intercompany clearing	100	C Ctr 2	2000
Debit	Expense GL 1	100	C Ctr 2	

Separate documents are created in each company code to represent the postings indicated in our example.

It is possible to define separate reconciliation accounts based on posting key (payables and receivables).

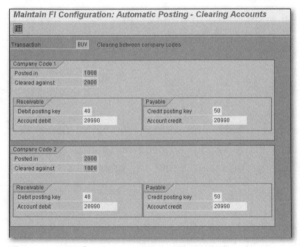

Figure 4.17 Define Intercompany Clearing Account

In our scenario, we have chosen to assign a single GL reconciliation account in both company codes, which will make reconciliation easier for us.

This step concludes our integration configuration for the new GL. We now look at the specifics of document splitting.

4.3.5 Document Splitting

For document splitting configuration, we move to a separate area of the **IMG** menu. The basic principle of splitting is to provide additional reporting analysis from the documents that have been posted. It is possible to split on different characteristics, but to explain this concept, we have chosen to split only on the profit center object. A common approach is to leave all existing objects as they are and use segments for splitting to provide segment financial statements.

The order shown in the SPRO is different, and experienced users may choose to follow that route if they are more comfortable with it. All activities are completed in the menu path **SPRO • Financial Accounting (new) • Financial Accounting Global Settings (new) • General Ledger Accounting (new) • Business Transactions • Document Splitting**.

Define Document Splitting Characteristics

This is where we specify the object upon which splitting occurs. For our scenario, we are only requesting splitting on the profit center, so this is the only characteristic that we activate here.

For each characteristic we need to define:

- **Zero-balancing**
  This characteristic should have a zero-balancing setting. The zero-balance flag ensures that any postings made balance within a document that is split. This is a form of double-entry accounting and ensures that any financial statements being produced are accurate.

- **Partner field**
  This field can be used to document the sender–receiver relationship in the (additional) clearing lines generated in the document.

- **Mandatory field**
  The system only accepts postings when this field can be filled with a value from document splitting. This ensures that the field is determined at the point of document entry.

The system itself will propose logical objects upon which splitting should occur, based on the scenarios you have selected. You can activate additional characteristics as long as these characteristics are active in your ledger.

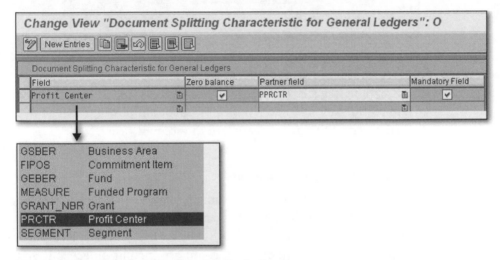

Figure 4.18 Document Splitting Characteristics for the GL

Figure 4.18 shows additional fields that can be used as splitting characteristics. You may choose additional characteristics for splitting if required.

Define Zero-Balancing Account

The zero-balancing account is defined in the system as a reconciliation account to balance lines within a journal. This is defined in the menu path **Financial Accounting (new)** • **Financial Accounting Global Settings (new)** • **Business Transactions** • **Document Splitting** • **Define zero-balance clearing account**.

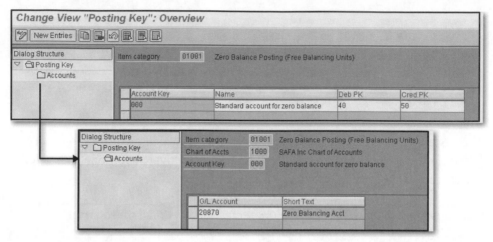

Figure 4.19 Define Zero-Balancing Account

The zero-balance account is posted to via specific posting keys, and we have defined the SAP standard posting keys (40 and 50) for this. All of our postings will go to a single reconciliation account to make clearing of the account easier.

Edit Constants for Non-Assigned Processes

In this SPRO activity we need to define a default account assignment object for lines that cannot be derived at the point of document creation. It is possible to define strict enough controls within your field status groups (see Chapter 3, Section 3.2.2) to prevent postings without an account assignment object, but you need to review this in line with your specific business requirements in terms of all interfaces having the correct information to pass to the GL.

You can set up different constants and within the splitting rules define different rules for different scenarios. Within the constant, you can define a default value for different fields, such as Segment. In our scenario we have chosen to only define a default profit center, as this is the catch-all for all transactions that do not derive a correct account assignment object. This is because for all expense postings, we have defined cost elements, which means the system does not allow you to post the transaction without assigning a cost center. Failures to derive can only be for income or balance sheet postings, which both look for profit centers. Figure 4.20 shows the combination of fields that need to worked through to complete this configuration activity.

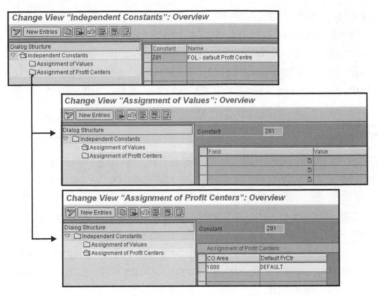

Figure 4.20 Define Constants for Non-Assigned Items

With this configuration setting, for any transaction that cannot derive a profit center, the system assigns this default account assignment to it. If you do not create the profit center (or other object), the transaction will fail, resulting in an error message requiring the user to enter a correct account assignment object. It is up to you how you use this transaction. In our example, we will allow the system to default a value for postings that cannot derive a profit center, and then as part of period-end reconciliations we will move this item to the correct account assignments.

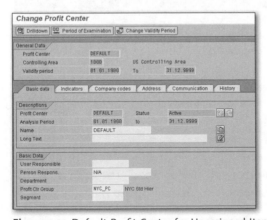

Figure 4.21 Default Profit Center for Unassigned Items

In figure 4.21, you can see that we have defined a DEFAULT Profit Centre which will accept these non-assigned lines.. Some organizations accept postings going to a default account assignment object, whereas some prefer not to allow such postings. A way around this is to define your default object and then block it for use, so any transaction lines that derive the default object cannot be completed.

Activate Document Splitting

We now need to ensure that our company codes are active for document splitting. When you define a new company code, a corresponding entry is created in this table with an inactive flag. We need to go into this table and ensure that there is not a deactivation flag against any of the company codes for which we are activating document splitting (see Figure 4.22). This is done in the menu path **SPRO • Financial Accounting (new) • Financial Accounting Global Settings (new) • General Ledger Accounting (new) • Business Transactions • Document Splitting • Activate Document Splitting**.

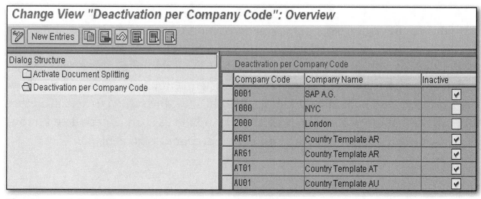

Figure 4.22 Activate Document Splitting per Company Code

This setting is client-wide and thus impacts all systems within a client.

Define Document Splitting Method

We will now explore the settings that need to be made to set up our splitting rules. All our splitting rules are collected within a splitting method. The easiest way to do this is to copy a standard splitting method so that all of the relevant settings below it are created. As you will see in the related configuration steps, a number of related objects need to be created to complete your splitting method, so taking a copy is the easiest approach to ensure that you don't miss anything.

Figure 4.23 shows how the different configuration activities so far combine to enable splitting to happen.

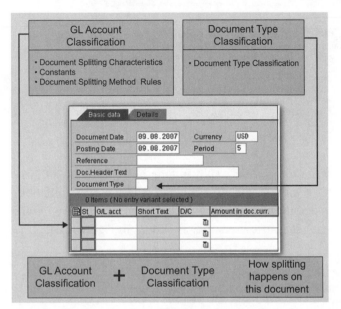

Figure 4.23 Relationship of Components within a Document Splitting Rule

In splitting configuration, you can activate inheritance, which ensures that additional lines within a document inherit account assignment objects. For instance, in a vendor invoice, the additional line items (e.g., tax line) inherit the account assignment object(s). The inheritance flag also enables zero-balance position within documents.

If you previously defined account determination without standard (as recommended), you should also activate inheritance.

Table 4.4 lists the differences in the GL view of this document with and without inheritance.

Classic GL Vendor Invoice				
Credit	Vendor	1160		
Debit	Expense	1000	C Ctr 1	P Ctr 1
Credit	Tax	160		

Classic GL Vendor Invoice				
Credit	Vendor	1160	C Ctr 1	P Ctr 1
Debit	Expense	1000	C Ctr 1	P Ctr 1
Credit	Tax	160	C Ctr 1	P Ctr 1

Table 4.4 GL View with Inheritance of account assignment

SAP ERP ECC is delivered with some standard splitting methods. Method 0000012 captures most organizations' requirements, as it includes the most combinations of transactions. The recommendation from SAP and the authors is for you to take a copy of this method and give it your own name, as shown in Figure 4.24.

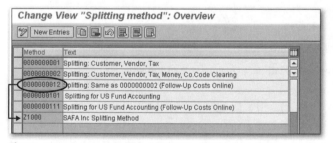

Figure 4.24 Create Document Splitting Method by Copying

We now look at the rules in this method that enable splitting to take place.

Define Document Splitting Rule

Document splitting is based on certain transactions that happen within the system. The GL is the heart of the system, and it has inputs that are business transactions. For these business transactions, we can define specific rules so the system knows where to look for account assignment objects.

Change View "Header data": Overview

Method	Splitting method	Transactn	Business transaction	Variant	Variant
Z1000	SAFA Inc Splitting Method	0000	Unspecified posting	0001	Standard
Z1000	SAFA Inc Splitting Method	0100	Transfer posting from P&L to B/S	0001	Standard
Z1000	SAFA Inc Splitting Method	0200	Customer invoice	0001	Standard
Z1000	SAFA Inc Splitting Method	0300	Vendor invoice	0001	Standard
Z1000	SAFA Inc Splitting Method	1000	Payments	0001	Standard

Figure 4.25 Business Transactions within a Splitting Method

From the list of business transactions shown in Figure 4.25, we should now copy across all of the business transactions that are necessary for our solution design. It is easy to copy all of the transactions across from the SAP-delivered splitting method. When you copy them, you should copy with dependent objects.

For each transaction, we define header information in terms of how the transaction is set up. In the header we have specified detail in terms of inheritance and default account assignment as discussed previously (see Figure 4.26). We also link the account determination for posting to zero-balance reconciliation account.

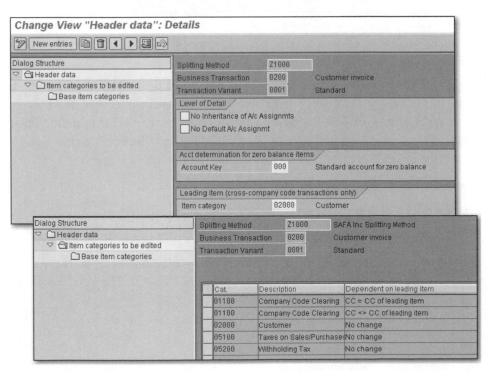

Figure 4.26 Copying Business Transactions

Within each business transaction are item categories (e.g., vendor, customer, asset, cash discount clearing, etc.). For each item category, we have a base item category.

Assign Document Splitting Method

Now we activate the constant to our splitting method, which is needed in line with our previous decisions about inheritance and default account assignment (see Figure 4.27).

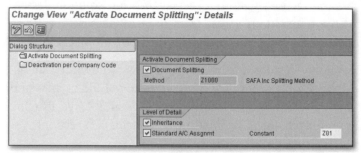

Figure 4.27 Assign Constant to Splitting Method

Define Business Transaction Variants

So far, we have explained how we set up our splitting method, and for most users, this is mostly a case of copying across the standard splitting method, as all of the settings are contained within it. Advanced users may want to define business transaction variants and specify fewer rules for their business transaction to restrict the possible entries. You do this by making the item category:

▸ **Mandatory:** It must exist.

▸ **Once only:** The item category must only appear once.

▸ **Not supported:** The item category is prohibited from this transaction.

In our example (Figure 4.28), therefore, if you look at the business transaction for vendor invoice, you can see a single variant is defined for it. The vendor field is defined as a mandatory field and therefore must exist.

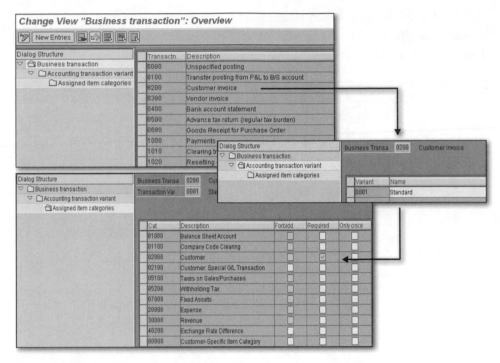

Figure 4.28 Business Transaction Variants

We now look at the configuration areas where you apply splitting settings for your GL accounts and document types that drives the transactional processing in the system.

Classify GL Accounts for Document Splitting

Having defined our splitting method and related rules, we will now assign GL accounts to splitting rules to control how transactions are split. This means that when you post to a GL account, the configuration settings determine what item categories exist and thus how splitting takes place. This is achieved by allocating a single business transaction to every GL account in use. The system then knows what rules are in place and can perform splitting accordingly. To do this, following the menu path **Financial Accounting (new) • General Ledger Accounting (new) • Business Transactions • Document Splitting • Classify G/L Accounts for Document Splitting**.

The entries in this table, like all account determination settings, are chart of accounts specific. You should make settings based on categories that exist as standard in the system (see Table 4.5).

Category	Description
01000	Balance sheet account
01001	Zero balance posting (free balancing units)
01100	Company code clearing
01300	Cash discount clearing
02000	Customer
02100	Customer: special GL transaction
03000	Vendor
03100	Vendor: special GL transaction
04000	Cash account
05100	Taxes on sales and purchases
05200	Withholding tax
06000	Material
07000	Fixed assets
20000	Expense
30000	Revenue
40100	Cash discount (expense, revenue, loss)
40200	Exchange rate difference
80000	Customer-specific item category

Table 4.5 Splitting Categories Available for GL Accounts

This list is standard and cannot be amended, so for each GL account or group of GL accounts, you need to define a category. It is better to make entries by group of GL account numbers, as this reduces the amount of manual maintenance needed when new GL accounts are created. This configuration screen can be seen in figure 4.29.

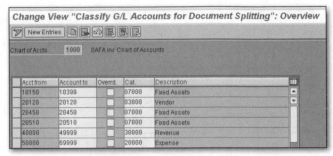

Figure 4.29 Assign Document Splitting Category to GL Accounts

You cannot post to GL accounts that are not entered in this table, and the system will give an error message saying it cannot determine the item category.

Classify Document Types for Splitting

You need to assign each transaction you enter in the system to a particular business transaction. This ensures that the settings made previously in terms of valid rules are adopted. The way to look at this is to consider what the first line of the transaction is that is being entered. For most document types, this is quite straightforward. Table 4.6 lists the transactions available to us in our splitting method. This list is dependent on the business transactions that you activated in your splitting method earlier in this section.

Splitting Transaction	Description
0000	Unspecified posting
0100	Transfer posting from profit and loss to balance sheet account
0200	Customer invoice
0300	Vendor invoice
0400	Bank account statement
0500	Advance tax return (regular tax burden)
0600	Goods receipt for purchase order
1000	Payments
1010	Clearing transactions (account maintenance)
1020	Resetting cleared items

Table 4.6 Business Transactions for Document Types

For journals we should adopt the unspecified posting transaction, as this is most appropriate. Figure 4.30 shows the settings made for standard document types in line with our business requirements.

Change View "Classify FI Document Type for Document Splitting": Overvi

Type	Description	Transactn.	Variant	Description	Name
KR	Vendor invoice	0300	0001	Vendor invoice	Standard
KZ	Vendor payment	1000	0001	Payments	Standard
ML	ML settlement	0000	0001	Unspecified posting	Standard
RV	Billing doc.transfer	0200	0001	Customer invoice	Standard
SA	G/L account document	0000	0001	Unspecified posting	Standard
SB	G/L account posting	0000	0001	Unspecified posting	Standard
SC	G/L account document				
SK	Cash document	0000	0001	Unspecified posting	Standard
SU	Adjustment document	0000	0001	Unspecified posting	Standard
UE	Data transfer	0000	0001	Unspecified posting	Standard
WA	Goods issue	0000	0001	Unspecified posting	Standard

Figure 4.30 Assign Business Transaction to Document Type

With this configuration activity, we have completed our configuration to enable document splitting. The rest of the chapter looks at some business processes and explains what to look for and expect in your system.

4.3.6 Parallel Accounting

The new GL allows you to operate non-leading ledgers to produce different financial statements based on different accounting policies. This was a real functionality gap for global organizations in previous versions of SAP ERP ECC. For instance, an American company with a German subsidiary would need to produce financial statements according to both the German Commercial Code and U.S. GAAP to satisfy both statutory and group reporting requirements. For this reason SAP ERP ECC provides functionality to enable parallel valuations through a number of methods.

Define Additional GL Accounts and Alternative Hierarchies

You can adopt one of two different approaches.

In a very complicated international SAP ERP ECC solution, you may want to maintain an overall group chart of accounts that is used by the entire corporate group.

You then define company–code-specific charts with the GL accounts needed for that company code. This function allows you to report in line with both the company code and group requirements. A simpler version of this has been adopted in some designs, where specific GL accounts are defined within the chart of accounts to allow different valuations to be posted. Either way, you need to maintain the different charts and understand which chart and GL accounts are relevant at any time.

Depending on your requirements, you can define alternative reporting hierarchies in line with the different accounting rules you are trying to satisfy. This is an easy solution to implement if your differences are based on accounting principles that define a different treatment of costs. You could also implement this solution with the definition of different financial statement versions. With the new GL, profit centers are within the GL reporting structure, so you can define different GL account groups (Transaction code KDH1) to report out of the GL.

Additional Ledgers

A key function of the new GL is the ability to setup additional ledgers, with the benefit being that your valuations exist in a completely separate ledger. SAP recommends this approach if this is more manageable than having additional accounts set up. This solution can be used in addition the creation of additional GL accounts and a group chart of accounts to provide the overall solution that best fits the organizations needs. New GL additional ledgers should not be confused with the functionality available in special ledgers in previous versions of SAP ERP ECC. You can supplement additional GL accounts with a different fiscal year variant, currency, or posting period variant in your non-leading ledger. Earlier in the chapter we looked at ledger definition. We will now revisit the same step and define an additional Ledger: AL. To do so, follow the menu path **SPRO • Financial Accounting (new) • Financial Accounting Global Settings (new) • Ledgers • Ledger • Define Ledgers for General Ledger Accounting**.

Next we define and activate non-leading ledgers, as shown in Figure 4.31.

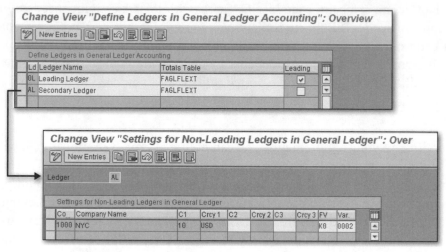

Figure 4.31 Define Settings for Non-Leading Ledgers

You can set up your non-leading ledger to record transactions in an additional currency. You can also assign a different fiscal year variant and posting period variant to comply with your requirement for reporting over different fiscal years.

The other advantages of non-leading ledgers is that they can use the standard reporting tools in the system.

Additional Company Codes

The third option available here is to define a dummy company code, which can be used to record additional financial information. This option again raises the need to create and maintain additional master data objects.

In reality, parallel accounting requires a combination of functionality to deliver a solution that best meets your requirements.

4.3.7 Controlling Component (CO) Transfer Postings

In Section 4.3.3 we introduced the configuration required to enable the integration between the Financial Accounting Component (FI) and the Controlling Component (CO). Any such postings made only in the Controlling Component (CO) trigger postings in the Financial Accounting Component (FI) GL that appear in GL via the Financial Accounting Component (FI) to Controlling Component (CO) reconciliation account (in Section 4.3.3 we defined this as GL account 20980). Common examples of such postings are Controlling Component (CO) settlements via secondary cost elements as well as allocations. Theses transactions are explained in detail Chapter 8.

GL Allocations

Previously, assessments and distributions were performed in the Controlling Component (CO) to provide management accounting analysis. With SAP ERP ECC, this functionality is now available in the GL, as the account assignment objects are also contained within the new GL. These can be used to allocate overhead costs to the correct account assignment objects. You may want to use this function to perform cost allocations within your organization.

4.3.8   Integration with Asset Accounting

In previous versions of SAP ERP ECC, asset accounting transactions such as depreciation did not fully integrate with the Controlling Component (CO). As part of the period-end process, you needed to run a transaction to transfer balances from Asset Accounting to Profit Center Accounting. With SAP ERP ECC 6.0, this integration occurs in real time, and there is no need to perform this information transfer at period end. This reduces the amount of effort needed at period end, thus enabling a faster period-end close. It also allows you to have accurate financial data in real time.

For this to occur, you need to ensure that the appropriate account assignment objects are activated, A cost center is a minimum requirement. In addition, it is possible to derive either profit center or segment if these are part of your solution design.

In this situation, an asset acquisition transaction triggers splitting with the inheritance of a profit center or segment from the asset to the vendor and tax line. Depreciation postings also inherit account assignment objects in real time.

Chapter 7 is completely devoted to Asset Accounting and provides a detailed explanation of how to process asset transactions as well as the configuration settings.

4.4 Summary

Having completed this chapter, we expect the reader to have a rounded understanding of the changes that come into effect as a result of implementing SAP ERP ECC 6.0. The reader should also have sufficient knowledge to design and configure a solution to meet requirements including:

▸ Activating the new GL

▸ Activating appropriate scenarios to enable document splitting

▸ Defining and deriving segments as a new account assignment object

▸ Defining additional ledgers for international accounting

▸ Understanding and making configuration settings in relation to integration between the Financial Component (FI) and the Controlling Component (CO)

▸ Creating allocations

This was a very important chapter to cover at this stage and in combination with the earlier chapters 2 and 3 you are in a good position to move onto chapter 5 where we look at the Accounts Payable component of Finance.

Accounts Payable is the sub-module that deals with the Vendor related business processes, i.e., Purchase Invoices and Purchase Payments. This chapter covers the process and configuration of Master Data, Vendor Invoices, and Vendor Payment Processing. You should be aware of previous chapters, specifically Chapter 3, that defined the Finance Global Settings.

5   Accounts Payable

The general function of the Accounts Payable (AP) component is to facilitate payments to vendors. There is a lot of integration of the Materials Management (MM) and Treasury (TR) components. In traditional finance terms, companies are organized so that the AP function sits alongside the core Financial Accounting Component (FI) function. From a business process point of view, accounts payable happens at the end of many procurement processes, so you may find that although this is a subcomponent of the Financial Accounting Component (FI), your AP team sits within the *Purchase to Pay* (P2P) process area (which we explain in the next section) When you understand the integrated nature of the SAP modules you will see that this approach makes a lot of sense and allows for better integration along the entire P2P business process.

The AP subcomponent covers the following:

▶ Creation and maintenance of vendor (supplier) master records

▶ Vendor transaction processing (including invoices and payments)

▶ Integrated nature within the MM component

▶ Invoice verification

▶ Outgoing Payment processing

The chapter starts with an overview of the P2P process and then discusses in detail the configuration required to deliver the SAP functionality listed above.

In this chapter we look at the three main aspects of AP, these being Master Data, Invoice Processing and Payment Processing. By the end of the chapter you should be able to understand the basic P2P cycle and be able to make configuration settings to satisfy your own design.

5.1 Overview of the P2P cycle

Business processes between your organization and your vendors are captured within the P2P cycle. The cycle picks up all of the business processes that occur from the point of purchase order creation to issuing payments to the vendor. Figure 5.1 provides a high-level view of the five key stages within this cycle and we explain the process behind each stage in the next section.

The stages include:

▶ Purchase order

▶ Goods receipt

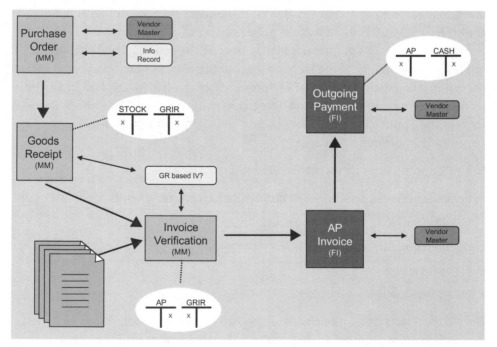

Figure 5.1 The P2P Cycle

SAP adopts a document principle, and along this process, you will create a number of documents, each with its own document number and document type. Let's look at the key stages of the process to understand the purpose of the different documents.

5.1.1 Purchase Order

A purchase order is created when you decide to purchase from a supplier (vendor). It is legal contract between the buyer (within your organization) and the vendor, who agrees to supply the goods. It contains a list of the items you are buying (materials), quantities, prices, and delivery information.

A purchase order may be created based on existing purchase orders or a purchase requisitions, which is used in some business processes. Information is pulled from info-records that contain purchasing-related information for the vendor-material combination.

In some scenarios, the creation of the (SAP) purchase order happens via a web-based frontend, such as *enterprise buyer professional* (EBP) or *supplier relationship management* (SRM). In these designs, you still have to create SAP purchase orders, so the process will reflect this.

The purchase order details the materials that you are procuring, and the summation of your materials is your stock held. A material is assigned an *account assignment* object (usually a profit center) that gives it a reporting dimension. A common requirement is to be able to split out your stock valuation by profit center, and many organizations design their solutions to get this figure. Material purchase price (standard cost) is also contained in the material master record.

5.1.2 Goods Receipt

A goods receipt is created when goods are received into stock. Its purpose is to ensure that the items received correspond to the information that was originally contained in the purchase order. For instance, you may have raised a purchase order for 100 items at $1 each, so your purchase order totals $100. You may, however, receive the items in more than one delivery, so the goods receipt is used to monitor the receipt of goods into stock.

When you receive the invoice for the items, you can see whether you are being invoiced for the full 100 items or just the items you have received. This is known as 3-way matching and is a control process used by many organizations. The name *3-way matching* refers to the fact that you are matching the original purchase order with the goods receipt and the vendor invoice. The 3-way matching is complete at the point of invoice verification.

5.1.3   Invoice Verification

Invoice verification is the process of validating your vendor invoices before they are released for payment. Most organizations choose to activate goods receipt–based invoice verification and operate a 3-way matching policy.

If you have activated goods receipt–based invoice verification, the system will check that the invoice you are entering corresponds to goods that have been received. In addition to checking quantities received, there is also a validation of the value of the invoice. Where there are variances in either price or quantity, the system generates variance postings. Organizations want to monitor these variances to keep a tight control over their buyers and procurement officers.

The posting of these variances to the GL is controlled by the settings made within the MM automatic account determination tables, which was discussed in detail in Chapter 4. Account determination by material is also used to determine which expense GL accounts are posted to.

5.1.4   AP Invoice

Invoice verification takes places within the MM component, but the process generates an AP invoice within the AP subcomponent. The purpose of the AP invoice is to create a document that is used to make a payment to the vendor, and as such, the payment information is stored in this document. When paying an invoice, the Payment Program determines the payment information (payment method, bank details, vendor address, etc.) from the vendor master record.

Some organizations may implement solutions that allow you to skip the purchase order steps and directly create an AP invoice. Normally, stock-related procurement is done via a purchase order, and nonstock procurement is done via AP invoicing. If you are entering an AP invoice directly, you are responsible for coding the invoice directly to the appropriate GL accounts.

5.1.5 Outgoing Payment

Outgoing payments can be generated manually, by user choice, or by use of the automatic payment program. We look at the payment program in more detail Section 5.11.6 and look at how it can be configured to meet your specific requirements. The key thing to note here is that it uses a combination of the selection criteria, the vendor master records, and the open items to make payments.

The payment document is matched against the AP invoice, which changes the unpaid AP invoice (open item) into a paid item (cleared item).

This section has explained the different stages of the P2P We will next look at the concept of building an AP business model.

5.2 Building an AP Business Model

We have previously spoken about having a straw man view of your system design early on, which helps shape the detailed decisions you need to make. Similarly, when you start your conceptual design of your AP solution, you should try to focus on the following key areas of the process, as these will have follow-up impacts on the detailed design:

▶ Design of your vendor master records

▶ Invoice processing control

▶ The payment process

We'll start with a discussion of the important aspects of the vendor master records. As mentioned already, the vendor master record has a lot of control over transactions processing, and you should consider which parts of the process relate to your organizations requirements and how the decisions you make impact the overall process.

5.2.1 Design of Vendor Master Records

Early on, you should decide on the process for procurement and how you will be using purchase orders. If you are using a traditional integrated solution involving purchase orders (as described in the P2P cycle), you will need to create the extended vendor master record to allow the creation of purchase orders against vendors. If you are using AP alone, you will enter your vendor invoices directly into AP.

A common approach is to use purchase orders for stock-related purchases (to provide stock analysis) and AP invoices for non–stock-related purchases.

5.2.2 Invoice Processing Control

The next question you have to answer is how will you process your vendor invoices for entering and release for payment? Will invoices be scanned or processed centrally, and what information will be required for entry? Some organizations require an authorization step before invoices can be released for payment. If your solution requires this, you may choose to use a parked document process to authorize invoices before they are released for payment.

This process has different levels of complexity depending on your specific needs and can be completely automated using SAP Business Workflow to pass invoices to nominated users for approval.

5.2.3 The Payment Process

Traditionally, organizations tended to make payment by check, but now more and more organizations implement an electronic bank transfer payment solution. Your choice will impact your controls over the master records and your need to create output. Will payments be made centrally or locally, and how does this differ from your current process?

If you have considered these areas as part of your solution design, you will have covered the main process areas required to deliver your AP solution. Lets now move onto the actual configuration of AP.

5.3 Master Data

Master data may seem to be the easiest part of your system design, but it is also the most important part of the system. You need to realize that master data is an important building block of your business process. Your master data will influence data flow through the system as well as out of the system. Reporting and external outputs are dependent on the way in which you structure your master data.

Some master data is created and used on an ongoing basis (operational master data), whereas some items are actually configured (static master data). We will look at both types in this chapter and explain the differences. We start with vendor masters which are operational master data as they may change over time.

5.3.1 Vendor Master Records

Vendor master records represent the key item of operational master data within the AP component. SAP business processes see the creation of vendors as being a function shared both the purchasing team and the finance team. Vendor master records are created to hold all of the information relating to that vendor in a single place. The vendor is assigned an account number, which you will use to refer to that vendor throughout the system.

In terms of creating your vendor master records, you need to consider whether you create them manually or through an automatic upload, as follows:

▸ **Manually**
Create your vendors manually if you have a small number of vendors and you want to use this process as a training process. Some organizations use the manual approach as a way of training staff. The risk here is of errors in data entry through manual keying, so some organizations prefer a different option.

▸ **Electronically**
Create your vendors electronically if you have a large number of vendors and creating all of them manually will not be possible within your project time constraints. Also, if you are migrating from a working legacy system, it may be reasonably easy to extract data from it and then load it to the SAP system. An electronic approach to upload your vendor records will provide you with a more accurate set of data, as your upload program will load exactly the values that are in your upload file.

Searching for Existing Vendors (Matchcodes)

The SAP system comes with a number of standard searches that you can use to find vendors in the database. These are known as "Matchcodes." In our business scenario, we don't have an excessive number of suppliers, but you may choose to use the "search term" function in a more inventive way to make searching for vendors more efficient. For example, the search term or the industry is used to classify your type of vendor, so you have additional search criteria. Figure 5.2 shows the additional Matchcodes available to search for Vendors. Using the Fuzzy Search option is the most flexible as this allows you to search by the different address attributes.

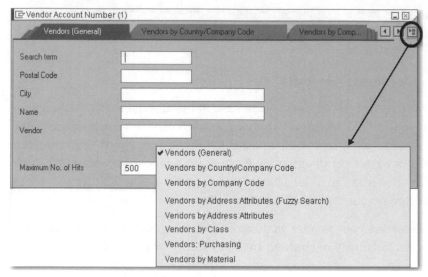

Figure 5.2 Searching for a Vendor Using Matchcodes

It is possible to create customized Matchcodes if you are using a specific field in the system that is not searchable via standard SAP matchcodes. For these, you need to identify the field you want to search by and request an ABAP developer to write some code.

To do this, follow the menu path **Financial Accounting (New) • Accounts Receivable and Accounts Payable • Vendor Accounts • Master Data • Matchcode • Maintain Matchcodes for Vendors** (see Figure 5.3) or use Transaction code OB50.

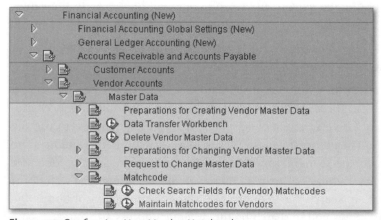

Figure 5.3 Configuring New Vendor Matchcodes

When you are creating a new vendor master record, the system will ask you to classify your vendor by specifying the account group to which it belongs. Account groups are explained in the next section.

5.4 Vendor Account Groups

The main control over the creation of vendor master records is within the vendor account group configuration. The vendor account groups have two main components:

▶ The account number given to your vendor master record (SAP-defined or user-defined)

▶ The fields that must be filled in when you create the vendor master record

Vendor account groups must first be configured and then assigned to the company codes you want to use. For SAFA Inc. we will classify our vendors as shown in Table 5.1.

Account Group	Description	Number Range	Usage
Z001	Domestic vendors	1000–1999	Vendors in the same country
Z002	International vendors	2000–2999	Vendors from another country
Z003	Nontrade vendors	3000–3999	Vendors who supply nontrade goods
Z004	One-time vendors	4000	One-off vendors

Table 5.1 Example of Vendor Account Groups Definition

Two configuration steps need to be completed here:

▶ Configure the vendor account groups

▶ Create number ranges for these account groups

The menu path to perform these steps is **Financial Accounting (New) • Accounts Receivable and Accounts Payable • Vendor Accounts • Master Data • Preparation for Creating Vendor Master Data**.

Vendor account group settings can be made specific per company code or per activity. These are discussed in detail later in this section.

We first concentrate on Define Account Groups with Screen Layout (Vendors) configuration activity which is found within the menu path described above. The account groups are defined as a four-digit alphanumeric reference and a description. SAP delivers standard groups, which you may use, or you can create your own. In our example we have chosen to create our own groups, which are created as copies of the SAP standard groups. This is demonstrated in figure 5.4.

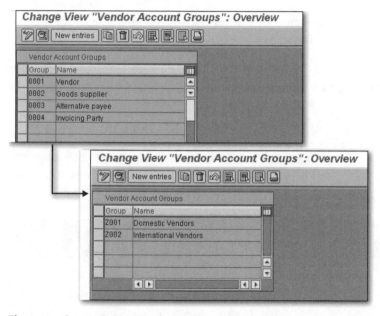

Figure 5.4 Create Custom Vendor Account Groups

<blockquote>

Note

The problem with using the standard SAP-delivered groups is that they show a wide range of fields on the vendor master record. Your particular business requirements may not require all of these fields, so most companies customize the account groups to re-move redundant fields. To configure your account group, double-click on it, and then you are taken into the screens behind it.

</blockquote>

The vendor master record is made up of three sections that are referred to as views (seen in figure 5.5), as follows:

▸ **General view**
  This contains the address information.

▶ **Company view**

This used to be referred to as the accounting view and controls the creation of AP invoices.

▶ **Purchasing view**

Information here controls the creation of purchasing.

For each area of the system, you need to determine the status of each field (hence the term *field status group*). For each field, you need to define whether the field is one of the following:

▶ Suppressed   When creating a customer, this field will be hidden

▶ Required   When creating a customer, this field must be filled in

▶ Optional   When creating a customer, this field will be available for input

▶ Display   When creating a customer, this field will be grayed out

These settings are made by selecting the appropriate radio button as shown in Figure 5.5.

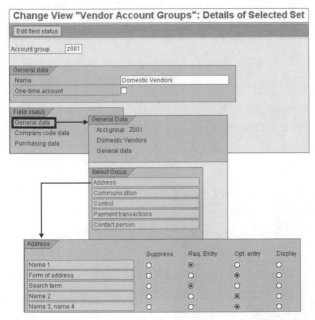

Figure 5.5 Editing Field Status behind Vendor Account Groups

> **Example: Editing Field Status within the Address Group**
>
> Going back to the application side, the settings you make here impact the business process when you are creating a new vendor master record. When you have a high-level view of your design, you will be able to make informed decisions in relation to which fields are required here.
>
> The options discussed here relate to generic requirements that should be applicable to most businesses. SAP caters for a large variety of industries and country variations that can be found in the SAP-delivered help files.

Let's look at the vendor master record views in more detail.

5.4.1 General Data View

The general data view holds the address information for the vendor. These fields are common for this vendor number, so if you create a vendor that is going to be used by different company codes, you can have a common vendor number, which means they all have the same general data. Within each field status group is a list of subgroups, which relate to the tabs on the customer master record. Figure 5.5 shows an example of the fields in the general data view.

General: Address

Figure 5.6 gives an example of how the settings you make in your field status groups influence the vendor master record. The 2 suppressed fields cannot be seen, whereas the 2 required fields must be filled in. The optional fields can be filled in if desired.

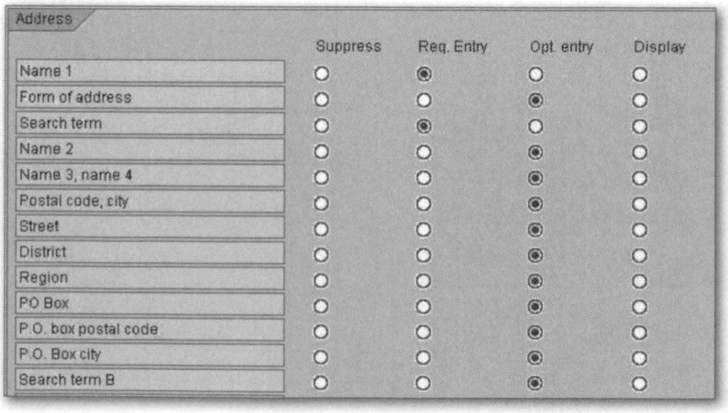

Figure 5.6 Vendor Field Status Group

When you are deciding which fields need to be populated, you need to consider the complexity of your organization and the requirements of your extended business process. Consider that the (address) information will be required for sending out correspondence with the vendor. For example, in Figure 5.7, you can see the relation between the field status settings and the create vendor process.

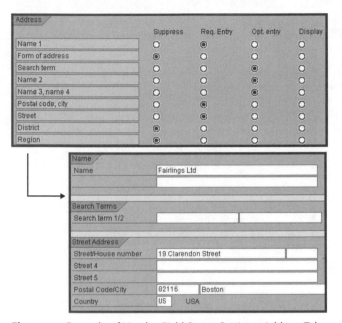

Figure 5.7 Example of Vendor Field Status Settings: Address Tab

For each field on these screens, SAP Help will provide you a detailed explanation of its use. Let's look at some of the key fields you need to be aware of on each of the fields in the vendor master record.

General: Control Data

Industry	You can use this field to group vendors together for reporting purposes.
Tax Nbr 1	You can use this field to group vendors together for reporting purposes.
Tax Nbr 2	This changes per country. In the United States this is the employee identification number. Across Europe it has different uses, and you need to refer to the help file to determine your specific country requirement. In the UK, for example, this is the national insurance (NI) number.

Payment Transactions

Country	This is the country the bank is in.
Bank	This is the bank key (or sort code).
Account	This is the bank account number
Holder	This is the name of the account. It is for information purposes, and there is no validation step here.

5.4.2   Company Code View

This is also referred to as the accounting view as this information relates the posting made to AP. Here you will see the following screens, which we'll look at in more detail in a moment:

- ▶ Account Management
- ▶ Payment Transactions
- ▶ Correspondence
- ▶ For each screen we again look at some of the key fields that are found on the screen.

Account Management

Reconciliation Account	This should always be a required (mandatory) field for all vendor master records. This is where you define the vendor reconciliation account within the GL balance sheet.
Previous Acct	You can use this to search for a vendor account. It can be used as part of data conversion, so the legacy system account number can be entered here.
Sort Key	This defines the value that fills in the assignment field in your transactions. Select 003 if you are unsure

Payment Transactions

Terms of payment	This should be the payment terms that have been agreed upon with this vendor.
Tolerance Group	This is the tolerances within which this vendor can transact. We explain the function of Tolerance Groups later on in this chapter.
Payment methods	Here you select the methods by which this vendor will accept payment.
House Banks	Here you select the bank account from which payments to this vendor will be made. We explain the function of House Banks later on in this chapter.

Correspondence

Correspondance	Here it is possible to enter contact information for the person who you deal with at the vendor's accounts department. Enter information here as required by your business process and speak with the output developers to link this information to the outputs

Two additional screens here relate to the procurement fields that we need to consider, as they relate to the process of invoice verification. Anything on these screens influences the documents that are created from the MM component (for example, purchase order, goods receipt, etc.).

5.4.3 Purchasing Data View

There are two screens in the purchasing view, and these are best discussed in conjunction with procurement. The key fields we need to highlight here are as follows:

▸ **Order Currency**
This is the default currency for this vendor.

▸ **Terms of Payment**
These are payment terms that default onto the MM documents for this vendor.

▸ **Control Data**
The relevant field here is the selection (or nonselection of the **GR-based inv. verif.** option.

The information in the purchasing view of the vendor is relevant for all purchasing documents created. If you buy different types of product from the same vendor, you may be offered different terms of payment. The AP sub-module can cope with having a different term on the purchasing and accounting views.

Partner Functions

SAP recognizes that third-party relationships can be complex, and you may be dealing with more than one address for a vendor. Each "partner" needs to exist as a separate vendor master record, and you can use the following business partners:

▶ **VN**

This is the main vendor. This is greyed out, as it is the master record in which you are currently.

▶ **PI**

This is the address to which invoices are presented.

▶ **OA**

This is the ordering address, which the vendor uses.

Within MM configuration, against a vendor account group, a partner procedure is assigned that controls which partner functions you can have for that type of vendor. A similar setting is assigned to the MM document types, which controls the type of partners that are relevant for this purchasing document.

5.4.4 Vendor Account Group Variations

There are two variations available here, which become excellent uses of functionality in a multi–company code environment. You should consider these options if you want to keep control of the number of account groups created. Different national legal requirements mean that fields can be used for different purposes, so you do need to consult SAP Help and OSS to find your country variations. This configuration activity is completed in the same area of the IMG as the other vendor master record configuration as can be seen in Figure 5.8. **SPRO • Financial Accounting (New) • Accounts Receivable and Accounts Payable • Vendor Accounts • Master Data • Preparations for Creating Vendor Master Data.**

Company Code Variant

You can define a different vendor account group setting per company code. That is, you can have the same account group ID but have a variation in the field status groups for the company code screens of this account group. In our scenario, a relevant example would be VAT registration, which is used in the UK but not in the United States.

Activity Variant

If you want to control the field status, based on activity, you can use this configuration step. This allows you to define the status of fields based on the transaction you are performing.

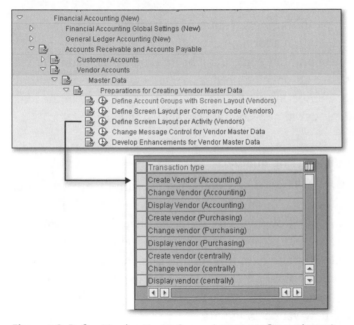

Figure 5.8 Define Vendor Master Screen Layout per Screen Layout

This concludes our review of the vendor master records. We now look at the configuration of vendor number ranges.

5.5   Vendor Number Ranges

When you create a new vendor, the system assigns it a vendor account number. As mentioned before when we were looking at vendor account groups, the number can be assigned by the SAP system automatically, or you can assign the number yourself (known as *external assignment*). The vendor number can be alphanumeric, so you may choose such a vendor numbering convention as your design.

Configuration is completed in the following area of the IMG: **Financial Accounting (new) • Accounts Receivable and Accounts Payable • Vendor Accounts • Master Data • Preparation for Creating Vendor Master Data**

Business Decisions

You will need to assess the specific business requirements here and understand what would be the best option. If your vendor base is small and stable, you may want to adopt an external assignment and put some thought into the naming convention. Most large organizations have an ongoing need to create new vendors, so putting too much thought into the numbering convention does not make sense in the long term. Some of the commonly asked questions are covered in the next section.

Q: Can we migrate over the existing numbers?

A: Yes you can. Just think about how you are going to deal with the new vendors that you create in your SAP system. For instance, your new vendors can be created with number ranges per account group, which may make them different from the migrated vendor numbers. Some users will argue that they want to retain the old numbers because they remember them. In this situation, migrate the old number to the Previous vendor number field on each vendor (as mentioned in section 5.4.2 earlier), and you can search for them then. You will be surprised how quickly users start memorizing the new vendor numbers.

Q: Can the User define the vendor number themselves?

A: For this is option, your account group must be assigned to an externally defined number range. Just think about creating a procedure that defines how to number the vendor so as to allow consistency.

Q: In our legacy system, we could identify the type of vendor by the vendor number. Can we introduce some logic into the vendor numbering convention?

A: This is possible. You need to have an account group for each vendor type you want to see and then set a different number for each vendor type. Again, think about the number of groups you want and the number of vendors that fit into each group.

5.5.1 Create vendor number ranges

The Create Number Ranges for Vendor Accounts node on the IMG allows you to create, display, and change the number ranges. Click on the **Maintain Number Range Intervals** button as shown in Figure 5.9 to amend an existing or create a new number range. From here, you need to select the **Interval** button, as shown in Figure 5.10, and then you can create a new range.

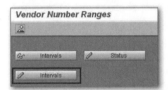

Figure 5.9 Vendor Number Range Maintenance

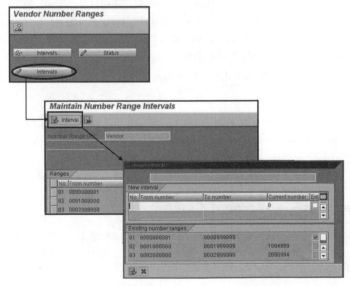

Figure 5.10 Insert New Interval

The system will not allow overlapping intervals and will give you a error message if you make a mistake here. If you want the user to decide the customer number, you need to select the **Ext** setting (External), to make the number range externally defined. You can use the **Ext** setting to have alphanumeric customer numbers.

The **Current number** indicates the last number that has been used. Be very careful here. If you are transporting this setting into a live environment, you need to check this setting. A classic error is when a new number range is transported to a production environment that is already live and current number buffer is overwritten.

In our fictitious company, SAFA Inc., we have the scenario that the same vendor supplies both company codes. As such, we will maintain the same vendor master record across company codes for their main supplier, Fairlings Ltd.

Configuration of any number range in the system requires the user to be careful as the settings can cause buffering issues as we explain in the next section.

5.5.2 Transporting Number Ranges

It is important to understand how transporting of number ranges works. The table you have just reviewed for creating new intervals is transported, along with the current number value. Therefore, in the example shown in figure 5.10, when this transport is applied to the target client, it will overwrite the Current Number of Range "02" with the value 1004869. Because it is very unlikely that your target system will have the same current number value, it will cause an error in the number range buffers.

For this reason, many projects do not allow the transport of any number ranges and prefer to have these as manual configuration tasks. Numerous OSS notes are associated with this and other number range issues.

5.5.3 Assign Number Range to Account Group

Having defined your account groups and number ranges, you need to assign the account group to the number range. We can see this activity in Figure 5.11.

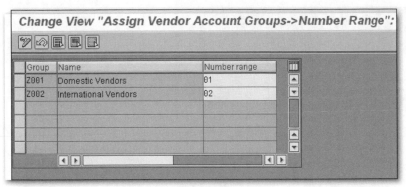

Figure 5.11 Assign Vendor Number Ranges to Account Groups

It is possible to assign the account group to more than one company code, as number ranges are company code independent. In this situation, in each company code, you could have the same vendor number assigned to different vendors. For our example, a number of vendors are common to both company codes, so we will apply the same vendor number to both of them, by *extending the vendor* into both company codes. To do this, you simply create this same vendor master record number in the additional company code by going to the Create Vendor screen. It is possible to do a mass creation (or extension) of vendors into additional company codes. In the next section we look at this process.

5.5.4 Extending Vendors to Additional Company Codes

If your business model uses multiple company codes, it is likely that the vendors are shared and used by more than one company code. SAP provides a standard transaction that extend vendors from one company code to another, avoiding the need to do this manually. It is also possible to extend a single vendor at a time, which is discussed at the end of this section.

The usual process would be to create the vendors for your initial company code and then use this function to extend them to other company codes (see Figure 5.12).

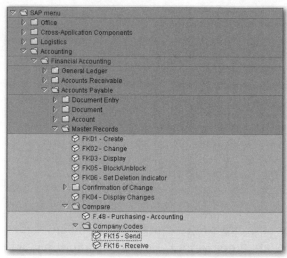

Figure 5.12 Extend Vendors to Additional Company Codes

In this transaction, you define the general selections, which are the source from which you are copying. You have two options to copy, depending on your target. If you are copying within the same SAP system, you can use the Transfer data directly option, which creates the batch session directly. If you are copying to another SAP system or client, you need to use the bottom option, Write data to sequential file (only for external SAP systems). This screen can be seen in Figure 5.13.

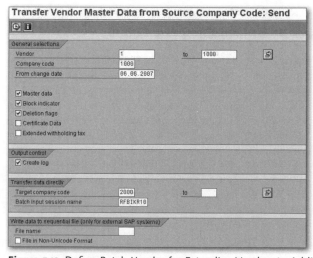

Figure 5.13 Define Batch Header for Extending Vendors to Additional Company Codes

If you have created the batch session directly, the transaction will generate a batch session that you need to process via Transaction code SM37 or SM35. If you are transferring to another SAP System, you need to Transaction FK16 and receive the information.

First, you need to specify the filename and the target company code to which you want to extend the vendors. The outcome of this transaction is a batch session that will create the vendors for you, and as such, SAP provides the program name. At the bottom of the screen, under the program control option, select **Check file only**. This first checks that the data is not corrupt. If this check is successful, you need to rerun this transaction without this option selected, and the system will generate the batch creation session. Figure 5.14 shows the screen that controls the receiving of the file.

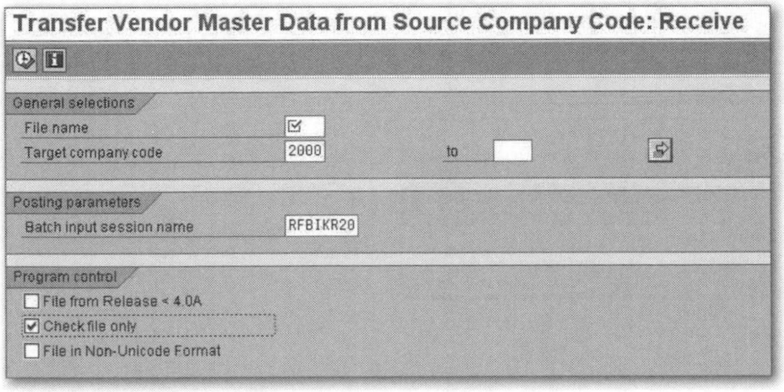

Figure 5.14 Extend Vendors: Receive Data File

If you only need to extend a single vendor, you simply need to create it in the additional company code. As the general view will already exist, you simply need to go into the Create Vendor screen and enter the new company code information. In the example below, we want to extend Fairlings into the London company code.

We have now covered vendor master records and their related configurations in sufficient detail. Next we move onto additional configuration activities in AP.

5.6   Accounting Clerks

Accounting clerks can be defined in the system and used to group vendors together. In a large organization, with many buyers, you may want to assign a vendor to a specific person. This flag can then be for reporting purposes, or you can display the relevant person's contact information on the output. In figure 5.15 we see the simple configuration screen that needs to be completed.

Accounting clerks are not an integral part of core SAP processes, so many organizations do not find a suitable use for them. This configuration activity is completed in the following area of the IMG: **Financial Accounting (new)** • **Accounts Receivable and Accounts Payable** • **Vendor Accounts** • **Master Data** • **Preparation for Creating Vendor Master Data** • **Define Accounting Clerks**

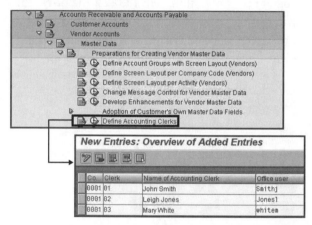

Figure 5.15 Create Accounting Clerks

The clerk ID is set by company code and can be alphanumeric. You may also want to link the SAP logon of the accounting clerk by entering it in the Office User field. This completes this simple configuration activity.

5.7 Define Sensitive Fields for Dual Control

In this activity, you can define fields for dual control within the vendor master record (this setting is also applicable for Customer master records). Dual control is very valuable for Sarbanes-Oxley compliance to ensure that vendors' bank details are not changed by fraudulent employees.

Once you have defined a field as sensitive, changes made to it within that company code are subject to additional confirmation steps. The actual confirmation step carries a separate transaction code, so it is possible to limit the users who have access to confirm changes to vendors.

The process would work as follows;

▶ A vendor master record is created or changed by an authorized user.

▶ Because impacted fields are marked as sensitive, the vendor cannot be used until an authorized approver confirms the changes made to the vendor master record.

▶ Users cannot approve their own changes.

An example of a control needed on the vendor master record is related to the control of outgoing payments. If you make payments by electronic bank transfer, you will want to mark the bank details on a vendor master record as sensitive. If you are making payments by check, you will want to make the address and, particularly, the name on the vendor master as sensitive, as these will control to whom the check is written and sent. The configuration is completed in the following area of the IMG and we see this example in Figure 5.16: **Financial Accounting (new) • Accounts Receivable and Accounts Payable • Vendor Accounts • Master Data • Preparation for Creating Vendor Master Data**

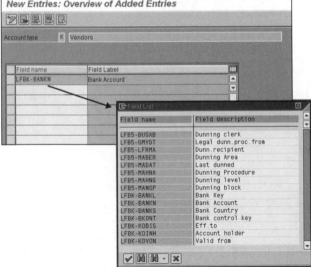

Figure 5.16 Define Sensitive Fields

Confirmation of vendor master record changes cannot be made by the person who originally made the changes to the vendor. This is a system control and you can where this is done in Figure 5.17.

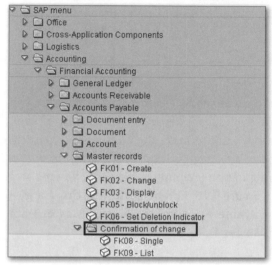

Figure 5.17 Confirmation of Changes Made to Vendors

You can make confirmations individually or approve a number of changes in a batch, using the List option.

In the next section we start looking at configuration related to Banks, which is an important part of the payment processing business process.

5.8 House Banks

Banks are included within the master data section of the AP component because they are normally static data.

It is usual for banks to be loaded into the system by most organizations, as they want to make automatic payments out of AP. It is possible to adopt a simple approach here or a more complicated design. This depends on the complexity of your organization and what analytic requirements you want to satisfy here.

In the first two examples above, you would most likely operate a single house bank. In the second example, you might adopt many accounts within that house bank. In the third example, you would need different house banks to satisfy the business requirements. It may become a complicated scenario when the same supplier is dealing with different business units. In that situation, you would need to configure bank ranking.

5.8.1 Configuring the House Bank

A house bank is configured in the system, whereas normal banks are created as master data. Let's assume the scenario where we are creating a single house bank with two paying bank accounts within it. Bank Accounts configuration is completed in its own area of the IMG as can be seen in Figure 5.18.

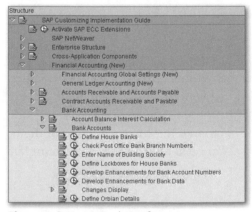

Figure 5.18 House Bank Configuration

In this situation, we would need to configure a single house bank. If you are operating many company codes, you need to create a house bank for each company code (see Figure 5.19). This is true even if you use the same bank for all your SAP company codes.

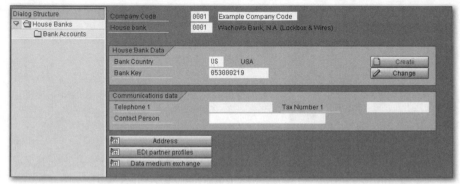

Figure 5.19 Define a New House Bank

Create the house bank at the level of the actual bank. Below the house bank, create the accounts that relate the actual bank accounts held at the physical bank. You need to give the house bank an ID that can be alphanumeric.

You may choose to enter the SWIFT (Society of Worldwide Interbank Financial Telecommunications) code. SWIFT codes are used internationally to identify banks. This is useful if you are conducting international transactions.

Once you have created the house bank and saved your changes, you can create your bank accounts below it. Double-click on the icon in the left-hand window. House banks can only be created once a Bank master record has been defined and we discuss this in the next section.

5.8.2 Bank Master Records

In our scenario, you need two bank accounts within the house bank (see Figure 5.20). Note that there is no way that SAP Bank Accounting Component would be able to validate the bank account information you are entering. It has a built in algorithm that can validate that you have entered the correct number of digits for the bank key and account number only. You need to give them an account ID, which you may decide.

Figure 5.20 Creating a Bank Account within a House Bank

Each bank account is linked to a GL account that maintains a record of the postings into and out of the bank account, based on the principles of double-entry bookkeeping. When designing your bank account's structure within the GL, you should bear this in mind.

Bank accounts need to exist in the system as master records if you are going to make electronic payments out of the system. If you are going to use the system only for check payments, you do not need to create each individual bank master record.

When you want to create these additional bank master records, as you are not making payments out of these, they do not need to be created and assigned to the house bank. They can be created directly within the application. In Figure 5.21 we show where these are created in the SAP Easy Access Menu.

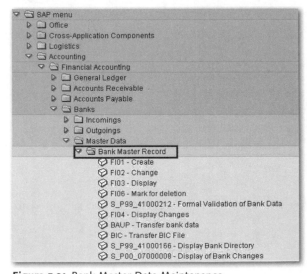

Figure 5.21 Bank Master Data Maintenance

For the remainder of this chapter, we will assume a business scenario where payments are made by check. We also make reference to payments using electronic transfer. If you do want to use an electronic bank transfer payment method you will need to consult your bank to ensure that the interface between the AP submodule and the bank is correct.

First we look at the configuration of our electronic check book, which is called the check lot.

5.8.3 Define Number Ranges for Checks

Checks can be printed on site if you purchase a micro-encoding printer (MICR) and use appropriate paper quality. This will be a dedicated printer that is used only for printing checks. Do not activate this printer in any system other than your production environment, or you may find checks being generated for fictitious companies. Figure 5.22 shows the configuration screen for creating your check lots, these should be in number ranges which should be defined having considered the number of checks you issue. This configuration is completed in the following area of the IMG: **Financial Accounting (new) • Accounts Receivable and Accounts Payable • Business Transactions • Outgoing Payments • Automatic Outgoing Payments • Payment Media • Check Management**

You can think of each check lot as a very large check book. You can create very few lots, with a lot of checks in each, or you may choose to have many lots, with fewer check numbers in them. A good guide is to create a lot equivalent to a year's processing.

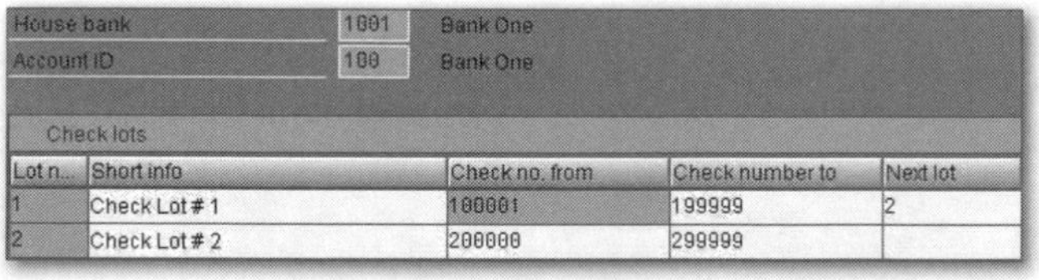

House bank	1001	Bank One		
Account ID	100	Bank One		
Check lots				
Lot n...	Short info	Check no. from	Check number to	Next lot
1	Check Lot # 1	100001	199999	2
2	Check Lot # 2	200000	299999	

Figure 5.22 Check Management Configuration

It is possible that sometimes you will need to void a check and so we need to define void reason codes next.

Check Void Reason Codes

Invariably, where you create a check, you will need to void a check. When you process a check void transaction, SAP Check Management component requires that a reason be assigned for it. You can decide how complex to make this selection by defining a number of reason codes (Figure 5.23). You can still control access to the check reason code.

Check Void Reason Codes		
Reason	Void reason cde	Reserved for print programs
1	Test printout	Sample printout
2	Page overflow	Page overflow
3	Form closing	Form closing
4	Ripped during printing	
5	Printed incorrectly	
6	Destroyed/unusable	

Figure 5.23 Define Check Void Reason Codes

We now take a break from configuration and look at the transactional side of Vendor Invoice Processing. This is a general look and is not intended to be a process definition. Before reading this section, it would be good to remind yourself of the process overview (Figure 5.1). The key transactions that happen in AP are the creation of the AP invoice and the payment of this invoice, both of which are covered in this section.

5.9 Invoice Processing

Usually vendors' invoices are sent through to the accounts payable department, which is responsible for loading them onto the system. There are different ways of processing the invoice, depending on the nature of the invoice.

The purpose of the AP document is to create something we can make a payment against. This satisfies related business requirements for reporting of creditors. If you are creating your invoice from a purchase order, the SAP software can draw information from the source document. If you are creating the AP invoice directly, you need to enter more details. It is common for solutions to be designed to use both methods.

We will consider two types of invoices: stock and non stock invoices.

5.9.1 Nonstock Invoices

Non stock invoices are raised for expense-type items. Usually they are used to pay for support-related services, for example, accounting, utility costs, and other overhead. For such costs, there is not usually a need to create a purchase order or make any stock adjustment, so we can create the AP invoice directly.

Non stock invoices are coded directly to the ledger and can be entered via transaction code FB60 (as seen in Figure 5.24), which is similar to a normal journal entry screen, which we have seen previously. Non stock invoices are basically finance documents and we reviewed the configuration of documents in chapter 3.

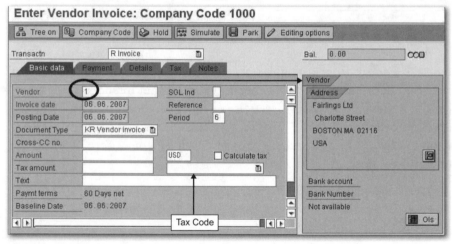

Figure 5.24 Enter Vendor Invoice (Nonstock)

Next we look at the process for entering invoices for stock items.

5.9.2 Invoice Verification (Processing Stock Invoices)

If we look back at our process overview (Figure 5.1), we will see that the AP invoice can also be created based on a purchase order. For stock items, invoices are entered in the logistics component, as these invoices are usually subject to invoice verification. For the purposes of this book, let's assume that you are subject to the rules of 3-way matching and you have selected GR-based Invoice Verification.

The two main objectives of invoice verification are to:

▶ Match the vendor invoice, in terms of what we ordered and what was delivered as well as prices charged

▶ Approve the payment of this invoice

The linkage across modules occurs through access of information as well as updating of information across modules.

Referring back to Figure 5.1, the process that is followed here is as follows.

1. Create the purchase order (no financial impacts). If you are using commitments (in the Controlling Component [CO]), this will generate a commitment.

2. Create the goods receipt whichgenerates postings in the stock and GRIR GL accounts (GRIR is the Goods Received−Invoice Received clearing account) . When the warehouse receives the items, process a goods receipt transaction within the MM module. This is, in reality, processing a goods movement transaction, but by using the movement type, it is possible to identify the type of movement, for instance a goods receipt. You process the goods receipt in reference to a purchase order, and once you enter the purchase order number on the screen, it will bring in the appropriate information directly from the purchase order.

3. Enter the invoice (generates an AP document and clears the GRIR account). The key here is the "traffic lights" in the top-right corner. While they are red, you cannot post this invoice because there is a problem. When the light switches to green, all of the details are matched and you can post it. An amber light indicates that you can post the invoice, but there is an problem that will block the invoice for payment.

A more detailed discussion of invoice verification is available in the special topics section at the end of the book.

When you enter the goods receipt and the invoice, the system determines postings to GL. These are controlled by the settings you make in the MM automatic account determination tables, which are discussed Chapter 9.

Purchase Price Variances

Sometimes differences are identified during the goods receipting and invoice verification stages. In these situations, variances are posted to the ledgers, and this is controlled by the account determination tables (see Chapter 9).

This concludes our brief review of the Vendor Invoice Processing and we return to configuration activities in the next chapter.

5.9.3 Duplication Invoice Check

It is important, when considering the overall model, to understand what information you want to have recorded on the invoice when it is entered into the system. The system requires certain mandatory fields, such as dates and amounts. In addition, you may want to use to the document type configuration to bring in the reference field (see Chapter 9). If you make this a mandatory field, you can use the duplicate invoice checking functionality (Figure 5.25).

The duplicate invoice check will validate if there already exists an invoice with the same criteria (as you configure in this configuration activity) and so give you a message to alert you to this.

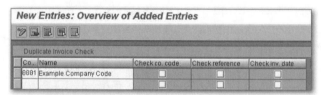

Figure 5.25 Configuration of Duplicate Invoice Check

This configuration is completed in the following area of the IMG: **Materials Management • Logistics invoice verification • Incoming Income • Set Check for Duplicate Invoice.**

This configuration screen will ask you which fields you want to incorporate into your duplicate invoice check:

- Company code
- Invoice reference
- Invoice date

The fields you select here will be used for the system to check to see if there has been another invoice of this amount to this vendor with these additional fields in the system. It is best to adopt all three options here and ensure that you identify as many instances of duplicate invoices as possible. This is also in line with Sarbanes-Oxley compliance. This setting can be made per company code.

Next we look at document parking which is relevant to the entering of vendor invoices into the AP component.

5.10 Document Parking

Document parking is function that can be used in different areas of the system. It is commonly used by organizations when processing invoices and journals.

There are two general scenarios in which a vendor invoice may be Parked;

▶ Organizations that use an approval process of document entry (manually or via SAP Workflow)

▶ Documents entered into the system, which cannot be completed as there is incomplete information or some other error with the invoice or the vendor master record.

▶ The park button is available in the normal vendor invoice entry screen and highlighted in figure 5.26.

Figure 5.26 Document Parking

In the first instance, assuming you are using a manual approval process, a clerk would only have access to Park a Document. It would then be to the responsibility of a senior person to post these documents once they are approved them. This process can be facilitated electronically using SAP Workflow.

In the second instance, a person entering a document, with a number of lines on it, may come to a point where he is unable to complete the entry and post it. If he simply cancels the transaction, he could lose the information that was already entered. In this situation, the user may choose to park the document. The advantage to this is that the document does not need to balance, as you can park an incomplete document.

It is possible to retrieve parked documents and then process them to completion or change them completely. It is possible to report on parked documents using standard SAP reports which are available in the SAP Easy Access Menu.

Once a vendor invoice has been entered onto the system the next step is to pay the invoice and we move onto the configuration of outgoing payments in the next section.

5.11   Outgoing Payments Processing

This section is the key area of the AP function for most businesses. Most organizations choose to operate the automatic payment program to generate a batch of payments based on invoices that have fallen due for payment.

The alternative is to process a manual outgoing payment, for example, where you have hand-written a check or made a cash payment. In the modern world, these instances are becoming less frequent.

5.11.1   Processing a Manual (Outgoing) Payment

It is possible to process a manual outgoing payment, which may be necessary when you have written a check or paid cash out of the petty cash box. Manual payments can be processed from transaction code f-53 (as seen in figure 5.27). Once you enter the header information, then you can select open items (unpaid invoices) which you make a payment against.

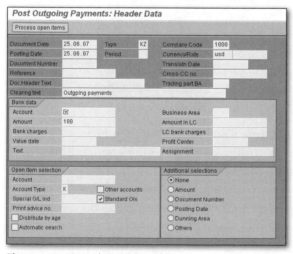

Figure 5.27 Manual Outgoing Payment

On the header screen, you enter at least the following information;

Document & Posting Dates	Here enter the document date (payment date) and the posting date (date of ledger entry).
Bank account	Here you should enter the bank (GL) account out of which you are making the payment
Amount	Here enter the payment amount, based on the currency that you have selected.
Open item selection account	Here you should enter the Vendor account against which you want to make the payment. From this account, the system will ask you to select open items in the next stage.
Open item selection account type	You need to select the type of account you are selecting, you can select from the drop-down menu. If you select D—Customers, the system allows you to make a payment to a customer (e.g., if you want to send a refund to a customer).
Additional Selections	It is possible to select your open items (invoices for payment) based on other criteria. If the account you are making this payment for have a number of open items, then you can select additional parameters from the additional selections.

Table 5.2 Manual outgoing payment header screen

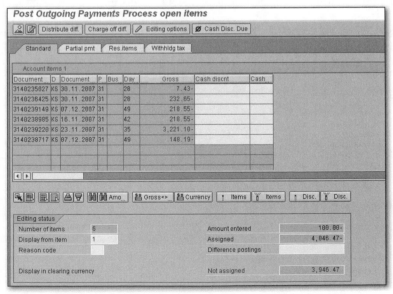

Figure 5.28 Select Open Items for Manual Payment

Processing of outgoing payments, both manual and automatic (which we look at later) is controlled by different configuration activities. We start by looking at vendor tolerances in the next section.

5.11.2 Vendor Tolerances

Vendor tolerances are defined for situations where payments are being allocated to vendor invoices. If the payment and invoice match within the tolerance set, then the small difference will be automatically written off to expense or revenue accounts when the open item clearing takes place.

This is configured in the following area of the IMG: **Financial Accounting (new) • Accounts Receivable and Accounts Payable • Business Transactions • Outgoing Payments • Manual Outgoing Payments • Define Tolerances (Vendors)**

The tolerance group is not given an ID, and this field is left blank. If you only create a single tolerance group, don't assign an ID to it. If you create more than one, you need to assign IDs to your tolerance groups and then separately assign users to those tolerance groups. All unassigned users will be subject to the "blank" vendor tolerance group.

Figure 5.29 shows the configuration of a Vendor Tolerance group

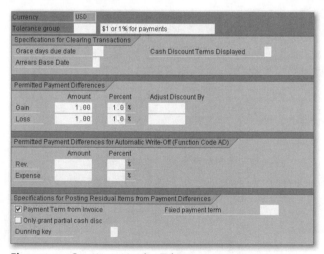

Figure 5.29 Creating a Vendor Tolerance

The permitted difference in this setting is very small, but if you want to extensively use the reason codes (which we cover in the next section), you can set larger tolerances in your system.

In addition, you specify settings here for the creation of the residual items. In Figure 5.29, we have specified that any residual item created will take its payment term from the original invoice.

5.11.3 Automatic Posting of Payment Differences

You may decide that all of these small differences are posted to a single GL account, and if so, you need to define a single account for all payment differences. Alternatively, you may want to classify the differences and then use this classification (reason codes) to determine to which account the payment difference is posted.

Define Reason Codes

Reason codes can be created to explain why there has been a payment difference on an invoice (see Figure 5.34). If you want to extensively use these reason codes, you should set your tolerances wider to enable larger differences to be posted. First you need to create your Reason Codes in the following area of the IMG: **Financial Accounting (new)** • **Accounts Receivable and Accounts Payable** • **Business Transactions** • **Outgoing Payments** • **Manual Outgoing Payments** • **Overpayment / Underpayment** • **Define reason codes (manual outgoing payments)**

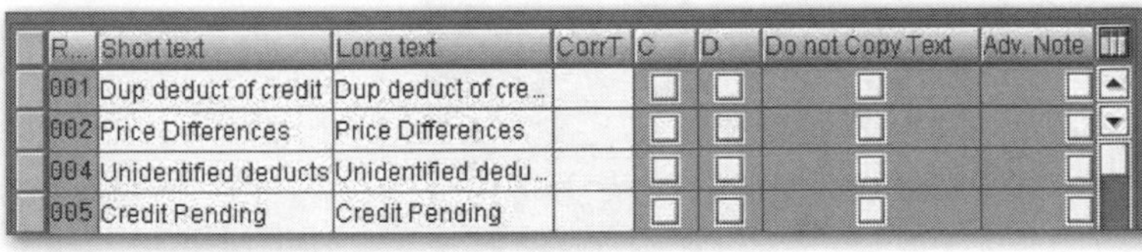

R...	Short text	Long text	CorrT	C	D	Do not Copy Text	Adv. Note	
001	Dup deduct of credit	Dup deduct of cre...		☐	☐	☐	☐	▲
002	Price Differences	Price Differences		☐	☐	☐	☐	▼
004	Unidentified deducts	Unidentified dedu...		☐	☐	☐	☐	
005	Credit Pending	Credit Pending		☐	☐	☐	☐	

Figure 5.30 Payment Difference Reason Codes

The additional options available here are summarized below, but you can refer to the SAP help files for a full description of each:

▶ **C:** Charge off difference via separate account

▶ **D:** Disputed item

▶ **Do not copy text:** Set this to enter the text manually, if you do not set this indicator, then the reason codes text will be copied into the line item text that this reason code is assigned to.

▶ **Adv. Note diff:** Payment advice note item

In the next step we can assign GL accounts for these reason codes, which will automatically control which GL accounts, these amounts are posted to.

Define Accounts for Payment Differences

If you have chosen not to use reason codes, you only need to make a single entry here, and all your payment differences (gains and losses) will be posted to a single account.

Financial Accounting (new) • Accounts Receivable and Accounts Payable • Business Transactions • Outgoing Payments • Manual Outgoing Payments • Overpayment / Underpayment • Define accounts for payment differences (manual outgoing payments)

In Figure 5.31, the first line, without the reason code, is the default setting. This is the setting you make if you choose not to use extensive reason codes. The other lines are indicative of the way in which you assign a specific reason code to an account.

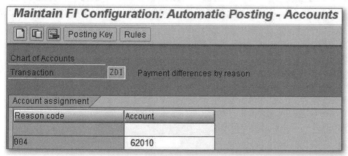

Figure 5.31 Assign GL Accounts to Payment Difference Reason Codes

On the second line, a reason code is specified and where this reason code is used, the difference is posted to this GL Account.

5.11.4 Cross-Company Code Manual Payments

In this same area of the IMG, you can use this configuration activity to setup inter-company payments and (therefore) clearing. In this situation, you need to simply identify which company codes make which transactions with other company codes. We do not cover this in our scope and more assistance can be obtained from SAP Help.

5.11.5 Payment Block Reasons

Invoices can be blocked for payment to ensure that a payment is not made in relation to them (Figure 5.32). This is a fundamental part of the payments cycle. It is possible that during invoice verification the system will automatically block an invoice to prevent it from being paid. It is also possible for an invoice to be manually blocked for payment. You may want to do this if you have an problem with the invoice or the vendor.

This is configured in the following area of the IMG: **Financial Accounting (new)
• Accounts Receivable and Accounts Payable • Business Transactions •
Outgoing Payments • Outgoing payments Global Settings • Payment Block
Reasons**

	Block ind.	Description	Change in pmnt prop.	Manual payments block	Not changeable
		Free for payment	☑	☑	☐
	*	Skip account	☑	☑	☐
	A	Blocked for payment	☑	☑	☐
	R	Invoice verification	☐	☐	☐

Change View "Payment Block Reasons": Overview

New Entries | BC Set: Field Value Origin

Figure 5.32 Create Payment Blocks

You can define a new blocking reason if required, but you should try to avoid creating an excessive number of blocks.

To block an invoice, you need access to change invoices, which is Transaction FB02 as can be seen in figure 5.33.

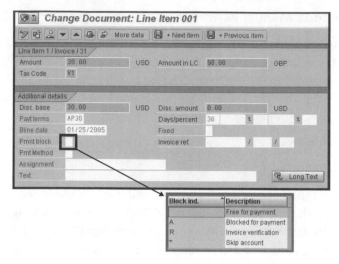

Figure 5.33 Block a Vendor Invoice for Payment

As you can see, a blank indicates that the invoice is **Free for payment**. If you want to stop this invoice from being paid, you need to apply one of the other blocks here.

To remove the block, you need access to the same transaction, unless the invoice is blocked as a result of invoice verification. We looked at the Document Change rules earlier in this chapter.

Default Blocks per Payment Term

An interesting piece of configuration is available that allows you to specify a payment block as a default for a specific payment term (Figure 5.38). You may find this useful for some business requirements.

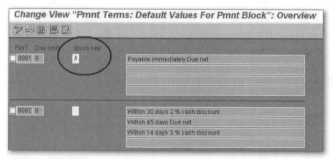

Figure 5.34 Assign a Default Block for a Specific Payment Term

This is configured in the following area of the IMG: **Financial Accounting (new)** • **Accounts Receivable and Accounts Payable** • **Business Transactions** • **Outgoing Payments** • **Outgoing payments Global Settings** • **Payment Block Reasons** • **Define default values for Payment Block**

Release Invoices Blocked by Invoice Verification

When an invoice has been automatically blocked by the system as a result of invoice verification failure, there is a transaction that is usually run in relation to this. The size and complexity of your organization determines how frequently this transaction is run. Figure 5.35 shows how to access this report in the SAP Easy Access Menu.

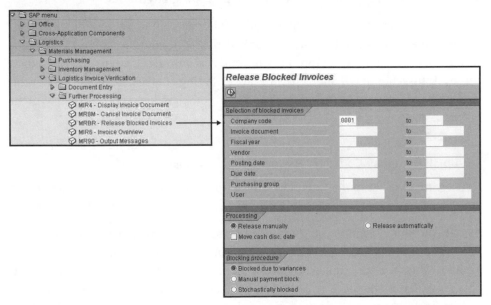

Figure 5.35 Release Invoices Blocked (MRBR) by Invoice Verification

This transaction is usually run by user, purchasing group, or vendor. You can also select invoices, by blocking procedure. If you want to analyze the invoices and release them after investigation, you should set the processing as **Release manually**.

The transaction returns all of the items that meet the specifications from the front page. From the next screen, you can click on the hyperlinks to view the documents. Selecting a line and then clicking on the green flag releases that invoice for payment.

We now move onto the configuration of the automatic payment program which is a major part of this chapter.

5.11.6 Automatic Payment Program

We now move on to the automatic payment program, which is essential to every Accounts Payable (AP) implementation in which you will be involved. the configuration steps are all held within the following area of the IMG: **Financial Accounting (new) • Accounts Receivable and Accounts Payable • Business Transactions • Outgoing Payments • Automatic Outgoing Payments**

The points made above concerning vendor tolerances and payment blocks are all applicable and important before we look at this configuration so you may want to refresh your memory before moving on. The automatic payment program is run by Transaction F110 and is part of most training courses. Lets first look at the configuration settings, and then we can highlight some key areas of the payment program itself.

Set up all Company Codes for Payment Transactions

First we need to setup the Company Codes for Payment Transactions as shown in figure 5.36.

As part of your system design, you need to review whether payments are being made out of a single company code or from many company codes. The first two nodes of this area are required to enable the required company codes for making payments. For each company code, you need to define who the sending company code is (ie the company code with the vendor invoices that need to be paid) as well as the paying company code (ie the company code which has the bank account that the payment is going to be made out of).

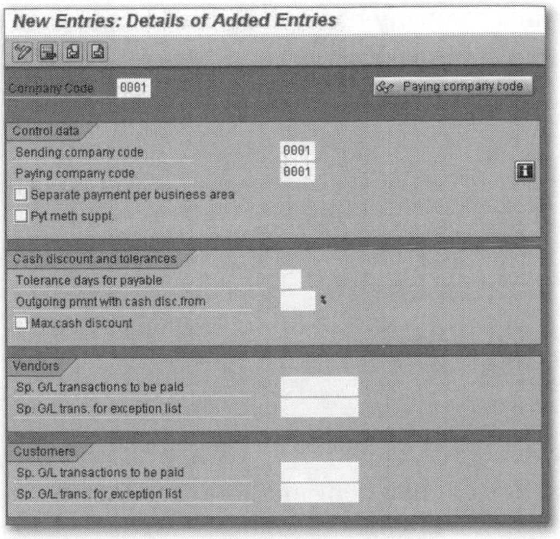

Figure 5.36 Configuration of Automatic Payment Program

It is possible to pay vendor invoices for another company code if you define that here.

Set up all Paying Company Codes for Payment Transactions

Next we need to setup the Paying Company Codes for Payment Transactions. So those company codes that we defined as paying company codes in the previous step, we need to make these settings.

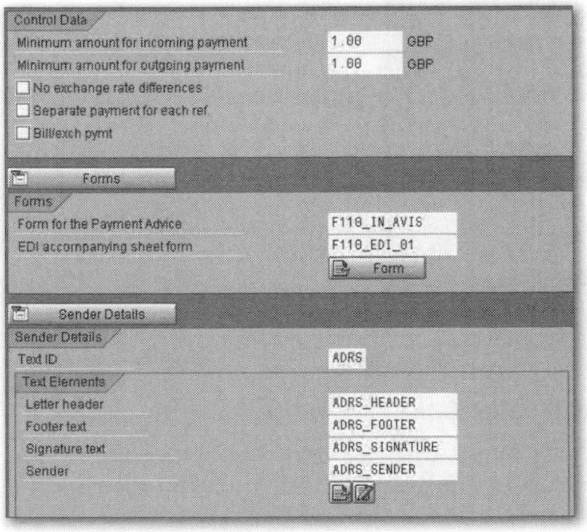

Figure 5.37 Set Up All Company Codes for Payment Transactions

This configuration step simply allows this company code to be used in the automatic payment program. In the next step, you make the settings to use this company code as a paying company code.

You must specify the following:

▶ Minimum amounts for a payment (incoming and outgoing)

▶ The forms to be used for the remittance advice

▶ The sender details (which link SAP fields). This information is used by the programmer who will create the remittance advice that you will send out to the vendor.

▶ We look at 2 payment method examples here, in figure 5.38 we look at payment method Check and in Figure 5.39 we look at payment method Bank transfer.

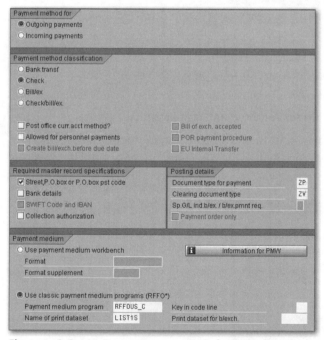

Figure 5.38 Set Up Paying Company Code for Payments

When comparing the 2 payment methods, you will see that it is possible to specify different rules for each payment method. We highlight some key points for the reader here.

▶ Payment methods are classified as being for Outgoing or Incoming payments.

▶ Required master record specification. The system uses this as a control, and when you are making a payment using this payment method, the system validates that this information exists in the master record. For checks, you need to have the address to which send the check, whereas for an electronic payment, you need the bank information.

▶ Posting details AP standard document types are ZP (payments) and ZV (clearing documents). It is possible to set up additional document types and assign them to a payment method to allow better analysis if needed.

▶ Classic payment medium programs are widely used:

  ▶ RFFOUS_T: bank transfers and bank direct debits

  ▶ RFFOUS_C: Check (with check management)

In Figure 5.39 we look at the payment method for bank transfer.

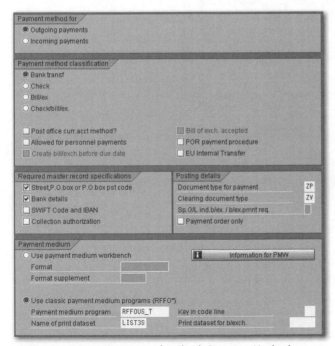

Figure 5.39 Country Settings for Check Payment Method

Set Up Payment Methods per Company Code for Payment Transactions

This is the second configuration activity for setting up payment methods. Here you define a payment method for each country from which you want to make payments (Figure 5.40). You will find standard settings within the system relating to different country requirements.

Figure 5.40 shows the settings for an electronic bank transfer payment.

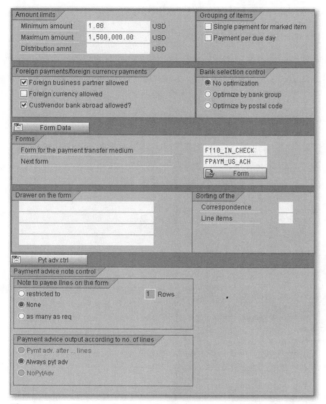

Figure 5.40 Country Settings for Electronic Bank Transfer Payment Method

It may appear that you are doing an additional piece of configuration, but some business requirements have multiple company codes in the same country.

In the company code settings, the most important setting you will make is the definition of the form that is relevant to this payment method. The form is developed using SAPScript and forms the payment advice (or remittance advice) that is sent along with the payment.

You can also set limits on the **Minimum amount** and **Maximum amount** that can be paid by this payment method, but this is a secondary control, as the automatic payment program has the primary controls.

If you want to create an individual payment for each line item in your payment run, select the **Single payment for marked item** option.

The **Payment per due day** field makes the system group together items by payment date. Thus, it groups together items that fall on the same due date and combine their payment.

Selecting **Foreign currency allowed** allows you to pay invoices that are in a currency other than your company code currency.

The **Cust/vendor bank abroad allowed?** setting needs to be activated if you will use this method to make payments in other countries.

Next we look at the configuration for setting up the ranking order for banks. This comes into play if you have many banks setup in your AP system.

Set Up Bank Determination for Payment Transactions

The last thing to configure in this section is the bank determination. In organizations that have a single house bank configuration setup, this is fairly straight forward

For each paying company code, you need to configure the following settings;

- **Ranking Order**

    If you have more than one house bank per payment method, you define the priority in which the system will look to make payments out of them (Figure 5.41).

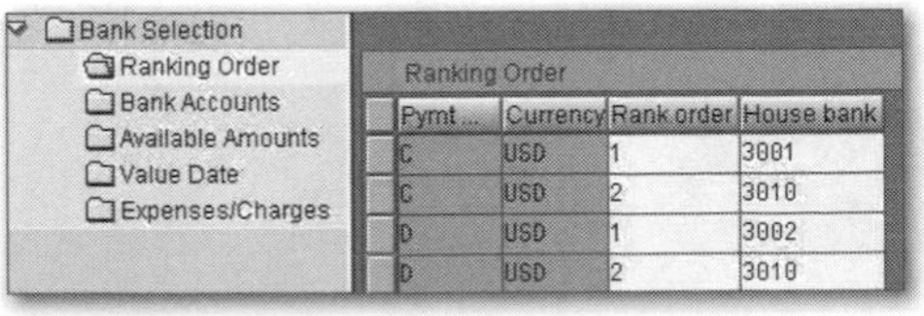

Figure 5.41 Configure Banks Ranking Order

- **Bank Accounts Available**

    This is where you list the available bank accounts for each house bank and the bank subaccount (GL account) to which it is assigned (Figure 5.42). (The NB charge indicator field is also available here, which is used with bills of exchange)

▽ ☐ Bank Selection						
☐ Ranking Order	Available Amounts					
☐ Bank Accounts	House ba...	Account...	Days	Currency	Available for outgoing p...	Scheduled incoming pa...
☐ Available Amounts	3001	100	999	USD		
☐ Value Date	3002	100	999	USD		
☐ Expenses/Charges	3010	100	999	USD	10,000,000.00	

Figure 5.42 Bank Accounts Available

▶ **Available Amounts**
Here you can define the maximum amount you want to be able to pay out of this bank account. The Days Until Value Date field is nullified if you enter 999 in it. Companies tend to set very large amounts here.

▶ **Value Date**
This should be the average amount of time it takes for a payment to clear. This is useful in treasury and cash management.

▶ **Expenses/Charges**
Here you configure charges that are to be made as part of the payment. This is used in Spanish bills of exchange scenarios.

Running the Automatic Payment Program

The last thing to discuss in this chapter is the actual running of Transaction F110. The following settings can be made to tailor your payment run to suit your organizational needs (Figure 5.43).

First, you can access all of the subtransactions using the menu within the payment program. Usually, you will be shown how to use the buttons on the screen, but not the menu bars.

Figure 5.43 Transaction F110 Menu Bar

Second, when you create your proposal, and your final payment list, it is possible to get a good report out of the system to analyze the items. When you create the proposal, instead of simply selecting the **Display Proposal** button, you can follow the menu path **EDIT • PROPOSAL • PROPOSAL LIST**. This will call report RFZALI20, which gives you a better layout of the proposal, and this layout can be printed or sent electronically for approval as part of your business process.

Figure 5.43 shows a link to the report from the menu path. If you follow this link, you can to create report variants that you can then use during the automatic payment program to generate customized output to meet your organization's requirements.

5.12   Summary

This was quite an extensive chapter which covered a lot of material within the Purchase to Pay process. Having completed this chapter the reader will now be able to configure SAP AP Component in relation to the following business process areas;

▶ Creation and maintenance of vendor master records

▶ Vendor transaction processing (including invoices and payments)

▶ Integrated nature within the MM component and relevant aspects of Logistics Invoice verification

▶ Outgoing Payment processing

In the next chapter we look Accounts Receivable which is the chapter that covers the sales ledger and customer transaction processing.

Accounts Receivable is the business process by which we collect money owed from our customers. Related to that are the business processes for debtor management for which we specifically use the Dunning functionality in our design.

6   Accounts Receivable

The overall objective of this chapter is to explain the functionality of the Accounts Receivable (AR) subcomponent, which is sometimes not given the credit it is due, as the work is seen to be done by the Sales and Distribution (SD) component. The function of the AR subcomponent is very important in the process chain because this is where a number of process controls are within the service-to-cash process. This chapter covers the following;

- ▸ Creation and maintenance of customer master records
- ▸ Customer transaction processing (including invoices, credits, and payments)
- ▸ Integrated nature with the SD module
- ▸ Debtors management, including credit control

The chapter starts with an overview of the order-to-cash process and then discusses in detail the configuration required to deliver the functionalities we outlined a moment ago. There are also a number of references to other chapters that are discussed throughout this chapter. Further, it is assumed that your solution is using core SAP ERP ECC functionality, so there is no discussion of SAP Customer Relationship Management (CRM). Let us first review the key points in your business blueprint to understand the type of solution that is possible within AR.

6.1   Overview of the Order-to-Cash Process

Business processes between your organization and your customers are captured within the order-to-cash business process. This process can start back as far as the first interaction with a customer, which may be a customer enquiry or quotation.

The level of detail depends on the volume versus the value of sales transactions, (i.e., "high value-low volume" sales transactions or "low value-high volume" sales transactions). The end of the process is the point at which a debt is cleared from the system either by the collection of the payment due, or the write off of it as a bad debt. Figure 6.1 summarizes the process.

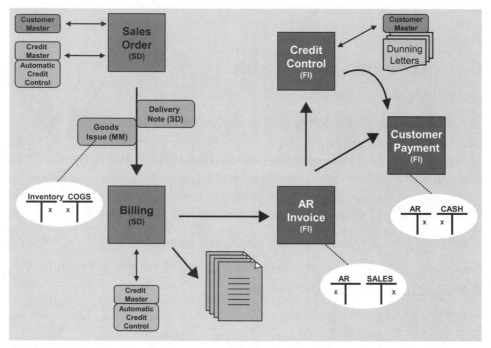

Figure 6.1 The Order-to-Cash Process

The SAP system creates documents along the process. Only some of the documents create financial postings, as indicated in Figure 6.1 by the accounts marked with a T. Let's look at some of the key stages in this process to understand the purpose of the different documents involved.

6.1.1 Sales Order

A *sales order* is created within the SD component, which supports the sales, delivery, and billing business processes. A sales order captures all of the essential sales information (including materials, quantity, prices, delivery dates) and is used as the basis for the follow-on documents.

A sales order may be created based on an existing sales order or from the information collected, for example, in a customer quotation. The way in which a sales order is created depends on the nature of your organization. For example, the capture of the information for the sales order may happen at the point of contact with your customer, so if you are a large retailer, this may be the retail outlet. In such an example, you may capture data and interface it into your SAP system and create sales orders as a result of your interface. Some organizations are selling in a high value-low volume situation and capture the information on a customer order form (paper-based or electronically). This information is then used to create a sales order. Or, you might have a customer service center, where customers call in orders, and sales orders are created while the customer is on the phone. Whichever method suits your business best, the sales order is the start of the process for the purposes of our discussions in this chapter.

6.1.2   Delivery Note

A *delivery note* is entered based on the information in the sales order. This initiates the shipping activities (e.g., picking and packing) associated with delivering materials to a customer. A single sales order may have many deliveries associated with it. Each delivery generates a goods issue transaction for recording changes in stock levels. Once a goods issue has been posted, no further changes can be made to the delivery note. The goods issue generates GL postings to record these changes in stock.

6.1.3   Billing Document

The *billing document* is the last document within SD and is the basis for the accounting documents that are created. The physical output is generated and created from the billing document once the customer is invoiced for the goods or services they have received. The GL postings in the accounting documents are generated based on complex account determination, as per the rules configured within the automatic account assignment tables (explained in Chapter 9).

6.1.4   AR Invoice

If the billing document generates the output, then what purpose does the AR invoice serve? The AR invoice represents the financial postings related to the sales order. The information in the sales order does not necessarily capture the ledger postings, and therefore you need the AR invoice. In addition, you use the AR invoice for the management of the debtor to collect cash due and to control your debtors. These points will be discussed in detail later within this chapter.

Now that we are clear on the principles and definitions, we talk about how we would build up our business model for AR.

6.2 Building an Accounts Receivable Business Model

We'll now look at building an AR business model. To start, a customer order is processed as a sales order, and when the customer is billed, postings are generated in AR. This part of the process is fairly common across implementations. The differences between implementations are around the management of debt and processing of customer payments. For this reason it is important to spend a lot of time on this topic in your blueprinting workshops to determine the business needs. Once these are clear, you can ensure that the setup of master data and transactional processing captures the correct level of detail.

From a high-level point of view, the following requirements should form an important part of your workshops with your business partners when creating a design for your AR solution:

▸ **What level of integration do you have with the SD component?**
Is your business selling stock or services? This should influence whether you want to use the billing functionality. In a standard integrated solution, you would expect to share your master data with the SD component,

▸ **What controls do you require over your customers, in terms of credit control and debt management?**
This is related to your current credit and bad debt issues. Organizations at this stage like to "blue sky" which means that they put all possible controls into the system. When it comes to the realization stage they sometimes find that they have lost flexibility or the system is too rigid to provide the best solution they initially wanted. If you have a small customer base and you want to maintain a personal relationship with your customers, you may choose to relax the system controls discussed in this chapter.

▸ **What should the design of your customer master records be?**

Based on the blueprinting discussions you should try to get a clear picture of the makeup of your customer master record and the fields that are to be included in it.

Although it is never possible to capture every answer you need by the end of blueprinting, if you have covered these main areas you should be well on your way to having a complete design. Next, we will start looking at the configuration of the accounts receivable subcomponent. We start by looking at the master data related configuration.

6.3   Master Data

Master data may seem the easiest part of your system design, but it is also the most important, as it is an important building block of your business process. Your master data will influence the data flow through the system as well as out of the system. Reporting and external outputs are dependent on the way in which you structure your master data. Some master data is created and used on an ongoing basis (operational master data), whereas other master data is actually configured (static master data). We will look at both types in this chapter and explain the differences. We start with the Customer Master Record.

6.4   Customer Master Records

The customer master record is a key element of operational master data within AR. SAP business process defines the creation of customers as being a function shared by the sales team and the finance team. The complete customer master record is made up of three component views, as shown in Figure 6.2:

▸ **General data**

▸ **Company code data (also referred to as the accounting view)**

▸ **Sales data**

The sales data view has a lot of influence on the overall makeup of the customer master record due to the heavy reliance on the information being passed from SD. All documents created in SD pull information from the sales view of the customer, and that is where you find the billing information. In the sales area view, you find the partner functions of the customer master record, as follows:

- ▶ Sold To: The person who orders the goods or services
- ▶ Ship To: The person who receives the delivery of the goods or services
- ▶ Bill To: The person who is invoiced for the goods or services
- ▶ Payer: The person who pays for the goods or services

Figure 6.2 shows the different components of the customer master record.

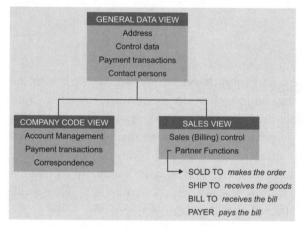

Figure 6.2 Different Components of the Customer Master Record

6.4.1 The Nature of the Customer Database

Because the management of customers is important to an organization, we will briefly investigate the nature of your customer database. Because each organization and the industry structure in which it operates is unique, we will examine two scenarios that represent both extremes:

- ▶ **My customers are large organizations.**
  You may find that you have complicated customer relationships. You may have contracts in place that define credit terms that you negotiated with the organization. The actual ordering is done by the customers' purchasing departments, and they may be ordering for a number of different sites. Delivery is made to one of their main distribution warehouses, from which the customer manages

the stock. Finally and most importantly, the bills are settled by the finance department, which is located in a building of its own.

▶ **My customers are small organizations.**
You know your customers fairly well, have decent relationships with them, and if they get behind making payments, you typically work out some terms over a period of time to enable them to get up to date. The same person who places orders negotiates terms. Another person in the same department releases bills for payment. Delivery is made to the same location as everything else and the invoice is usually sent out with the delivery.

These two scenarios represent completely different business requirements and would require significantly different configurations to be completed. Also, we have not mentioned a hybrid customer that could be internal to your organization, and that has its own set of configuration requirements. Whatever your customer scenario, the SAP system works on the assumption of having a single customer master record in the system.

6.4.2 Manual or Automatic Creation of Customer Master Records

We will now examine the way in which you will create your customer master records in your new system and migrate from your old system.

Creating Customers

You need to consider whether you create your customers manually or through an automatic upload:

▶ **Manually**
Use this option if you have a small number of customers and you want to use this process as a training process. Some organizations use the manual approach as a way of training staff. The risk here is of errors in data entry through manual keying.

▶ **Electronically**
Use this option if you have a number of customers, and creating all of them manually will not be possible within your project time constraints. Also, if you are migrating from a legacy system, it maybe relatively easy to extract data from it and then load it into your SAP system.

An electronic approach to upload your customer records will provide you with a more accurate set of data, as your upload program will load exactly the values that are in your upload file.

When you are creating a new customer, the system will ask you for certain information, for example, **customer** and **account group**, as shown in Figure 6.3. We talk about their purpose in the next section as we look at the related configuration activities.

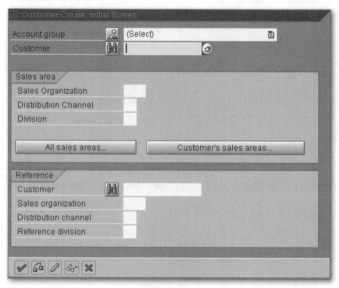

Figure 6.3 Create Customer (Centrally)

6.4.3 Searching for Existing Customers (Matchcodes)

The SAP system comes with a number of standard searches that can be used to find customers from the database. These searches are known as *Matchcodes*, and they let you search for customers in different ways other than by searching the usual name and address, as shown in Figure 6.4. You may want to consider how you would usually search for customers based on your own organizational requirements. You may want to make use of the Industry field (which we explain in later in this section) and so want to have a Matchcode for Industry.

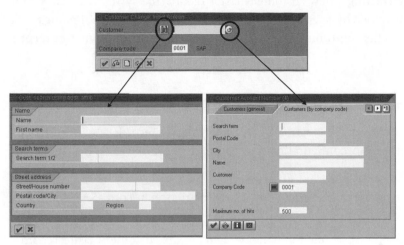

Figure 6.4 Examples of Standard Matchcodes

You can create customized Matchcodes if you are using a specific field in the system that is not searchable via standard SAP searches. For these, you need to identify the field you want to search by and request an ABAP developer to write some code. This is configured using the menu path **Financial Accounting (New) • Accounts Receivable and Accounts Payable • Vendor Accounts • Master Data • Matchcode • Maintain Matchcodes for Vendors** or by using Transaction code FD01. Figure 6.5 gives an example of a customized Matchcode being created;

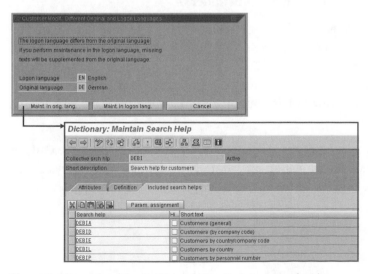

Figure 6.5 Example of the Creation of New Customer Matchcodes

When you are creating a new customer master record, the system will ask you to classify the customer by specifying the account group to which it belongs. The account group is the controlling object for the creation of customer master records and is discussed next.

6.4.4 Define Account Groups

The main control over the creation of customer master records is within the customer account group configuration. A customer account group has two main components:

▸ The account number given to your customer master record (SAP-defined or user-defined)

▸ The fields that must be filled in when you create the customer master record

Customer account groups must first be configured and then assigned to the company codes for which they are relevant. With vendors, you create your own account groups based on purchasing requirements. For customers, the decision about account groups should be influenced by the integration with the SD component, as mentioned earlier. Therefore, we will use the SAP standard account groups. Account groups are configured by following IMG path **Financial Accounting (New) • Accounts Receivable and Accounts Payable • Vendor Accounts • Master Data • Preparations for Creating Customer Master Data • Define Account Groups with Screen Layout (Customers)**.

Account groups are defined as a four-digit alphanumeric reference with a description. We are going to use the standard SAP account groups to make full use of the business partner functions. You could create your own classification of customer, (e.g., customer location, type of product they purchase from you, etc.). This is done by clicking on the **New Entries** button and following the screens as shown in Figure 6.6.

In the **General data** section of the account group, you need to select the **Output determ. proc.** (output determination procedure), which links your business partner from the billing process to the relevant output (i.e., invoice, delivery note, etc.).

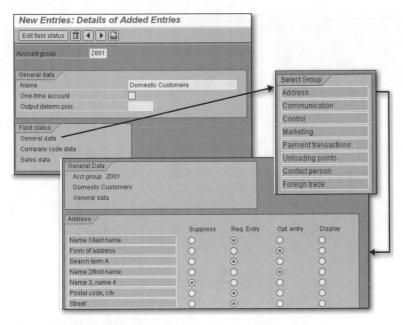

Figure 6.6 Configuration of Customer Account Groups

Within the account group, the **Field status** is split into three component views of the customer master record (**General data**, **Company code data**, and **Sales data**, as discussed earlier in this chapter). Double-click a view to see the list of subgroups, which relate to the tabs on the customer master record. For each field, you need to determine its status (hence the term **Field Status Group**). You do this by selecting the appropriate radio button for each field, as shown in Figure 6.7 (which uses the example of the **Address** tab):

▶ **Suppress:** When creating a customer master record, this field will be hidden.

▶ **Req. Entry:** When creating a customer master record, this field must be filled in.

▶ **Opt. Entry:** When creating a customer master record, this field will be available for input.

▶ **Display:** When creating a customer master record, this field will be grayed out.

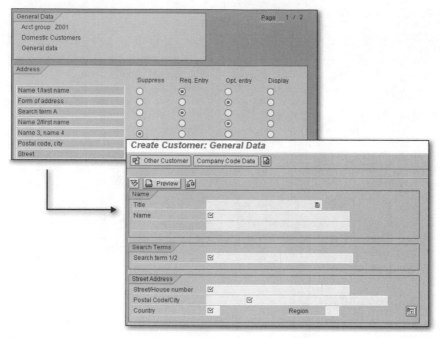

Figure 6.7 The Customer Address Tab is Controlled by the Settings Made within the Vendor Account Group

Setting Field Status

When you are deciding which fields need to be populated for the address information, you need to bear in mind the discussion earlier in the chapter regarding the complexity of your organization. If you are working with a small number of customers, the address need not be complicated. If you are dealing with a complicated set of customers, you need to make use of a greater combination of fields to capture the master data correctly.

What Field Status Would You Set for these Business Requirements?

Look at the two examples below of different organizations and their varying levels of information needs:

▶ A professional cleaning company that provides office cleaning services to a university. Each faculty pays its own bills, customer correspondence needs to include information to the level of building, floor, and room number.

▶ A national retailer that operates a franchise model. In this situation, there will be a controlled number of customers. The level of address information needed for each customer is street (including house number), and the town, city, and zip code combination.

You need to think about what you are going to use a piece of master data for, before deciding what information to record.

Table 6.1 identifies the key fields available in the customer account group.

Address Tab	Holds the address information for the customer. This depends on the partner function that you are creating, so for the ship-to, you should enter the warehouse address, and for the bill-to, you should enter the accounts payable department.
Name	This is the main name the customer is known by. Two lines are given here, and you can use both lines.
Search term	Short name that is used to set up a matchcode
Street	Street address
Postal code or PO box Pcode	Zip code
Country	Two-digit country identifier
Region (state)	Two-letter state abbreviation
Language	Two-letter language code
Control Tab	Holds information about tax for which you should consult your local tax rules.
Vendor	If this customer is also a vendor, you can indicate this here. This allows you to match payables and receivables against each other if you adopt this policy.
Industry	You can use this field to group together customers for reporting purposes.

Table 6.1 Key Fields Available in Customer Account Groups

Control Tab	Holds information about tax for which you should consult your local tax rules.
VAT Reg No	Customer VAT registration number, which is important to collect in some countries, to be able to charge them tax. You should consult your local tax laws on this matter.
Tax Number 1	The use of this field changes by country; in the United States this is the social security number (SSN). Across Europe it has different uses, and you need to refer to the help file to determine your specific country requirement.
Tax Number 2	The use of this field changes by country; in the United States this is the employee identification number. Across Europe it has different uses, and you need to refer to the help file to determine your specific country requirement. In the UK, this is the national insurance (NI) number.
Payment Transactions	For customers, bank information is not necessarily important, as you do not pay them. For customers who pay you via electronic bank transfer, you should require a reference to be supplied with the payment.
Country	Country of bank
Bank Key	Bank sort code
Bank Account	Bank account number
Acct holder	Bank account holder
Co	Not required
Bank Type	Not required

Table 6.1 Key Fields Available in Customer Account Groups (cont.)

The fields listed in Table 6.2 are within the company code data view of the customer master.

Account Management	
Reconciliation account	This should always be a mandatory field, as it controls the posting between the AR subledger and GL. This is explained in some detail later on in this chapter.
Sort Key	When an AR document is created, a value is entered into the assignment field on that document. This field is the default sorting parameter when running a customer line item report. Whatever you select as the sort key is the value entered into this customer's assignment field.

Table 6.2 Key Fields Available within the Company Code View

Account Management	
Head Office	The head office functionality is used to group together customers for reporting and analysis purposes. An example is where certain customers use different factor companies to pay their bills on their behalf (this is a debt collection process used by some companies). The partner function controls the information that is stored on the output. You can use Head Office within AR solely to collect the debt from another person. This concept is explained in more detail in the section on debtor management later in this chapter.
Previous Account Number	This is sometimes a useful field to populate in an exercise of migrating customers from an old system to a new system. It may also be used over time for customers who have had their account number changed in the SAP system itself.
Planning Group	If you are using the Treasury component, this field can be used to control the update of the receivable section of liquidity-forecast reporting.
Interest Calculator	This lets you calculate and charge customers interest on late payments.
Payment Transactions	**This tab on the company code data view controls the processing of items within AR only.**
Terms of payment	Agreed payment terms with the customer should be used here. This value defaults into each customer invoice you create. It is possible to change the payment terms in the invoice, so you are not restricted to this value.
Clearing with vendor	Selecting this field, along with the assignment of a vendor on the previous screen, allows you to net off payable and receivable items. Both fields need to be complete to allow this to happen. Most organizations want to keep their records separate, and very few use this functionality. It may be something you find useful for your internal trading scenarios, however.
Tolerance Group	A tolerance group can be assigned to a customer to control the value of transactions that can be processed, as well as the tolerance within which small differences can be written off. This is explained in more detail later in this chapter.
Lockbox processing	This is a predominantly U.S. functionality that is explained later in this chapter.

Table 6.2 Key Fields Available within the Company Code View (cont.)

Correspondence	This tab is used for recording important information in relation to the dunning- related correspondence with the customer (dunning is a function of credit control).
Dunning Area	Dunning is a process whereby you monitor outstanding invoices and produce SAP-generated reminder letters to be sent out to the customer. Dunning is explained in detail toward the end of this chapter. Dunning area is an assignment made of this customer to a rule within the Dunning Procedure which is explained towards the end of this chapter.
Dunning Proc	Here we assign the dunning procedure relevant to this customer.
Correspondence	There are some additional fields on this screen to enter customer contact information. You should use these fields only to record the customer credit control department contact information.

Table 6.2 Key Fields Available within the Company Code View (cont.)

In addition to these fields, there is also sales data view-related information that needs to be completed. However, this is beyond the scope of this book. The only point we will make here is that the fields are important to the AR process, so you should try to get involved with this as much as you can.

In this section we have explained in some detail the configuration of customer account groups. This should be sufficient information for you to be able to configure most business requirements. As you can see, the SAP system is flexible enough to be applicable for a wide range of industries.

Note
Some of the fields that we have not covered may be applicable to your specific business requirements, so you should check all fields before suppressing any.

6.4.5 Company Code or Activity Account Groups

In the same area of the IMG **Financial Accounting (New) • Accounts Receivable and Accounts Payable • Vendor Accounts • Master Data • Preparations for Creating Customer Master Data)**, you can see that there are two variants for the creation of account groups: the company code variant and the activity variant, shown later in Figure 6.8, which become excellent uses of functionality in a multi–company code environment. You should consider these options if you want to keep control of the number of account groups you create.

Different countries' legal requirements mean that fields can be used for different purposes, so you do need to consult the SAP Help and OSS to find your country variations.

OSS is the Online SAP Support network that allows you to obtain help and support from SAP in terms of technical and configuration issues you may have.

Company Code Variant

You can define a different customer account group setting per company code, that is, you can have the same account group ID, but have a variation in the field status groups for the company code screens of this account group. In our scenario, a relevant example would be VAT registration, which is used in the UK but not in the United States.

Activity Variant

If you want to control the field status, based on activity, you can use this configuration step. This allows you to define the status of fields based on the transaction you are performing. A good use of this is the activation of all fields in display mode so you can see which other fields are available but have not been used or have been suppressed. The different activities (transaction types) are shown in Figure 6.8.

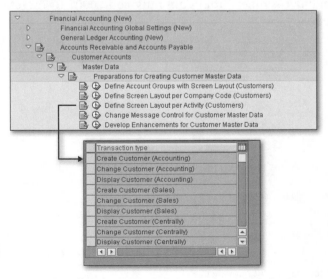

Figure 6.8 Different Activity-Based Layouts Available for Customer Account Groups

Behind each activity you will see the same customer account group field status variant configuration, as already discussed.

In our scenario, we have two company codes that operate in two different countries. As a result, the customer base is not common to both company codes. If your own scenario is such that different company codes do sell to the same customers, then you may want to learn about an easy way of "extending" your customers into additional company codes. The next section explains how this can be achieved (although it is not relevant to our example).

6.4.6 Extending your Customers to Additional Company Codes

The transaction to extend your customer master records is not a configuration but instead is part of the application side of the system. SAP provides a standard program to extend customers from one company code to another, eliminating the need to do this manually. The usual process would be to create the customers for your initial company code first; this can be done manually or via a custom upload program. The program is accessed in the folder **SAP MENU • Accounting • Financial Accounting • Accounts Receivable • Master Records • Compare**, or by using Transaction code FD15.

Here you must select the source of the data and define the target to which you want to send it. We have given an example of how to use this screen in Figure 6.9. In this example, we are sending customers from **Company code 0001** to **Target company code 0002** and **0003**.

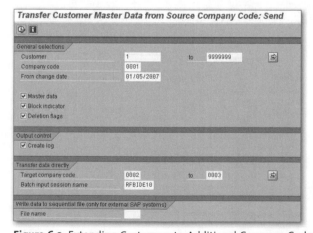

Figure 6.9 Extending Customers to Additional Company Codes

We have selected the option to create the data within the same SAP client, so we can transfer data directly via a batch session **RFBIDE10**. We can also use this program to transfer data to an external SAP client by writing the data to a sequential file. Either way, you need to execute the program that will transfer the data from the source to the target. If you created a batch session, you need to process the batch (Transaction SM35). If you created a sequential file, you need to use Transaction FD16 to *receive* the data in the target SAP client.

This step is dependent on the same customer number ranges being available in the target company code and the source company code. For this reason, we will look at the configuration of customer number ranges next.

6.4.7　Customer Number Ranges

When you create a new customer, the system assigns it a customer account number. This number is allocated based on the number range that is assigned to the account group that you have selected for this customer, so all customers within the same account group follow the same numbering convention. If you don't want to assign any logic to the numbering of customers, then you can assign all your account groups to the same number range.

Business Decisions

You need to review with your business partner what the requirements are for the number ranges. Common requests include the following:

- ► **Q: Can we migrate the existing customer numbers?**
  A: Yes you can. Just think about how you are going to deal with new customers you create in the SAP system. For instance, your new customers may be created with number ranges per account group and you may not have had the account group concept in your legacy system.
- ► **Q: User must define the customer number**
  A: This is an option. Your account group must be assigned to a number range that is externally defined (see below).
- ► **Q: Can we identify the type of customer by the customer number, as we could in our legacy system?**
  A: This is possible. To do so, you need to have an account group for each customer type you want to see and then set a different number for each customer type.

Once you have decided your customer number ranges you can configure them in the system.

Create New Number Ranges

To create, display, and change the number ranges, follow these steps:

1. Use IMG path **Financial Accounting (New)** • **Accounts Receivable and Accounts Payable** • **Vendor Accounts** • **Master Data** • **Preparations for Creating Customer Master Data** • **Create number ranges for customer accounts**.

2. Click on the **Intervals** button (with the pencil), as shown in Figure 6.10.

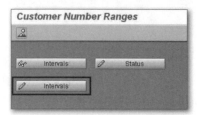

Figure 6.10 Create Customer Number Range

3. The screen **Maintain Number Range Intervals** displays, as shown in Figure 6.11. This screen shows you the available number ranges. Select the **Interval** button (with a plus and page icon) and then create a new range in the **Insert Interval** screen that displays.

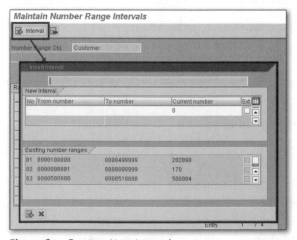

Figure 6.11 Create a New Interval

The system does not allow overlapping intervals and will give you an error message should this happen. If you want users to decide the customer number, you need to select the **Ext** setting to make the number range externally defined. You can use the **Ext** setting to have alphanumeric customer numbers.

The **Current number** column indicates the last number that has been used. Be very careful here. If you are transporting this setting into a live environment, you need to check this setting. A common error is when a new number range is transported to a production environment that is already live, and the current number buffer is overwritten. Now, let's take a look at transporting number ranges.

Transporting Number Ranges

It is important to understand how the transporting of number ranges works. The table you have just reviewed for creating new intervals is transported, along with the **Current number** value. Therefore, in the example shown in Figure 6.11, if this transport is applied to another client, it will overwrite the **Existing Number Range 02** with the value **170**. As it is very unlikely that your target system will have the same current number value, it will cause an error in the number range buffers. For this reason, many projects do not allow the transport of number ranges and instead prefer to have these manually configured.

Assign Number Range to Account Group

Having defined your customer account groups and number ranges, you need to link the two together using the IMG path **Financial Accounting (New) • Accounts Receivable and Accounts Payable • Vendor Accounts • Master Data • Preparations for Creating Customer Master Data • Assign number ranges for customer accounts**.

We will finish this section by looking at a method called accounting clerks for grouping together customers for internal control purposes.

6.4.8 Accounting Clerks

Accounting clerks can be defined in the system and used to group together customers. For example, in large organizations, where you have many credit controllers, you may want to assign customers to specific controllers. You can then use this to group these customers together for reporting purposes, or you can display the relevant credit controller's contact information on any output (e.g., customer statement) that you send to this customer.

Accounting clerks are not an integral part of core SAP processes, so many organizations choose not to use them. They can, however, be very useful for reporting and control purposes. Figure 6.12 shows the creation of a sample accounting clerk for a company code. You can make as many entries in this table as you require. To configure accounting clerks, use the path **Financial Accounting (New) • Accounts Receivable and Accounts Payable • Customer Accounts • Master Data • Preparations for Creating Customer Master Data • Enter Account Clerks Identification code for customers**.

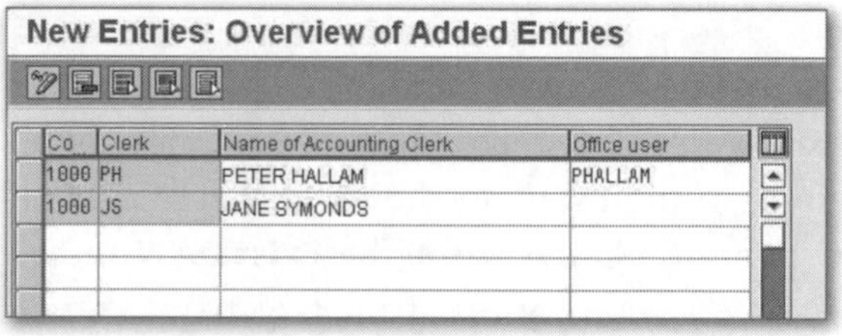

Co	Clerk	Name of Accounting Clerk	Office user	
1000	PH	PETER HALLAM	PHALLAM	
1000	JS	JANE SYMONDS		

New Entries: Overview of Added Entries

Figure 6.12 Create Accounting Clerks

The clerk ID is set by company code and can be alphanumeric. You may also want to link the SAP logon of the accounting clerk, by entering it in the **Office user** field. This field is optional, so it is possible to create clerks that don't represent people but represent teams or departments. You can make this flexible to suit your own requirements.

We have now completed our discussions and the setup of AR-related master data. Next, we will examine the configuration requirements around the processing of customer transactions.

6.5 Finance Documents Global Settings

There has already been some detailed discussion in this book of the setup of the general configuration needed to post documents (see Chapter 3, Section 3.2). In this section, we will review the configuration areas that are specific to AR and confirm the AR-specific tasks that need to be completed.

6.5.1 Document Types and Number Ranges

This topic was discussed as part of the financial accounting global settings. The AR-specific document types are usually found within the D* range. In our design, we expect customer invoices to be generated from the SD module, and this assumption is also valid for credit notes being issued. The main documents created in our AR solution will be based on incoming payments from customers, so we will only spend a little bit of time talking about customer invoices.

6.5.2 Document Posting Keys

Document posting keys were discussed in detail in Chapter 3. The advice here is to use the standard posting keys provided in the system unless you can find a very good business reason for creating additional posting keys. You may want to make changes to the settings behind posting keys to change the field status variants associated with them. A common use of this functionality is to make certain fields optional depending on the posting key you choose. For instance, later on in this chapter, we talk about the use of reason codes, and you may choose to change the field status setting for reason codes on customer-related posting keys.

6.5.3 Payment Terms

The payment terms of an invoice are defined as "the agreement between yourself and a third party to confirm the due date of payment." The payment terms also include an element of discount that may be on offer. There is no differentiation between payment terms for customers and vendors, and they are both configured in the same area of the IMG. Invoice payment terms are discussed in detail in Chapter 9 because they impact both Accounts Payable (AP) and AR. Next, we will turn our focus specifically on customer invoice processing.

6.6 Customer Invoice Processing

Our overall solution has been to implement a sales order processing route to invoicing the customer. Specifically, we have used the billing functionality off the back of the sales order to generate a bill for the customer. This solution has the benefits derived from the extensive sales functionality within the SD module. Referring back to Figure 6.1, the AR invoice is created from the billing document. This process is automatic and happens when you release the billing document to accounting. The release to accounting is an internal interface within the SAP system and it is controlled by three elements, as shown in Figure 6.13. If you have an error in releasing the billing document it will usually be as a result of one of these elements.

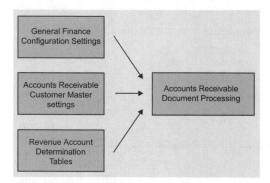

Figure 6.13 Control of Document Processing in Accounts Receivable

Figure 6.14 shows the layout of a customer invoice where you can see that the layout is very similar to that of the other finance documents (journals and vendor invoices).

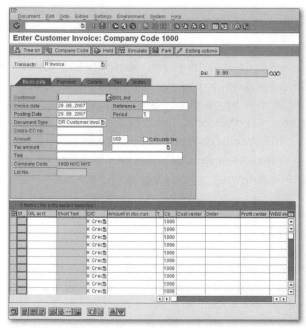

Figure 6.14 Accounts Receivable Invoice Entry Screen

The minimum controls required have been discussed previously and would enable you to either create new AR invoices or pass sales order-generated invoices. We will now look at the processing of customer payments, which is a common requirement of most AR solutions.

6.7   Customer Payments

When processing incoming payments from customers, depending on the size of your organization, you may want a manual process or an automatic process. Most organizations choose to follow a manual process so that they are able to allocate the payment, fully or partially, to the correct customer invoice. Large retailers and organizations with a large number of customers generate large numbers of receipts, in which case automatic customer payment processing is likely preferable. In Figure 6.15 we can see the customer payment processing transaction.

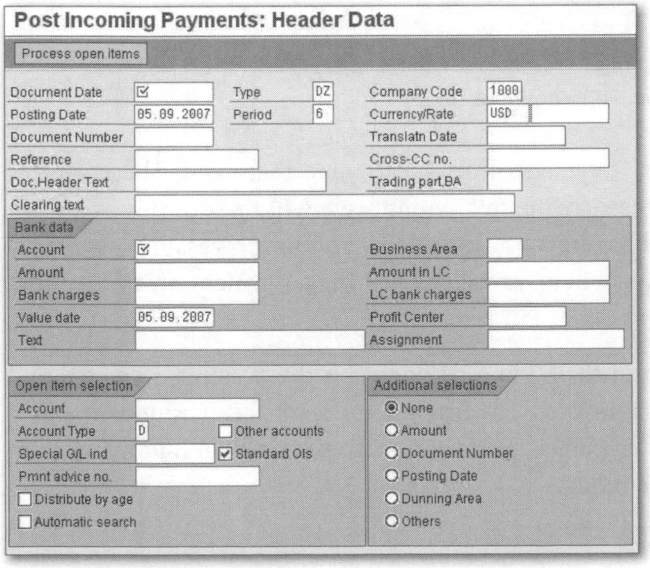

Figure 6.15 Post Incoming Payment Screen Layout (F-28)

This transaction allows you to post a payment to the system, by referencing a customer invoice that is on the system. Once you reference an existing invoice, then the system will match the payment against the invoice and this process is known as *clearing* and is very important in maintaining a record of your debtors' positions. Figure 6.16 shows the screen from where you can select a customers unpaid invoices (also known as open items). Clearing can be performed manually or automatically. The choice depends on the best fit from a process point of view.

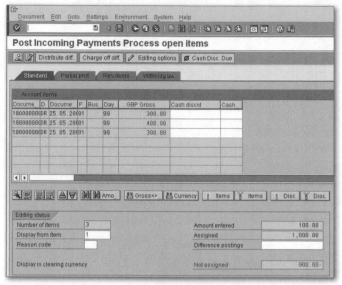

Figure 6.16 Open Item Selection: Payments Processing

When processing incoming payments from customers, there could be instances where the customer does not pay the full amount (we will refer to this as a short payment). If this occurs, there are tabs available to you for processing of a partial payment or creating a residual item, as well as posting a payment on an account:

▸ **Partial payment**
The invoice remains untouched, but a payment on the account is created and referenced to the original invoice. The original invoice is seen as unpaid and is free for dunning. If the customer is dunned, both the original invoice amount and the payment are identified.

▸ **Residual item**
During payment processing, the SAP system clears the old invoice and creates a new document for the balance unpaid. The new document references the original invoice but has a new set of dates.

▸ **Payment on account**
The third option is the simplest and maybe least frequently used. You can simply create the payment on the account, by posting a payment without referencing it against an invoice. When you then issue a customer statement, this pay-

ment on account will also be listed. Once the customer makes the full payment for the remainder of the amount due, you can manually clear the invoice with the partial payments that the customer has sent you.

Short payment is common for a number of reasons such as on-the-spot discounts granted, faulty or underdelivery of goods, or even good faith discounts. In the next section we look at the further processing options for these instances.

6.7.1 Defining Customer Tolerances

We have previously discussed the need to create tolerance Groups to enable postings to take place in GL and in AP. Within the AR module, you need to create customer tolerance groups to create AR postings. The purpose of tolerance groups is to control the amount of payment differences that can be processed in the system, as follows:

▶ Maximum payment differences that can be applied through clearing

▶ Maximum discounts that can be given

At least one customer tolerance group must be defined to enable transactions to be processed and was introduced in Chapter 3 (Section 3.2.12). As can be seen in Figure 6.17, there are several tolerances that can be defined, they are collectively referred to as a *tolerance group*.

The role of a tolerance group is best explained by using an example. Consider a scenario where the invoice amount due is $123.05, and the customer sends a check for $123.00. In this scenario, there is not much business benefit in keeping this unpaid balance of $0.05 on the ledgers and chasing the customer for it. Some businesses may therefore decide to write this amount off to a write-off GL code. In this situation, we would say that the customer has made a payment that is within tolerance, and this invoice will be completely cleared.

To define tolerances, follow the path **Financial Accounting (New) • Accounts Receivable and Accounts Payable • Business Transactions • Incoming Payments • Manual Incoming Payments • Define Tolerance Groups • Define Tolerances (customers)**.

This configuration screen, shown in Figure 6.17 is irrespective of currency and always looks at the local currency in the company code. In this example, the **Permitted Payment Differences** are configured as 0.02 units of currency or 1.0% of the invoice value. The lower limit is valid. If you only want to use absolute amounts or percentages, you must enter the maximum value.

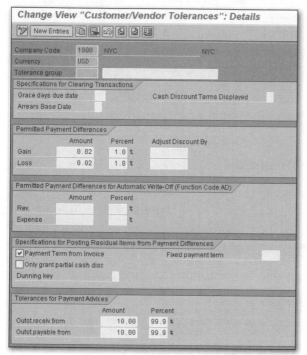

Figure 6.17 AR Tolerance Group

Some of the key fields in this configuration screen are explained in Table 6.3.

Field	Description
Grace days due date	If a value is entered here, this will be the additional grace period given to customers to make their payments.
Permitted Payment Differences	In this section you define the permitted payment differences that are allowed. This may be specified as an amount or a percentage. The usual method is to define both a percentage limit and an absolute amount as a limit. Whichever is reached first will restrict the permitted payment difference.
Specifications for Posting Residual Items from Payment Differences	The settings you make here influence the residual item that may be created if you are processing a short payment from a customer.
Tolerances for Payment Advices	A residual item will automatically be created for anything that is above the tolerance amount entered in this section. Usually you would set the amount here to be the same as the amount in the **Permitted Payment Differences** section.

Table 6.3 Customer Tolerance Group settings

It is important to be clear on what value you assign, as you could assign a high value, which at the end of the accounting period might add up to a large amount of cash that you are prepared to write off. Once you have defined your tolerance group, you can assign customers to it and therefore control the processing of customer payments. You may also want to create customer tolerance groups to be able to treat groups of customers differently.

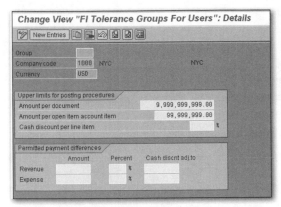

Figure 6.18 Example of a Customer Tolerance Group

The example in Figure 6.18 shows a customer tolerance group without a name, which is the default customer tolerance group assigned to all customers when they are created. If you choose to create additional groups, they must be assigned directly to the Customer master record.

Now that we have explained how you can provide boundaries for processing customer payments, we will next look at what you can do with these tolerances and how to automatically account for them.

6.7.2 Write-off Amounts within Tolerance

In this section, we are going to discuss the configuration for over- or under-payments made by customers using IMG path **Financial Accounting (New) • Accounts Receivable and Accounts Payable • Business Transactions • Incoming payments • Incoming payments global settings • Overpayment / Underpayment** or Transaction code OBBE. The configuration you make here applies if a payment amount is not the exact amount of the invoice but is within the tolerance difference you have defined for this customer.

Figure 6.19 shows the configuration screen where you can either identify a specific account that should receive all over- or underpayments, or specify an account by reason code (we'll examine reason codes in more detail in the next section).

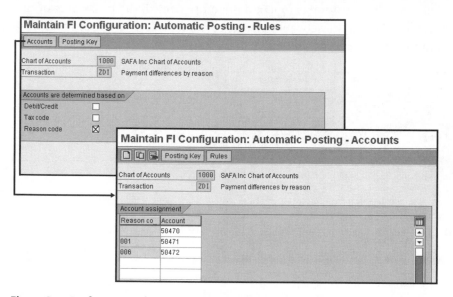

Figure 6.19 Configuration of Customer Over- and Underpayment Account Determination

The account determination transaction behind this screen is called **ZDI**. If you want to post to different GL accounts based on the reason code, then you need to have selected **Reason code** on the **Automatic Posting—Rules** screen, as shown in Figure 6.19. The blank setting configured in the **Account assignment** section of the **Automatic Posting—Accounts** screen (also shown in Figure 6.19) means that the default account for this account determination will be **50470**. If a difference arises due to reason codes **001** or **006**, however, these will post to **50471** and **50472**, respectively.

In this same configuration area, you can configure account determination settings for cash discounts. This uses account determination Transaction SKT and is configured the same way as over- and underpayments. In Chapter 9, we will discuss all of the available account determinations you can use, and you should consult that chapter to see which other options are available to you. For instance, if you are selling or purchasing from overseas, you may want to configure accounts for exchange rate differences. Next, we will explain the configuration of reason codes.

6.7.3 Reason Codes

Reason codes can be used to provide a reporting dimension on document line items. For any document you process, you can assign a reason code that allows you to label a reason for the line. This functionality is frequently used on payment lines to assign reasons for short payment. The field first needs to be activated in the field status variant to allow postings to be made to the field (see Chapter 3, Section 3.2.2). Also, the account to which the difference is assigned needs to have the appropriate field status to enable the reason code posting to take place.

At this point, you need to understand how to create reason codes. As you read the following sections, you will see how to expand the functionality. Reason code configuration is completed using the path **Financial Accounting (New) • Accounts Receivable and Accounts Payable • Business Transactions • Incoming payments • Incoming payments global settings • Overpayment / Underpayment** or Transaction code OBBE.

Reason codes are company code specific; therefore, it is possible to create different reasons in each company code as can be seen in Figure 6.18. Because the code can be applied to any Financial Accounting Component (FI) document, you may find that there are additional codes in this table that are not specific to AR.

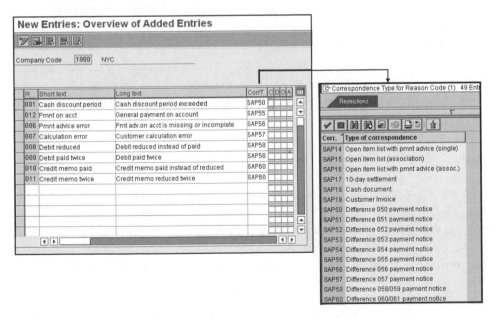

Figure 6.20 Configuration of Reason Codes

Table 6.4 lists the columns used to configure reason codes, as shown in Figure 6.20, along with their descriptions.

Column Name	Description
Reason Code (R)	Three-digit alphanumeric code.
Short text	Enter the short description of the reason code.
Long text	Enter the long description for the field. It is possible to have this information brought into the line item text field on the document line item against which you are using this reason code (see the option "Do not copy text").
Correspondence Type (CorrT)	The process we are working with is based on a customer who does not pay the full amount due on their invoice, and you may want to send correspondence to the customer based on the type of short payment they are making. Here you can specify the technical name of the correspondence you want to associate with this reason code.
Charge off difference via separate account	Use this option to post the difference to a specific GL account, as defined for this reason code.
Do not copy text	You can define some standard text for the reason code. If you select this box, you can enter your own text.
Do not consider tolerances	If you select this option, you will create a residual item with the reason code.

Table 6.4 Reason Code Configuration Options

The last section in this chapter looks at the management of debtors, which is the final piece of the sales order to cash cycle outlined earlier in Figure 6.1.

6.8 Debtor Management

This section looks at the processes associated with the management of your debtors. This is an important area for any organization because most organizations rely on efficient payment collection from customers to retain liquidity. Different options are available for you to use, and organizations need to select those most appropriate to them. In this section, we will cover the following items:

- Credit control and credit limits on customers
- Automatic credit control
- Dunning
- Interest calculation and other charges

You should first review and understand the functionality that is available to you. It is very easy to decide to implement all of the debtor management functionality we cover, but you should decide if this is really relevant to your organization. For instance, if you are delivering a public service, you are less likely to restrict services to your customers. In this industry, you may be less likely to implement strict credit controls, as you may be obliged by law not to restrict the delivery of your service.

The controls you chose will also be dependent on the nature of your relationship with your customers. If you have a small customer base and a good relationship with your customers, you may prefer to monitor credit limits and have direct conversations with your customers rather than just send them letters. We start this section by reviewing the functionality of Credit Limits.

6.8.1 Credit Limit Business Process

A common approach to credit limits that businesses use is the creation of a sales order by sales team, who receive a system message if a customer has exceeded their credit limit. They then need to contact the credit controller, who is responsible for adjusting this customer's credit limit. If your business partner does not like this process and is worried about delays in the process, you need to review the objectives of this process. Do you want to enforce credit controls in the system, and if so, how low do you want to set your credit limits?

If you want to avoid blocked invoices, you may need to set a high credit limit. The consequence is that customers may exercise more credit than you want them to. If you want to keep a tighter control on the system, but keep your customers happy at the same time, you may need to review the business process to ensure that the "releasing of blocked invoices" happens more quickly.

Some clients we have worked with have set up a process in which the credit controller checks for blocked invoices several times a day. Other clients have a simpler process, where a phone call is made to the credit controller, who can release a blocked invoice over the phone. Different options have different merits; you need to decide which is relevant to your specific business requirements.

You should evaluate how much it costs to chase a customer for a debt and what policy you want to have on this matter. Blockbusters for instance will generate reminder letters for all late rental returns. The question to ask is, how does the value of the debt, compare to the cost to send a letter and compare to the policy you want to put in place in terms of chasing debtors.

Before you get into the configuration settings, you need to decide how you want to split up your customers. You may want to group your customers into those with whom you are strict and those with whom you are more flexible. This can be achieved in different ways. For instance, you may choose to have strict rules for new customers and more flexible rules for existing customers. You may then realize that corporate customers should be excluded from this credit control process altogether, so you now have three groupings. For each group, define the following configuration elements that are related to each other as shown in Figure 6.21:

▶ Credit control area

▶ Risk category

▶ Credit representative group

▶ Credit master

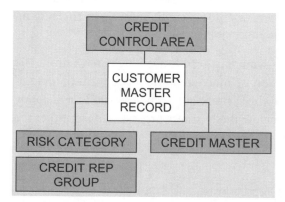

Figure 6.21 Hierarchy of Configuration Elements within the Automatic Credit Control Settings

We will look at the configuration of the three groups of customers (new, existing, and corporate) to explain the different configuration settings you can make. Configuration is completed within the following area of the IMG path: **Financial Accounting (New) • Accounts Receivable and Accounts Payable • Credit Management • Credit Control Account**. This configuration is shared between AR and SD, and you can find some elements of configuration within the AR area of the IMG.

First, we will look at the configuration of the building blocks for credit control, and then we will move on to the settings for automatic credit control.

Credit Control Area

The *credit control area* represents a basis control for restricting your credit exposure. We introduced the credit control area as part of our enterprise structure configuration in Chapter 2 (see Section 2.5.5), and it is configured within the enterprise structure area of the IMG. The credit control area is used to control the processing of transactions with customers. It is a way of defining an overall credit limit for a defined group of customers. You define here the total value of credit that can be given to customers within this credit control area. Most organizations operate a simplistic view and define one credit control area per company code.

You can also define the default risk category, credit limit and representative group that is assigned to all new customer master records created for a credit control.

Risk Category

To define a risk category, use Transaction code OB01. Consider risk categories as a way of segregating your customers. Review your organization and decide what different levels of risk you want to operate. You may have a very diverse range of customers and thus need to have several levels. In our scenario, we are only going to create two levels, these being high risk and low risk customers, as shown in Figure 6.22.

When you create a new customer, you can default assign a risk category (as mentioned previously in Chapter 2 [see Figure 2.13]). The configuration settings we have made will mean that new customers will be created without any default credit limit or risk category.

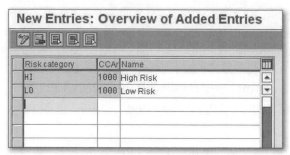

Figure 6.22 Define Customer Risk Categories

Credit Representative Groups

Treat credit representative groups as another way of grouping your customers together. For instance, you can group these customers together from a credit controller's point of view. If you have more than one credit controller, you can assign customers to different credit controllers. Use this configuration setting to create controllers, who can run reports on their group of customers. You can also group your customers together based on the customer type, to allow you to treat each group differently. Overall, you will use the **Credit rep. group** to distinguish credit control settings for different customers, using Transaction code OB02, as shown in Figure 6.23.

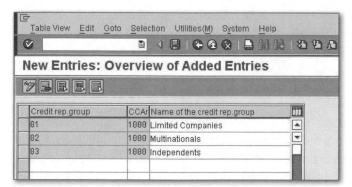

Figure 6.23 Define Credit Rep Groups

Credit Masters

For our scenario, we have chosen to operate credit controls within the system, which will restrict our ability to generate new customer orders if there are problems with the customer credit limit exposure, and so we need to assign credit limits to our customers. This is done through the creation of a customer credit master, which is attached to a customer master record.

The following steps explain how we intend to deliver our business requirements. We start by clearly stating the business requirements we intend to configure. The business process should be a two-step process:

1. Create the customer

2. Update customer credit master

Once you create a customer master record, you need to change the credit master to activate the credit limits. All customer master records are automatically linked to a credit master. To assign credit limits to customers use the path **SAP MENU • Accounting • Financial Accounting • Accounts Receivable • Credit Management • Master Data • Change** or Transaction code FD23.

The credit master carries the same number as the customer master you have created. You can define a credit master per controlling area, so if the customer transacts in different credit controlling areas, you can assign a separate credit limit for each. The credit limit information is stored within a customer master record. The key pieces of information for you to complete are located in different screens within the credit master and are summarized in the following list:

▶ Credit Limit: You can define an overall credit limit for this customer. This limit is defined for an individual amount (i.e., per invoice) and for a total amount (total value of open invoices).

▶ Credit Exposure: The total amount for which the customer is indebted.

▶ Risk Category: Lets you group customers together.

▶ Credit Rep Group: Lets you group customers together.

▶ Blocked: When this box is checked, the customer is blocked from ordering due to credit problems.

This information is summarized on the credit master **Overview** screen, an example of which is shown in Figure 6.24.

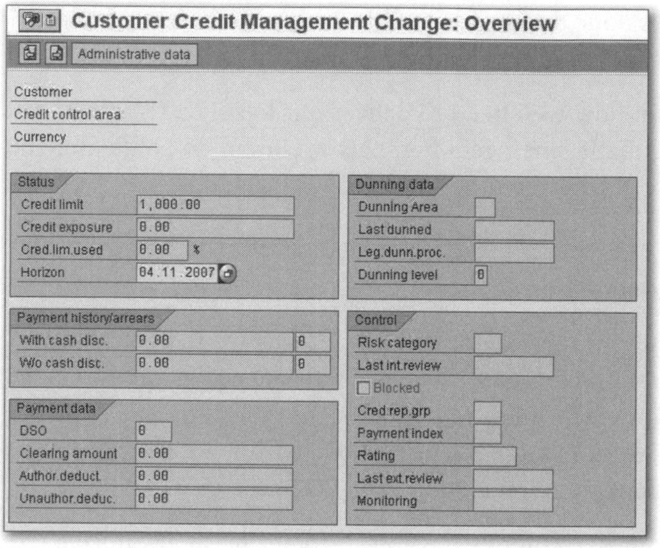

Figure 6.24 Credit Master Overview Screen

6.8.2 Automatic Credit Control

Once you have the master data objects in place, you can define the settings for automatic credit control following the IMG path **Sales and Distribution • Basic Functions • Credit Management / Risk Management • Credit Management • Define Automatic Credit Control** or using Transaction code OVA8.

> **Note**
>
> Automatic credit control is a feature of the system that is shared between the AR component and the SD component. Depending on the rules you configure, at the point of raising a sales order or an AR invoice, the system will determine the customers credit exposure and then depending on the customers risk, respond with a warning or an error message.
>
> For this reason, configuration settings are found in different areas of the IMG. For example, sales orders are created in SD, but the customer credit limit is held on the credit master, which is part of AR.

Here you define the rules for automatic credit control based on the combinations of master data objects we have defined so far. So, for a customer item, the system determines the action to take by a combination of the customer's credit limit exposure, risk category, and credit representative group. You'll see two examples in a moment. The action can take place at the sales order creation stage or at the AR invoice creation stage, depending on the settings you make for the credit control area and your overall solution design.

The options available are described in Table 6.5, and examples are given of how to use the combined settings to achieve settings for types of customers.

Field	Possible entries	Effect
Reaction	<BLANK> A B C D	No message (no credit check occurs) Warning Error Warning + value that is exceeded by Error + value that is exceeded by
Status/Block	Checkmark	If you select this option, a block will also be applied to sales documents.
Static	Checkmark	The system will look at the value of: Open S/orders* + Open delivery docs* + Open billing docs + Open AR items (* these two values are optional)
Dynamic	Checkmark	The only checks Open Sales order value
Document value	Checkmark	This option will enable a credit check based on a maximum document value.
Critical fields	Checkmark	This setting checks whether critical fields (payment terms, additional value days, fixed value date) have been changed within the sales document.
Number of days	Checkmark	If a released sales order is subsequently changed, it is rechecked for credit after this number of days (default value = 3 days)

Table 6.5 Automatic Credit Control settings

To explain how these settings impact the processing, we have created some default settings for two different customer types (bad and good customers), which you can use to guide your own settings. Always consider the settings in line with the specific requirements of your organization and the solution design that best suits them:

▶ **Bad customers**

The settings made in our example for Bad customers, shown in Figure 6.25 do not allow you to process a delivery for a customer who has exceeded their credit limit. The sales order goes into credit hold and needs to be released by an authorized person. You may choose to apply similar settings to new customers, for example.

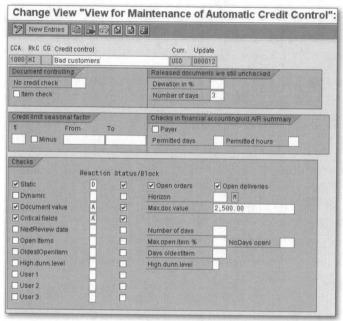

Figure 6.25 Settings Made for Bad Customers

▶ **Good customers**

The settings made for Good customers (Figure 6.26) has fewer restrictions in it, and most importantly it will only give warning messages when a Good Customer exceeds their credit limit. You may chose to apply similar settings to New Customers and so include them in the default settings on the Credit Control area as we mentioned in Chapter 2 earlier.

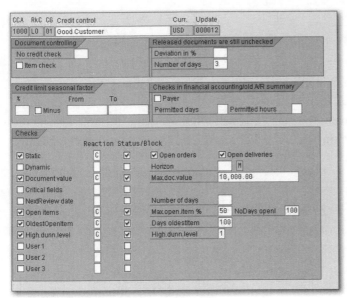

Figure 6.26 Settings for Good Customers

For customers that you don't want to undergo credit checking then you should not assign any Credit Representative Groups to them.

6.8.3 Dunning

Dunning is the business process by which the system determines customer items that are overdue for payment. The dunning program can then produce letters which are sent to these customers requesting payment. In the configuration of the dunning program you define ageing buckets for invoices and you configure which letters are sent out for each bucket. This will become clearer as you work through this chapter.

The dunning program can be configured to produce letters (via SAPScript forms) that can be sent to customers requesting immediate payment. In this section we'll look at several topics including business decisions regarding dunning, dunning areas, dunning blocks, configuring the dunning procedure (including dunning levels, dunning charges, minimum amounts, and dunning texts), assignment of the dunning procedure to customers, and other related topics. Let us get started.

Business Decisions

As part of your business blueprint design you need to agree with your business partner the specific requirements for chasing customer debts.

You should think about the state of your current aged debtors status (i.e., how many old debts you have on your ledger) and whether you have a target debtors days situation that you want to reach. This will influence your dunning design and help you decide the dunning levels and dunning areas that are needed (explained later on in this section).

Additional requirements might include the following:

- ▶ **Q: How can I control the output of letters to customers and stop certain customers from receiving letters?**
  A: Use the dunning block function at the Invoice or customer level.

- ▶ **Q: How can I create a different dunning process for my domestic customers?**
  A: You can create different dunning procedures and assign them to customers. Also, use the dunning areas function to control which customers you want to dunn more frequently.

Dunning configuration is completed by following IMG path **SPRO • Financial Accounting • Accounts Receivable and Accounts Payable • Business Transactions • Dunning**.

Dunning Areas

Dunning areas can be set up as ways of splitting up the treatment of your customers during dunning. This is applicable in large organizations, with central credit control functions. Alternatively, you may want to use dunning areas to group customers together in categories, where you want to split them up for dunning purposes, that is, you may want to dunn some customers now and some later.

Dunning Blocks

Dunning blocks are used to prevent items from being dunned, in scenarios where you want to exclude a customer or some items from the dunning program. A dunning block can be applied to an individual invoice or to the customer directly, which will apply to all of the customer's open invoices.

By default, all customer invoices and customer master records are created with the dunning block field blank. You can then go into the invoice and change the field to select your block reason, which you configure as shown in Figure 6.27.

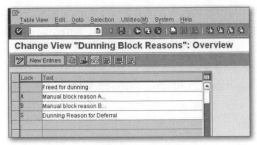

Figure 6.27 Dunning Blocks

Both the dunning blocks and dunning areas can be used as selection criteria in SAP standard reports. If you are looking at a customer line item report, you can use the dynamic selections option to restrict your query by a specific dunning block reason.

Dunning Procedure: Overview

The *dunning procedure* is where we define the dunning rules for how you want to "dunn a customer." It is possible to have multiple dunning procedures in the system, each is company code independent. A customer can only be assigned to a single dunning procedure at any time and this can be changed.

In our scenario, we are going to configure a dunning procedure (**Dunn.procedure**) **0001** with a **Name** of **Four-level dunning notice, every two weeks**, as shown in Figure 6.28.

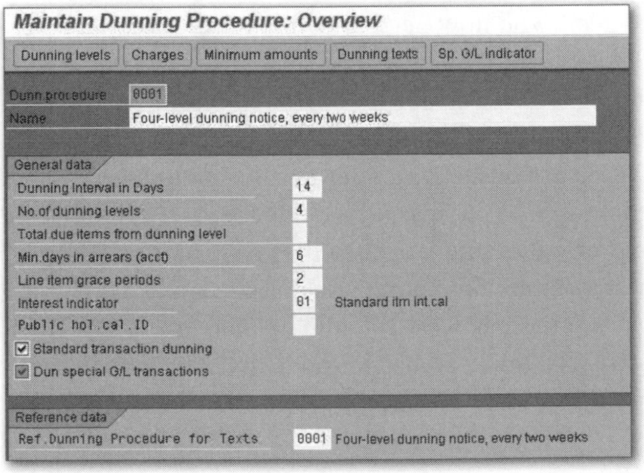

Figure 6.28 Overview of Dunning Procedure

The settings configured on the **Maintain Dunning Procedure: Overview** screen shown in Figure 6.28 are for a four-level dunning procedure, which means that customers assigned to this dunning procedure can have their invoices progress through a maximum of four levels. This allows you to differentiate between the responses to customer items that apply to different levels. Basic configuration settings include the following:

- ▶ **Dunning Interval in Days**
  If an invoice has been dunned, the system will not dunn it again until the interval time specified in this setting has elapsed.

- ▶ **Min. days in arrears (acct)**
  This is the minimum number of days that an item must be in arrears before it will be selected for output. In this example, an invoice that is only two days overdue will not be considered.

- ▶ **Line item grace periods**
  This setting is used if you are granting a grace period. An item whose days in arrears are less than or equal to the grace period will not be dunned.

- ▶ **Standard transaction dunning**
  This should be selected for dunning of normal customer items.

The next configuration item for the dunning procedure is dunning levels:

Dunning Procedure: Dunning Levels

Having defined the basic settings of the dunning procedure in the **Maintain Dunning Procedure: Overview** screen, you now need to configure the *dunning levels* in the **Maintain Dunning Procedure: Dunning levels** screen shown in Figure 6.29. The purpose of dunning levels is to be able to enable different controls for invoices depending on how late they are. A dunning level is triggered when an invoice becomes so many days late. For instance your first dunning level maybe two days. You may want to identify these items and include them in a report, but you may not want to send out any dunning letters to these customers. You may chose to only send out dunning letters for invoices which are older. This is an important part of your design, as you may want to build up some early levels for your own internal reporting analysis. Invoices that go above that level and become very late can then be configured to trigger output that you send to the customer. Settings include:

► **Days in arrears**

This is the number of days overdue that controls at which dunning level an invoice is.

► **Calculate interest?**

Not every organization charges interest to their customers who make late payments on the basis of good-will or likely response of the customer to pay the additional interest.

► **Always dun?**

Where there has been no change to the dunning level of a customer invoice, you may choose not to send out a letter. You need to use this setting in combination with the **Dunning Interval in Days**" option configured on the **Overview** screen.

► **Print All Items**

If you select this option for a dunning level, the system prints all open items on the account (except dunning blocked items) for this dunning level.

► **Payment deadline**

You can add a line of text in your output, indicating a payment deadline (e.g., "Please send payment for these items within the next 10 days"). This needs to be included within the SAPscript.

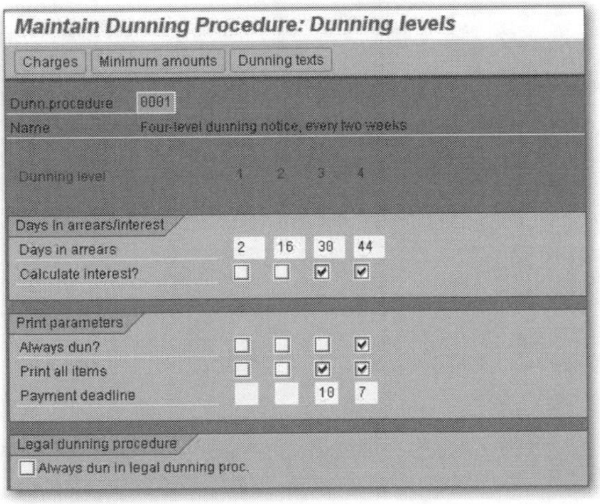

Figure 6.29 Dunning Levels

Next, we'll look at configuring dunning charges.

Dunning Procedure: Dunning Charges

Dunning charges are fixed amounts of (interest) charges you want to charge your customers for being late. In that way, dunning charges are a form of administration charge. Think very carefully about making such (interest) charges to your customers in terms of the (lack of) good-will you might create. Dunning charges are configured on the **Maintain Dunning Procedure: Charges** screen, as shown in Figure 6.30.

Many organizations want to issue interest charges to customers but rarely make the charge permanent. Some organizations have used dunning charges as a threat to customers, to encourage them to pay on time. If this is what you want to achieve, then you can get this coded into your dunning letter layout. You can choose to use a percentage charge instead of a fixed amount, which is calculated based on the amount that is overdue.

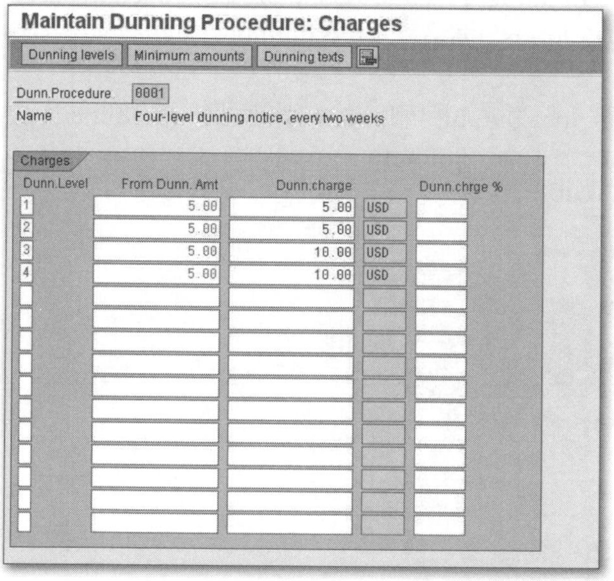

Figure 6.30 Dunning Charges

Dunning Procedure: Minimum Amounts

In the **Maintain Dunning Procedure: Minimum Amounts** screen, shown in Figure 6.31, you can define the minimum value invoice that can be dunned. This functionality ensures that you are not sending letters requesting payment for a few dollars. You can set a **Minimum amount**, or a percentage of the total open items

(**Min. percentage**). You should define a minimum amount for dunning based on the nature of your business.

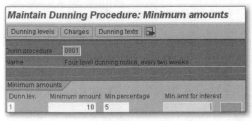

Figure 6.31 Define Minimum Amounts for Dunning

Dunning Procedure: Dunning texts

In the screen **Maintain Dunning Procedure: Dunning texts**, shown in Figure 6.32, developers (or you) assign SAPScripts to the correct dunning levels. In the example shown, we have assigned standard SAPscripts, but the usual procedure is for you to create your own, with your organizations logo's on them.

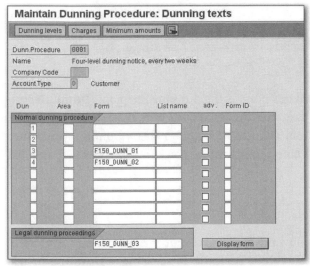

Figure 6.32 Assign Dunning Texts to Dunning Procedure

This concludes the dunning procedure configuration and makes the procedure available to assign it to customers in the customer master record, which we'll discuss next.

Assignment of the Dunning Procedure to a customer

Once you have created your dunning procedure, you will want to assign customers to it. If you want to dunn a customer, you need to have a dunning procedure assigned to that customer. Figure 6.33 shows where you assign dunning procedures to customers. If you have chosen to use dunning areas as well, you can select these for your customers.

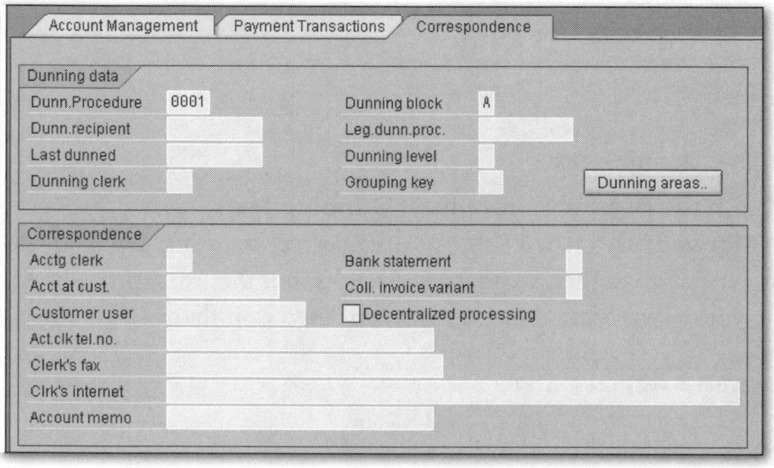

Figure 6.33 Assignment of a Dunning Procedure to a Customer

Another field available to you at this point is the dunning recipient (**Dunn. Recipient**). You can assign another customer master record here that should receive all dunning notices for this customer. Once a customer has a dunning procedure assigned to it and it has open invoices against it, you can run a dunning due list for the customer.

Creating a Dunning Due List

To create a dunning due list, follow the path **SAP Menu • Accounting • Financial Accounting • Accounts Receivable • Periodic Processing • Dunning** or use Transaction F150. The process you need to follow is:

1. Define your parameters

2. Edit or confirm the proposal

3. Generate output

At the point of editing your proposal, you may choose to block or unblock customer items for dunning. It is also possible to force dunning letters to be generated for customer items. If you go into a customer invoice and look at the customer line, you will see a field called "Last Dunned." This carries a date for the last dunning run, and next to it is a field that carries the dunning level that was reached as part of the last dunning run. If you want to raise the invoice to a higher dunning level, change these values so that when the invoice is next dunned, it achieves the desired level. An example of this is shown in Figure 6.34.

Figure 6.34 Manually Editing Dunning Levels on a Customer Invoice

Changing the Dunning Proposal List Layout

When you review your dunning (proposal) list, the system references report RFMAHN21 (which can be seen in Figure 6.34). If you go into Transaction SE38 and run this report, you can create a report layout variant that you can then use when you review your dunning proposal.

We have spent a fair amount of time covering the functionalities available to you to for the management of your debtors. The choices you make in terms of your design will be specific to your organization and are likely to be unique to your own situation.

6.8.4 Head Office Functionality

We have already talked about the use of business partners in defining complex relationships within an organization. However, business partners only really come into play if you are adopting a sales order-based process. If you are implementing a finance-only solution, you may need to look at alternative ways in which to define customers' relationships. In a finance-only solution (only utilizing the AR subcomponent for customer invoicing), then you can use the head office function for grouping customers together.

We have also already talked about the use of a dunning recipient to send your dunning correspondence to a different person. You can use the head office functionality with the customer master record to group together different customer accounts. For instance, if you receive orders from several customer locations, and the bills are paid centrally, you can create all of them as customer master records. By entering the head office customer number for these master records you can group them together. The benefit is that when you create an invoice against individual locations, all of the items are grouped together under the single head office account.

6.9   Summary

The AR subcomponent is an important component of your overall business processes. This chapter built on the foundations established in the Enterprise Structure and Financial Accounting Global Settings chapters to complete the configuration required to deliver a complete AR solution based on our business requirements. The key learning points of the chapter were:

▶ Review of the sales order to cash process cycle

▶ Explanation of the use and configuration of customer master records

▶ Explanation of the use and configuration of the main documents processed in AR, including customer invoices and customer payments.

▶ Review of the functionality available to you to manage your outstanding debtors, followed by an explanation of the configuration you need to complete to make use of this functionality and align it with your business requirements.

In Chapter 7, we configure the Asset Accounting subcomponent, a process that is usually seen as a challenge to new users. The challenges are partly due to a lack of understanding of the complexities of the process, and thus we will explain the process in detail.

This chapter explains the mysteries of Asset Accounting, which many SAP Financial Accounting Component (FI) consultants struggle to cope with. Asset Accounting is very different from the other Financial Accounting Component (FI) subledgers, and good process and configuration knowledge in this area is a valuable asset.

7 Asset Accounting

The objective of this chapter is to explain the functionality of the Asset Accounting subcomponent (often referred to as Fixed Assets). Asset Accounting functionality is designed for the management and supervision of an organization's fixed assets and is a GL subledger. Asset Accounting is sometimes seen as a specialist topic, as many SAP professionals do not understand the processes within this component from a company or a statutory point of view. For this reason, in this chapter, we provide a lot of information to help explain this area to beginning users, including the following:

▸ An explanation of the link between the different organizational elements within Asset Accounting

▸ Configuration of asset master records

▸ Configuration of depreciation methods and postings to the General Ledger (GL) in line with statutory requirements

▸ Detailed explanations of how to process asset acquisition, transfers, and retirement transactions.

▸ Asset depreciation processing

The order in which this chapter progresses is important, as it follows the IMG, which is organized by type of activity. Following this order (which is also the order in which steps are processed) ensures that you complete the configuration in the order required by SAP to take into account the dependencies between the different objects. This also ensures that less experienced users do not miss any steps or get confused with the different dependencies.

The chapter begins by presenting the main concepts of Asset Accounting. We then look at the key points that should form part of your workshops with your business partners when creating a design for your Asset Accounting solution in your business blueprint. After that, we take a detailed look at configuring Asset Accounting.

7.1 Overview of Asset Accounting

SAP Asset Accounting covers the complete lifecycle of an asset, which may start when the purchase order is created or capitalized, to its retirement at the end of its useful life. During this time, the system calculates appropriate depreciation values and interest amounts and presents this information in many different reports. The asset lifecycle is shown in Figure 7.1.

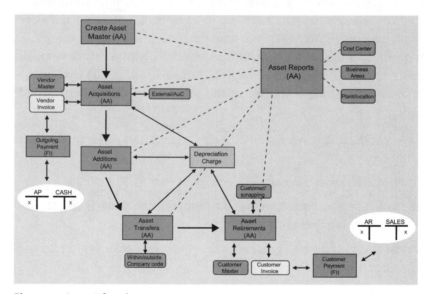

Figure 7.1 Asset Lifecycle

7.1.1 Implementation Considerations

As with any SAP component, you should always be clear on what aspects of functionality you want to implement before you start the configuration. This is certainly true for Asset Accounting, as SAP has designed this component so that it can be used internationally in many countries. The changes in statutory requirements in different countries require the module to be flexible enough to mold to your country- or industry-specific requirements.

You should also ensure that no country-specific settings are hard-coded when you configure your system. Where appropriate, SAP delivers many country-specific settings that can be copied to reduce the effort required in implementations.

7.1.2 Integration

Asset Accounting is fully integrated with other components, as indicated in Figure 7.1. At all times, postings to assets are integrated with the GL, so the value of your assets is reflected correctly in your balance sheet.

7.2 Building Blocks of Asset Accounting

In Chapter 2, we defined the enterprise structure for our SAP solution design, which outlined the basic building blocks needed to build our solution. Let us first refresh our memory of this diagram, shown in Figure 7.2, before we look at the Asset Accounting-specific objects.

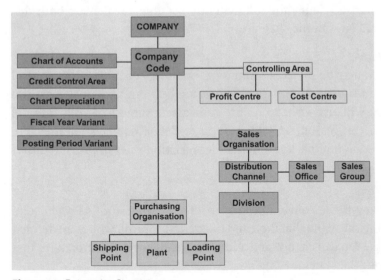

Figure 7.2 Enterprise Structure

In Chapter 2, we decided not to include the Asset Accounting elements, as they would be explained better in this chapter. You will see that the setup of Asset Accounting is based on its own mini-organizational structure, which is in turn influenced by your organizational design as well as your statutory reporting requirements. This section will provide you with a basic definition of how asset accounting is built and structured. This is needed to design your Asset Accounting blueprint.

7.2.1 Chart of Depreciation

The chart of depreciation is the organizational element used to manage various legal requirements for the depreciation and valuation of assets. Like company code, these are usually country-specific but do not need to be aligned with any other organizational units. A chart of depreciation, for example, can be used for all of the company codes in a given country.

Country-Specific Charts of Depreciation

In a simple scenario, you may have one or more company codes in the same country. These can be assigned to the same chart of depreciation because they are all governed by the same legal requirements for asset valuation. Within your chart of depreciation, you need to define the following two settings, which are both discussed in more detail later in the chapter:

▶ **Depreciation Areas**
Your organization may be subject to statutory reporting constraints that control what rules you must obey. Your organization may be a multinational organization, and so you will also want to report your assets subject to your internal conventions. For this reason, SAP allows you to define depreciation areas, in which you can set up internal and external depreciation rules to provide different analyses.

▶ **Depreciation Keys**
A depreciation key is the convention under which depreciation is calculated. Your key holds the calculation method and the period control, which are defined at the client level. You can change and add to the standard calculation keys that are delivered with the system.

> **Note**
>
> SAP supplies a number of charts of depreciation relating to different countries, which you can copy; however, it is not possible to use them directly. It is a good idea to make a copy of the appropriate chart of depreciation for your country, as this will contain all of your statutory requirements and provide you with a good base from which to start.

Integration between Company Code and Chart of Depreciation

In Asset Accounting, you are required to assign company codes to exactly one chart of depreciation. For your company, you should keep the number of charts of depreciation to a minimum to keep your asset values uniform. Country-specific company codes with similar asset accounting requirements use the same chart of depreciation, and the same applies for industry-specific company codes.

Integration between Chart of Accounts and Chart of Depreciation

The assignment of a company code to a chart of accounts is independent from its assignment to a chart of depreciation. This means that several company codes can use the same chart of accounts, although they have different charts of depreciation (and vice versa). This link is where financial information is passed from Asset Accounting to GL accounts. The GL account assignment is controlled by means of the asset class in Asset Accounting. You have to specify an account determination in each asset class. In this account determination, you specify the GL accounts in which automatic posting takes place for different transactions.

7.2.2 Asset Assignment to Organizational Units

In Asset Accounting, the asset master record serves as a basis for assignments of assets to different organizational units. These assignments are not only important from an asset accounting point of view because they can be used in many reports but are also important for other applications for detailed analysis. The following assignments are possible:

▸ **Assignment of company code**
As already mentioned, you must make assignments to company codes based on the information we have provided with relation to charts of depreciation.

▶ **Assignment of business area**

This assignment is necessary if your design is to deliver business area balance sheets. Assets can be assigned to a business area directly during master record creation, or they can be derived automatically from the cost center that you entered. As long as a fixed asset is assigned to a business area, the system makes account assignment of all postings to this asset to this business area, including depreciation and gain, or loss postings on asset retirement.

▶ **Assignment to plant, location, and address**

The definitions of the plant and location organizational units are primarily specified in the SAP logistics components. In Asset Accounting, plant has no relevance, but it can be used as a sort and selection criteria for reports. You can assign an asset to one plant for a specific period of time in its master record. This assignment can be changed directly in the asset master record.

▶ **Assignment to cost center and profit center**

We have already mentioned that GL postings are integrated by asset class. If you think about the account assignment object, you will agree that an asset may belong to a specific department. For this reason, the financial transactions must also be assigned to that department, and assets are assigned to a cost center on their master record. It is important to understand that an asset can only be assigned to one cost center at a time. This assignment enables the following:

  ▶ Assignment of all costs (depreciation and interest charges) related to the asset to the correct cost center

  ▶ Planning for future depreciation or interest for the asset

  ▶ Assignment of gain or loss from the sale of asset to the correct cost center

You can assign fixed assets to a cost center from a specific point in time, and if there is change in assignment, the system is smart enough to distribute the depreciation or interest amount to the subsequent cost center. Profit center assignment is achieved through the cost center–profit center assignment in the cost center master record. There is no direct assignment to a profit center.

7.2.3 Integration with the GL

From a high-level point of view, your Asset Accounting solution needs to provide you with two pieces of information:

▶ An asset register that provides an analysis of the assets you own, along with their original cost and net book value

▶ An accurate financial position in terms of the current gross book value of your assets

   ▶ The real-time integration with the GL is straightforward because Asset Accounting is a subledger of the GL.

7.2.4 Structuring Your Fixed Assets Design

You have different options as to how you want to see figures reported on your asset statements. You should consider the current conventions in place at your organization before making a decision. The following are common approaches:

▶ **Balance sheet approach**
If you want to structure assets according to the structure of your balance sheets, you have three options available in the standard system:

   ▶ Use the financial statement version

   ▶ Use balance sheet items

   ▶ Use GL accounts

▶ **Asset class approach**
Asset classes can represent the structure of your assets. Every asset you create in the system is created with reference to an asset class. You use the settings of account determination in the asset class to assign each asset to an item in the balance sheet.

▶ **Asset approach**
This approach is more practical and may be more relevant for organizations with many assets that can be combined due to the size and nature of the assets. For instance, a laboratory may be an asset as a whole that is made up of many smaller assets. In this scenario, we would have the following:

   ▶ The asset "main number," which represents the overall asset.

   ▶ Below the main asset, you can use asset "subnumbers" to represent the many component parts, and you have the flexibility to depreciate them individually if their acquisition dates are different from the original asset.

> **Note**
>
> You can use an asset main number to represent a fixed asset if your requirements are simple.

In the next section, we will look at how to build an Asset Accounting business model.

7.3 Building an Asset Accounting Business Model

Once you understand the main concepts in Asset Accounting, you should think about the questions you need to ask your business partners as part of your workshops to in turn understand their requirements from an Asset Accounting point of view. The answers to these questions will help you build an Asset Accounting model according to the exact requirements of your business partners. Examples of the questions could include:

▶ **How many different types of assets do you have?**
This will help you determine the number of asset classes you need in the system to represent their current structure within the SAP system.

▶ **Do you want to represent different types of assets with individual balance sheet accounts in your financial statements?**
This will determine if you need to create separate account determinations for every type of asset and also for the same type of assets with different useful lives, or if you can assign the same account determination to an asset, for example, furniture and fixtures, with different useful lives. This would mean that you don't have to create a separate account determination for this asset with different useful lives. Most companies prefer to use one account determination for each type of asset and use the Asset Accounting reports to view more details about asset types with different useful lives.

▶ **Do you want your different asset types to have unique number ranges?**
This will help you to determine if you need to add more number ranges so they can be assigned to different types of assets using their respective asset classes. Most of the time, companies want to assign a different number range to different types of assets so that they can easily be identified.

▶ **How many different types of depreciation calculations are required?**
This will help you determine how many different depreciation areas are

required within your chart of depreciation and which of these will post to the GL and which will post, for example, only to the Controlling Component (CO) for Cost Accounting purposes. Remember that the settings required for straight-line depreciation as well as for declining methods and so on are also connected to the depreciation area through the depreciation key. Settings such as when to start or stop depreciating assets (when they are acquired, transferred in or out, or retired) are also linked to the depreciation key. These settings are also determined at this stage so that the same could be reflected when the configuration of depreciation keys are done.

We have now spent some time explaining the concepts of Asset Accounting to provide you with a solid understanding of the key elements involved. Asset Accounting is sometimes seen as a specialist subject that will start making sense as we begin our configuration activities.

7.4   Asset Accounting Configuration

In this section, we will look at the important Asset Accounting configuration steps, following a logical sequence. This ensures that you don't miss any important steps while also making sure that after following these steps, your Asset Accounting component is fully functional. We'll start by copying a reference chart of depreciation to define your own chart of depreciation.

7.4.1   Copy Reference Chart of Depreciation

To define your chart of depreciation, you copy a reference chart of depreciation, including all of the depreciation areas from the reference chart. As already explained in the previous section, your chart of depreciation is a directory of depreciation areas arranged according to your business and legal requirements. You can use the chart of depreciation to manage all different types of valuation rules for your assets in a specific country or economic region.

If necessary, you can delete any depreciation areas that you do not need in your copied chart of depreciation.

The IMG path for this configuration step is **SPRO • Financial Accounting (New) • Asset Accounting • Organizational Structure • Copy Reference Chart of Depreciation/Depreciation Areas**, or you can use Transaction code OAP1. A screen with Activities including Copy Reference Chart of Depreciation will appear as shown in Figure 7.3.

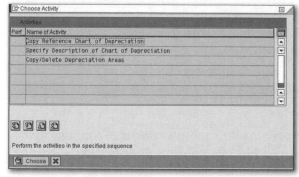

Figure 7.3 Copy Reference Chart of Depreciation

If you are creating a chart of depreciation for a country for which SAP has not delivered a standard country-specific chart of depreciation, you can save a lot of time by copying a chart of depreciation with similar depreciation parameters and then making changes to it. To copy a chart of depreciation:

1. In the **Organizational object Chart of depreciation** screen, click on the copy icon, as shown in Figure 7.4.

2. In the **Copy** dialog box that appears, specify the chart of depreciation from which to copy and the chart of depreciation to which to copy (the latter is a number you assign, such as 1000 in our example.

3. Click on the checkmark icon.

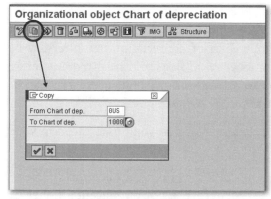

Figure 7.4 Copy Chart of Depreciation

The system returns a message related to the transport of number ranges and addresses. Click on the checkmark icon on the message and we recommend that you maintain the number ranges and addresses manually.

Once you have created your copy, you need to go back into the same transaction and change the name of your chart of depreciation. In our scenario, we will create two charts, copied from the U.S. and UK templates, as shown in Figure 7.5.

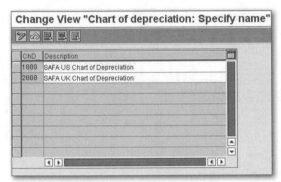

Figure 7.5 Chart of Depreciations Created for SAFA Inc.

Behind each chart, you will find the valid depreciation areas for it, as shown in Figure 7.6. Delete the depreciation areas that are not needed from your new chart of depreciation or add new depreciation areas by copying them.

Change View "Define Depreciation Areas": Overview

Chart of dep.   1000   SAFA US Chart of Depreciation

Define Depreciation Areas

Ar.	Name of depreciation area	Real	G/L	Trgt Group	
1	Book depreciation in local currency	☑	1		
10	Federal Tax ACRS/MACRS	☑	0		
11	Alternative Minimum Tax	☑	0		
12	Adjusted Current Earnings	☑	0		
13	Corporate Earnings & Profits	☑	0		
30	Consolidated balance sheet in local currency	☑	0		
31	Consolidated balance sheet in group currency	☑	0		
32	Book depreciation in group currency	☑	0		
40	State modified ACRS	☑	0		
80	Insurance values	☑	0		

Figure 7.6 Depreciation Areas for Your Chart of Depreciation

Next, we will look at assigning the chart of depreciation to a company code.

7.4.2 Assign Chart of Depreciation to a Company Code

In this step you assign your chart of depreciation to your company code so that the relationship between chart of depreciation and company code is complete from an Asset Accounting point of view.

The IMG path for this configuration step is **SPRO • Financial Accounting (New) • Asset Accounting • Organizational Structure • Assign Chart of Depreciation to Company Code**, or you can use Transaction code OAB1. In this screen, you enter the relevant chart of depreciation in the **Chrt dep** column for your company code, as shown in Figure 7.7. This completes the assignment step.

Change View "Maintain company code in Asset Accounting": Overview

Co	Company Name	Chrt dep	Description
0001	SAP A.G.	0DE	Sample chart of depreciation: Germany
0100	ACME Inc		
0MB1	IS-B Musterbank Deutschl.		
1000	NYC	1000	SAFA US Chart of Depreciation
2000	London	2000	SAFA UK Chart of Depreciation
FI01	Country Template FI		
FR01	Country Template FR		
GB01	Country Template GB		
HK01	Country Template HK		
HU01	Country Template HU		
ID01	Country Template ID		

Figure 7.7 Assignment of Chart of Depreciation to Your Company Code

Now, let's look at specifying a number assignment across company codes.

7.4.3 Specify Number Assignment across Company Codes

In this step, you define a cross-company code assignment of the main asset number. You need to perform this step only if you want a cross-company code number assignment; otherwise, you can skip this step. In Asset Accounting, you have an option to allocate the main asset number across different company codes, so for every company code, you can determine from which other company code the number assignment will be carried out.

The IMG path for this configuration step is **SPRO • Financial Accounting (New) • Asset Accounting • Organizational Structure • Specify number assignment across Company Codes**, or you can use Transaction code AO11.

In the screen that displays, shown in Figure 7.8, specify which company code you want to use for the cross-company code number assignment for your company codes in the **No. Co Cd** column.

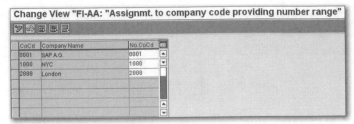

Figure 7.8 Assignment of Number Range to Company Code

Based on the settings in this screen, the system assigns the main asset number from the number range of the assigning company code to these company codes. If a cross-company code number assignment is not required, you must enter the company code key in the **No. Co Cd** column that you are currently configuring.

Next, we'll look at the specify account determination step.

7.4.4 Specify Account Determination

In this step, you create the base for establishing a link between Asset Accounting and the GL by defining the account determination keys and description that will be used later in the implementation to include the GL accounts to which to post. Once these keys are created, you can configure additional settings for the controls these keys represent.

> **Note**
>
> The key of an account determination must be stored in the asset class. In this way, the account determination links an asset master record to the general ledger accounts to be posted for an accounting transaction using the asset class.

You should create at least the same number of account determinations as your asset balance sheet accounts in the GL. SAP supplies many standard account determinations, and you can use them if they meet your requirements.

The IMG path to configure settings for account determination is **SPRO • Financial Accounting (New) • Asset Accounting • Organizational Structure • Asset classes • Specify Account Determination**. The screen that displays, where you configure the settings, is shown in Figure 7.9. Select the New Entries button and enter the account determination key and its description.

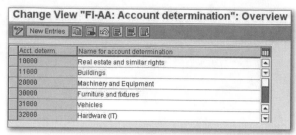

Figure 7.9 Define Account Determination

Next, let's look at creating screen layout rules.

7.4.5 Create Screen Layout Rules

You can create screen layout rules for each key you have created. The screen layout determines the status of the fields appearing in the asset master record. You use the screen layout to determine if fields are required, optional, or suppressed. There are two steps for creating the screen layout rules:

1. Create the keys and descriptions of the screen layout controls using IMG path **SPRO • Financial Accounting (New) • Asset Accounting • Organizational Structure • Asset classes • Create Screen layout rules**. The rules you define in the screen shown in Figure 7.10 define the field status when you create a new asset master record for the selected account determination.

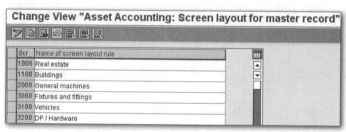

Figure 7.10 Defining Screen Layout Rules

2. Define the details of the screen layout control for asset master data, which controls the settings for the field groups in the asset master record. This step allows you to structure the asset master record individually for each asset class. For each field group you define, you specify the following:

▸ The characteristics of the master record screen, that is, whether the fields are going to be required, optional, displayed, or suppressed

▸ The maintenance level, that is, the main asset number or subasset number

▸ A copy option at the time of creating a new master record using another master record as a reference

Use IMG path **SPRO • Financial Accounting (New) • Asset Accounting • Master Data • Screen Layout • Define Screen Layout for Asset Master Data** or Transaction code OA77.

The screen layout is defined for each key that was created in step 1 and for each screen of an Asset Master Record, as shown in Figure 7.11.

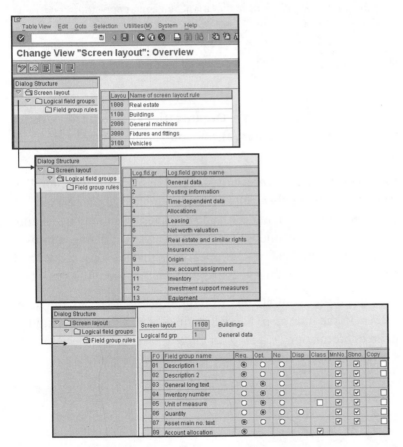

Figure 7.11 Defining Screen Layout for Asset Master Records

Next, we'll look at defining asset number range intervals.

7.4.6   Define Asset Number Range Intervals

In this step, you define the number ranges for your company code for assigning the main asset number. Many companies use their asset numbering convention to categorize their asset portfolio. In the asset class, you can specify the number range for the assignment of numbers for that asset class. You have an option to create number ranges using internal as well as external assignment.

> **Note**
>
> You should use number ranges with internal assignment to keep administration needed for the number assignment to a minimum.
>
> Also, SAP provides standard number ranges you can use, or you can create your own number ranges if required.

The IMG path for defining the number range intervals is **SPRO • Financial Accounting (New) • Asset Accounting • Organizational Structures • Asset Classes • Define Number Range Interval**, or you can use Transaction code .AS08.

From the **Maintain Number Range Intervals** screen that displays, shown in Figure 7.12, you can either copy number ranges from a template company code, or you can create your own numbers in line with your business requirements. Figure 7.12 shows the creation of custom number ranges. If you want to define your own asset record numbers, you should define a number range that is externally defined by selecting the External (**Ext**) box for the appropriate number range.

We have now completed the requirements to define the asset classes for Asset Accounting purposes. In the next step, we will define the asset classes using the previously configured information.

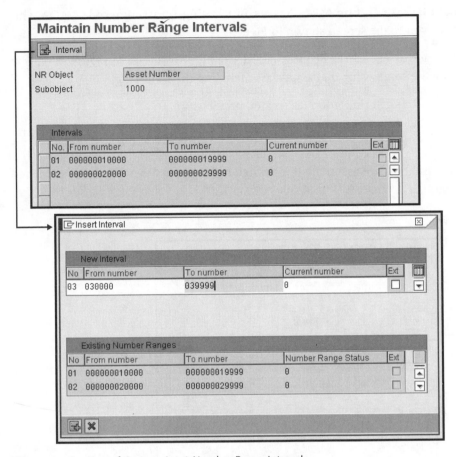

Figure 7.12 Creation of Custom Asset Number Range Intervals

7.4.7 Define Asset Classes

In Asset Accounting, the most important means of structuring your assets is using the concept of asset classes. You can define as many asset classes as you require in accordance with your legal requirements. You define asset classes at the client level, and they apply to all company codes. This statement is true even for company codes that have different charts of depreciation and therefore different depreciation areas.

Configuration of asset classes is completed by following the IMG path **SPRO** • **Financial Accounting (New)** • **Asset Accounting** • **Organizational Structures**

• **Asset Classes** • **Define Asset Classes**, or by using Transaction code OAOA. This will take you to the screen shown in Figure 7.13.

Behind each asset class is a configuration screen, also shown in Figure 7.13, that contains the settings for that asset class including the following:

▶ The account determination (as created previously)

▶ The screen layout rule for maintaining the asset master record (as created previously)

▶ The number range assignment for assigning the main asset numbers (as created previously)

▶ Whether the asset class is blocked

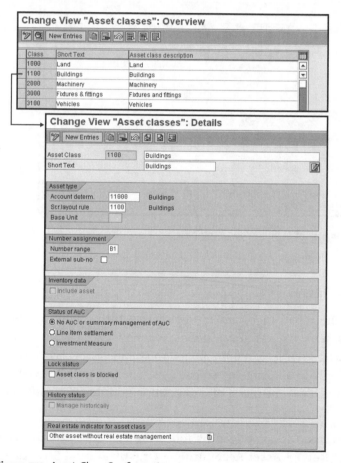

Figure 7.13 Asset Class Configuration

Next, we'll define depreciation areas.

7.4.8 Define Depreciation Areas

In this step, you define your depreciation areas according to your legal or business requirements. Depreciation areas are identified by two-digit numeric keys. You can enter the different depreciation terms (explained in the next section) in the asset class or directly in the asset master record of the particular asset. This enables you to use straight-line depreciation for your internal accounting and declining-balance depreciation for external reporting.

You can go to the configuration screen, shown in Figure 7.14, for defining depreciation areas using IMG path **SPRO • Financial Accounting (New) • Asset Accounting • Valuation • Depreciation Areas • Define Depreciation Areas**.

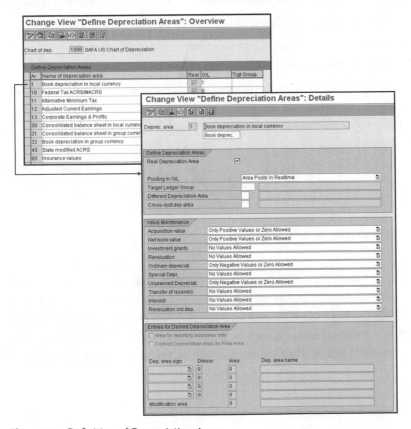

Figure 7.14 Definition of Depreciation Areas

You'll need to determine if transfer of asset values or depreciation from a depreciation area will be done automatically to the general ledger. You also need to remember that the system can only post asset balance sheet values from one depreciation area online. In most implementations, this is the book depreciation area 01.

Configure the settings for your depreciation area in the **Details** screen as follows:

1. In the **Value Maintenance** section, define the type of value management that is allowed for **Acquisition value** and **Net book value**. The standard setting is **Only Positive Values or Zero Allowed** in all areas in which you want to depreciate your asset.

2. If you need depreciation areas that derive their values from other depreciation areas, you can define derived depreciation areas by configuring these settings in the **Entries for Derived Depreciation Area** region of the **Details** screen:

   ▸ Enter the depreciation areas that will form the basis for its values.

   ▸ Enter whether the values from these areas should be included as positive or negative values in the formula.

   ▸ Ensure that the indicator **Real Depreciation Area** in the **Define Depreciation Area** of the screen is not activated, as the derived depreciation area can only be used for reporting purposes, and its values are not posted to asset reconciliation accounts.

Next, we'll configure the transfer of Acquisition and Production Costs (APC) values.

7.4.9 Specify Transfer of APC Values

In this step, you define the transfer rules for posting values of depreciation areas. These settings allow you to ensure that certain depreciation areas have identical asset values posted to them. You can configure the settings for the transfer of APC values through IMG path **SPRO • Financial Accounting (New) • Asset Accounting • Valuation • Depreciation Areas • Specify Transfer of APC Values**, or use Transaction code OABC. Either way you'll see the screen displayed in Figure 7.15.

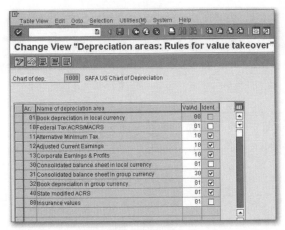

Figure 7.15 Define Depreciation Areas

Select the depreciation area that would be used for adopting values for your selected depreciation area. The standard system setting copies the asset balance sheet values from depreciation area 01 to all other depreciation areas during postings.

> **Note**
>
> You only need to carry out this step if you want to copy posting values from a depreciation area other than depreciation area 01.

Next, let's look at specifying the transfer of depreciation terms.

7.4.10 Specify Transfer of Depreciation Terms

In this step, you can ensure that certain depreciation areas are uniformly depreciated by defining transfer rules for the depreciation terms from one depreciation area to another one. The IMG path for this step is **SPRO • Financial Accounting (New) • Asset Accounting • Valuation • Depreciation Areas • Specify Transfer of Depreciation Terms**, or you can use Transaction code OABD. In the screen that displays, shown in Figure 7.16, specify the depreciation area in the **TTr** column from which the depreciation terms should be copied for the dependent depreciation areas.

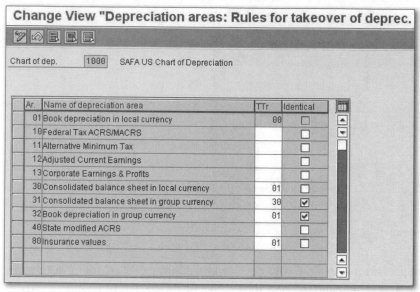

Figure 7.16 Transfer of Depreciation Terms

You also need to determine whether this copying is mandatory or optional. If you specify optional copying, the proposed depreciation terms in the dependent areas can be changed in the asset master record. Next, we'll look at determining depreciation areas in the asset classes.

7.4.11 Determine Depreciation Areas in the Asset Classes

In this step, you configure the settings to determine the depreciation terms that will be used in your asset classes. The assets in an asset class normally use the same depreciation terms, that is, depreciation key, useful life, and screen layout. At the time of creation of new assets in the system, you don't have to maintain the depreciation terms because these values are defaulted from the settings in the asset classes. Use IMG path **SPRO • Financial Accounting (New) • Asset Accounting • Valuation • Determine Depreciation Areas in the Asset Classes** or Transaction code OAYZ to access the configuration screens shown in Figure 7.17.

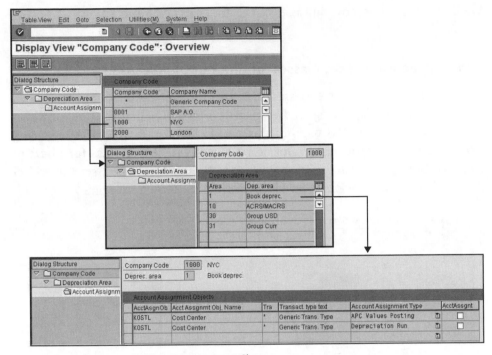

Figure 7.17 Define Depreciation Areas in Asset Classes

In the area specifications of your asset class, enter the depreciation key, useful life, and screen layout rule, as shown in Figure 7.18. (The settings for the depreciation key will be explained in detail in the next steps.)

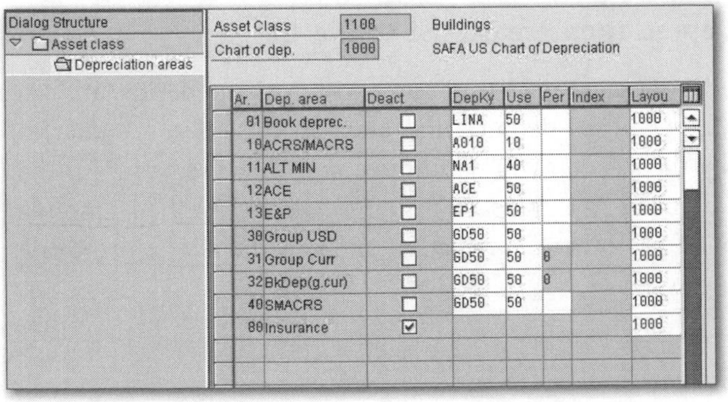

Figure 7.18 Summary of Depreciation Areas within an Asset Class

We'll now look at deactivating asset classes for charts of depreciation.

7.4.12 Deactivate Asset Classes for Chart of Depreciation

In this step, you can lock asset classes for entire charts of depreciation. This reduces the risk of an asset class being used by mistake in a chart of depreciation for which it is not created. The IMG path for this step is **SPRO • Financial Accounting (New) • Asset Accounting • Valuation • Deactivate Asset Class for Chart of Depreciation**, or you can use Transaction code AM05. To lock an asset class, select the checkbox in the **Lock** column for the asset class, shown in Figure 7.19.

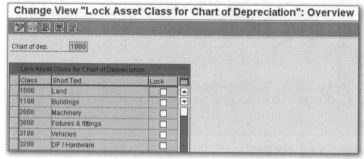

Figure 7.19 Deactivate Asset Class

Now, let's define how depreciation areas post to the GL.

7.4.13 Define how Depreciation Areas Post to the GL

In this step, you define how the depreciation areas will post the depreciation to the GL. If you look at the standard depreciation areas in the reference chart of depreciation provided by the system, you will notice that they are set up so that book depreciation area 01 posts APC transactions automatically to the GL online. You can post transactions from other depreciation areas to the GL automatically using periodic processing.

> **Note**
>
> You always have to use periodic processing to post depreciation to the GL.

The IMG path for this configuration step is **SPRO • Financial Accounting (New) • Asset Accounting • Integration with the General Ledger • Define How Depreciation Areas Post to General Ledger**, or you can use Transaction code OADX.

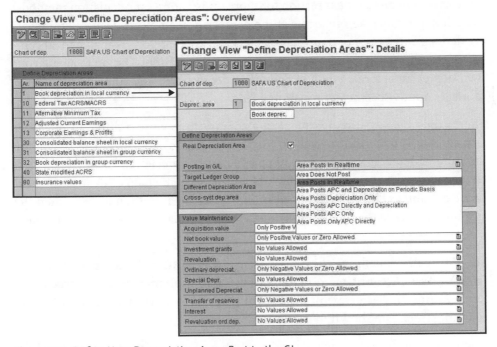

Figure 7.20 Define How Depreciation Areas Post to the GL

Specify how your depreciation areas should post to the GL by selecting from these options, shown in Figure 7.20:

▶ **Area Does Not Post** (no values are posted to general ledger)

▶ **Area Posts in Realtime** (post assets in GL in real-time)

▶ **Area Posts APC and Depreciation on Periodic Basis** (post assets periodically in GL)

▶ **Area Posts Depreciation Only** (only depreciation posted in GL)

Next, we'll look at maintaining the depreciation key.

7.4.14 Maintain Depreciation Key

The depreciation key contains the settings necessary for determining the depreciation amounts for your assets. It contains calculation rules that are used for the automatically calculating different depreciation types. You assign calculation methods (please refer to the next section for more information on calculation methods) to each depreciation key to arrive at the depreciation amounts. Depreciation keys are defined at the chart of depreciation level and are therefore available in all company codes. If you are using the SAP-delivered charts of depreciation to create your own depreciation areas, you will find many depreciation keys that are predefined to meet country-specific depreciation needs.

There could be a legal requirement in a country to have two different depreciation methods in the life span of an asset. In an SAP system, you can divide the duration of depreciation into several phases in the depreciation key. If you enter a changeover method for one of these phases, the system changes over to the next phase as soon as the event specified in the changeover method occurs. Then the system starts using the next type of depreciation calculation specified for that next phase.

The IMG path for defining the depreciation key is **SPRO • Financial Accounting (New) • Asset Accounting • Depreciation • Valuation methods • Depreciation Key • Maintain depreciation Key**, or you can use Transaction code AFAMA. The relevant screens are shown in Figure 7.21.

Defining the depreciation key is a step you can perform once you have defined the underlying items including base method, double declining method, period control, and so on. We will discuss these items in the next sections.

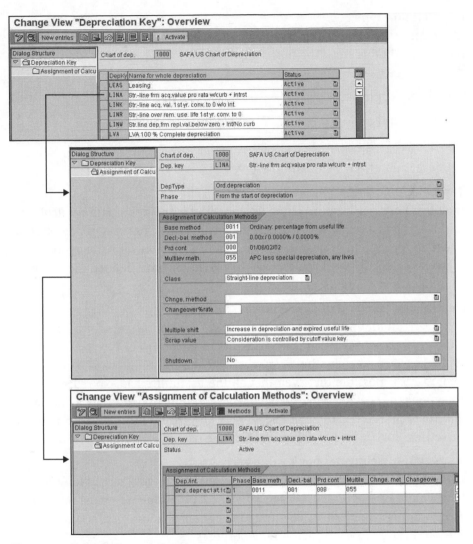

Figure 7.21 Maintain Depreciation Key

7.4.15 Define Base Method

The base method contains the settings required for calculating depreciation, and you enter the base method in a depreciation key. The base method is independent of the chart of depreciation and does not contain any country-specific settings. In defining the base method, you specify the following items:

▶ **Depreciation type**
You identify the depreciation types and valuation types allowed for each depreciation area in this step. The following depreciation types are used in the SAP system:

- ▶ Ordinary depreciation
- ▶ Special depreciation
- ▶ Unplanned depreciation
- ▶ Depreciation from write-off of reserves

▶ **Depreciation calculation method**
The most important feature of the base method is the depreciation calculation method, as it makes it possible to calculate many different types of depreciation values in the system. The system determines other control parameters in the depreciation key by assessing the way in which you have defined the depreciation calculation method.

▶ **Treatment of the end of depreciation**
In asset accounting, you generally want to see the depreciation of a fixed asset being finished when the net book value has reached zero or the end of the useful life has been reached. However, when you use certain types of depreciation methods, it is possible that even though the useful life has expired, the book value might not have reached zero. You can continue to depreciate a fixed asset after that point to reach the net book value of zero by making adjustments in the settings for the end of depreciation in the base method.

▶ **Depreciation below net book value zero**
It is also possible to continue depreciating your asset below zero as long as your depreciation area settings allow a negative net book value. You must set an indicator in the base method to allow this kind of depreciation. Depreciation below zero can be useful for cost-accounting purposes.

The IMG path for maintaining these details is **SPRO • Financial Accounting (New) • Asset Accounting • Depreciation • Valuation methods • Depreciation key • Calculation methods • Define base methods**, and the relevant configuration screen is shown in Figure 7.22.

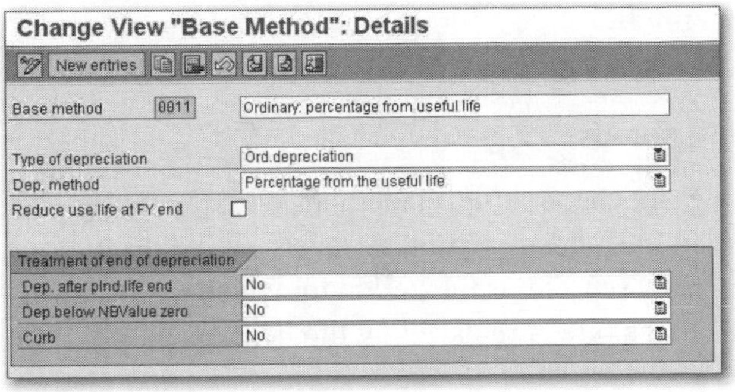

Figure 7.22 Define Depreciation Base Method

We'll now look at defining the declining balance method.

7.4.16 Define Declining Balance Method

The *declining balance* method as well as the *sum of the year digit* method are diminishing-rate depreciation methods. In arriving at the depreciation value for the declining-balance method, the system multiplies the straight-line percentage rate based on the useful life of the asset by an agreed factor. The system also provides upper and lower limit percentages rates because it is possible to have a very large depreciation rate with a shorter useful life and a very small depreciation percentage rate with a very long useful life. As shown in the Figure 7.23, the agreed factor is entered in the column Dec. factor and upper and lower limit percentages are entered in the columns Max. perc. and Min. perc. respectively.

This configuration is completed by following IMG path **SPRO • Financial Accounting (New) • Asset Accounting • Depreciation • Valuation methods • Depreciation key • Calculation methods • Define Declining-balance methods**, or by using Transaction code AFAMD, to access the screen shown in Figure 7.23.

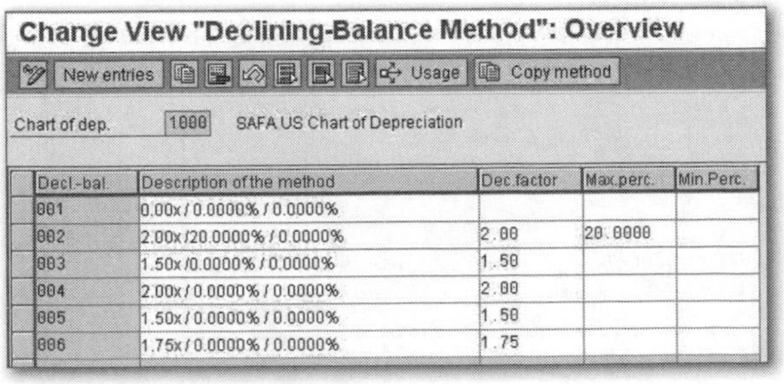

Decl.-bal	Description of the method	Dec.factor	Max.perc.	Min.Perc.
001	0.00x / 0.0000% / 0.0000%			
002	2.00x /20.0000% / 0.0000%	2.00	20.0000	
003	1.50x /0.0000% / 0.0000%	1.50		
004	2.00x / 0.0000% / 0.0000%	2.00		
005	1.50x / 0.0000% / 0.0000%	1.50		
006	1.75x / 0.0000% / 0.0000%	1.75		

Figure 7.23 Declining Balance Method

Now, let's define multi-level methods.

7.4.17   Define Multi-Level Methods

In this step you configure settings for the multi-level method. With the multi-level method, you can have a calculation divided into many levels according to your requirements. In this context, a level represents the period for which a certain percentage rate is valid. This percentage rate is replaced by the next percentage rate when its period of validity has expired.

The IMG path for this configuration step is **SPRO • Financial Accounting (New) • Asset Accounting • Depreciation • Valuation methods • Depreciation key • Calculation methods • Define Multi-Level methods**, or you can use Transaction code AFAMS.

In the first screen, shown in Figure 7.24, you define the multi-level method key and description and the validity start date for the different levels in the multi-level method, that is, from capitalization date, from ordinary depreciation start date, or from special depreciation start date, and so on.

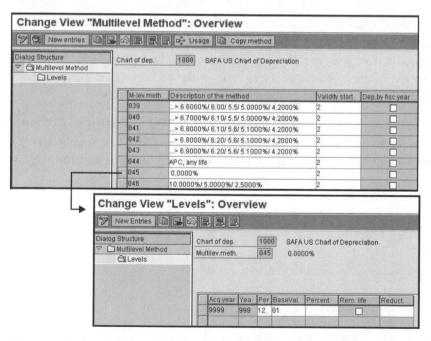

Figure 7.24 Define Multi-Level Methods

The next step, shown also in Figure 7.24, is to define the **Levels**, which require the following settings:

▸ Validity period in calendar months for percentage rate.

▸ Base value for the calculation of depreciation. This could be the acquisition value, net book value, replacement value, and so on, depending on the requirements of your depreciation calculation. In some depreciation methods, you must change the depreciation method from, for example, the double declining method to straight-line when the straight-line depreciation value is more than the double declining method and then use the net book value as the basis of change to the method of depreciation calculation.

▸ Percentage rate for the calculation of depreciation. The system uses this rate as well as the base value to determine what should be the total depreciation amount for an asset.

▸ Remaining useful life indicator. Set this indicator if you want the system to determine the periodic depreciation percentage based on the remaining life of the asset. It should only be used for depreciation keys in which the base method uses the "percentage from the useful life" depreciation calculation method.

> **Note**
>
> The SAP system provides a number of methods as standard, and you can use these methods or create your own based on your specific requirements.

Next, let's examine maintaining period control methods.

7.4.18 Maintain Period control Methods

For determining the depreciation start and end date for asset transactions, you can set an appropriate period control in the period control method for the most commonly used transaction categories:

▸ Acquisitions

▸ Additions (subsequent acquisitions and post-capitalization)

▸ Retirements

▸ Transfers (e.g., intra-company transfers)

You have many different options in setting the depreciation start date for assets acquired within the same year. Examples include the following:

▶ Starting the depreciation from the start of the month in which acquisition is taking place

▶ Starting the depreciation from the start of the next month from the month of purchase

▶ Starting the depreciation from the start of the year if the asset is purchased during the year

Using the asset value date of a transaction (acquisition or retirement), the system determines the start date or end date of the depreciation calculation using the period control.

The IMG path for carrying out this configuration is **SPRO** • **Financial Accounting (New)** • **Asset Accounting** • **Depreciation** • **Valuation methods** • **Depreciation key** • **Calculation methods** • **Define Period Control methods**, or you can use Transaction code AFAMP. You'll be working with the screen shown in Figure 7.25.

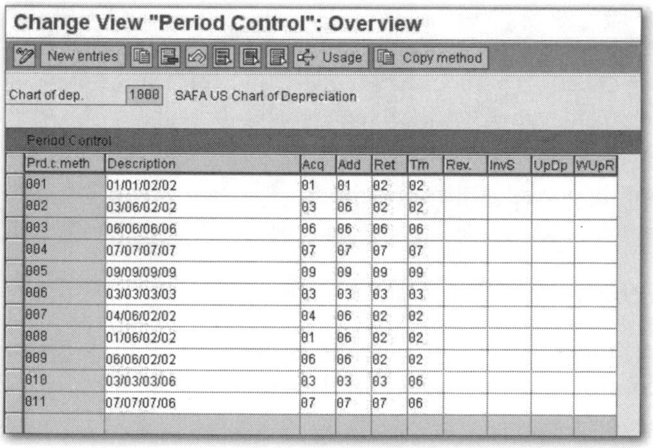

Change View "Period Control": Overview

New entries | Usage | Copy method

Chart of dep. 1000 SAFA US Chart of Depreciation

Period Control

Prd.c.meth	Description	Acq	Add	Ret	Tm	Rev.	InvS	UpDp	WUpR
001	01/01/02/02	01	01	02	02				
002	03/06/02/02	03	06	02	02				
003	06/06/06/06	06	06	06	06				
004	07/07/07/07	07	07	07	07				
005	09/09/09/09	09	09	09	09				
006	03/03/03/03	03	03	03	03				
007	04/06/02/02	04	06	02	02				
008	01/06/02/02	01	06	02	02				
009	06/06/02/02	06	06	02	02				
010	03/03/03/06	03	03	03	06				
011	07/07/07/06	07	07	07	06				

Figure 7.25 Maintain Period Controls

Next, let's examine activating account assignment objects.

7.4.19   Activate Account Assignment Objects

In this step, you configure settings for additional account assignment objects (for example, cost center, fund centers, internal orders, etc.) during posting in Asset Accounting.

Note

To enable the posting of transactions to the GL, you have to ensure that the account assignment objects you want to use are available for input by using the field status of posting keys 70 (debit asset) and 75 (credit asset).

You can configure the field status settings of posting keys using IMG path **SPRO • Financial Accounting • Asset Accounting • Integration with the General Ledger • Change the Field Status Variant of the Asset G/L Accounts**.

The IMG path for activating the account assignment objects is **SPRO • Financial Accounting (New) • Asset Accounting • Integration with GL • Additional Account Assignment Objects • Activate Account Assignment Objects**, which will lead you to the screen shown in Figure 7.26.

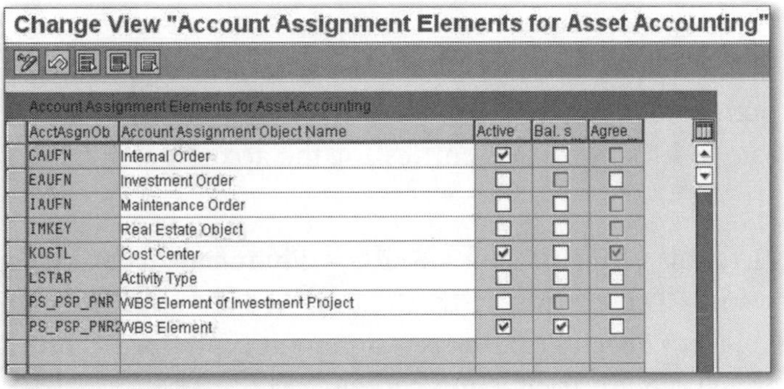

Change View "Account Assignment Elements for Asset Accounting"				
AcctAsgnOb	Account Assignment Object Name	Active	Bal. s	Agree
CAUFN	Internal Order	☑	☐	☐
EAUFN	Investment Order	☐	☐	☐
IAUFN	Maintenance Order	☐	☐	☐
IMKEY	Real Estate Object	☐	☐	☐
KOSTL	Cost Center	☑	☐	☑
LSTAR	Activity Type	☐	☐	☐
PS_PSP_PNR	WBS Element of Investment Project	☐	☐	☐
PS_PSP_PNR2	WBS Element	☑	☑	☐

Figure 7.26 Assign Account Assignment Elements for Asset Accounting

For each account assignment object, you can make the following selections:

► **Active**
Activate the account assignment objects you need for Asset Accounting.

► **Balance sheet**
Indicate whether the account assignment object is relevant to the balance sheet. If you have specified this, you can no longer change the account assignment

object directly in the asset master record once the asset has been capitalized and you are required to create a new asset and transfer that asset to the new one to make this change.

▶ **Agreement**
Specify whether the account assignment object you entered at the time of posting should match the account assignment object entered in the asset master record. If you set this indicator, you cannot change the account assignment object when posting.

We'll now look at specifying the account assignment types for account assignment objects.

7.4.20 Specify Account Assignment Types for Account Assignment Objects

In this step, you assign account assignment types to the account assignment objects of company code, depreciation area, and transaction type. The possible account assignment types for account assignment objects are:

▶ Periodic postings

▶ Account assignment of depreciation

If you want to assign both account assignment types to an account assignment object, you have to create at least two table entries for the account assignment object as shown in Figure 7.27.

The IMG path to complete this configuration is **SPRO • Financial Accounting (New) • Asset Accounting • Integration with General Ledger • Additional Account Assignment Objects • Specify Account Assignment types for Account Assignment Objects**, or you can use Transaction code ACSET.

You should create a generic entry using an asterisk (*) for the transaction type, as the system will use the account assignment type you entered for all transaction types for that account assignment object in both the company code as well as the depreciation area.

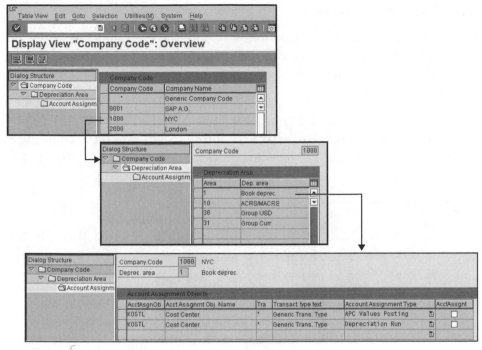

Figure 7.27 Account Assignment Types for Account Assignment Objects

In this configuration activity, you should activate all of the account assignment types you need, although cost center is usually sufficient for most solutions. You do not have to delete the ones you do not need; you can deactivate them, and activate them again later if you need them.

> **Note**
>
> You need to complete the configuration of activating account assignment objects and specify account assignment types for account assignment objects before you can run the new depreciation program RAPOST2000, as the system will otherwise give you error messages related to missing cost centers or internal orders assignments at the time of depreciation run.

Now, we'll look at assigning GL accounts.

7.4.21 Assign GL Accounts

In this step, you assign the GL accounts (the balance sheet accounts, special reserve accounts, and the depreciation accounts) for Asset Accounting. Earlier we defined the account determination and explained that we will be using them to link the Asset Accounting with the GL.

This configuration is completed using the screens shown in Figure 7.28, by following the IMG path **SPRO • Financial Accounting (New) • Asset Accounting • Integration with General Ledger • Assign G/L Accounts**, or using Transaction code AO90.

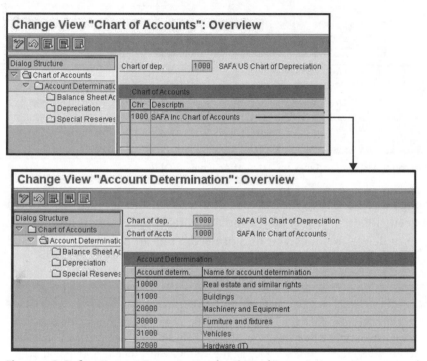

Figure 7.28 Define Account Determination for Chart of Depreciation

For each asset class, you need to specify the GL accounts that are posted to for transactions related to acquisition (balance sheet), depreciation, and revaluation, as we'll see next.

Balance Sheet Accounts

In the left pane, select **Balance Sheet Accounts** in the **Dialog Structure**, as shown in Figure 7.29, and enter the GL accounts to which you want to post the acquisition and production costs, down payment accounts, and gain and loss accounts on sale of fixed assets, and so on.

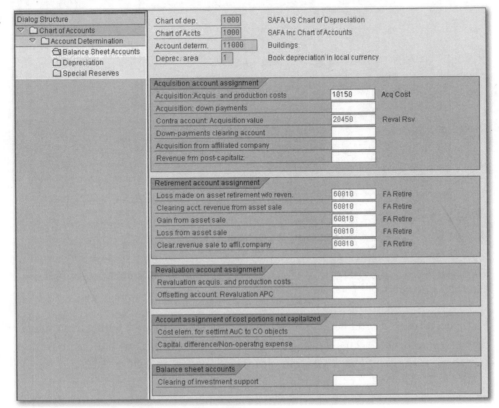

Figure 7.29 Balance Sheet Accounts for Acquisition

Depreciation Accounts

Next, select **Depreciation** in the **Dialog Structure**, as shown in Figure 7.30. In the fields on the right, you define the accumulated depreciation account, depreciation expense account, unplanned depreciation accounts, and so on.

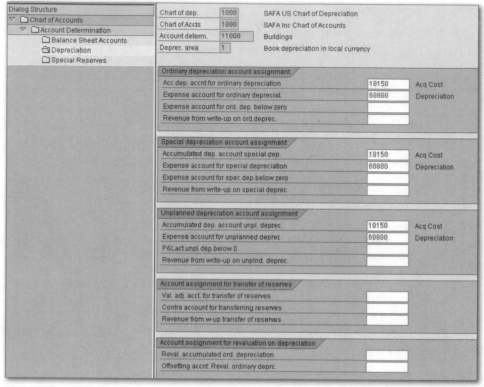

Figure 7.30 Accounts for Depreciation Postings

For special reserves you need to select the depreciation area for which this calculation applies. In our scenario, we do not define this setting, but the configuration
screen is the same as the two examples we looked at in Figure 7.29 and Figure
7.30. We'll now look at specifying the document type for posting depreciation.

7.4.22 Specify Document Type for Posting Depreciation

In this step, you assign the document type to your company code that should be
used for posting depreciation in the system. The standard document type provided
by SAP is "AF."

The IMG path to complete this configuration step is **SPRO • Financial Accounting (New) • Asset Accounting • Integration with General Ledger • Post Depreciation to General Ledger • Specify Document Type for Posting of Depreciation**, or you can use Transaction code AO71. From the screen shown in Figure

7.31, you can define a new document type if needed. If an appropriate document type exists, you can assign it by company code.

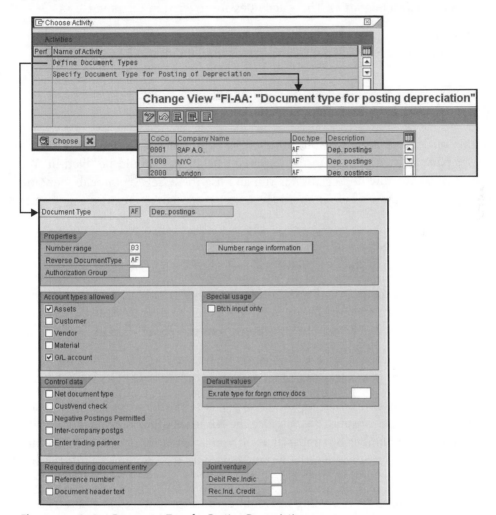

Figure 7.31 Assign Document Type for Posting Depreciation

To post depreciation successfully using the new depreciation program RAPOST2000, you need to remove the **Batch input only** flag in the document type AF, as this new program does not create a batch session, and the depreciation run will fail with this setting active.

This completes the configuration of the Asset Accounting subcomponent. There are additional activities, however, that you'll need to complete for most projects that relate to data migration. These activities are covered in Chapter 10.

We will now spend some time looking at the transaction processing steps in Asset Accounting so that you can get a complete picture of this component.

7.5   Asset transaction processing

In this section, we will look into some of the commonly used transactions from a user perspective and explain the important fields that should be filled in. We will also look at how depreciation is run and use the Asset Explorer to view the results of activities we have done so far. Let's get started by creating a new asset master record.

7.5.1   Create New Asset Master Record

After completing the previous activities, you are now ready to create your new asset master record in your SAP system. The menu path is **SAP Easy Access •** **Accounting • Financial Accounting • Fixed Assets • Asset • Create • Asset**, or you can use Transaction code AS01.

Follow these steps to create a new asset master record:

1. In the Create Asset: Initial screen that appears, select the asset class, company code and number of similar assets. Use the **Number of Similar Assets** field to state the total number of similar assets if you are creating multiple assets that are similar to each other, and the system will create asset master records for that number of assets with similar information.

   You could also enter an existing asset number in a company code as a reference to create your asset quickly.

2. Figure 7.32, Figure 7.33, and Figure 7.34, respectively, contain important fields you need to populate for the asset you are going to create, as outlined in Table 7.1.

General tab (holds the General Data for the Legacy Asset)	Description
Description	This is the name of the new asset. Two lines are available here, and you can use both the lines.
Acct determination	This is taken from the asset class entered in the first screen. Note that this cannot be changed in this screen.
Inventory number	You can use this field to enter the manufacturer's serial number, as it will help you enquire about this asset from the manufacturer.
Quantity	You can enter the quantity that the system manages for this asset. Note that this quantity field can be used at the time of partial retirement, and the system will update the asset accordingly.
Capitalized on	This date is the value date for this asset. When first postings are made to the asset, the system uses this field to assign the value date to the asset.
De-activation on	The system posts the value date of the retirement in this field when is asset is completely retired.
First Acquisition on	This field is automatically set with the asset value date of the first acquisition posting.
Time-dependent tab (holds important information about assignments to objects like cost center, internal order, etc.)	Description
Cost Center	You enter the cost center in this field to which the postings are made for this asset.
Internal Order	You can allocate an internal order using this field.
Plant	Use this field to enter the plant assignment for this asset. This information could be used in asset accounting for further analysis.
Location	You can enter the location of this asset in this field.
Origin Tab (holds the information about the origin of this asset)	Description
Vendor	Enter the vendor from which this asset was purchased.

Table 7.1 Create New Asset Master Record

Origin Tab (holds the information about the origin of this asset)	Description
Manufacturer	Enter the manufacturer details in this field, as it will help in making enquiries about this asset.
Original Asset	You can use this field to enter the legacy asset number to create a link with the SAP asset number.
Deprec. Areas tab (Displays information about different depreciation areas and settings within depreciation areas)	Description
Valuation	This tab displays settings for different depreciation areas such as the depreciation keys, useful life in years and period, ordinary depreciation start date [which is defaulted from the capitalization date entered in the General tab], etc.

Table 7.1 Create New Asset Master Record (cont.)

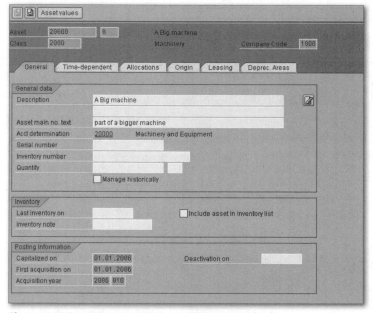

Figure 7.32 Create New Asset Master Data: General Tab

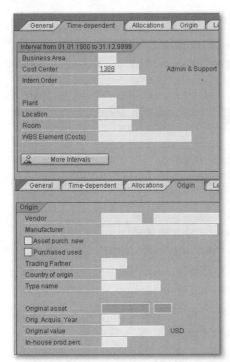

Figure 7.33 Create New Asset Master Data: Time-dependent Tab

Deact	A	Depreciation area	DKey	UseLife	Prd	ODep Start
☐	01	Book deprec.	LINA	50		
☐	10	ACRS/MACRS	A010	10		
☐	11	ALT MIN	NA1	40		
☐	12	ACE	ACE	50		
☐	13	E&P	EP1	50		
☐	30	Group USD	GD50	50		
☐	31	Group Curr	GD50	50	0	
☐	32	BkDep(g.cur)	GD50	50	0	
☐	40	SMACRS	GD50	50		

Figure 7.34 Create New Asset Master Data: Depreciation Areas Tab

Once you have entered this information, you can save your asset master data, and the system will generate an asset number from the number range assigned to the asset class to which this newly created asset belongs.

7.5.2 Post Values to Asset Using External Acquisition

After you have created an asset master record, you now have to post values to it. That is, in the previous step we simply created an asset shell into which we still have to enter values.

Note

There are certain transactions within Asset Accounting where you can use the same transaction to create an asset master record and post values to it, but we will explain each step using different transactions, as it will help you in understanding the whole process more easily.

The menu path for posting values to an asset using external acquisition with vendors is **SAP Easy Access • Accounting • Financial Accounting • Fixed Assets • Postings • External Acquisitions • With Vendors**, or you can use Transaction code F-90. To perform this action, follow these steps:

1. Use Table 7.2 to enter the information in the screen **Acquisition from purchase w. vendor: Header Data**, as shown in Figure 7.35.

Field	Description
Document Date	Enter the document date.
Type	Enter the document type, which in our case is vendor invoice "KR."
Company Code	Enter your company code.
Posting Date	Enter the posting date.
Period	Enter the posting period. The system defaults this field when you enter the posting date.
Currency/Rate	Enter the currency in which the invoice will be created.
Reference	This is a freely definable field and can, for example, be used to enter the vendor invoice number for future reference.
Doc. Header Text	This is also a freely definable field and could be used to enter a specific reference to this asset.
PstKy	Enter the posting key "31," that is, credit vendor.
Account	Enter the vendor account number from which the asset is purchased.
TType	Enter transaction type "100," which is external acquisitions. SAP has provided standard transaction types that can be used and are more than sufficient to meet your requirements.

Table 7.2 Acquisition from purchase w.vendor: Header Data

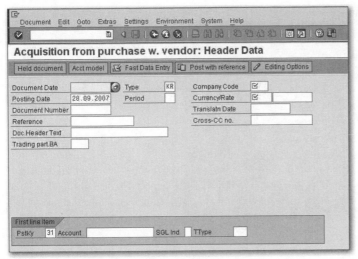

Figure 7.35 Acquisition of Asset with Vendor: First Screen

2. Use Table 7.3 to complete the page **Enter Vendor Invoice: Add Vendor Item**, as shown in Figure 7.36.

Field	Description
Amount	Enter the amount of the invoice.
Calculate tax	If the invoice is tax-related, select this checkbox, and the system will calculate the tax accordingly.
Payt Terms	The system will default the payment terms from the vendor master record in this field.
Bline Date	The system will default the baseline date from the payment terms settings.
Text	Enter any useful information in this field that would help you identify this transaction in the future.
PstKy	Enter the posting key "70," which is debit asset, as we are posting values to the asset.
Account	Enter the asset number you created in the previous step.
TType	Enter the transaction type "100" in this field.

Table 7.3 Enter Vendor invoice: Add Vendor item

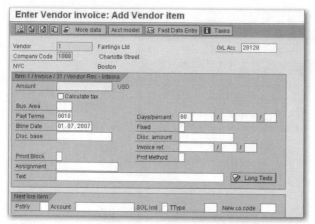

Figure 7.36 Acquisition of Asset with Vendor: Second Screen

3. 3. Use Table 7.4 to complete the fields in the **Enter Vendor invoice: Add Asset item** screen shown in Figure 7.37.

Field	Description
Amount	Enter the amount that should be posted to the asset.
Calculate tax	Select this checkbox to have the system automatically calculate the tax amount.
Text	Enter any useful information in this field that would help you identify this transaction in the future.

Table 7.4 Enter Vendor invoice: Add Asset item

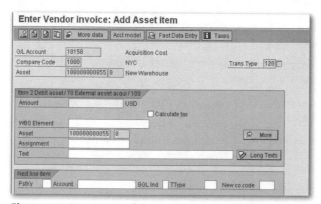

Figure 7.37 Acquisition of Asset with Vendor: Third Screen

4. Simulate the transaction, and you will see that the system has generated another line with the tax amount.

5. Post your document, and a document number will be generated. You have now successfully posted values to your asset.

7.5.3 • Working with Asset Explorer

After you have created the asset in the system and posted values to it, you should use Asset Explorer, a very useful tool in Asset Accounting, to view the details of the asset just created with some additional information made available to you by your SAP system. The menu path for Asset Explorer is **SAP Easy Access • Accounting • Financial Accounting • Fixed Assets • Assets • Asset Explorer**, or you can use Transaction code AW01N.

Details of Asset Explorer

When you access the **Asset Explorer** screen, shown in Figure 7.38, the system shows the last asset created as a default. The screen has three visible sections:

▶ **Depreciation areas**
In this section, you can see the values posted for the asset, the depreciation calculation, and a comparison for the coming years for each of the depreciation areas in your chart of depreciation (e.g., if you have two depreciation areas, one is straight line and the other is reducing balance; by clicking on each of them, you can see the relevant values calculated by the system under these two methods including the depreciation calculation).

▶ **Objects related to asset**
In this area, you can see what objects are connected or related to your asset such as vendors, cost centers, internal orders, and so on.

▶ **Information tabs (with an option to specify a fiscal year)**
   ▶ Planned values
   ▶ Posted values
   ▶ Comparisons
   ▶ Parameters

   Each of these tabs contains specific information that is explained next.

Planned Values

The **Planned values** tab, shown in Figure 7.38, gives you the planned values for an asset for a given year. You can see the APC value, the accumulated depreciation, the ordinary depreciation for the year, and the net book value at the end of the year. In the lower half of the screen, you can see the transactions that have been posted to this asset during the given year. These transactions include acquisitions, transfers, retirements, and so on, and you can view the original document posted by clicking on these transactions.

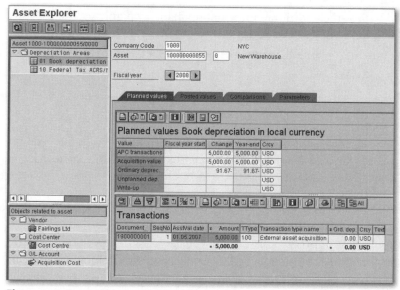

Figure 7.38 Asset Explorer: Planned Values Tab

Posted Values

On the **Posted values** tab, shown in Figure 7.39, the system tells you what is the value of depreciation (posted or planned) for posting on a periodic basis, and you can also see what would be the yearly charge of depreciation for the given asset.

> **Note**
>
> For the periods for which depreciation has already been posted, you will see a green signal in the Status column, which indicates that the run was successful.

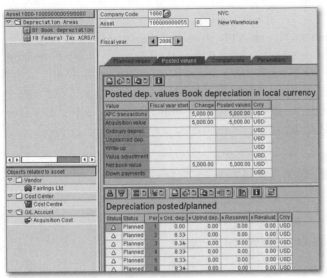

Figure 7.39 Asset Explorer: Posted Values Tab

Comparisons

On the **Comparisons** tab, shown in Figure 7.40, the system gives you a comparison of the yearly depreciation charge including the net book value over the entire life of an asset. You can also see on this tab when your asset will be fully depreciated.

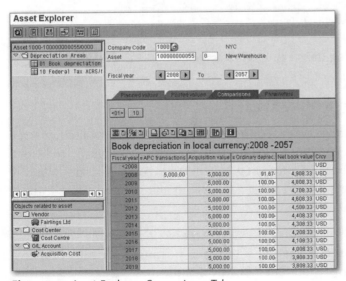

Figure 7.40 Asset Explorer: Comparisons Tab

Parameters

The **Parameters** tab, shown in Figure 7.41, shows you a summary of all of the parameters that have been used by the system to calculate the values shown on the other tabs we've discussed. Looking at this tab, you can easily see that the settings we have configured in the previous steps are all summarized (wherever applicable). Examples include depreciation key, useful life of the asset, ordinary depreciation start date, and an option to view the depreciation key settings.

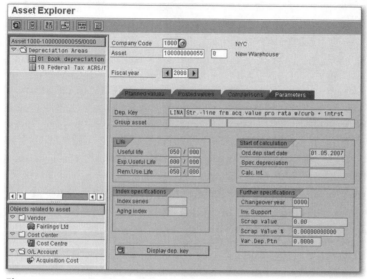

Figure 7.41 Asset Explorer: Parameters Tab

Next, we'll look at posting transfers to other assets.

7.5.4 Post Transfers to Other Assets

In this transaction, we are going to see how to transfer one asset to another asset in Asset Accounting. The example we'll look at is one within a company code, but the same logic can be used to transfer assets between two company codes. We will also explain how to create a new asset master record and transfer values using a single transaction.

The menu path for this transaction is **SAP Easy Access • Accounting • Financial Accounting • Fixed Assets • Posting • Transfer • Transfer within company code**, or you can use Transaction code ABUMN. Follow these steps:

1. Use Table 7.5 to complete the first tab, **Transaction Data**, as shown in Figure 7.42.

Field/Section	Description
Document Date	Enter the document date.
Posting Date	Enter the posting date.
Asset value date	This is the value date for this asset in Asset Accounting. The system will use this date to calculate the amount of depreciation for this transferred asset.
Text	Enter any useful information in this field.
Transfer to	**Existing asset**: If you want to transfer this asset to an existing asset number, enter the asset number. **New asset**: If you want to create a new asset and transfer values to it, enter the description of the new asset, the asset class in which it should be created, and the cost center.

Table 7.5 Transfer within Company Code: Transaction Data

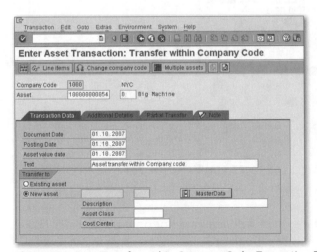

Figure 7.42 Asset Transfer within Company Code: Transaction Data Tab

2. If you post your document at this stage, the system will completely transfer the values to the new or existing asset.

3. If you want to partially transfer the asset, use Table 7.6 to complete the **Partial Transfer** tab, as shown in Figure 7.43.

Field/Section	Description
Amount posted	Enter the partial amount in this field, and the system will only transfer this value to the new asset.
Percentage rate	If you want to transfer a certain percentage to the new asset, enter the percentage amount to be transferred.
Quantity	If you have maintained the quantity field in the asset master record, you will have an option here to transfer an amount using quantity as the basis for calculating the transfer values.
Related to	Select the relevant option depending on whether the transaction is related to prior or current year acquisitions.

Table 7.6 Transfer within Company Code: Partial Transfer

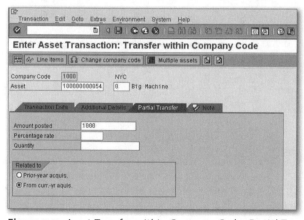

Figure 7.43 Asset Transfer within Company Code: Partial Transfer Tab

4. Post your document, and the system will generate not only the transfer document but also a new asset number if you specified to transfer the values to a new asset.

5. Use Asset Explorer for both the assets created in the above-mentioned step to see the results of this transaction.

7.5.5 Post Retirements with Scrapping

So far, we have created the asset master record, entered values into it, and posted transfers within a single company code. Now we are ready for posting retirements to an asset using the scrapping transaction.

> **Note**
>
> You do have other options available for retiring assets, such as retirement with a customer where the asset is sold to an outside customer for a given price. We will use the scrapping option because retiring an asset with a customer is very similar to creating a customer invoice and as such wouldn't add any value.

The menu path is **SAP Easy Access • Accounting • Financial Accounting • Fixed Assets • Posting • Retirement • Asset retirement by scrapping**, or you can use Transaction code ABAVN. Follow these steps:

1. Use Table 7.7 to complete the information on the **Transaction data** tab, as shown in Figure 7.44.

Field	Description
Document date	Enter the document date.
Posting date	Enter the posting date.
Asset Value date	This is the value date for this asset in Asset Accounting. The system will use this date to calculate the amount of depreciation for this retiring asset.
Text	Enter any useful information in this field.

Table 7.7 Asset Retirement by Scrapping: Transaction Data

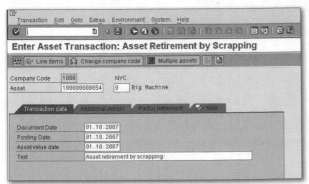

Figure 7.44 Asset Retirement by Scrapping: Transaction Data Tab

2. If you post your document at this stage, the system will completely retire the asset and post the Net Book Value (NBV) of the asset as a loss to the profit and loss account (maintained in the configuration step assign GL accounts)

3. If you want to partially retire the asset, use Table 7.8 to configure the **Partial retirement** tab, shown in Figure 7.45.

Field/Section	Description
Amount posted	Enter the partial amount, and the system will only retire this value of the asset.
Percentage rate	If you want to retire a certain percentage of this asset, enter the percentage amount to be retired,
Quantity	If you have maintained the quantity field in the asset master record, you can retire a partial amount using **Quantity** as the basis for calculating the values to be retired.
Related to	Select the relevant option depending on whether the transaction is related to prior or current year acquisitions.

Table 7.8 Asset Retirement by Scrapping: Partial Retirement

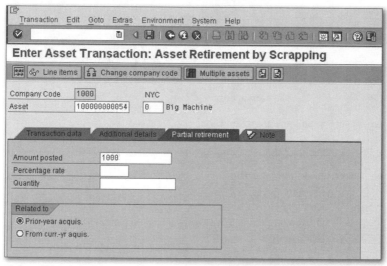

Figure 7.45 Asset Retirement by Scrapping: Partial Retirement Tab

4. Post your document, and the retiring document will be generated.

5. Use Asset Explorer to see the results of the retirement on your asset.

Next, we'll look at posting depreciation in the system for your assets.

7.5.6 Post Depreciation Run

To post depreciation in the system, you need to execute a depreciation run on a periodic basis for your assets within your company code. The menu path to do so is **SAP Easy Access • Accounting • Financial Accounting • Fixed Assets • Periodic Processing • Depreciation run • Execute**, or you can use Transaction code AFAB. Follow these steps:

1. In the **Depreciation Posting Run** screen shown in Figure 7.46, enter the **Company Code**, **Fiscal year**, and **Posting Period** for which you want to run the depreciation.

2. Select **Planned posting run** from the options for **Reasons for posting run**.

> **Note**
>
> You normally use the option **Planned posting run** for posting depreciation in the system. You can use **Repeat** if you have made corrections to manual depreciation or depreciation terms and want to complete the postings. The system only posts changes to the depreciation in this case. Use **Restart** when there was an error in the previous run and you have corrected it (such as a missing cost center in the asset master).

> **Tip**
>
> You need to execute the depreciation run in the background because the system does not let you run it in the foreground. You should use the **Test Run** option first to identify any problems before you do a live run.

3. Once you have checked that the depreciation run was complete using Transaction SM37, go to the Asset Explorer and check the asset you created in the previous steps. You will see that on the **Posted values** tab, depreciation will be posted for the period for which you have executed the depreciation run, with a green signal to indicate that the depreciation run was successful.

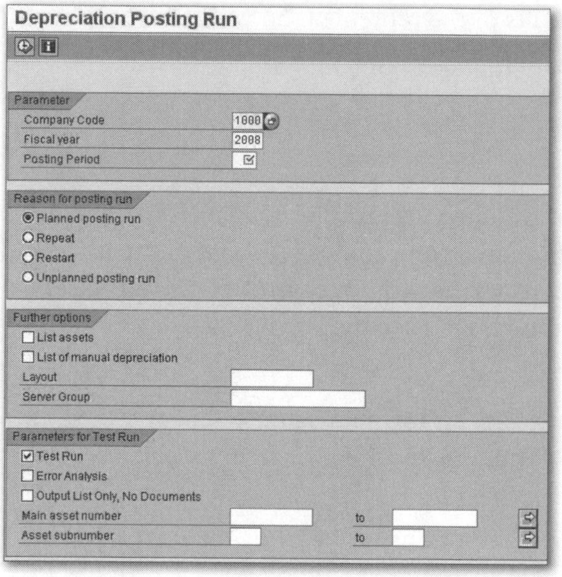

Figure 7.46 Depreciation Run

7.6 Summary

This concludes our review of the main transactions within Asset Accounting that you may need to process. An understanding of these will enable you to make informed decisions in relation to the overall process. Asset Accounting must always be considered in line with the statutory requirements of your country and the business requirements of your organization. The areas covered within this chapter provide you with a solid base from which to configure most solutions.

The Asset Accounting subcomponent is a complex area because of the differences in statutory requirements of different countries. In addition, accounting principles need to be adhered to. As such, it is important to understand the SAP functionality and the requirements from an organizational and statutory point of view. We have deliberately gone into additional detail in this chapter to help the reader, as we feel this area is often confusing.

The key learning points of this chapter were:

▸ Understanding the lifecycle of an asset

▸ Understanding the basic concepts of Asset Accounting and developing a business requirement document based on your understanding of this module

▸ Understanding the configuration of the main components of the Asset Accounting subcomponent

▸ Explanation of the key business transactions related to Asset Accounting

We will work with additional Asset Accounting configuration options in Chapter 10, when we look at the settings required to transfer legacy assets.

Next, in Chapter 8, we will provide you with an overview of the Controlling Component (CO) to get sufficient areas of it working to support our SAP ERP Financials solution.

Although this book is focused on SAP ERP Financials, it is impossible to remove all reference to the Controlling Component (CO) because we require some controlling to make our financial solution work. This chapter provides an overview of this component to get sufficient areas of it working to support our SAP ERP Financials solution. For a full explanation of the Controlling Component (CO), you should consult a book that focuses on this topic.

8 Controlling Component (CO) in SAP ERP

The objective of this chapter is to provide an overview of the functionality of the Controlling Component (CO) in SAP ERP. Although this is a separate component, it is integrated with SAP ERP Financials, and we need to include for you sufficient information about it to enable SAP ERP Financials to work.

The objectives of this chapter are as follows:

- Provide an overview of the Controlling Component (CO)
- Explain the basic concepts in this component, including master data and document flow
- Basic configuration settings for the following:
  - Cost Element Accounting
  - Cost Center Accounting
  - Internal Orders
  - Classic Versus New Profit Center Accounting

> **Note**
>
> It is important to know that with the introduction of the new GL, the use of the Controlling Component (CO) has changed, specifically Profit Center Accounting, which is now contained within the new GL component. We have already included this aspect in our discussion in Chapter 4. As explained in that chapter, you do have the option of using classic GL instead of the new GL, and for that reason we discuss Profit Center Accounting in this chapter as it exists within a classic Controlling Component (CO) scenario. Cost Center Accounting and Internal Order Accounting have not been effected by the new GL changes.

8.1 Overview and Diagram

Before SAP ERP Enterprise Central Component (ECC), the Controlling Component (CO) existed to provide organizations with additional account assignment objects needed to produce management-focused financial analysis. From SAP ERP Financials, organizations would create their financial statements such as balance sheets and profit-and-loss statements. This is referred to as external reporting and is always subject to certain standards and legal requirements.

Most companies divide their accounting function into internal and external, and the Controlling Component (CO) represents the internal accounting, as it provides the necessary information to those people who are responsible for managing and controlling the company's operations. This component is not governed by legal requirements and hence provides management with a very flexible tool to obtain reports in many different dimensions. Figure 8.1 shows a diagram that helps explain how data flows from SAP ERP Financials to the Controlling Component (CO), in a classic GL scenario.

For our new GL scenario, we have already configured some aspects of the Controlling Component (CO) in Chapter 4 because the former Profit Center Accounting component is part of the new GL. In addition to this, we will also need to configure Cost Element Accounting and Cost Center Accounting to enable postings to cost centers and internal orders; both of these are covered within this chapter.

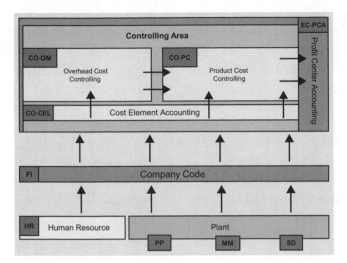

Figure 8.1 Data Flow to the Controlling Component (CO) in a Classic GL Scenario

In a classic Controlling Component (CO) solution, you also need to configure Profit Center Accounting separately as a subcomponent, and this is covered within this chapter also, to explain a scenario where the new GL and document splitting is not activated. We'll start by reviewing the key components of the Controlling Component (CO) that fall within our scope.

8.2 Subcomponents of the Controlling Component (CO)

Like SAP ERP Financials, the Controlling Component (CO) also has a number of subcomponents that you need to be aware of, including Cost Element Accounting, Cost Center Accounting, Internal Orders, and Profit Center Accounting. We'll look at each in more detail next.

8.2.1 Cost Element Accounting

Within the Controlling Component (CO), cost elements are equivalent to GL accounts and help in the flow of data from SAP ERP Financials to this component. A cost element's full name is primary cost element because you also may create secondary cost elements. You can only create a cost element for an income-expenditure GL account and not for balance sheet GL accounts. This has not changed from classic GL to the new GL.

> **Note**
>
> No primary cost element can exist without a twin (GL account) being represented in SAP ERP Financials.

8.2.2 Cost Center Accounting

Cost Center Accounting was created for internal controlling purposes because it provides a tool that can collect costs. If you are coming from a non-SAP background, you may have used cost centers before. In an SAP system, cost centers can be configured to collect both costs and revenues, but they should only be used for costs.

8.2.3 Internal Orders

Internal orders can be used to represent individual tasks or projects that you want to report on in addition to the other account assignment objects already mentioned. Internal orders can support task-oriented planning, monitoring, and allocation of costs. They can be real (in which case they collect costs while the task or project is going on) or statistical (in which case they can exist for long periods of time to provide an additional reporting dimension). (We will provide a more in-depth explanation of real and statistical postings in a moment.)

8.2.4 Profit Center Accounting

Classic Profit Center Accounting allows you to analyze income and expenditure for profit centers that represent an independent subunit within an organization. You link cost centers to profit centers and you can have a one-to-one or many-to-one relationship. In classic Profit Center Accounting, you can transfer some balance sheet items such as inventories, accounts receivables and payables, and fixed assets from SAP ERP Financials on a periodic basis and prepare financial statements. As mentioned in Chapter 4, with the new GL this is no longer required because active splitting is available.

There are many other subcomponents, but they are not within the scope of this book. Based on the subcomponents we discussed, we will now consider how you can bring them together into a controlling model.

8.3 Building a Controlling Model

It is correct to say that you cannot build any area of Financials independently of other subcomponents. This is very true in the case of the Controlling Component (CO). This component is very integrated with the other SAP ERP Financials components, and it is important to design it together with the same people who are designing your GL solution. Some questions you need to consider during your design include the following:

▶ **When should I create a controlling area for more than one company code?**
If you are planning to make cross-company code postings to allocate activities or periodically allocate costs, then you should consider creating one controlling area that is assigned to multiple company codes.

▶ **What restrictions do I need to take into account if I set up only one controlling area?**
Using one controlling area in your structure will restrict other settings, as follows:

  ▶ **Chart of accounts:** The chart of accounts should be the same in the company codes assigned to the controlling area.

  ▶ **Fiscal year variants:** The fiscal year variants must have the same number of posting periods regardless of the number of special periods.

  ▶ **Closing process:** You cannot carry out Controlling Component (CO) closing before final SAP ERP Financials closing has taken place.

  ▶ **Performance issues:** With one controlling area, the volume of data increases manifold, and there might be performance issues as a result.

▶ **How would you structure your hierarchies?**
It is possible to create a hierarchy or group for every master data object, and the same rules apply to all. You should assign each cost center within the hierarchy somewhere. Although there is no hard and fast rule in defining your cost center structure, you should define it so that it reflects your organization's areas of responsibility. Remember that the hierarchy is going to be used for reporting purposes. Some organizations will maintain more than one hierarchy to provide different reporting analysis.

▶ **How can internal orders be used?**
Internal orders make it possible for management to carry out detailed costing analysis for a particular activity. All costs and revenues relating to that activity

are assigned to the order created for that purpose, and you can use that information to see what costs have been incurred for that activity and what revenues have been generated. You can also see whether you made any profit or loss during the time the activity was performed.

▶ **How would you structure your Profit Center Accounting?**
For both classic and new Profit Center Accounting, you decide on your profit center to cost center assignment in a number of different ways. Some designs define profit centers at points that receive income and then assign the cost centers to the profit center(s) that contribute to the generation of that income. In such a scenario, you will have more cost centers than profit centers, which is a correct reflection of how many organizations operate. It is, however, possible that the profit center is set to an equivalent level as the cost center, so throughout the organization there is a one-to-one relationship. Keep in mind that profit centers are also needed to post balance sheet items to, so your balance sheet debtors and creditors can only be analyzed at the profit center level.

Examples of where organizations choose to define their profit centers include the following:

▶ On the basis of geographical locations or regions

▶ On the basis of product line or segments

▶ On the basis of functions such as production, research, and so on

You can also have a combination of these structures if your organization is structured that way.

8.3.1 Concept of Real and Statistical Postings

Before we get further into this chapter, we need to review the concept of real and statistical postings, which we've mentioned once already and will mention several times throughout the chapter. When you make entries in SAP ERP Financials related to expenses and income, they give rise to real and statistical postings in the Controlling Component (CO). It is important to understand the concepts of real and statistical postings, as many people find this very confusing:

▶ You can further process real postings and use them for cost allocations within the Controlling Component (CO), using distributions and assessments. One rule of thumb is that only one real posting takes place in this component, and that all other postings for that transaction become statistical.

▶ Statistical postings are only used for information purposes, and there are no restrictions for you on making statistical postings in the system.

The most important point is that whether a posting is statistical or real is determined by the account assignment object, that is, cost center, internal order, and so on, and not by any other criteria. We will try to explain this concept further by giving some examples.

In scenario 1, shown in Table 8.1, the real posting is determined by the cost center, and the statistical posting is received by the profit center.

Posting in SAP ERP Financials	Posting in CO	
	Real	**Statistical**
1) Expense GL account 2) Cost center	Cost center	Profit center as derived from cost center master record

Table 8.1 Scenario 1: Only Cost Center Assignment

In scenario 2, shown in Table 8.2, an internal order has determined the real posting, and both cost center and profit center have received the statistical postings. This means that if the order is real, the cost center will automatically take the statistical posting, and for the profit center, postings are always statistical.

Posting in SAP ERP Financials	Posting in CO	
	Real	**Statistical**
1) Expense GL account 2) Cost center 3) Internal order (real)	Internal order	Cost center Profit center as derived from cost center master record

Table 8.2 Scenario 2: Real Internal Order and Cost Center Assignment

In scenario 3, shown in Table 8.3, the internal order has again determined the posting by taking the statistical posting, as it is a statistical order, and the cost center has taken the real posting.

Posting in SAP ERP Financials	Posting in CO	
	Real	Statistical
1) Expense GL account 2) Cost center 3) Internal order (statistical)	Cost center	Internal order Profit center as derived from cost center master record

Table 8.3 Cost Center and Statistical Internal Order Assignment

You should now be comfortable understanding the components of the Controlling Component (CO) that we will need to support an SAP ERP Financials solution and the concept of real and statistical postings. We will now take a detailed look at the configuration settings in the Controlling Component (CO).

8.4 Configuration Settings in the Controlling Component (CO)

In this section, we will go over the configuration discussed in Chapter 2. We are reviewing this to explain the differences from a classic GL point of view. First, we will briefly review our sample company, SAFA Inc., which we will use for this configuration.

SAFA Inc. is a U.S.-based company with U.S. dollars as its base currency. It has another office in London (created as a separate company code as explained in Chapter 2), and we have assigned the two company codes to the same controlling area. We will now look at basic controlling area settings.

8.4.1 Basic Controlling Area Settings

We first discussed controlling area configuration in Chapter 2, and you may choose to refer back to that chapter as you read through the information presented here.

Define a Controlling Area

The *controlling area* is the organizational unit that allows you to carry out cost controlling. It also defines the boundary in which you can allocate costs, as it is not possible to allocate costs outside its boundaries. Controlling areas structure the internal accounting operations of an organization within the Controlling Component (CO). The menu path used to define controlling areas is **SPRO • Enterprise Structure • Definition • Controlling • Maintain Controlling Area**, or you can use Transaction code OX06. Our controlling area was already defined in Chapter 2, Section 2.4.9.

Activate Controlling Area Components

We now need to activate the controlling area components that are relevant for our solution. From our design point of view, we only activate a few components using the menu path **SPRO • Controlling • General Controlling • Organization • Maintain Controlling Area** or Transaction code OKKP. In Chapter 2, we activated components as shown in Figure 8.2. These settings are valid if we are implementing the new GL.

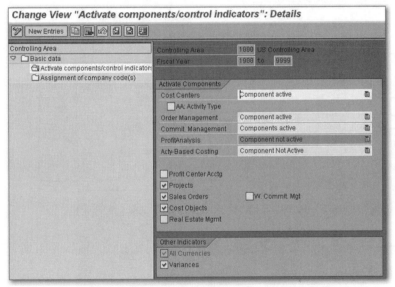

Figure 8.2 Activate Controlling Area Components

In a classic GL scenario, however, we would need to activate Profit Center Accounting (**Profit Center Acctg**) as well to enable Profit Center Accounting postings. This configuration would therefore need to change in a classic GL implementation. Next, we will examine assigning a number range to the controlling area.

Assigning a Number Range to a Controlling Area

Controlling Component (CO) postings are tracked through the assignment of document numbers. The number range assignment could be internally generated by the SAP system or set for manual update, that is, external number assignment. We recommend using internal number generation to keep administrative tasks to a minimum.

Controlling Component (CO) document number ranges are created in the same way as SAP ERP Financials number ranges (see Chapter 3, Section 3.2.5): you can create them from scratch or by copying from an existing controlling area. The copying option is recommended, as this ensures that you copy all required number ranges. The menu path is **IMG • Controlling • General Controlling • Organization • Maintain number ranges for CO documents**, or you can use Transaction code KANK. Figure 8.3 illustrates the process.

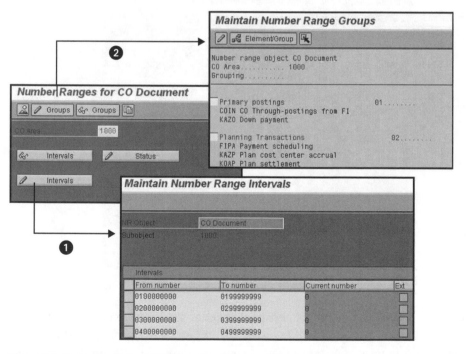

Figure 8.3 Create Profit Center Accounting Document Number Ranges

Once you have created your number ranges, you also need to assign the number range to a transaction group. As you can see in Figure 8.3, both of these actions can be performed from the same transaction screen. Next, we will look at maintaining Controlling Component (CO) versions.

Maintaining Controlling Component (CO) Versions

SAP uses versions in the Controlling Component (CO) to allow you to maintain different plan or budget numbers to be able to monitor actual numbers against different scenarios. You must define a minimum of one version, usually version 0, known as the plan/actual version. The version ensures that data is consistent among, for example, cost center accounting, internal orders, profit center accounting and profitability analysis.

> **Note**
>
> When we previously created our controlling area, the system automatically created version 0, which is valid for five fiscal years. The standard setting within SAP is that the system will always use version 0 when referencing actual postings.

To complete the base Controlling Component (CO) enterprise configuration, you have to configure settings for at least version 0 for currency, fiscal year, and Profit Center Accounting. The menu path is **IMG • Controlling • General Controlling • Organization • Maintain versions**, or you can use Transaction code OKEQ. The screens used to maintain versions are shown in Figure 8.4.

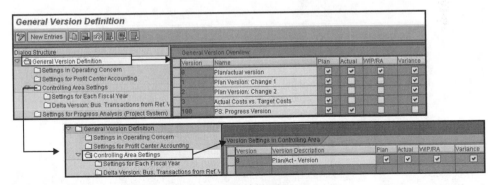

Figure 8.4 Maintain Controlling Component (CO) Versions

Settings for Each Fiscal Year

To configure the version 0 settings for your controlling area:

1. Select version 0 in the **General Version Definition** screen

2. Click on **Settings for Each Fiscal Year** in the **Dialog Structure**, and the screen shown in Figure 8.5 appears. As mentioned earlier, when you created your controlling area, version 0 was created within it and as a default, five years were made available at the same time. Some of the important fields are discussed in Table 8.4.

> **Note**
>
> If you want to add more years later, click on the **New Entries** button, and the detailed screen for a new fiscal year will appear.

Field	Description
Year	Enter the fiscal year for which you are maintaining these settings in version 0. You will have to make these settings for each fiscal year.
Version Locked	Set this flag if you want to freeze the version after a certain time of the year. If selected, you cannot make changes to the planning anymore.
Integrated Planning	Set this flag if you want to transfer plan data from cost centers to profit centers. Because you are using profit centers and cost centers in your organization, you need to select this checkbox.
Copying Allowed	Set this flag if you want to copy plan versions from one to another to create different planning versions in which you can make version-specific changes.
Exchange Rate Type	Enter the key for how you will store exchange rates in the exchange type system. For our scenario, select P—Standard translation for cost planning.
Value Date	You can enter a specific date if you want that same date to be used for the planning translation. If you leave this field blank, the SAP system will calculate the exchange rate on a periodic basis and track any currency fluctuations.
Integrated planning with cost centers/bus processes	Set this flag if you want to integrate cost center planning with internal orders and WBS elements. By setting this flag, you are ensuring that planned order settlements (cost allocations) will be picked up in Cost Center Accounting.

Table 8.4 Settings for each fiscal year

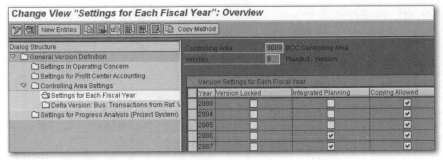

Figure 8.5 Settings for Each Fiscal Year: Overview

After completing your settings, save your version. In the next step, we will maintain the settings from a Profit Center Accounting point of view.

Settings for Profit Center Accounting

You will use the same screen as before (Transaction code OKEQ) to configure the Profit Center Accounting settings:

1. Select the version you are maintaining and then select the settings for Profit Center Accounting.

2. Click on the **New Entries** button and enter the information shown in Table 8.5 in the relevant fields, shown in Figure 8.6.

Field	Description
Year	Enter the fiscal year for which the version settings are valid.
Online transfer	Activate this setting if you want all transactions to update Profit Center Accounting automatically.
Version Locked	Set this flag if the version should be protected from entries or changes.
Line items	Set this flag if you want to use line item processing for all planning transactions.
ExRate Type	Enter the exchange rate type in this field. In our scenario, we are using exchange rate type "M" which is "Standard translation at average rate".

Table 8.5 Settings for Profit Center Accounting

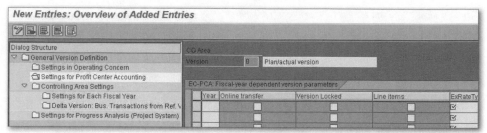

Figure 8.6 Settings for Profit Center Accounting: Overview of Added Entries

3. Save your entries after completing the configuration settings.

This concludes our configuration of the basic controlling area settings. We now move onto the next component, cost element accounting.

8.4.2   Cost Element Accounting

As mentioned previously, cost elements are created as the equivalent of GL accounts in the Controlling Component (CO), and this section looks at their related configuration.

Cost Element Types

Cost elements describe the origin of costs. They are defined as either primary or secondary. *Primary cost elements* represent costs that are incurred from outside of your company. *Secondary cost elements* typically represent activities incurred within your company. The chart of accounts contains all of the GL accounts belonging to SAP ERP Financials.

Cost and revenue accounts in SAP ERP Financials have an identical twin in the Controlling Component (CO) in the form of revenue and cost elements. This ensures that postings from the former are transferred to the latter in real time. This also means that when you create a GL account in SAP ERP Financials, you must create a primary cost element for it in the Controlling Component (CO) so that expenses and so on can be reconciled in both components. Note that you must create the primary cost elements in SAP ERP Financials as GL accounts before you can create them in the Controlling Component (CO), and that you can create secondary cost elements only in the Controlling Component (CO) (they are not represented by a GL account in SAP ERP Financials). You use secondary cost elements to record internal flow of values for activities such as assessments in Cost Center Accounting and settlements in internal orders.

Once you have created a primary cost element for a GL account, it is important to assign an object, such as cost center or internal order, to it so that when the information flows to the Controlling Component (CO) from SAP ERP Financials, you know exactly where the cost originated. Also, at the time of creation of cost elements, you are required to assign a cost element category that actually determines the type of transactions for which you can use that cost element. One example would be category 01 primary cost elements used for expense postings.

There are two methods for creating cost elements in the system. One is to create them automatically, and the second is to create them manually. In the next steps, we will explain both of these methods.

Creating Cost Elements Automatically

You can create cost elements automatically by creating a batch run. For this, you provide the default settings for the cost element or the cost element range you want to create and enter the cost element types for the cost elements.

Primary cost elements are only created when the respective GL account exists in the operational chart of accounts, and the SAP system takes the cost element name from the GL account master data in SAP ERP Financials. You can, however, change the name in the Controlling Component (CO).

You can also configure that when you create a GL account, a cost element is automatically created. If you use this function, you need to ensure that the range mentioned for the creation of cost elements includes the account numbers that might trigger creation of cost elements automatically.

You can create secondary cost elements for all cost elements you have defined in the settings. The system takes the description from the cost element category. Once you have entered your default settings, a background session starts that generates the cost elements.

Follow these steps to configure the default settings for automatic cost element creation:

1. Follow the path **IMG • Controlling • Overhead cost controlling • Cost and revenue element accounting • Master data • Cost elements • Automatic**

creation of cost elements • **Make default settings**, or use Transaction code OKB2.

▶ In the screen that displays, as shown in Figure 8.7, enter the information as explained in Table 8.6.

Field	Description
Account from **Account to**	Enter the range of the accounts in these two fields.
CElem cat.	Enter the cost element category that corresponds to the account range specified in the **Account from** and **Account to** fields.
Short text	The short text will be defaulted from the category specified in the **CElem cat.** field.

Table 8.6 Automatic Cost Element Generation Settings

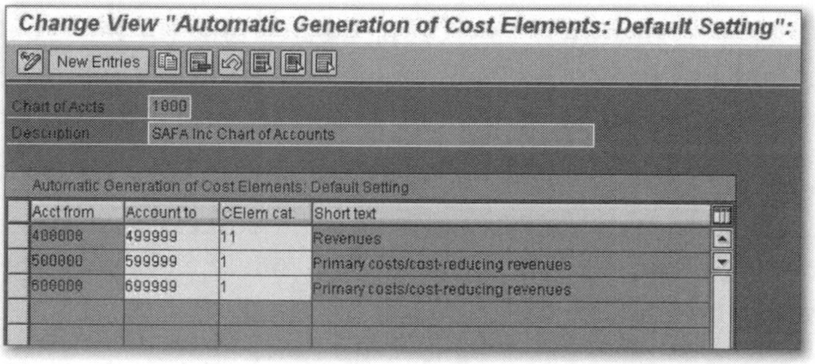

Figure 8.7 Automatic Generation of Cost Elements: Default Setting

After completing the default settings, you are now ready to create the batch input session for creating the cost elements:

2. Follow the menu path **IMG • Controlling • Overhead cost controlling • Cost and revenue element accounting • Master Data • Cost Elements • Automatic creation of cost elements • Create batch input session**, or use Transaction code OKB3.

▶ Enter the information in the fields as detailed in Table 8.7 and shown in Figure 8.8.

Field	Description
Controlling Area	Enter the controlling area ID in which the cost elements should be created.
Valid from	Enter the date from which the cost elements will be valid.
Valid To	Enter the date to which these cost elements will be valid.
Session Name	The ID of the person who is creating this session will be defaulted into this field. You can also make any other entry in this field.
Batch input user	The ID of the person who is creating this session will be defaulted in this field. You can also make any other entry in this field.

Table 8.7 Create Batch Input Session to Create Cost Element Settings

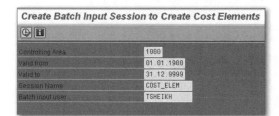

Figure 8.8 Create Batch Input Session to Create Cost Elements

▶ Click on the execute icon to create the batch input session. A session log will appear with details of the cost elements to be created.

▶ Review this log to identify any missing or unnecessary entries.

You run the batch job either online or in the background:

3. Follow the menu path **IMG • Controlling • Overhead cost controlling • Cost and revenue element accounting • Master Data • Cost Elements • Automatic creation of cost elements • Execute batch input session**, or use Transaction code SM35.

▶ Select the batch session you created earlier and execute it. To run the batch session in the background, select the **Background** option in the dialog box that displays and then click on the **Process** button.

This completes our discussion of creating cost elements automatically. Next, we will create cost elements manually.

Note

Manual creation of cost elements is not a configuration step and is processed through the **User** menu in Cost Element Accounting.

Creating Cost Elements Manually

To create a cost element manually:

1. Follow the SAP menu path **SAP Easy Access • Accounting • Controlling • Cost Elements • Master Data • Cost Elements • Create primary/secondary cost elements**, or use Transaction code KA01 (primary cost element) or KA06 (secondary cost element)

2. In the screen that displays, **Create Cost Element: Inital Screen**, shown in Figure 8.9, enter the information as explained in Table 8.8.

Field	Description
Cost Element	Enter the number of the primary or secondary cost element.
Valid from	Enter the validity from period.
Valid to	Enter the validity to period.
Cost Element	You can enter the number of the cost element from another controlling area as a reference to create the new cost element.
Controlling Area	You can enter the number of the controlling area that contains the cost element to use as a reference to create the new cost element.

Table 8.8 Create Cost Element: Initial Screen Settings

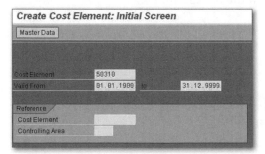

Figure 8.9 Create Cost Element: Initial Screen

3. Press Enter to move to the next screen.

4. Enter the information outlined in Table 8.9, on the corresponding tabs shown in Figure 8.10 and Figure 8.11.

Basic Data tab	
Field	**Description**
Name	Enter the name of the cost element you are creating.
Description	Enter the description of the cost element are creating.
CElem Category	As explained earlier, select the cost element category from the options available, such as 1 for primary cost elements and 11 for primary revenue elements, as shown in Figure 8.10.
Default Acct Assgnmt tab	
Field	**Description**
Cost Center **Order**	If you have a GL account to which you want to default a specific cost center or internal order, you can define it here. Whenever this GL account is posted to, the system defaults the account assignment you specify here.

Table 8.9 Create Cost Element: Basic Screen Settings

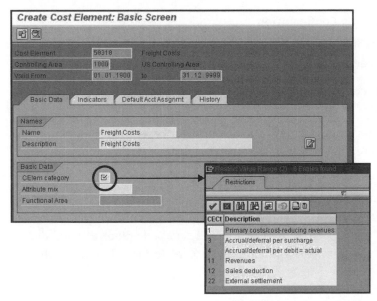

Figure 8.10 Create Cost Element: Basic Data Tab

Figure 8.11 Create Cost Elements: Default Acct Assgnmt Tab

Now you have learned how to create cost elements both automatically and manually and how to create a link between SAP ERP Financials and the Controlling Component (CO), as these cost elements are the carriers of cost from the former to the latter. This concludes our discussion of Cost Element Accounting. Next we look at Cost Center Accounting.

8.4.3 Cost Center Accounting

Cost Center Accounting is used to collect and report cost activity for defined locations or activities. Cost centers are maintained within a hierarchy structure that reflects internal reporting requirements. This hierarchy development is the key to all of the cost accounting reporting within the Controlling Component (CO).

Cost Center Accounting Configuration

Before we start our configuration of Cost Center Accounting, recall some of the key assumptions we made at the start of this chapter:

▸ Cost will flow directly to the responsible cost centers, so no cost allocations are required at the end of the month.

▸ Because we are not making any cost allocations, concepts such as statistical key figures and activity types that are used to trace costs as well as allocating internal activities are not discussed in this chapter.

One of the most important areas in the configuration of Cost Center Accounting is the standard hierarchy. This will be your backbone for reporting operating costs as part of your internal reporting analysis and will act as one repository for all cost centers. In the next section, you will learn how to create a standard hierarchy.

Standard Hierarchy for Cost Center Accounting

Cost centers cannot be created within the Controlling Component (CO) unless you have completed the standard hierarchy. Earlier in the chapter when we were configuring settings for the controlling area, we entered the hierarchy name for our cost centers and said that this will be used as the topmost (main) node in our hierarchy. However, cost centers cannot be attached to the main node; therefore, you have to create lower-level nodes to which you assign cost centers.

> **Note**
>
> The hierarchy structure needs to reflect your internal reporting requirements and should be finalized at the blueprint stage; otherwise it would be very time consuming to make changes to the hierarchy later.

The standard hierarchy can be developed from either the IMG or the user menu, as follows:

1. Use the path **SAP Easy Access** • **Accounting** • **Controlling** • **Cost Centers** • **Master Data** • **Cost Center Group** • **Change** or Transaction code KSH2. The Change Cost Center Group: Initial screen will appear.

2. Enter the top node mentioned when you created the controlling area in this field.

3. Add new hierarchy nodes to this structure. Within this structure, you should include all cost centers, so it is important that your hierarchy represents your organization's internal structure accurately.

Ultimately, your hierarchy should look similar to that shown in Figure 8.12.

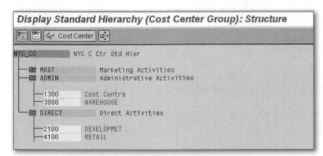

Figure 8.12 Standard Hierarchy for Cost Centers

Next, we need to talk about cost center categories.

Create Cost Center Category

For our purpose, the use of cost center categories is restricted to providing default control indicators to cost centers at creation time and at the time of assigning functional areas and reporting. Like many other standard settings provided in the system, you have an option to use the SAP-delivered cost center categories (which are changeable), or you can create your own categories if the ones provided by the SAP system are not sufficient. Follow these steps to create your own cost center categories:

1. Follow the path **IMG • Controlling • Cost Center Accounting • Master data • Cost Centers • Define cost center categories**. The screen shown in Figure 8.13 appears.

2. Click on the **New Entries** button and configure the fields as explained in Table 8.10.

Field	Description
CCtC	Enter a single character category ID in this alphanumeric field.
Name	Enter the name of the category.
Qty	Set this indicator if you want to retain quantity. information in the cost center.
ActPri	Set this flag if you want actual primary costs to be tracked.
ActSec	Set this flag if you want actual secondary costs to be tracked.
ActRev	Set this flag if you want to restrict the posting of revenues to a cost center created under this category.
PlnPri	Set this flag if you want to block the category from planning costs.
PlnSec	Set this flag if you want to block the category from planning secondary costs.
PlnRev	Set this flag if you want to block the category from planning revenues.
Cmmt	Set this flag if you want commitments to be tracked on the cost centers. This setting makes sense if you have activated commitment management.

Table 8.10 Create Cost Center Categories—Settings

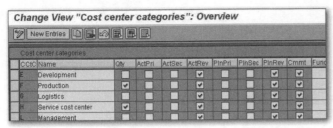

Figure 8.13 Create Cost Center Categories

We are now ready to create cost centers in our controlling area, so we will do this next.

Create Cost Centers

To create cost centers, follow these steps:

1. Follow the User menu **SAP Easy Access • Accounting • Controlling • Cost Center Accounting • Master Data • Cost Center • Individual processing • Create**, or use Transaction code KS01. Alternatively, you can create cost centers from the IMG.

2. The **Create Cost Center: Initial Screen** will appear, as shown in Figure 8.14. Use the information shown in Table 8.11 to complete this screen.

Field	Description
Cost Center	Enter the cost center number you are creating.
Valid From **to**	Enter the validity period during which postings can be made to this cost center.
Cost center (in **Reference** area)	You can use an already created cost Center as a reference to create a new cost Center. To do so, enter the cost Center number you want to use as a reference.
Controlling area (in **Reference** area)	Enter the controlling area in which this reference cost center is created.

Table 8.11 Create Cost Element: Initial Screen—Settings

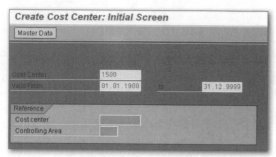

Figure 8.14 Create Cost Center: Initial Screen

3. Press enter, and the **Create Cost Center: Basic Screen** will appear, with the **Basic data** tab active, as shown in Figure 8.15. Complete the fields on the **Basic data** tab using the information provided in Table 8.12.

Field	Description
Name	Enter the name of the cost center in this field.
Description	Enter the description of the cost center in this field.
Person responsible	Enter the name of the person in charge of this cost center.
Department	Enter the name of the department to which this cost center relates.
Cost Center Category	Enter the cost center category you created earlier.
Hierarchy area	Enter the cost center hierarchy node under which this cost center is going to be attached.
Business Area	If you are using business area functionality, enter the business area.
Functional Area	Enter the functional area.
Currency	Enter the currency. Remember that this field will only be available for input if all of the company codes have the same currency as that of the controlling area; otherwise this field will be grayed out, and the currency of the company code will be defaulted in.
Profit Center	If Profit Center Accounting is active, enter the profit center to which this cost center belongs.

Table 8.12 Create Cost Center: Settings

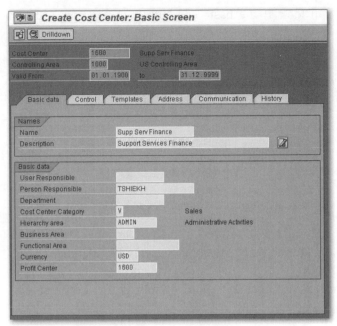

Figure 8.15 Create Cost Center: Basic Screen

4. On the **Control** tab, you have certain activities related to cost centers that you can **Lock** depending on your requirements. Remember that the settings we configured at the time of definition of the cost center category are reflected in this part of the screen. For our cost center, we will lock the revenue postings to this cost center, that is, both actual as well as planned, as shown in Figure 8.16.

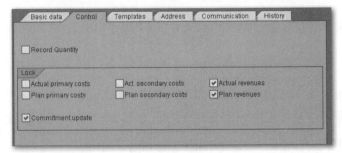

Figure 8.16 Create Cost Center: Control Tab

We have now created a cost center and completed the basic configuration for the cost center. You can now start using it for postings in SAP ERP Financials as explained in Chapter 4.

In the next section, we will look at the basic configuration steps for internal orders.

8.4.4 Internal Order Accounting Configuration

As we have already seen in Section 8.4.1, we have activated order management for SAFA Inc. because we would like to use internal orders for tracking costs for specific activities.

Order Types

One of the most important concepts in internal order accounting is order types. You always create an internal order with reference to an order type. Order types pass on certain settings to the internal orders that are created with reference to that order type. Order types are also created at the client level and are available to any controlling area within that client. In general, there are four types of orders.

▶ **Overhead cost order**
These monitor costs related to internal activities settled to cost centers.

▶ **Investment order**
These monitor costs related to internal activities settled to fixed assets.

▶ **Accrual order**
These offset postings for accrued costs calculated in the Controlling Component (CO).

▶ **Orders with revenues**
These capture revenue that is not part of the core business of the company's operations.

To define order types:

Follow the IMG path **IMG • Controlling • Internal Orders • Order Master Data • Define Order types**, or use Transaction code KOT2.

1. The **Change View "Order Types": Overview** screen appears. To create a new order type, click on the **New Entries** button.

2. In the next screen, enter the order category "01" for internal orders and press Enter.

3. The New entries: Details of Added Entries screen will appear. Enter the information in the respective sections, as outlined in Table 8.13.

General parameters section	
Field	**Decscription**
Settlement prof.	Enter the settlement profile ID. The settlement profile controls the settlement logic and origin structures. You can use the standard settlement profiles provided by SAP.
Planning profile	Enter the planning profile ID that would be the default setting for this order type. The planning profile controls the settings for planning with internal orders associated with this order type.
Budget Profile	Enter the budget profile ID for this order type. The budget profile controls the budgeting-related settings within orders, and you use this to activate the budget availability control settings for your orders.
Control indicators section	
Field	**Description**
CO Partner Update	You configure this field for updating orders during Controlling Component (CO) cost allocations. You have three options: **Active**, **Semi-active**, and **Not Active**. The standard system setting is **Semi-active**, which means that during settlements between orders, both records will be updated, however during settlement between cost centers and internal orders, cost center record will not be updated with the order details.
Commit. management	If you want to activate commitment management, set this flag. This lets you track commitments at the time of purchase requisitions, purchase orders, and so on.
Revenue postings	If you want to post revenues to your orders, you need to set this flag.
Integrated planning	You set this flag if you want Profit Center Accounting to be updated with internal order planning.
Status management section	
Field	**Description**
Status Profile	If you have activated general status management, you must enter the status profile ID.
Release immediately	If you set this flag, orders with this type will be released immediately upon creation.

Table 8.13 Create Order Types: Settings

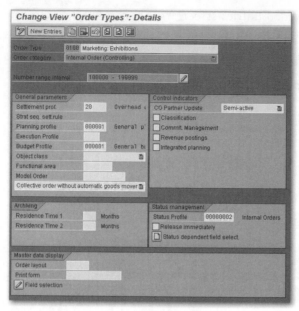

Figure 8.17 Create Order Types: Details

Order Number Range to Order Type Assignment

Next, you need to assign an order number range to the order type:

1. Use the same screen you used to create the new order type and click on the **Number range interval** button, shown earlier in Figure 8.17. This opens the **Maintain Number Range Groups** screen, shown in Figure 8.18. You can use the already created number range groups from this screen, or, if you want to create a new number range, use the **Groups** button on the menu path and select Insert option and then enter the text and the number range interval for this group in the appropriate fields.

2. You can now assign the order type to a number range group. You will find the order type in the Not-Assigned section of the **Maintain Number Range Groups** screen.

3. Select the order type by using the "Select element" icon which highlights the selected order type and then place a checkmark next to the number range group that you created in the previous step.

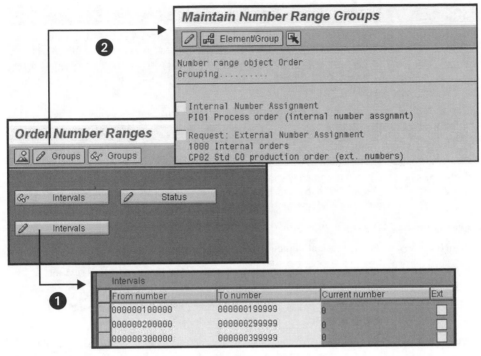

Figure 8.18 Create Internal Order Number Ranges

4. Click on the **Element/Group** button to assign the order type from the Not-Assigned section to the new number range group.

5. Save your settings.

Create Internal Order

You are now ready to create internal orders. These are created in the application side of the system, based on the internal order type.

1. Use the path **SAP Easy Access • Accounting • Controlling • Internal Orders • Master Data • Special functions • Order • Create** or Transaction code KO01. The Create Internal Order: Initial screen will appear. Enter the **Order type** in this screen and press Enter.

2. Use the information in Table 8.14 to configure the **Assignments** tab in the screen shown in Figure 8.19.

Field	Description
Order	Enter the order number in this field. If the order number assignment is an internal number, then this field will be grayed out (unavailable). You will only be allowed to configure this field if the external number assignment is selected for the number range assigned to the number range group settings explained earlier.
Description	Enter the short text for the order in this field.
Assignments tab	
Field	**Description**
Company Code	Enter the company code to which this order would be assigned and remember that you will be required to complete this assignment of an order to a company code at the time of creation of an internal order.
Business Area	If you are using business areas, enter the business area.
Plant	Enter the plant number if you are using production orders.
Functional Area	Enter the functional area in this field (if you are using the cost of sales accounting option in SAP ERP Financials).
Object Class	Select **Overhead**. You could also select **Production**, **Investment**, and **Profit Analysis**.
Profit Center	If Profit Center Accounting is active, enter the profit center to which this order will be assigned.
Responsible ctr	Enter the cost center number that is responsible for this order.
Sales Order	Enter the sales order number for which the internal order will collect costs.

Table 8.14 Create Internal Orders: Assignments Tab Settings

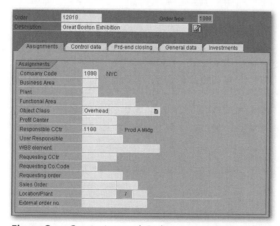

Figure 8.19 Create Internal Order: Assignments Tab

3. Use the information in Table 8.15 to configure the **Control Data** tab in the screen shown in Figure 8.20.

Control data tab	
Field	**Description**
System status (in the **Status** area of the screen)	Shows the current status of the order. The four options are **CRTD** (created), **REL** (released), **Tech Comple** (technically complete) and **CLSD** (closed). You can manually select one of these options depending on the status of the order at that time.
Currency	Enter the currency in which you would like to maintain the order, but the system will default the company code currency in this field. You will only have this option if you are not using cross-company code controlling.
Order category	This field is grayed out (unavailable), as the system has taken this setting from the previously defined order type settings.
Statistical order	This is the setting that determines if the internal order is real or statistical. If you select this checkbox, all of the postings to this order will be for information purposes only, and you will not be able to settle them to other cost objects in the Controlling Component (CO).
Actual posted ctr	Enter the cost center to which this posting will be made (in addition to the statistical order as set in the previous field).
Plan-integrated order	If you set this flag, the planned data will be passed on to Profit Center Accounting.
Revenue postings	This setting will be defaulted from the settings made in the order type. If you want to post revenues to your orders, the same setting should be configured at the time of order type creation so that all orders created with that order type have an option of revenue postings.
Commitment update	This setting will also be defaulted from the order type.

Table 8.15 Create Internal Order: Control Data Tab Settings

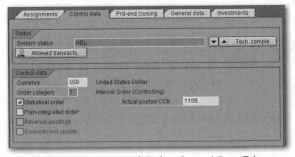

Figure 8.20 Create Internal Order: Control Data Tab

Internal Orders represent a very useful account assignment object in the system to monitor and record costs.

This concludes our discussion of internal orders. We will now look at Profit Center Accounting.

8.4.5 Profit Center Accounting Configuration

In terms of our new GL solution, Profit Center Accounting is not configured separately, as it now exists within the new GL. In a classic Profit Center Accounting scenario, however, an SAP ERP Financials posting will also generate a corresponding Profit Center Accounting posting document. In this section, we cover the steps needed from a classic Profit Center Accounting perspective. The first step is defining a Profit Center Accounting hierarchy.

Define Profit Center Accounting Hierarchy

Because Profit Center Accounting is active within your controlling area—as established earlier—you must create the standard hierarchy from the Profit Center Accounting point of view and create a dummy profit center and assign it to that hierarchy.

> **Note**
>
> The Profit Center Accounting hierarchy is different from the cost center hierarchy, but if the reporting structure requires it to have the same structure, you can create it accordingly.

We have already explained the configuration required to create the Profit Center Accounting standard hierarchy and the default profit center in Chapter 2, Section 2.4.12. These both need to be assigned to the Profit Center Accounting controlling area. The standard hierarchy is shown in Figure 8.21.

This configuration is set in the **SPRO • Enterprise Controlling • Profit Center Accounting • Basic Settings • Controlling Area Settings • Maintain Controlling Area Settings** area of the IMG, or by using Transaction code 0KE5.

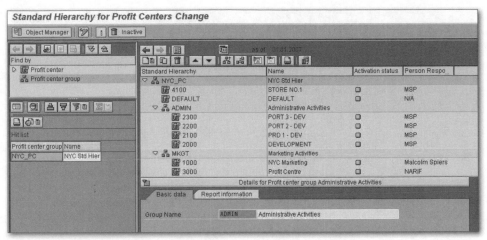

Figure 8.21 Standard Hierarchy for Profit Centers

To enable postings in Profit Center Accounting, you need to configure document types and number ranges that are independent of SAP ERP Financials document types and number ranges. We'll look at this next.

Define Document Types

It is possible, using Profit Center Accounting, to post to an unbalanced entry because the document types typically fall outside the range of those assigned by SAP ERP Financials and the Controlling Component (CO). Therefore, it is important to use the transaction balancing feature in Profit Center Accounting, together with the required document types and number ranges, to enable proper posting.

To define document types for actual postings to Profit Center Accounting:

1. Follow the path **IMG • Controlling • Profit Center Accounting • Actual Postings • Basic Settings: Actual • Maintain Document Type**, or use Transaction code GCBX.

2. The **Change View "Valid Document Types": Overview** screen appears, as shown in Figure 8.22. You can see that SAP has delivered the standard document type **A0**, which can be used if required.

3. If you want to create your own document types, click on the **New Entries** button and enter the information in the fields as outlined in Table 8.16.

Field	Description
Doc. Type	Enter the two-character document type ID.
TC	Set this flag if you want to store the transaction currency at the time of postings.
C2	Set this flag if you want to store postings in a second currency.
C3	Set this flag if you want to store postings in a third currency.
Bal. check	As mentioned, it is possible to post unbalanced entries in Profit Center Accounting, and this is where you configure this function. You can select from three options: 0—This setting will ensure that all entries in Profit Center Accounting are balanced and will give an error message if they are not. 1—This setting will warn you if the entries are not balanced but will still let you post. 2—This setting will not carry out any balance check at the time of postings.
Description	Enter a description for the document type.

Table 8.16 Create Document Type for Profit Center Accounting: Settings

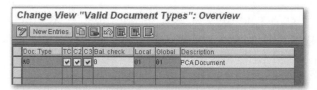

Figure 8.22 Create Document Type for Profit Center Accounting

Number Range Assignment

After completing the definition of your document type, you need to assign a number range to it. To complete this configuration step:

1. Follow the path **IMG • Controlling • Profit Center Accounting • Actual Postings • Basic Settings: Actual • Define Number Ranges for Local Documents**, or use Transaction code GB02.

2. In the **Number ranges for local GL documents** screen, shown in Figure 8.23, click on the Maintain Groups (with pencil icon) button, and the **Maintain number range group** screen will appear. The document type created in the previous step appears in the **Not-Assigned** section of that screen.

3. To assign your document type to a number range group, select the document type by clicking on the **Select Element** button.

Mark the number range group to which your document type should be assigned and then click on the **Element/Group** button. The document type will move to the assigned number range, and you can now create Profit Center Accounting documents.

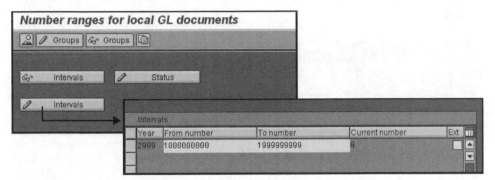

Figure 8.23 Define Number Range for Local GL Documents

We will now look at setting up master data to enable postings.

Create Profit Centers

You create a profit center using the same process as when we created the dummy profit center earlier (see Section 8.4.5 and Chapter 2, Section 2.4.12). The menu path is **SAP Easy Access • Controlling • Profit Center Accounting • Master Data • Profit Center • Individual Processing • Create**, or you can use Transaction code KE51.

In the next section we will establish how the postings from other areas pass through to Profit Center Accounting.

Profit Center Determination

As you have already seen, when a cost center or internal order is created, we have assigned a profit center in the object's master record. This means that when any entry is made in the cost center or internal order, profit center information is updated automatically. This also ensures that if you are reviewing the postings in

Profit Center Accounting, you can tell which cost object was used at the time of the original entry, that is, the cost center or the internal order. Further, this means that all of the entries come from postings from other objects, and they are only mirrored in Profit Center Accounting.

Before looking at some more steps required to ensure that all entries pass through to Profit Center Accounting without errors, you need to understand the rules for profit center determination, in order of their priority. Table 8.17 explains these rules briefly.

Scenario/Rule	Description
Substitution rule exists in SAP ERP Financials or in the Controlling Component (CO)	If you have set a substitution rule in SAP ERP Financials or the Controlling Component (CO) to determine the profit center, this will have the highest priority at the time of profit center determination.
Entry using cost or revenue element	If the data is transferred using a cost or revenue element, the profit center will always be determined from the master records of cost centers or internal orders assigned to them at the time of entry.
Entry using balance sheet accounts or profit and loss accounts	If at the time of entry to a balance sheet account or profit and loss account, no profit center was mentioned and you have configured a setting in the configuration step "Choose additional balance sheet and profit and loss accounts" (explained later in this chapter), then the system will determine the profit center using this setting.
No profit center is mentioned in the posting document	The system will post to the dummy profit center where it cannot determine the profit center from the posting document.

Table 8.17 Rules for Profit Center Determination

After you have established the rules for Profit Center Accounting determination, you can define some more settings in Profit Center Accounting to ensure that the profit center is determined properly. We need to cover two main steps, including automatic account assignment and choose additional balance sheet and profit and loss accounts as explained below.

Automatic Account Assignment

In this setting, you enter the company code and cost element combination and configure default settings in the system to specify that for this combination of company code and cost element, if the system cannot find a valid profit center, the entries should go to a specific profit center. Again, the idea is to ensure that no postings are made in the system without assignment to a valid profit center. Proceed as follows:

1. Follow the path **IMG • Controlling • Profit Center Accounting • Actual Postings • Maintain Automatic Account Assignments**, or use Transaction code OKB9.

2. On the **Change View "Default account assignment"** screen, click on the New Entries button and the New Entries: Overview of Added Entries screen will appear as shown in Figure 8.24. Enter the relevant information in this screen, as explained in Table 8.18.

Field	Description
Company code	Enter the company code ID for which you are maintaining this setting.
CostElem.	Enter the cost element that will derive the assignment.
BA	Set this indicator if you are using business areas and would like a business area posting with the entry.
Cost Ctr	Enter the cost center the system will use as a default.
Order	Enter the order the system will use as a default.
Profit Ctr	Enter the profit center the system will use as a default. This setting can be configured for revenue elements only.
Acct assignmt detail	Three settings are available: **Valuation area is mandatory** **Business area is mandatory** **Profit Center is mandatory** This setting lets you carry out account assignment by valuation area other than business areas and company code.

Table 8.18 Default Account Assignments: Settings

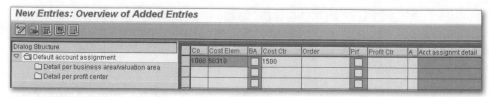

Figure 8.24 Maintain Automatic Account Assignments

Choose Additional Balance Sheet and Profit and Loss Accounts

We will now take profit center determination one step further by defining balance sheet accounts and profit and loss accounts in a table where they will have an assignment to a specific profit center. This ensures that all entries flow to Profit Center Accounting without any errors should a profit center not have been specified at the time of data entry. The path is **IMG • Controlling • Profit Center Accounting • Actual postings • Choose Additional Balance Sheet and P&L Accounts • Choose Accounts**, or you can use Transaction code 3KEH. You'll see the screen shown in Figure 8.25.

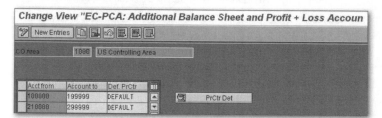

Figure 8.25 Choose Additional Balance Sheet and Profit and Loss Accounts

In this table you enter the account number range and the profit center to which it should post if a profit center is not entered at the time of document entry.

> **Note**
>
> Remember that you can transfer certain balance sheet accounts, such as fixed assets, materials, and work in process, to Profit Center Accounting on a real-time or periodic basis. However, accounts receivables or accounts payables can only be transferred to Profit Center Accounting on a periodic basis.

8.5   Summary

In this chapter we have looked at the Controlling Component (CO) settings from a very simplistic point of view. In reality, it is a very comprehensive area, and even if your internal reporting requirements are complex, it has all of the necessary tools to meet your requirements.

The key learning points of this chapter were:

- ▶ Understanding the basics of the Controlling Component (CO)
- ▶ Understanding the concept of real and statistical postings
- ▶ Understanding the basic configuration settings for cost element accounting, cost center accounting, internal orders and Profit Center accounting
- ▶ Understanding how to create the master data in these components
- ▶ Understanding how profit centers are determined

In Chapter 9, we look at the integration areas of SAP ERP Financials to understand how different components interact with this component.

A huge selling point of SAP ERP is its integrated nature, and in this chapter we review integration configuration functionality. This chapter includes the complex area of Account Determination, and for the reader this is an excellent chapter of knowledge to acquire.

9   ERP Financials Integration

One of the main reasons organizations decide to implement an Enterprise Resource Planning (ERP) solution is to use a single application to deliver the organizations desired business functionality. Historically, organizations installed applications called "best of breed," for example, the best accounting software package alongside the best sales ledger software, alongside the best financial software, and so on. Best of breed implied that each software package was the best at its specific function. The communication between these individual systems occurred through a number of electronic interfaces.

ERP systems, on the other hand, typically provide an integrated solution for all of the business processes, that is, procurement, stock management, logistics, invoicing and accounting, and so on, and a good ERP system should deliver a "seamless link" between the components for these different business functions in terms of navigation and communication.

To this end, implementing an SAP system offers organizations the opportunity to have all of the key business functions integrated within a single application. We refer to this as the integrated solution that SAP offers organizations.

Beyond just the ability to integrate, it is very important for different functionalities to integrate well. This is a classic issue in large projects where individual teams sometimes end up working in isolation, and the eventual solution you put together does not work. If you are new to SAP projects, this may not seem like a huge issue, but let us give you an example that may seem a little comical but represents a good analogy to what can happen if integration isn't happening or being considered.

> **The Car Project**
>
> I hired a group of external consultants to help with a car-building project. The consultants were split into teams, reflecting their individual skills and experience. Within each team, some of my own organization's employees were added, to provide business knowledge and represent my views.
>
> Further, I gave each team a name depending on the team's role. The fuel tank and tires were being designed and built by a team called MM. The external design and color, which we wanted to be attractive to potential customers, was handled by the SD team. The engine was built and designed by the FI team. All of these teams had a significant number of members, so they were accommodated in the same open plan office area on the same floor in one of our company's offices. Since they had a significant amount of work to do, they also had use of meeting rooms where they could have the space to finalize their designs and test their builds.
>
> After many months of work, each team completed their design, and built and tested it within their areas. The time had come for all of the teams to bring their prototypes together and combine the parts of the car. Because all of the teams had confirmed that their individual designs worked, what could go wrong?
>
> Because the individual teams built their designs in isolation and did not spend any time confirming whether their solutions fit within the collection, the following ended up happening:
>
> ▸ The gas tanks were small because the MM team didn't believe that they should hold a lot of gasoline.
>
> ▸ The tires were large and provided a lot of stability, but the design hindered the ability to accelerate.
>
> ▸ The outside of the car looked extremely modern and was very pleasing to the eye. The team also added in as many luxuries to the car as possible, which, however, increased the fuel consumption levels drastically.
>
> ▸ The engine, the heart of the car, was very small and modern in design to provide efficiency. Its cost efficiency was, however, achieved by running on solar power.

From this slightly comical example, you can see the lack of an integrated approach to design and the resulting non-integrated solution. The obvious question arises, why don't consultants just talk to each other?

In a successful project, integration must occur on three levels:

▸ **Process**
The business processes need some alignment to ensure that there is end-to-end cohesion in your design. The common approach is to create process flow diagrams, which summarize the overall blueprint documents. A common flaw is to

not link the flow diagrams together. For instance, having an "end node" saying "see other process" is not sufficient. You should be able to match an end node on one diagram to a point on another diagram.

▶ **Functionality**
A consistent use of functionality is important to ensure that the overall solution is consistent. In our car-building example, all teams should have agreed that the car would be powered by a solar power source, in which case all designs would have been based on a consistent functionality basis.

▶ **Technology**
This may appear to be the most obvious, but it is critical to the overall integration of the final solution. The technologies involved in any interfaces, printers, scanners, or point of sale equipment should all integrate to your SAP system. Sometimes there are issues in communications even with your desktop software due to firewalls or other technology. These all need to be addressed.

Of these three, in this chapter we are concerned primarily with the functionality integration. Technology is outside of our scope, but there will be some discussion of process. More specifically, the scope for this chapter covers the following areas:

▶ Automatic account determination

▶ Master data

▶ Internal and external interfaces

At the end of this chapter you will be aware of the key integration points related to finance. In addition, the chapter will explain configuration as well as the impact of the choices you make. We will now start by looking at our first topic, automatic account determination.

9.1   Automatic Account Determination

SAP ERP is completely integrated across all modules, which means that transactions in the Materials Management or Sales and Distribution components will generate appropriate postings in GL. In configuration you can define rules which are based on the transaction in the Stock and Sales component to determine which GL Accounts are posted to, and this is what we call Automatic Account Determination.

We will review the main areas by subcomponent; you should select those that are relevant for your own organization. We will start by looking at the purchase to pay (P2P) related account determinations. To understand this, we first remind ourselves of the P2P cycle in Figure 9.1.

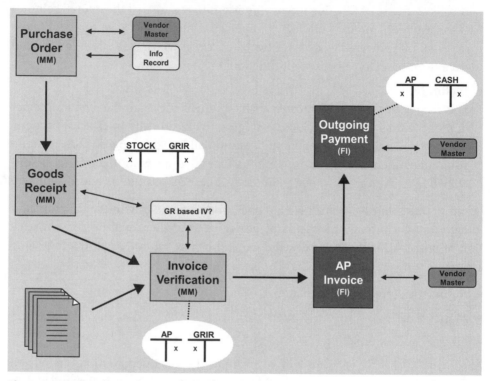

Figure 9.1 The Purchase to Pay Cycle

Two sets of account determination occur within this area: inventory movement-related and outgoing payments-related. First, we will look at inventory movement-related account determination.

9.1.1 Inventory Movement–Related Account Determination

The movement of inventory generates a range of GL postings. In this section, we summarize the key inventory-related transaction keys that you can use. These transaction keys are initiated within the Materials Management (MM) component. For each transaction key, there is a related movement type that is related to one of the transactions listed in Table 9.1.

When you configure each key, you need to first define the rules for the key. Under the rules you select the subdivisions for that key. For instance, for the BSX key, you may decide that there needs to be a different GL account defined for different valuation areas that are defined within MM. You may also decide for some keys to define different accounts depending on whether the transaction line posting to them is a debit or a credit entry. The transaction key is triggered by a movement type, and it is possible to configure customized movement types and transaction keys to meet your specific requirements.

For each key, you should consider your own business requirements and be aware of the overall project design across the purchase to pay cycle. For a complete understanding of this process, you should consult an MM configuration guide.

GL Account Name Purpose	SAFA Inc. Account Number	Transaction Key
Stock *This account is the stock GL account which reflects the value of stock held in the system.*	15510	BSX
Stock take on *This is the data migration used for the take on account for the migration of stock items from the legacy system.*	15511	GBB-BSA
Stock write off *This is the expense GL account to which we write off stock value due to destruction or obsolescence.*	60380	GBB-VNG
Material consumption *The material consumption account is where we expense materials which are consumed by the business. We have two material consumption accounts that will be posted to, depending on the materials valuation class.*	50111 50112	GBB-VBR
Goods received invoice received *This is the clearing account that is posted to (see chapter 5, section 5.1).*	15650	WRX
Freight charges *This account receives all planned and unplanned freight charges.*	50310	FR1 & UPF
Customs charges *This account is where all customs charges will be posted to.*	50320	FR3

Table 9.1 GL Accounts Assigned for Inventory-Related GL Postings

The GL accounts shown in Table 9.1 should be known to you to complete this configuration. For our sample scenario, we have also included the appropriate GL account number from the SAFA Inc. chart of accounts. This configuration is controlled at the chart of accounts level, so all company codes assigned to this chart of accounts are affected by these settings.

Inventory-related account determination is configured using the path **IMG • Materials Management • Valuation and Account Assignment • Account Determination • Account Determination without Wizard • Configure Automatic Postings.** From within the screen that displays, click on **Account Assignment** and you will be taken to the screen as seen in Figure 9.2. I tend to go straight to this screen via Transaction code OBYC.

Note

If you find the MM area of the IMG a little confusing, you might find accessing this screen from the OBYC Transaction code a little easier.

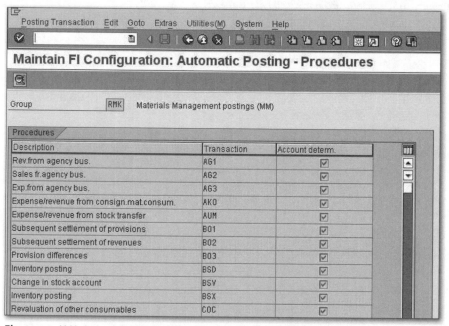

Figure 9.2 MM Automatic Posting Procedures: Configuration Table

The configuration of each key is based on three screens:

▸ **Posting Key**
Lets you define the financial posting keys that are triggered by this key.

▸ **Rules**
Lets you select the relevant rules for this key. For instance, against BSX you can select **Valuation modif.** (valuation modifier) and **Valuation class**, which allow you to enter a GL account for this combination.

▸ **Accounts**
Lets you assign the actual GL accounts that are posted to, based on the combination specified within the rules.

Figure 9.3 shows an example of the first key we are configuring, **Transaction** key **BSX**. Note, here you only see two buttons, **Accounts and Posting Key** as we are already in the **Rules** as you can see by the screen heading.

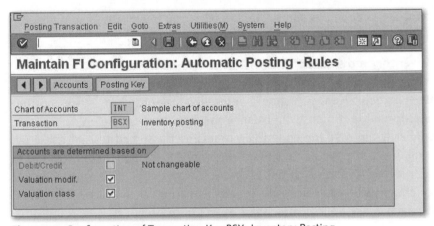

Figure 9.3 Configuration of Transaction Key BSX: Inventory Posting

We mentioned in this example the use of valuation classes, which lets you segregate postings based on the type of material being used in the transaction. If you have activated this field as a rule, you can assign different GL accounts for each valuation class. Figure 9.4 shows several standard valuation classes. Because every organization is different, you are also able to configure your own valuation classes to suit your own requirements. Also note that material master records are assigned to valuation classes.

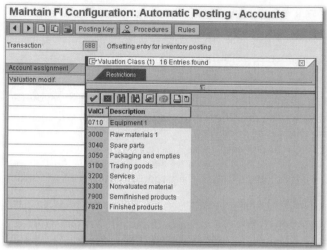

Figure 9.4 Examples of Material Valuation Classes

The following are some of the transaction keys that you may want to configure for your own solution:

▶ **BSX—Inventory movement**
This transaction key is used to post the value of incoming materials to your nominated account. Here you should enter your balance sheet stock account. In standard solution designs, the balance sheet account can reference a profit center. Your design may incorporate a profit center assigned to each material, which will then be derived onto any inventory postings made with reference to this material. The limitation of this is that you may not be able to divide your range of materials for specific profit centers. If you want to divide your stock, you may need to use the valuation class as an indicator.

▶ **WRX—GR/IR clearing account (GRIR)**
This transaction key is used in all solutions that involve the implementation of MM. This account is a clearing account that allows you to reconcile the receipt of goods (into stock) and the appropriate payment of invoices that vendors send you in relation to these goods. Refer back to Figure 9.1, which shows the postings made to the GRIR account:

▶ **Goods Receipt**

   ▶ Debit   Stock

   ▶ Credit   GR IR

▶ **Invoice Verification**

    ▶ Debit   GR IR

    ▶ Credit   Vendor

You should periodically reconcile and clear off your GRIR account. This can be achieved by running Transaction MR11.

▶ **UPF — Unplanned Freight, Customs, and Delivery Costs**
This transaction key is used to post freight, customs, and delivery costs. These costs are defined as separate lines on the purchase order and thus post to the FR1 (Freight) and FR3 (Customs) accounts. Unplanned delivery charges are captured at the point of invoice entry (as part of the MIRO transaction).

▶ **UMB Stock Revaluation or Price Change**
This transaction key is triggered by changing the standard price of materials, you transact a gain or loss in the value of your stock of materials if you are using a standard price solution. If you are adopting a moving average price scenario, then your stock value and material price will automatically be in line. Material price changes can be achieved through Transaction mr21.

▶ **PRD/PRA Purchase Price Variance**
This transaction key is triggered when there is a difference in the price of a material that occurs at any time after a purchase order is created. Such a change will then effect the value of goods being receipted — this difference triggers this key. This is slightly different from UMB, which is a specific revaluation of stock.

▶ **GBB Inventory Offsetting**
This transaction key is used to determine the offset account for inventory postings for valuated stock. There are numerous sub-keys within the GBB area that you may choose to use.

▶ Table 9.2 is a comprehensive list of sub-keys and their purposes. You should enter the GL accounts you want to post to if the relevant key is triggered. Leave those you don't want to use untouched.

▶ The rules for all of these sub-keys are defined under the superior key, in that you can segregate the postings rules by:

▶ Debit and credit

▶ General modifier (subkey, e.g., AUA)

- ▶ Valuation modifier
- ▶ Valuation class (configurable for materials)

Sub-key	Description
AUA	For order settlement.
AUF	For goods receipts for orders (without account assignment) and for order settlement if AUA is not maintained.
AUI	Subsequent adjustment of actual price from cost center directly to material (with account assignment).
BSA	For initial upload of materials to the SAP system. This is explained in more detail in Chapter 10, Data Migration.
DST	For physical stock adjustments that may occur on a periodic or ad hoc basis.
INV	For assigning the GL account relevant for posting any gains or losses due to inventory differences.
VAX	For goods issues for sales orders *without an* account assignment object. This posting must go to a balance sheet code only.
VAY	For goods issues for sales orders *with* an account assignment object. This posting must go to a balance sheet code only.
VBR	For internal goods issues for internal consumption. This key confirms the account to which your material is being consumed. In our example, we have specified two "cost of sales" accounts to which we will post our costs, and which are dependent on the valuation class.
VKA	For sales order account assignment in a make to order scenario (for example, for an individual purchase order).
VKP	For project account assignment (for example, for an individual purchase order).
VNG	For defining the GL account that is posted to for any scrapping or destruction write off of stock.
ZOB	For goods receipts without purchase orders (mvt type 501).
ZOF	For goods receipts without production orders (mvt types 521 and 531).

Table 9.2 Inventory Offsetting, transaction GBB Sub-Keys

In this section we have looked at the direct approach to configuring the automatic account determination rules. You can use the **MM Account Determination Wizard**, shown in Figure 9.5, to complete the configuration.

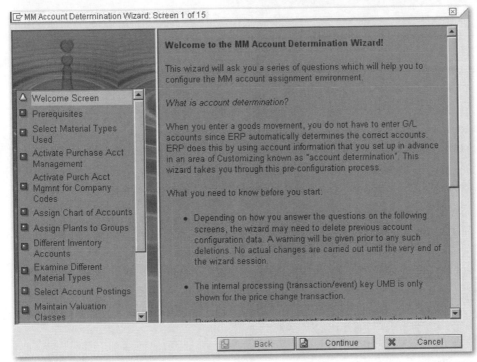

Figure 9.5 MM Account Determination Wizard

Checking your Configuration

Within the same area of the IMG, the system provides you with a tool to check the settings you have made to see which accounts will be determined from your settings. Perform these steps:

1. Follow the path **IMG • Materials Management • Valuation and Account Assignment • Account Determination • Account Determination without Wizard • Configure Automatic Postings.**

2. You will see the Automatic Posting screen shown in Figure 9.6.

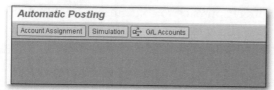

Figure 9.6 MM Automatic Postings

3. If you click on **Account Assignment**, you will find the MM automatic posting procedures (shown earlier in Figure 9.2), as already discussed.

4. If you click on the **Simulation** and **GL Accounts** buttons, you can find useful tools to allow you to test what account determinations will result from your configuration settings.

5. Figure 9.7 shows the use of both of these options. You should use them to test your configuration settings before you release your configuration for testing.

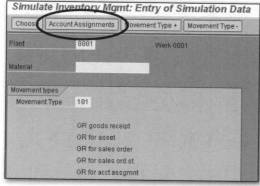

Figure 9.7 Simulate Tools to Test MM Account Determination Settings Made

Next, we will look at order-to-cash account determination. We will come back to look at payments processing at a later point in this chapter.

9.1.2 Billing: Revenue Account Determination

As we discussed in Chapter 6, Billing is a part of the Order to cash cycle, and so the postings to GL will be revenue related. Before looking at the configuration settings for revenue account determination, let us first refresh our minds about the process we are configuring, as shown in Figure 9.8.

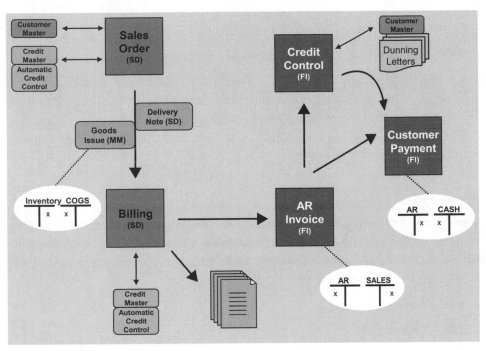

Figure 9.8 The Order-to-Cash Cycle

Since Billing is part of Sales & Distribution (SD) this configuration activity is sometimes configured by a combination of the FI and SD consultants.

Within this cycle, two sets of account determination are configured; the main area is for customer billing purposes, which we will look at first.

Billing is the process by which we convert a customer sales order into an invoice that the customer will pay. Billing can be a very complicated process if you are dealing with a multicountry customer base. In that scenario, complications arise around the treatment of your customers in terms of taxes, freight charges, customs charges, and so on. For the purposes of our discussion, we have assumed that SAFA Inc. only bills customers within their own region. This assumption provides an explanation of how this configuration works. If your scenario is more complicated than this, you need to review your information with your SD configuration consultant to understand the differences that arise.

The configuration for revenue account determination is completed in the following part of the IMG: **IMG • Sales and Distribution • Basic Functions • Account Assignment / Costing • Revenue Account Determination**.

Whereas procure to pay worked off movement types, in SD, the basic configuration object is the account determination procedure. This drives the controls from which we determine the account determination. These procedures are assigned to billing types (e.g., invoice, credit, etc.), which are similar to Financial Accounting Component (FI) document types.

Account Keys

The default SAP revenue account determination procedure that can be used by most implementations is known as KOFI. Within this procedure you have available to you predefined account keys that represent different types of revenues, and will meet most of your requirements:

- **ERF**—Freight revenues
- **ERL**—Revenues
- **ERS**—Sales deductions
- **EVV**—Cash settlement
- **MWS**—Sales tax

For each of these you need to determine which GL account should receive the posting. If you need additional keys, you can create them to provide additional coding requirements.

In our example, we have chosen to assign sales within the 40000–44999 GL account number range, so the revenue key should point in this range. Specifically, we want to provide the analysis shown in Table 9.3 from our sales, and we also want our account determination to be posted to automatically.

GL Account	Description
40000	Sales—general
41000	Domestic sales
41100	Domestic—electronic
41200	Domestic—household
42000	International sales
42100	International—electronic
42200	International—household
43100	Miscellaneous—domestic
43200	Miscellaneous—international

Table 9.3 GL Accounts used for Revenue Account Determination

In most instances, all of your revenues will not be posted to a single code, however. To provide subdivisions of these keys, you can define account assignment groups for your customers and materials, as you will see next.

Account Assignment Groups for Customers

You can assign a flag to group together your customers for revenue reporting purposes to the customer master record. You should use this in line with your reporting requirements. For instance, you may want to group your customers into domestic and foreign customers, or you may want to group them by some other category.

For our requirements, we need to have two account groups defined: domestic and international customers. This group is assigned to the customer master record by selecting the correct **Acct assgmt group** field on the customer master record as shown in Figure 9.9.

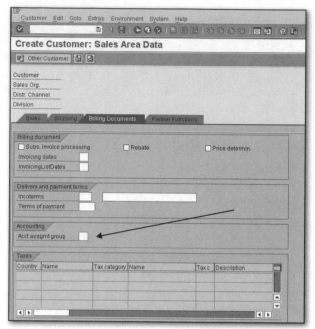

Figure 9.9 Customer Account Assignment Group

Account Assignment Groups for Materials

You can assign a similar flag to your materials, which lets you provide analysis of the sales of these materials. For our requirements, we need three groups for materials: electronic products, household products, and miscellaneous products.

The information we have discussed so far represents the theory behind how billing account determination works from a finance point of view. To deliver these requirements, we now need to make configuration entries into our table using the path **IMG • Sales and Distribution • Basic Functions • Account Assignment/ Costing • Revenue Account Determination • Assign GL Accounts**, or Transaction code VKOA.

Here, as shown in Figure 9.10, you can use tables (levels) to rank the order in which to determine the correct account. You can think of the these tables as a series of sieves, through which you pass conditions, with Table 5 being a pot that catches anything that hasn't been caught by a table above it. As you proceed through the levels, the complexity is reduced in terms of the combinations of characteristics that determine the relevant account, with Table 1 (Cust.Grp/Material/Grp/AcctKey) being the most complex and Table 5 (Acct Key) being the least complex.

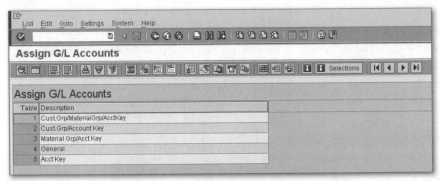

Figure 9.10 Revenue Account Determination Tables

Our configuration requirements are outlined in Table 9.5.

Ref	Key	Customer AAG	Material AAG	GL Acct	Description
1	ERL			40000	Sales—general
2	ERL	1		41000	Domestic sales
3	ERL	1	1	41100	Domestic—electronic
4	ERL	1	2	41200	Domestic—household
5	ERL	2		42000	International sales
6	ERL	2	1	42100	International—electronic
7	ERL	2	2	42200	International—household
8	ERL	1	3	43100	Miscellaneous—domestic
9	ERL	2	3	43200	Miscellaneous—international

Table 9.5 Configuration Design for Revenue GL Accounts

Line 1 in this table represents our previously mentioned "catch-all" scenario. This entry has the lowest level of complexity and means that if no other account is determined, the system will post to account 40000. This entry would be made in **Table 5 Acct Key**.

Line 2 is a catch-all scenario for having a material or customer that does not have an AAG assigned to it and thus ensures that all **domestics sales** are captured within the range 41000–41200.

Line 3 specifies that any items for which the customer has AAG = 1 (domestic customer) and a material AAG = 1 (electronic goods) will post to account 41100. The same logic is applied to explain line 4. Both of these lines would be entered at the top level, **Table 1 Cust Grp/Material Grp/Acct Key**.

In Figure 9.11, you can see some of these entries being made accordingly.

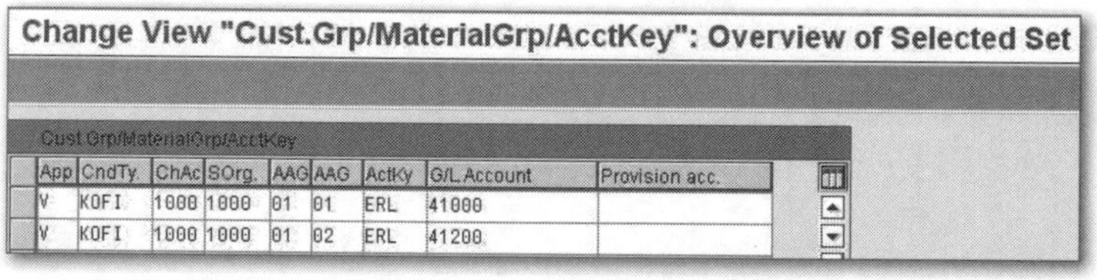

App	CndTy	ChAc	SOrg.	AAG	AAG	ActKy	G/L Account	Provision acc.
V	KOFI	1000	1000	01	01	ERL	41000	
V	KOFI	1000	1000	01	02	ERL	41200	

Figure 9.11 Entries made to Table 1, of SD Revenue Account Determination Table

This concludes our discussion of the configuration needed to complete SD revenue account determination.

9.1.3 Payment Processing Account Determination

This configuration is common to both incoming and outgoing payments, and was covered in detail as part of the Chapters 5 and 6. Therefore, we are only going to review the various settings you may want to configure here without going into detailed explanations.

The configuration of outgoing payments is completed by following the path **IMG • Financial Accounting (New) • Accounts Receivable and Accounts Payable • Business Transactions • Outgoing Payments • Outgoing Payments Global Settings**.

The configuration of incoming payments is completed by following the path **IMG • Financial Accounting (New) • Accounts Receivable and Accounts Payable • Business Transactions • Incoming Payments • Incoming Payments Global Settings**.

Configuration Steps

The following configuration items are available to you, and you should configure those items that are relevant for your business requirements.

▶ **Cash Discounts taken (SKE)**
Lets you define the GL account to which you post any cash discounts that are taken as a result of early payment. This is usually triggered from Payment Terms. Here you can also activate the Posting Key rule to determine if this is a discount given or taken.

▶ **Overpayments and underpayments (ZDI)**
Lets you define the GL account to which you assign the gains or losses that arise from under- or overpayment by the vendor. The difference must be within the agreed tolerance limits. You specify this based on the chart of accounts, so in our example, this same account would be relevant for both company codes, since they both use the same chart of accounts. Figure 9.12 shows the configuration screen for Transaction key ZDI. We also saw in previous chapters how this can be integrated with Reason Code configuration.

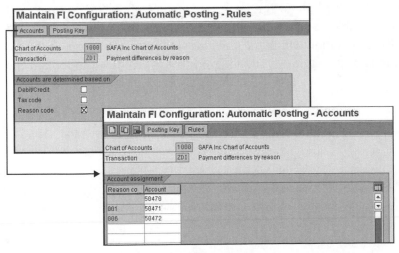

Figure 9.12 Maintenance of Payment Differences Key

▶ **Exchange rate differences and foreign currency revaluation (CEX)**
Lets you define the GL Account to which you assign the gains or losses which arise due to differences in Exchange Rates in the system.

▶ **Rounding differences (RDF)**
Rounding differences are created in the system due to the activation of tax summarization (which summarizes the tax amount from different lines into a single line). There may be a small gain or loss from this step, and this would be posted to this GL account.

▶ **Bank charges**
Here you can define the GL accounts that are posted to for bank charges. Although this is a configuration step, bank charges are usually posted manually, based on the amounts that appear on the bank statement. Because banks take the charges themselves, you only need to make a posting to confirm the amount that was charged.

We have spent a considerable amount of time looking at the configuration of Automatic Account Determination rules in this chapter, and there is a lot of value to the reader to gain this knowledge. In the next section, we look at Integration in the Master Data area.

9.2 Master Data

We have previously talked about the integrated nature of an SAP system, and this integration is enabled by configuration and master data. We have discussed some aspects of configuration within the previous sections when we reviewed the account determination functionality. In addition to this, we need to look at the following:

▶ Account assignment objects

▶ Document types and number ranges

▶ Payment terms

▶ Journal entry screen layouts

9.2.1 Account Assignment Objects

Previously, we have also looked at the integration between the SAP ERP Financial Accounting (FI) and Controlling (CO) components. For this integration to take place, we needed to create cost elements, which facilitated postings from the Financial Accounting Component (FI) to the Controlling Component (CO). If we have activated the Controlling Component (CO), we must assign Controlling objects to our postings, and this sometimes causes issues due to a confusion in understanding, as SAP users cannot always grasp which account assignment object is relevant. Our basis position, originally described in Chapter 3, is stated in Table 9.6.

Type of Posting	Primary Object	Possible Account Assignment Object
Balance sheet	GL account	Profit center
Income	GL account Revenue element	Profit center Profitability analysis Revenue project
Expenditure	GL account Cost element	Cost center Internal order Capital project
Internal settlements Internal allocations and assessments	Secondary cost element	

Table 9.6 Common Account Assignment Objects

We start by looking at integration from the Purchase to Pay process.

Purchase to Pay

When creating a purchase order, you must assign cost objects at some point in the process before the AP invoice is created. If we have a standard purchase order and invoice processed (as shown in Figure 9.1), then this cost assignment comes at the point of invoice verification. At this point, you assign the cost to an expense GL account and a cost object (cost Center, WBS, or internal order).

If, however, you have instances where transaction keys are triggered (e.g., Transaction key GBB), then the system will require an additional account assignment object. If your transaction key triggers a balance sheet GL code, you need to supply a profit center. If it triggers an income-expenditure GL code, you need to supply a cost center.

For most of your MM transaction keys, you will be triggering balance sheet GL codes. For these you should maintain a profit enter against your material master that will be derived on any balance sheet account determination transactions.

> **Note**
>
> Remember, for income-expenditure GL codes, you can default a cost object using Transaction code OKB9.

The creditor that is created when you create the invoice is also a balance sheet GL account. If you are using splitting configuration, this profit center for this posting is derived from the expense posting. If you are not operating splitting, you need to configure settings in Transaction code 3KEH and transfer balances to Profit Center Accounting as part of your period-end process.

Order to Cash

When creating a sales order, you must assign a revenue object. The common object used is the profit center. This posts to a revenue GL account, which is linked to a revenue cost element (type 11).

Any associated discounts or customer payment differences written off for this customer usually post to an income-expenditure account. For these accounts, you need to ensure that a cost center is referenced for these postings, in line with the information explained in Chapter 8, Section 8.4.2.

The other account assignment that may be triggered is a CO-PA segment. If your solution includes this component, you need to account for this object.

Customer and Vendor Master Records

As part of Chapters 5 and 6, we introduced customer and vendor master records. These are important integration objects within the system, as they both generate postings to GL. This integration is enabled by the allocation of a reconciliation account to each record, and this enables the posting to GL.

There are also other integration points that influence account determination, as mentioned earlier in this chapter. These need to be considered from a high-level point of view across components to ensure that the internal interface is passing information that is wanted.

The design of customer or vendor master records without any finance input is not good for overall integration, and you should ensure that this is dealt with appropriately within your project.

Material Masters

Because material masters impact a number of different areas, you need an integrated approach to the fields on the material master. From a finance point of view, you should input information in the finance and costing views to ensure that overall integration is achieved.

9.2.2 Document Types and Number Ranges

In Chapter 3, we talked about the configuration of document types and number ranges. It is important to give a lot of thought to the use of document types because there are integration points with the Financial Accounting Component (FI).

In sales order billing, you can configure billing document copy control rules. You specify which Financial Accounting Component (FI) document type is created for a particular billing type, and you can define additional information that is copied into the AR document.

> **Tip**
>
> You should define the AR document number range as the same range as that for the SD billing documents, and also flag the range as externally defined. The reason for this is that the billing document number will be the "invoice number" that the customer sees. Subsequent processes (e.g., dunning) are based on the AR document number, so it is good to keep the same reference in SD and AR. This ensures that any correspondence with your customer will reference the same document numbers.

9.2.3   Payment Terms

Terms of payment are defined in the system within the outgoing invoices section of the IMG. They are common to both AP and AR and are used on both sets of invoices. On an AP invoice, they determine when the invoice should be paid, and on a AR invoice, they define by when the customer should make the payment.

Each country tends to have standard terms of payment that are part of the culture of that country. In the United States and the UK, terms are often 30 days or 60 days from date of invoice. In Europe, many countries adopt a policy of requiring their payments at the end of the next month from when the invoice was created, that is, a January invoice is due February 28.

It is important to look to your local customs and those of your industry sector. The purpose of the terms of payment is to ensure that you can maximize your cash flow position. The ideal position would be to have an adequate number of payment terms to get your customers to pay quickly and for you to pay your vendors by taking maximum advantage of discounts on offer. Review your requirements before you start this piece of configuration, as you may be in danger of creating too many payment terms.

The payment terms appear on the customer master record, and when an invoice or a sales order is created for this customer, the customer's terms are defaulted into the sales documents. These terms can be overwritten within a sales document. Associated with the payment terms are discounts you want to offer the customer for early payment.

The configuration is completed using the path **Financial accounting (New) • Accounts Receivable and Accounts Payable • Business Transactions • Outgoing Invoices/Credit Memo's • Maintain Terms of Payment**, or by using Transaction code OBB8.

When you first enter the overview screen, shown in Figure 9.13, you will see that there are already a number of standard payment terms in the system. Each payment term has no restriction on it, in terms of company code, so anything in the system is available for all to use. So, you should look at the existing values in the system to see if there is a standard payment term that you can use.

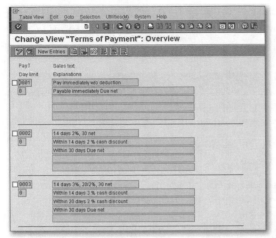

Figure 9.13 Standard Payment Terms within the System

Payment terms are defined by a four-digit alphanumeric code. You may choose your codes based on a convention that reflects the purpose of that payment term. Each payment term is defined on a vendor or customer master record, which defaults into the invoices created for them. The payment terms can be manually overwritten on the invoices by the person creating the invoice. The combination of baseline date and payment terms determines the due date. The payment terms shown in Figure 9.14 provide discounts for early payment, which can be seen at the bottom of the screen.

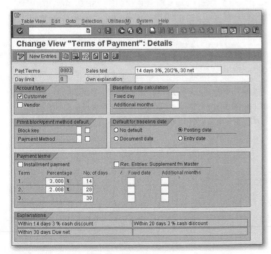

Figure 9.14 Configuration of a Payment Term

If you have payment terms that consist of only 14 days net, then you only need to enter a single line for this configuration. Table 9.7 explains the additional functionality available to you to configure your payment terms.

Field/Section	Description
Sales text	Enter the short description of the payment term that you want to print on any output.
Own explanation	Enter your own longer explanation of what the payment terms actually are.
Day limit	Lets you link your payment terms to a day of the month. In our example of European payment terms, you would enter 28 in this field. This would apply the rule for all items created before the 28th of the month, which would be due next period.
Customer or Vendor	Select for whom this payment term is valid. You may chose to have a small list of payment terms that are valid for both AP and AR.
Fixed day	If this field is used, it will override the default baseline date that is proposed by the system.
Additional months	Lets you define the number of periods plus the baseline date to calculate the payment due date.
Block key	You can use this option to cause the delivery (for customers) or payment (for outgoing payments) to be blocked. This only happens if the payment term is entered on the customer or vendor master record. Enter the specific block you want to be assigned.
Payment Method	You can specify a specific payment method that should be used for this payment term.
Default for baseline date	The baseline date is the date from which you calculate your due date. You can define the baseline date as the **Posting date** or the **Entry date** (document date).

Table 9.7 Configuration of Terms of Payment

If you are operating in different countries, which require different translations, you can assign different translations. This is done in the main payment terms screen. First you select your payment term, and then you assign your translation as shown in Figure 9.15.

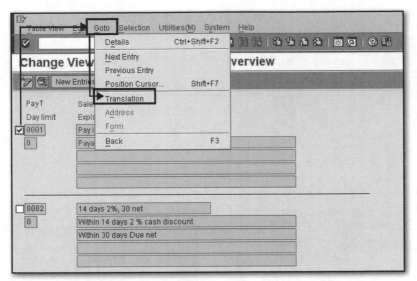

Figure 9.15 Adding Translations to Payment Terms

9.2.4 Journal Entry Screen Layouts

The last item in this section that we will talk about does not really fit into master data, but this is an appropriate place to talk about it.

The document entry screens we have looked at as part of journal and invoice entry can be changed to remove any fields that are not required. The standard settings include a number of fields that are not required for your design. You can drop and drag the fields into an order that best suits your requirements, and change the width of the fields to represent the length of the codes that go into them. In addition to this, you can configure administrator-level settings to hide fields that are not required and should be removed completely from the layout.

> **Note**
>
> Any fields you remove will be hidden for all finance document entry, specifically journal entry and invoice entry (for GL, AP, and AR).

Once made, these settings should be saved either as a local variant or a standard setting for all users in the system as can be seen in Figure 9.16.

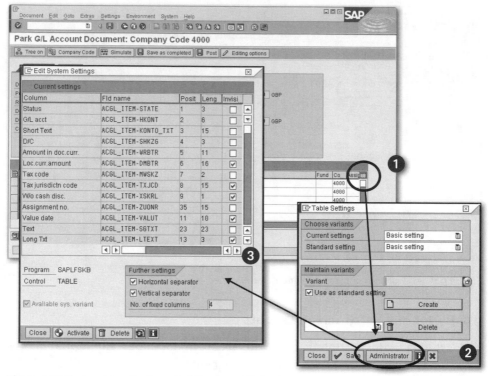

Figure 9.16 Customizing the Layout of Document Entry Screens

This section has provided some explanation of the master data that needs to be in place for an integrated solution to be configured. We have also looked at the dependencies between the different master data objects and explained which aspects you need to pay attention to. Let us now turn our attention to our next topic, interfaces.

9.3 Interfaces

This section is intended to provide you with an understanding of the key concepts for consideration when designing an interface. An *interface* is any connection or communication point between two different entities. An example of an interface is the SAP GUI, which is the software that is on your PC and allows you to log onto the SAP system. GUI stands for graphical user interface, and it provides the connection between the user and a piece of software.

Interfaces exist within SAP in terms of communications that are sent between modules. Billing, for instance, is in an internal interface that communicates between the SD and Financial Accounting (FI) components. For example, if there is a failure in the creation of the accounting document, you may hear the term failure of the billing interface.

At the beginning of this chapter, we talked about implementing an SAP system to replace individual "best of breed" systems that may have existed previously. However, despite best intentions, sometimes your solution must retain a legacy system. In this case, for example, if you have a legacy system you feel you cannot replace by using the SAP system instead, or that it is not cost effective to replace the legacy system, you will need to define an external interface for use with the SAP system, so that the information can be transferred.

In defining interfaces there are three key stages:

- ▸ Identifying the purpose of the interface
- ▸ Designing the interface
- ▸ Testing the interface

9.3.1 Purpose of the Interface

It may sound obvious, but you need to be clear about the purpose of the interface. Sometimes an interface is needed to represent information being passed from third-party software, so there is no choice but to keep the interface. Also, the role of the legacy system may be different now from what it was previously, so its use may also be different. You should assess the role of the interface in line with the scope of your implementation and understand what you want it to do. Common reasons for keeping legacy systems and the corresponding purposes of interfaces include those shown in Table 9.10.

Reason for Legacy System	Purpose of Interface
The legacy payroll system is being retained due to the size of the migration of the data and the historical information.	Provide financial information to be included within the accounts. A simple approach would be to create a GL journal from the interface.
Point of sale systems are installed in all retail sites across a company's network. These point of sale systems are customized for the company's products, and replacing them would represent a high level of risk.	Create sales information as well as cash taken analysis. Sales information is needed for sales analysis, cash banked information is needed for GL. A simple approach would be to create a consolidated AR invoice from the interface.
A monthly file (e.g., fuel invoice) is sent from a major supplier, which is easier than the supplier printing hundreds of individual invoices and sending them. This electronic file is interfaced in to save the time needed to manually enter this information.	This will create GL expense postings (post expenses to the relevant cost centers that have incurred the cost) as well as a creditor who we must pay. A simple approach would be to create a consolidated AP invoice.

Table 9.10 Common Reasons for Keeping Interfaces

You need to be aware at all times of the cost-benefit analysis of the interface, alongside the costs—and Benefits of retaining or retiring your legacy systems.

As part of identifying the purpose of the interface, you also need to know the source system, the information that is being passed along, and the target system to which the information is being delivered. Then, you can begin to design your interface.

9.3.2 Interface Design

To design your interface, you need to consider the following points:

- **Data mapping requirements**—The mapping of data from the source system to the target system, along with any conversion of data that needs to be performed (discussed in detail later in this section)

- **Volumes**—Requirement for line item information or summarized data (consolidated documents)

- **Frequency**—In terms of keeping systems synchronized and up-to-date

- ▶ **Balancing and reconciliation**—Ensuring that the information being transferred is correct and we are not losing or adding information during the interface (discussed in detail later in this section)
- ▶ **Security**—Data integrity and confidentiality

Interface Definition

First, you should decide whether you want a specific document type for your interface, or, if there are numerous interfaces, you may chose to share document types. You may also need to maintain a link between your SAP document and the source system. This may be through the passing of information onto the line item text or document header text of the SAP document. Another approach is to use a document type with external document numbering. This would allow you to use the document number that is sent in the interface file.

Next, you want to be clear on what information is being passed through the file. Interface files usually have three components: a header, the data, and a footer section. The header should carry all of the file classification information such as document type, dates, and any header text information. It is possible to put in validations as part of the header to check that specific information is available before a file is processed. The purpose of the footer is to signify the end of the file. In addition, you may add code to allow a balancing entry to be made. For instance, your file may only carry a list of cash sales made (credit sales), but for double entry purposes, you would need to have a balancing entry to cash (debit cash). This logic may be part of your footer section.

Conversions and Mappings

The actual information contained in the body of the interface is used to generate the lines of your SAP posting. For this information to post, it needs to use the correct coding conventions that you use for your GL accounts, cost centers, customers, vendors, and so on. Most likely, the system you are interfacing from will not have these codes. You will therefore need to perform a mapping of the data so that the information is in a convention that can be uploaded to and accepted by your ledger codes. This mapping can occur at the point of file creation (i.e., when the file is produced from the source system the codes will be converted to your codes), or it can be mapped at the point of upload.

Where should this mapping take place? This depends on your level of control over the source system. This also depends on the frequency of changes that are likely to occur in the future, that is, do you want to control these changes yourself? If so, the owners of the data objects should always maintain a mapping table, which they are responsible for keeping keep updated. You should decide on the best process for this, depending on the frequency of changes to your master data and the importance of these changes.

Point of sales interface scenarios

In our examples outlined earlier in Table 9.10, the retail customer is likely to post to a single customer for all postings (perhaps a one-time customer). For example, if you imagine a large retailer such as Wal-Mart sending such an interface from one of their stores, there is minimal benefit to the company or to the customer at the check-out to be set up as a customer master record. In addition, the GL postings made will be fairly simple.

In the fuel car example, however, it would make sense to have a vendor set up for the fuel supplier and to have a mapping between the person who has purchased the fuel (perhaps by their car vehicle registration number) and the cost center that should be charged for the expense.

You need to assess your individual business requirements to determine the decisions you make, keeping in mind the volume of data you want to see generated in your system.

Balancing and Reconciliation

The responsibility for the balancing and reconciliation of any interfaces being passed should be shared between two groups of individuals. The technical or infrastructure teams are responsible for ensuring that all records are processed without errors. This information may be part of the header or the footer section of the interface to confirm the number of lines that are in the file. If there are any failures in the posting of a line, your interface design should define what happens to that file. You could choose to reject the whole file, reject the individual lines, or maybe post the failing lines to a suspense code. Once an interface file is processed, you would expect a trailer report to be produced that summarizes the postings made. This trailer report is the reconciliation from the IT and infrastructure point of view.

What happens, however, with the actual value of items being posted? Who should reconcile this? This depends on your organization because some will require users to do this, and other organizations will require the infrastructure team to do this. Whatever your decision on this, you may choose to produce a reconciliation as part of the trailer report to make this process easier.

Also, some solution designs that incorporate SAP Workflow and Webflow may require the lines of large interface files to be approved before they are released for payment.

Security

Security may be the most important aspect of your interface design in order to maintain data integrity and prevent fraud. For a payables interface, for example, you should prevent the possibility of someone intercepting the file and adding their own details into the file as the person to be paid. Your security design needs to be confirmed with your security and authorizations team. Perhaps you will decide on file encryption, or maybe you will look to storing the files on secure servers where they cannot be intercepted. Whatever measures you implement, make sure they address your organization's security needs.

Outbound Interfaces

So far, we have talked about incoming interfaces, but you may also need to maintain outbound interfaces to target systems. If so, the same principles apply in terms of identifying an interface purpose and interface design (including data mapping).

9.3.3   Interface Testing

The final stage is the testing of your interface. Interfaces should be tested in line with your other configuration testing to ensure that you test the information being passed as well as further processing of the data to provide complete integration with your system.

If your file is being passed to or from a third-party system, it is important to test this step as well to overcome any communication issues. Simply testing your file locally will not suffice.

This section has provided you with an overview of the key concepts within interface design. Like with many other things, as you gain more experience, you will probably feel that your interface designs get better, and when you become aware of the types of issues you face, you will start incorporating these into your designs.

9.4   The Value of Integration Testing

As a closing statement, never forget the importance of integration testing. There simply is no substitute for testing a fully integrated process, especially as the Finance area is often held accountable if things don't work properly.

A lot of testing will be done within the individual areas of MM and SD, and those areas will be happy once an accounting document is created. From our point of view, however, we need to ensure that the accounts that are determined from the account determination reflect the process that is being followed. The only way to properly test this is to run as many end-to-end test cycles as possible, with business users present to authorize and confirm that the postings are correct.

9.5   Summary

This chapter was directed at and will be very valuable to more advanced users who are tasked with providing integrated solutions. It built on individual functionalities we discussed in earlier chapters, and provided detailed explanations of the key integration areas within our scope.

Having completed this chapter, the reader should now be in a position to:

▶ Understand the integration points between MM and the Financial Accounting Component (FI) and design and configure the automatic account determination settings

▶ Understand the integration points between SD and Financial Accounting (FI), and design and configure the automatic account determination settings

▶ Speak with confidence about integration issues that may occur between these components

▶ Understand the key concepts of interface design and be able to write functional specifications for most interfaces

In Chapter 10, we will look at how to make use of the standard reporting options available to you in the SAP ERP Financials component.

Data migration is a topic that impacts every project and has a large influence on the final financial solution being delivered. This chapter introduces the concepts you need to be aware of and defines a framework model that walks the reader through the process. We also take a look at component-specific migration activities that need to be completed as appropriate.

10 Data Migration

The management of data in your system is very important to support the overall design you have configured. This starts with the initial creation of data in the system. If you are moving to an SAP system from a legacy system or are migrating to a new instance, you need to do some form of data migration activity. Data migration is the process through which we transfer information from the old system into our new SAP system to prepare it for our use.

> **Note**
>
> In our discussion in this chapter, we will use the generic term data migration to represent the process of migrating existing master data (customers, vendors, GL accounts, cost centers, etc.) and include the subsequent need to migrate transactional information relating to these objects.

Data migration is a fundamental part of any project. If the transfer of data is done badly, this will seriously devalue your solution even if you have the best solutions in place. The process is usually very involved and requires a significant amount of time being invested by the client. It is also unlike other areas of the project, as you are largely reliant on the client's input, because they know their data best.

The objective of this chapter is to provide you with an understanding of how to set up and execute the migration of data from a source system to SAP ERP ECC. In addition, we will also look at other important aspects of managing your data after go-live that you should be aware of.

In this chapter, we will do the following:

- Define the key criteria that should form the basis of your data migration strategy

- Explain concepts and processes for data migration, including reconciliation

- Provide you with an understanding of the tools available and the choices that need to be made

- Take a specific look at new GL and Asset Accounting migration

We will also provide you with a number of templates that you can reference for your own use.

> **Note**
>
> Make sure that any template you use works for your own scenario because for the purposes of this book, we are looking at things from the point of view of a generic SAP solution. For example, you should ensure that your own fields and mappings are reflected in the templates you use and not just accept our example templates.

We will start this chapter by taking a look at some fundamental principles for data migration.

10.1 Key Principles of Data Migration

When examining the key principles of data migration, let us first look at the scope of your project. It should cover the scope of objects you need to migrate, as well as the transactional information that needs to be included within your data migration activities. This may be influenced by your decisions to retain or retire legacy systems, as mentioned previously in Chapter 9. The overall objective is to migrate all transactional information from your legacy systems to enable you to operate on your new SAP system with a minimum number of issues. To migrate the transactional information, you need to have the data objects in place and have a clear mapping of old objects to new objects.

The set of data objects you create must support your solution and must therefore be fit-for-purpose, i.e., be in the correct configuration status for our organizations use. You must adopt an approach that will standardize all data objects within the system to conform to the same common design principles, as follows:

► **Common design**

Include the contents of master data as well as the use of master data in all of your blueprint discussions. This should be an active part of your solution design.

► **Reduce risk where possible**

Build in as many reconciliations and checks as possible.

► **Reduce the amount of manual intervention**

Automate as much as possible, and reduce the number of points at which manual intervention is required. Manual intervention creates opportunities for human error.

► **Improve data quality**

Don't simply move bad data from source to target. Aim to improve the quality of the data as part of your overall solution.

► **Have the client take ownership**

Impress on your clients that it is important that they understand the data that is being migrated. Make sure they don't expect you to take care of this. It's their data, and they know it best!

It is important to involve your client in the migration process as much as possible. Although they may initially struggle with the technical aspects, they need to fundamentally understand the mapping of fields and records. Because, as we said previously, it is their data and they know it better than you; they should drive the nontechnical aspects of this work.

The stages for migrating data can be consolidated into a six-step migration process that you need to follow to successfully migrate data from legacy systems to SAP systems. We will now take a closer look at this process.

10.2 The Six-Step Migration Model

Based on our experience we have defined a six-step data migration model which can be adopted by any organization. The six-step migration process shown in Figure 10.1 is valid for both upgrades and new implementations.

> **Note**
>
> Although we consistently refer to the migration from a non-SAP system point of view, the basic principles are the same whether you are migrating data from an old SAP system or a non-SAP system.

You should review and understand all of the stages in this process in order to make informed decisions. Because the terms are somewhat self-explanatory, you may immediately have an idea of what each of these stages implies. In this section, however, we will give you a clear definition of what activities each stage should include, so that you will know exactly what to do at each stage.

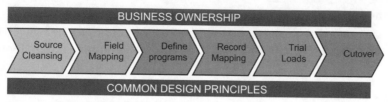

Figure 10.1 The Six-Step Migration Model

10.2.1 Source/Data Cleansing

Source cleansing, often called *data cleansing*, is a term used to represent different activities. In our process, we define data cleansing as the process of cleaning your legacy data in preparation for the migration. Initially, this may seem like a redundant exercise, but in reality many systems are cluttered with master data that is not needed. The migration to a new SAP system is a good opportunity to remove redundant data so that only clean data is available in the new system.

Data cleansing usually applies to master records. For instance, in your current system, you may have accounts that are not valid, and there is no need to bring these over to the new system. You may also need to make changes to your existing master data to accommodate new functionality, or you may want to reduce the number of records you have. Reducing the number or records is called legacy data rationalization, and it is a common exercise. Reasons for rationalization tend to be the excess number of records in the legacy system. This applies to all types of master data. Examples include:

▶ Customer or vendor master records

▶ GL master records

▶ Material master records

▶ Cost centers

▶ Payment terms

You can make these changes in your legacy system if possible. Codes to be deleted should be marked for deletion so that they are not used in the new system. In some instances it is not possible to make these changes in your legacy system, and you will have to make them outside the system in Microsoft Excel or Access.

10.2.2 Field Mapping

Field mapping is an important step that is reliant on your design being finalized. It is the process of matching the fields in your legacy master records to the corresponding SAP fields of your master record. This may seem easy at first, but issues arise when the legacy system does not have a field the SAP system requires. These fields then need to be generated by a "local" rule that is defined as part of the mapping process. For instance, when creating vendor master records, you need to define the vendor account group and vendor reconciliation account. Most legacy systems do not carry this information, so you need to define rules for these fields.

The ideal procedure for this is to create a spreadsheet for each master data object that lists all of the fields that are part of your design and then map them to your legacy fields. Examples of vendor, customer, and GL master record mapping templates are provided with this book, and you may choose to use them as a starting point for your own data mapping exercise. If you are involved in a multicountry rollout, the ideal approach is to create a single spreadsheet that includes all of the fields that you will need and then use the same format for all of your countries. This means the load into the system can happen via a single load program, which is what you'll need to define next.

10.2.3 Define Programs

The process of loading your data into the system can be manual or automatic. Either way, you should have completed the previous two steps (data cleansing and field mapping) to have a definite list of records that need to be created. Most organizations request an automatic load process to ensure that data is loaded in an efficient manner without a chance of user error.

Automatic load programs can be created using several methods, including the following:

- ABAP programming
- Legacy System Migration Workbench (LSMW)
- CATT (Computer Aided Test Tool)

The first two methods are the most popular. Many organizations choose to create ABAP programs for their data migration activities, and while there is no technical or functional drawback to this, do keep in mind that if you need changes to be made to the program, you will need an ABAP resource to do so.

We prefer and recommend the tool provided by SAP specifically for migration purposes: The Legacy System Migration Workbench (LSMW). LSMW is a very flexible tool that can be used to post repeat transactions from a spreadsheet format that you create. The biggest benefit is that you do not need to know any ABAP code—an LSMW program is created by recording a transaction, so the system repeats the transaction. The LSMW tool first uploads your data, runs any conversions that you have specified, and then creates a batch session for you to load the data.

In the Special Topics section we run through the steps needed to define a Create GL Account LSMW program that will demonstrate the tool.

If you are familiar with the CATT tool, you can use it to create master data from a spreadsheet format. We do not cover this in this book, as the LSMW is considered a superior tool to use.

> **Note**
>
> Whichever tools you use, in addition to having a "Create" program, you should also have a "Change" program, as there will be many occasions when you will perform a load and realize that changes need to be made.

10.2.4 Records Mapping

You will likely also need to map master records from your legacy system to your SAP system. This scenario arises when an old code is not being mapped directly to a new code. For instance, as part of your migration exercise, you may decide to reduce the number of cost centers you have, so many old cost centers now map to a single new cost center. The same could be true for GL account codes. In terms of vendors and customers, you may be mapping your old records in line with the functionality available in SAP in terms of business partners (customers) or one-time vendors (vendors).

The deliverable for this activity is a mapping table that maps old records to new records. This mapping table is used for the control of migration of balances from your legacy system.

An important aspect of record mapping is to identify the accounts that require data take on accounts to be set up. These are required for accounts where you want to do more than transfer a balance. Common examples include *inventory take on* and *open item take on*. We will discuss the topic of data take on accounts in more detail later in the chapter.

10.2.5 Trial Loads

Everything is now in place for you to migrate some of your data. You should approach this exercise in stages:

▶ **Unit test load programs**
Load small volumes of data to check that all fields work and that the load program can handle variations.

▶ **Volume test load programs**
Check to see that the system can handle large volumes. For instance, if you want to load 10,000 open items, can your load program handle it?

▶ **Trial cutover**
Take real extracts from your legacy system and see that the information can be loaded with your load programs.

The two main questions to have answered when you are testing your load programs are:

▶ **What happens when there is an error in the file or the program?**
Do you want to send an error report out, or do you want to be able to fix it at the point of finding the error?

▶ **What is the reconciliation process for each load?**
You should be clear on what reports you run or what tables you need to extract to reconcile the load.

The last thing to say here is that your trials are the only chance you have to test the process, so you should test as thoroughly as possible. Once data is loaded to your production system, it is very difficult to get it out. Our recommendation is to get to the point where trial cutover files are not changed once they are loaded and reconciled, and these are the same files that are loaded into the production system.

10.2.6 Cutover

Data migration can be a stressful and sometimes thankless task. The emphasis is usually on the configuration work. Often, the only time data migration becomes a hot topic is when it goes wrong. Therefore, when you get to cutover, you want to minimize the risk to your data by doing the following:

▶ **Prepare files in advance**
Take as much time as possible to check the load files before you load. If possible, load the same file you loaded and reconciled for trial cutover.

▶ **Don't change files**
Once you have prepared your load file, if you need to make changes to records, try not to make them in your load file. Make a separate task list and make these changes manually after loading. If you need to make significant changes, you may have to create a new extract or create a second load file to reflect these changes.

▶ **Use your tried and tested process**
Don't bring anything new into the process at this stage.

▶ **Use the same reconciliation process**
Don't cut corners and try and do it faster due to time constraints.

If you have followed all of these steps, you should execute a controlled migration of data from your legacy system to the SAP system. It is possible to use variations of the process we have defined; for example, some projects make use of data repositories to store and manipulate data. The overall process will not change, however, and this six-step migration process will deliver positive results.

Next, we will look at the topic of inventory transfer.

10.3 Inventory Transfer

The transfer of inventory happens as part of a specific migration process, and, as mentioned, requires the setup of a data take on account. We have already seen how to configure the settings for this in Chapter 9 (see Section 9.1.1), when we defined account determination. The complete steps for the migration are as follows:

▶ Define account determination (see Section 9.1.1).

▶ Migrate and load GL balances. The inventory value is loaded against the inventory take on account 15511 in SAFA Inc.'s chart of accounts.

▶ Migrate and load material masters. At this point, there is no stock value.

▶ Migrate and load inventory. Each item is created with the following double entry: debit stock, credit take on account.

   ▶ The net effect is that the take on account is cleared to zero and the correct balance exists on the inventory account. This activity needs to be coordinated with your colleagues in the materials management team.

10.4   Open Items Transfer

In terms of migrating open items, you can manage your debtors on your legacy system or you can migrate them to SAP ERP ECC. Some organizations migrate a balance to reflect their outstanding debtors at cutover and then clear their debtors in their legacy system. This approach can work for organizations with a small number of debtors. For larger organizations, it is not practical, especially because management of debtors in this case is a manual task. Migration of open items is therefore required for larger organizations, and you will need to create AP and AR documents to reflect these open items.

For open item migrations, you may choose to create data take on accounts to which to migrate balances. These take on accounts need to be in place so that a two-stage migration can take place. That is, as part of the GL balances migration, you post a balance that reflects the closing balance in the old system. You then post the open items to the customer or vendor in question, with the other side of the entry going to the take on account. The net effect is that the open item is created with reference to the customer or vendor, and the take on account has been automatically cleared.

> **Note**
>
> Open item migration should have a posting date that is the same as the cutover date. You need to use a combination of the document date, the baseline date and the payment terms to indicate how old the open item is.

We will now look at the specific requirements when upgrading to the new GL, as opposed to installing a new SAP ERP ECC 6.0 system.

10.5 Upgrade to SAP ERP ECC 6.0

As outlined in the previous sections, if you are migrating from a legacy system, you should follow the steps already identified. If, however, you are upgrading your SAP system (i.e., you are staying in the same SAP instance), then you need to follow a different process. The new GL, which you can activate because you are implementing SAP ERP ECC 6.0, uses a different set of tables, which we introduced previously in Chapter 4 (see Section 4.1.3), and therefore, in addition to the upgrade of software, you also need to migrate this data.

This is a major undertaking, so you need to allocate sufficient time and resources to achieve it. SAP restricts access to the migration cockpit, which you will use for the migration, to people who have either attended the correct SAP course or are engaging SAP to support them in their migration. For this reason, we will only summarize the key points you need to be aware of. For a complete explanation, you will need to complete SAP Course AC210 or contact SAP directly.

Note
It is also possible to upgrade to a new SAP instance, that is, install a completely new system and then migrate to it, as it is a new system. This should be approached in the same way as a move from a legacy system to a new SAP system.

Implications of an Upgrade of SAP Software

If your project is implementing SAP ERP ECC, SAP recommends that you treat this as a two-stage process including an implementation exercise and a data migration exercise. Also note that SAP provides a migration service to help you with the process if you need it.

For customers who are new to SAP, that is, moving from a legacy system, you need to transfer the data to the new GL after it has been activated. For existing SAP users, upgrading from a previous version of SAP requires particular thought to be given to the process due to the differences in the new GL (as identified in Chapter 4).

Designing your GL Migration Exercise

Based on your overall GL solution design, you will have already determined what account assignment objects you are implementing, and answered the following questions:

▶ On what objects are you splitting?

▶ Are you implementing segment reporting?

▶ Are you moving to multiple ledgers, and if so, how do you determine the source of this information?

A mapping of objects must happen first to ensure that the migration exercise you are performing is built in a logical manner. The following outline provides an overview of the stages involved in the overall process of GL Migration:

▶ Complete the system configuration

▶ Configure the settings needed for migration

▶ Complete carry-forward and close down the old fiscal year in the legacy system

▶ Start the migration

▶ Create Worklists

▶ Transfer open items with a posting date for the previous fiscal year

This concludes our upgrade-related discussion. We direct the reader to consult the online material (see *www.SAP.com*) or SAP Course AC210, which provide a complete explanation of the upgrade process.

10.6 Asset Accounting Legacy Data Transfer

Asset Accounting data migration is slightly more complicated than migration of other master records due to the accounting treatment of annual depreciation and net book value. The process for migrating assets requires you to first create *asset shells* (referred to as the *legacy assets*) and then to populate them with values, as you will see in the coming sections.

10.6.1 Define Asset Transfer Date

First, we need to define in our configuration the date on which we are going to transfer our assets. This date controls how the asset values are recorded in the new system. It is usually aligned with the cutover date and is defined by following the path **IMG • Financial Accounting (new) Asset Accounting • Asset Data Transfer • Parameters for Data transfer • Date specifications • Specify transfer date/last closed fiscal year**, which will take you to the screen shown in Figure 10.2.

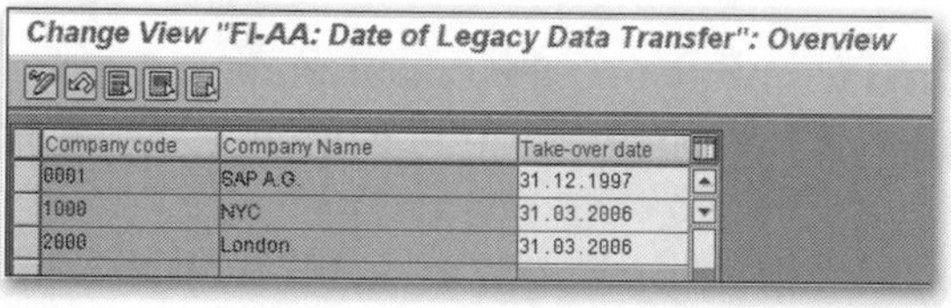

Company code	Company Name	Take-over date	
0001	SAP A.G.	31.12.1997	▲
1000	NYC	31.03.2006	▼
2000	London	31.03.2006	

Figure 10.2 Specify Transfer Date for Legacy Data Transfer

Note that any assets you create will only be classified as a legacy asset if they are capitalized before this asset transfer date. If there are any assets that were capitalized after the transfer date specified in this configuration step and you need to transfer them to the new system, they will need to be migrated as normal fixed assets. In the same area of the IMG, using the path **IMG • Financial Accounting (new) Asset Accounting • Asset Data Transfer • Parameters for Data transfer • Date specifications • Specify last period posted in previous system**, you also need to specify the last period in which depreciation was posted in the legacy system, as the system will use this as a basis for calculating depreciation for transferred assets in the SAP system from that point on. This is shown in Figure 10.3.

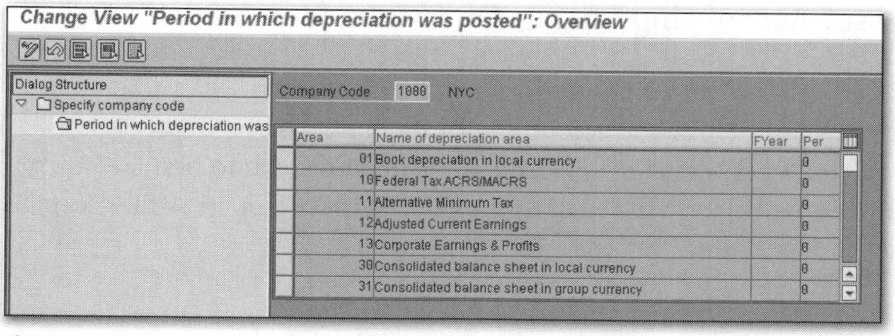

Figure 10.3 Specify Last Period Posted in the Previous System

Having completed these two settings, you can now create legacy asset shells.

10.6.2 Create Legacy Assets

The process of creating legacy assets is most easily completed by defining a load program, especially if you have a large number of assets. You can create the assets manually if you feel that your volume of data is low enough. Our recommendation, however, is to create an LSMW program because creating even 30 assets manually in each client will take time and is prone to errors.

The process of legacy asset creation is very similar to creating a normal asset, as already discussed in Chapter 7 (see Section 7.5). The differences are in the manual assignment of values with which you want to populate the assets.

Follow the path **IMG • Financial Accounting (new) Asset Accounting • Asset Data Transfer • Manual Online Transfer • Create/Change/Display Legacy Asset**, or use Transaction code AS91 to access the screen shown in Figure 10.4.

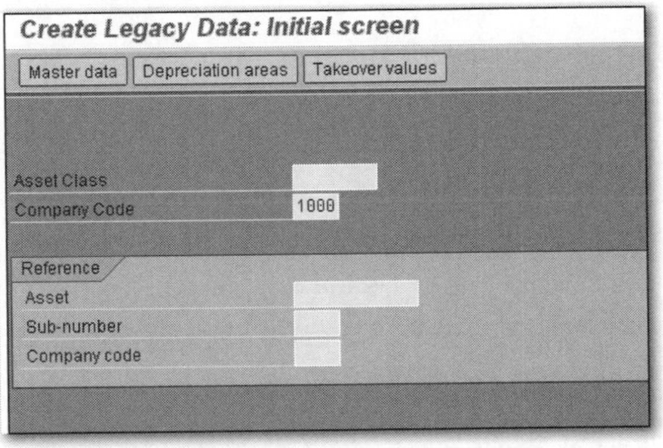

Figure 10.4 Create Legacy Data Initial Screen

In Figure 10.5 we can see the different screens which need to be complete for this legacy asset master record. We highlight some key fields in Table 10.1, full definitions were given previously when we looked at asset master records in Chapter 7.

Tab/Field	Description
General Tab	
Description	Enter the name of the legacy asset. You can use both lines.
Acct determination	Taken from the asset class entered in the first screen.
Inventory number	Use this field to enter the manufacturer's serial number. This will help you enquire about this asset with the manufacturer.
Quantity	You can enter the quantity that the system manages for this asset. This field can be used at the time of partial retirement, and the system will update the asset accordingly by only retiring the partial quantity specified during the entry.
Capitalized on	This date is the value date for this asset. When first postings are made to the asset, the system uses this field to assign the value date to the asset.
De-activation on	The system posts the value date of the retirement in this field when the asset is completely retired.
First acquisition on	This field is automatically set with the asset value date of the first acquisition posting.
Time-Dependent Tab	
Cost Center	Enter the cost center to which the postings are made for the asset.
Internal Order	Allocate the asset to an internal order using this field.
Plant	Enter the plant assignment for the asset. This information can be used in Asset Accounting for further analysis.
Location	Enter the location of this asset in this field.
Origin Tab	
Vendor	Enter the vendor from which this asset was purchased.
Manufacturer	Enter the manufacturer details, as they will help when making inquiries about this asset in the future.
Original Asset	Enter the legacy asset number in this field to create a link between the SAP asset number and the legacy asset number.
Depreciation Areas Tab	This tab displays information about different depreciation areas and settings within depreciation areas such as the depreciation keys, useful life in years and period, ordinary depreciation start date (which is defaulted from the capitalization date entered in the General Data tab using the period control settings explained in the previous section), etc.

Table 10.1 Fields to be Completed for Setting Up Your Legacy Asset

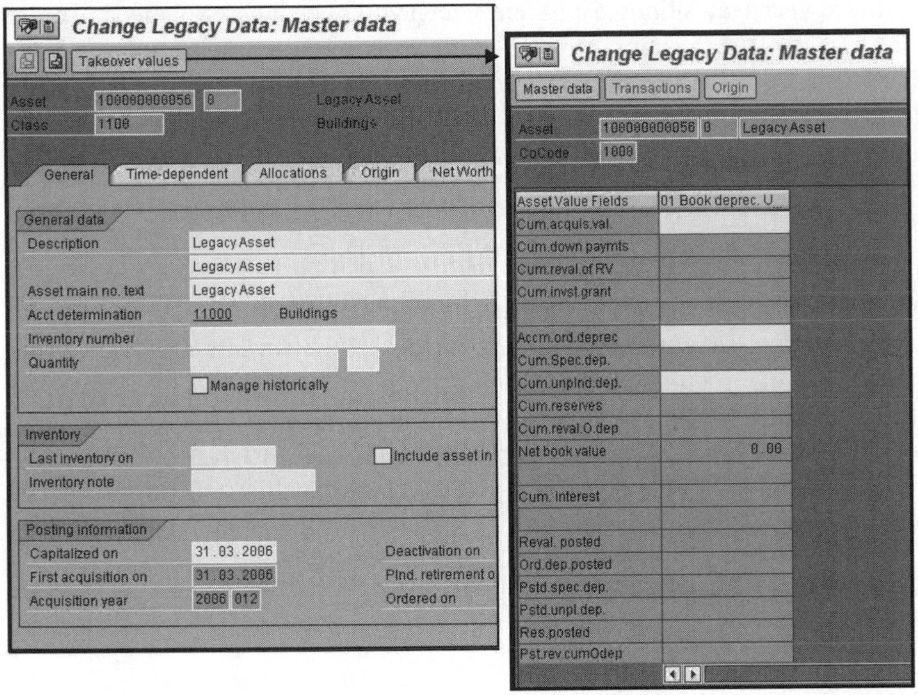

Figure 10.5 Create Legacy Asset Detail Screen

In addition, you need to define the asset takeover values. These include amounts related to the asset costs, accumulated depreciation, depreciation charge for the year, and the net book value. This is controlled within the takeover values screen (click on the Takeover Values button) that you go to once you have entered all of the required information in your legacy asset. Enter the information based on the information outlined in Table 10.2.

Field	Description
Cumulative Acquisition Value	Enter the total cumulative value of the asset you are transferring.
Accumulated ord depreciation	Enter the accumulated depreciation value up to the last fiscal year.
Ordinary depreciation posted	Enter the total depreciation charged for the current year for your asset.

Table 10.2 Define Legacy Asset Takeover Values

For current year acquisitions, a different screen will open where you need to enter the asset value date, the transaction type for acquisition (i.e., 100,) and the acquisition value, as there will not be any accumulated depreciation amount for it. Click on the Save icon, and an asset number will be generated for this asset within the SAP system.

10.6.3 Transfer Balances

In the previous steps, we created assets and populated them with values only in Asset Accounting. They are not yet reflected in the GL, however. We will now bring Asset Accounting in line with the GL by making entries in the IMG as explained below using the path **IMG • Financial Accounting (new) • Asset Accounting • Preparing for Production Start-up • Production Start-up • Transfer Balances**, or Transaction code OASV. This path will take you to the screen shown in the left portion of Figure 10.6.

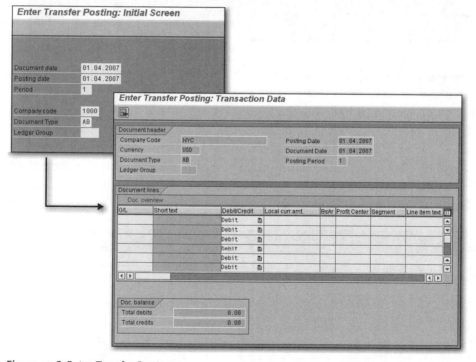

Figure 10.6 Enter Transfer Postings

Postings should be between the assets balance sheet reconciliation accounts (as identified in the account determination and assign GL accounts steps explained in Chapter 7, Section 4) and the asset take on accounts. This transaction posts a document that updates the asset balance in the asset GL accounts. When you compare the GL balances now with any report in asset accounting all of the balances will match, and both of the modules are now in sync with each other.

This concludes our review of data migration. Approach your migration with caution to ensure that you carefully design the migration of each object. If you follow the steps we have identified, and pay attention to testing and the quality of your data, you should be able to achieve a successful migration to support your technical solution.

10.7   Summary

The objective of this chapter was to provide you with the knowledge to prepare for a data migration exercise. Because most implementations of SAP involve the migration of data, the chapter should be useful to all who are involved in an SAP implementation. Key learning points of this chapter include the following:

- ▶ Understand what a data migration exercise involves and be prepared for it
- ▶ Understand the six-stage migration process
- ▶ Understand the specific issues involved with a new GL upgrade
- ▶ Understand the specific activities that need to be completed in relation to an Asset Accounting migration

Next, in Chapter 11, we will review period-end process and its related activities.

This chapter is designed to introduce some of the key activities that organizations run as part of their period end. We will work toward the creation of a period-end timetable based on the solution that we have designed, and you can use this to create your own period-end timetable in line with your organization's needs.

11 Period-End Closing

Period end is the process your organization adopts to complete the activities needed to close your books for a given period. A common approach is to consider a month as being an accounting period, so you produce 12 period ends in a year. At the end of the year, you perform a year end and produce your financial statements that represent your performance over the period of one year. Period ends provide management information about how the organization is progressing part way through the year. The year end provides more external analysis to shareholders and other stakeholders about how the organization has performed over the year.

The specific definitions of period end and year end, however, are dependent on your organization, and it is difficult to define what activities it should contain. The objective of this chapter is to explain different activities you can consider as part of your period end or year end

This chapter will provide the reader with the following:

▶ An understanding of the key SAP requirements for period end and year end

▶ An explanation of the configuration needed to set up your system to perform period end and year end

▶ An explanation of the SAP activities that need to be completed, based on your organization's needs

▶ An explanation of the non-SAP activities you should consider

As we mentioned previously, it is important that you consider this chapter from your own organization's point of view to be able to define a valid procedure for your needs.

11.1 Fast Close with the New GL

As we discussed in Chapter 4, with the implementation of the new GL, you can now complete period-end activities much quicker than before, which is helpful because the U.S. Securities and Exchange Commission (SEC) now requires the completion of financial statements faster than in the past. In previous versions of SAP software, the fact that data was stored in different ledgers meant that it took longer to produce a set of financial and management accounts. With the new GL, many time-consuming activities have become redundant and were thus eliminated, enabling a faster close. Examples of time-saving changes include the following:

▶ Real-time document splitting allocates the correct account assignment object to each GL line, which means all balances are correct at the point of document entry.

▶ As a result of document splitting, there is no need for periodic transfer of payables, receivables or assets to Profit Center Accounting to produce profit center-based balance sheets.

▶ Profit Center Accounting allocations have been replaced with GL allocations, so you now operate a single ledger, where the financial and management accounts are the same.

▶ Real-time integration with CO means that CO only postings, such as settlements can now update GL to ensure that financial and management accounts are the same.

▶ Segments have been introduced, which can be aligned to provide performance analysis by business segment. Segment is a new account assignment object which was not available before.

In Chapter 4 (Section 4.3.3) we looked at the integration with the Controlling Component (CO), which ensured that we can now have all of our reporting needs met by a single ledger. Previously, the common approach was to produce financial accounts and trial balances from the GL and management accounts (departmental or divisional analysis) from the Controlling Component (CO) (and Profit Center Accounting).

11.2   Key Elements of a Period End Timetable

The objective for your work in this area should be to produce a period end timetable that lists all of the activities by date that need to be complete. This timetable should list at least the following items:

▶ Person or department who will complete each action

▶ The date(s) on which the action is due to start and finish

▶ The dependencies that influence each task

The timetable should include all transaction codes (including reports), so that it represents a single point of reference for all who are part of the process. If your organization adopts a form of quality management and procedure management process, this timetable should form part of it.

11.3   Dependent Activities Already Completed

Period end is dependent on configuration elements that we have covered in previous chapters:

▶ Fiscal year variant (Chapter 2, Section 2.4.2)

▶ Posting period variant (Chapter 2, Section 2.4.3)

At this point, you should refresh your memory of these activities, and consider the current period-end processes that exist in your organization. Each company performs certain processes, and uses its own acronyms or names to refer to deliverables of period end.

11.4   Analysis of Period-End Activities

The period-end timetable that we are proposing is intended to provide guidance to the types of activities you might need to complete. However, as we've mentioned, you should determine how our suggestions fit in with your own organization's needs to develop your own period-end timetable.

Prior to SAP ERP ECC, SAP Schedule Manager was available to you to help to coordinate and control your period end, so this has now been replaced by the closing cockpit. There is also no problem with using a spreadsheet process, and this may be the most practical solution for most organizations. More information on the Closing Cockpit can be obtained from *www.SAP.com*

Note

A number of activities appear in the period-end timetable that are not restricted to the end of the month. For instance, journals may be entered at time, or vendor payments may be created more than once in the period.

For our example company SAFA Inc., we have split the timetable into three sections: the preparation work that goes on all month, batch jobs that run overnight at the end of the month, and fast close activities, which usually occur on the first two days of the next period. These activities are outlined in Table 11.1, Table 11.2, and Table 11.3

	Day	Task Nr.	Activity	Transaction Code (incl. Variants)	Responsibility
PREPARATION	–3	1	Run all interfaces	Interface	Support team
		2	Reconcile all interfaces	Interface	Support team
		3	Start control account reconciliations	Manual	Finance department
		4	Start clearing account reconciliations	Manual	Finance department
	–2	5	List of parked journals checked by departments	S_ALR_87012291 S_ALR_87012347	Finance departments
		6	Run customer billing	SD	Customer billing team
		7	Run vendor payments	F110	Payables
	–1	8	Produce all inter-department transfer journals (Controlling Component [CO] allocations)	FV50 and CO Allocations	Finance departments
		9	Run final sales figures	User-specific report	Sales team(s)
		10	Run customer dunning report	F150	Debtors team

Table 11.1 Preparation Tasks

In this section, we will look at each table independently and identify in more detail what you need to do for each associated task. We will start with the preparation phase, shown in Table 11.1:

▶ **Tasks 1 and 2: run all incoming interfaces**

Many SAP system implementations do not result in the end of life for all interfaces. Therefore, it is likely that you will still need to run interfaces to receive data.

▶ **Tasks 3 and 4: reconciliation of control and clearing accounts**

Every accountant wants to reconcile accounts. With the implementation of the new GL, there is not a reconciliation ledger anymore, but there are still accounts that need to be reconciled. In addition, you will now have an FI-CO reconciliation account (or multiple accounts, depending on your configuration). For clearing accounts, you are looking for a zero balance, so you should check any accounts that have balances. To do so, use either a trial balance report or (new) GL balances report (FAGLB03).

Reconciliation of accounts requires you to run different reports depending on which reconciliation you are completing. If you are working with a clearing account, you should run the (new) GL line items report (FAGLL03) that allows you to look at open and closed items.

▶ **Task 5: approval of all parked documents**

If your process includes approval processes, it is likely that you will use the *parked document* functionality. Common examples are the approval of vendor invoices for payment and the approval of journals. Before you complete period end, you should ensure that all parked documents that should be posted are actioned; otherwise, they will not be reflected in your period accounts. Two reports you may choose to run are S_ALR_87012291 and S_ALR_87012347.

▶ **Task 6: run customer billing**

As discussed in Chapter 6, *Billing* is the process by which customers are invoiced for goods or services you have supplied to them. Many organizations perform frequent billing runs; others may run billing less frequently. Before the end of the accounting period, you should ensure that all customers are invoiced for as many items as are relevant for that period so that this revenue can be included in the period end.

▶ **Task 7: run vendor payments**
As discussed in Chapter 5, vendor payments can be automatically generated by the *automatic payment program*. You will run this program as part of the periodic processing using Transaction F110.

▶ **Task 8: produce interdepartmental transfers**
Many costs that are centrally invoiced to a company need to be allocated to lower levels departments. You should ensure that periodically you allocate costs to the correct cost centers. This should include all cost allocations and any internal trading that would result in interbusiness transfers. For this, you can use the new GL allocation functions, or you can use journals to apportion costs.

▶ **Task 9: run final sales figures**
As you get ready to close the old period, you may want to get an early indication of how sales are looking by running final sales figures before you close the period. If you can see anything that is missing, it gives you an opportunity to react. Sales figures may be produced from either SD or from the Financial Accounting Component (FI), depending on the analysis you want to generate.

▶ **Task 10: customer dunning**
Before the end of the period, once you have received all receipts from your customers, you should generate your dunning proposal. You may define your own dunning cycle, which may run weekly depending on your business needs. This was discussed in Chapter 6.

It is also common to run some aged debtor analysis at some point in the period to analyze your performance in retrieving old debts. This will probably be linked in with dunning to the customer debt management process.

Next, we will look at a number of activities that can be set up as batch jobs, as shown in Table 11.2. Configuring activities to run as batch jobs removes the need for manual intervention, and the system will perform the task as per the configured schedule. The activities involved must be the kind that you can schedule, for instance, running reports or executing transactions. In our schedule, some activities are defined for day 0; these are jobs that are scheduled to run overnight as batch jobs and are relevant examples.

	Day	Task Nr.	Activity	Transaction Code (incl. Variants)	Responsibility
BATCH	0	11	Open new period	OB52	Batch job
		12	Close old sales period	OB52	Batch job
		13	Close material period	MMPV	Batch job
		14	Run all settlements in CO		Batch job

Table 11.2 Batch jobs

▶ **Task 11: open new period**

At some point, you might want to have two accounting periods open at the same time. The open and closed accounting periods control which periods are available to receive GL postings. This includes goods movements. For example, if your period is closed, you cannot book goods into the system. Some organizations therefore have one or two days when both accounting periods are open, so adjustments can still be made in the old period during period end, as well as valid entries being entered into the new period.

▶ **Task 12: close old sales period**

Although you may be happy to be able to have two accounting periods open, you will probably want to close sales quickly so any sales invoiced in the next month go into the next accounting period. It is usually acceptable to receive vendor invoices late, so these may need to be posted back into the old period.

▶ **Task 13: close material period**

In Materials Management (MM), you have a period control (Transaction code MMPV) that needs to be maintained in line with the accounting period. This controls the booking in of stock. Therefore, you cannot book stock into a closed period.

▶ **Task 14: run all settlements in the Controlling Component (CO)**

If your solution involves project systems or internal orders, you should have procedures in place that define and control the settlement of these account assignment objects. It is likely that settlement will happen when a project or job is complete, but there should be periodic processing to ensure that jobs are settled to the periods to which they relate.

Now, let us look at the fast close tasks, as outlined in Table 11.3.

	Day	Task Nr.	Activity	Transaction Code (incl. Variants)	Responsibility
FAST CLOSE	1	15	Customer balances reconciliation		Debtors team
		16	Vendor balances reconciliation		Payables team(s)
		17	Update foreign currency valuation rates		Financial controller
		18	Run GR/IR reconciliation	MR11	Financial controller
		19	Run depreciation		Financial controller
		20	Post final adjustments and corrections		Payables team(s)
	2	21	Close old period	OB52	Support team
		22	Produce trial balance	S_ALR_87012277	Financial controller
		23	Produce final period accounts		Financial controller
		24	Issue final accounts		
	3	25	Reverse all prior period accruals	f.80	

Table 11.3 Fast Close Activities

▸ **Task 15 and 16: reconcile vendors and customers**
At some point in the period, you will need to reconcile the sales and purchase subledgers. This is easy because you operate reconciliation accounts, and therefore by definition, the postings between subledgers and the GL are reconciled. All you need to do is compare the value of the vendor or customer balances to the balances on your corresponding reconciliation accounts.

▸ **Task 17: update foreign currency valuation rates**
Depending on the number and volume of your foreign currency transactions, you should regularly update the currency rate that is configured in the system. Your business process design should determine how important it is to maintain an up to date rate in the system, and based on this, you should update the rates (Transaction code S_BCE_68000174).

▶ **Task 18: run GR/IR reconciliation**

You should reconcile the open items in your GR/IR (goods received—invoiced received) GL account on a regular basis. This transaction checks for all open items against this GL account and matches them. Any unmatched items represent invoices received with the goods or goods received but not invoiced. You perform this reconciliation with Transaction code MR11.

▶ **Task 19: run depreciation**

Depreciation should be run periodically to allocate costs to the periods to which they relate. This is usually seen as a cost imposed on departments, because there are fixed rules that determine what depreciation charges are incurred. Depreciation was discussed in depth in Chapter 7.

▶ **Task 20: post final adjustments and corrections**

At this stage, all transactions that are expected to post into the period have been posted, and you can now close down the period. Any final adjustments should be made, and at the end of day 1, you should have a complete set of accounts ready.

▶ **Task 21: close old period**

At a point in time scheduled in the timetable, the old finance period should be locked so that final accounts can be produced. Locking the period ensures that no uncontrolled changes can be made to the numbers you produce.

▶ **Task 22 and 23: produce trial balance and final period accounts**

The trial balance shows the balances on all accounts and will always add down to zero. Along with this you will produce your final accounts and do any further variance analysis that is required as part of your process. The production of accounts can be manual or automatic, and it may be done locally or centrally.

▶ **Task 24: issue final accounts**

Once the final accounts have been issued, your period end is concluded, and you can move into the next period's activity.

▶ **Task 25: reverse all prior period accruals**

The new period's activity should commence with the reversal of all prior period accruals, and with this the period-end cycle begins again.

In addition to the period-end activities, there are activities you need to perform for year end. We will look at this next.

Additional Activities Needed for Year End

As we have discussed, you will complete a period end at the end of every month. Then, in the twelfth month, you will also need to complete your year-end activities, which vary widely from organization to organization. Generally speaking, however, there are certain year-end activities that need to happen from a system point of view and certain activities that need to happen from a process point of view:

▶ **System-driven**
The minimum system activity you need to perform at year end is the carry forward of GL balances (Transaction code f.65). This is a basic accounting step that needs to be completed that carries forward your net result as a balance brought forward on the balance sheet. *Net result* is also referred to as the excess income over expenditure and profit (or loss) for the year. In our solution, we also need to complete the fixed asset year change (Transaction code ajrw).

▶ **Process-driven**
In terms of process, you will probably want to make changes to master data records that have become redundant and hierarchies that have changed. You may also have an annual inventory count which requires that you make changes to inventory levels or the standard price of your materials (Transaction code mr21). The process aspect needs to be looked at carefully within your organization to understand what is needed and who needs to be involved.

11.5　Summary

This short chapter identified key activities that need to be run to complete period end, and some general information about running year end. The schedule we have produced is based on the solution relevant for our fictitious company SAFA Inc. and provides a good base from which you can base your own organizations period end timetable.

When considering your period end process, you will have a lot of interest in the reports that can be run from system and this what we cover in Chapter 12 next. In particular we look at the functionality available to you to create your own customized report painter reports.

This chapter on SAP ERP Financials reporting should be relevant for all readers. For new SAP users, it explains the approach to adopt for collecting reporting requirements, as well as identifying some of the common reporting requirements. For experienced SAP users, it provides a step-by-step explanation of how to create a report using the powerful Report Painter tool. In addition, we talk about the new reporting dimensions and reports available to you with the new GL.

12 SAP ERP Financials Reporting

When we started looking at the enterprise structure earlier in this book, a key message we conveyed was the importance of knowing the reporting requirements of the organization. These requirements come from internal and external stakeholders and need to be satisfied for your system to be perceived as adding value. This chapter therefore covers the following topics:

- Satisfying your organization's reporting requirements
- Identifying common requirements within the processes in scope
- Using Report Painter to deliver monthly management accounts

The key reports for finance are usually centered around the production of financial and management accounts. Organizations use different terms to refer to these reports, but all provide a detailed analysis of combinations of GL accounts and account assignment objects (cost centers and profit centers).

We start this chapter by working on building your *reporting suite*, which is how we refer to the complete set of reports you consider to be part of your process design.

12.1 Building Your Reporting Suite

When building your reporting suite, the most important thing to keep in mind is the purpose of reporting. Reporting is the tool through which internal and external stakeholders can understand the organizations financial performance as a result of the business decisions made by management in the period defined. The simplest scenario, for example, the result of an advertising campaign should be to see improved sales. This result should then be reflected in your reporting analysis. Also, you may find that you have reports that are no longer required, and, on the other hand, that you need to implement new processes that require new reports to be developed.

You should therefore approach this area as you approached the blueprint for the functional modules discussed in previous chapters. Start by understanding the current "as-is" reporting suite. Gather reporting requirements from all processes that are in scope. You should also consider changes that are being made to supplementary processes, for instance, processes and systems that are outside of the implementation scope, but are directly influenced by your changes.

The deliverable from your data gathering will be a spreadsheet listing all of the reporting requirements you gathered, so once you have gathered a list of reports, combine them into a spreadsheet-based reports database where you record how each of these reporting requirements are satisfied. For each report, capture the information outlined in Table 12.1.

Characteristic	Example data
Process area	Finance
Report name	Departmental Cost Analysis
Characteristics	GL account Cost center Actual Budget
Dimensions	Period Fiscal year
Frequency	Monthly
Priority	Hi, Med, Low
Delivery method (solution and report name if known)	Report Painter report Z-CCTR1
Report owner (For example, the person who is going to provide the explanation of the report and its purpose as well as sign it off once it is tested.)	Naeem Arif

Table 12.1 Sample Reports Database Information

By capturing this minimum information, you can group together reports that are similar and then combine their requirements. Also, SAP lets you run reports by master data groups and hierarchies, which means the same report structure can be combined with different master data groups or hierarchies to provide different sets of analyses.

When we talked about the implementation process in Chapter 1, we talked about testing of the solution by the user community. Reports usually impact a wide range of users, so it is a good idea to form a reporting user group that is involved in the development and approval of all finance reports. This ensures that reports are built to the same set of standards. This simple approach is a tried and tested approach which enables you to create a single point of reference for all your reporting requirements, which we have referred to as your reporting suite. You should keep this log as the record of what decisions were made and who made them in terms of delivering reports as after go-live users may want to know what happened to their reports and what decisions were made.

Next, we will look at the tools you have available to you to deliver your reporting requirements.

12.2   Reporting Tools

Once you have created your spreadsheet of reporting requirements, you should go through the process of evaluating your reports. Group together the reports whose requirements are similar to reduce the number of reports you will ultimately build. Some reports may have existed previously for system control and performance purposes. SAP Integration often removes the need for these reports. Finally, and this may be the most difficult task, you need to rank the reports in terms of business priority.

Once you have finished these tasks, you can start converting reporting requirements into solutions. The solutions available to you fall into the following categories and should be documented in the database:

▶ **SAP standard report**
SAP has thousands of reports available to you to use. While there is no single catalog to list all of these, within each subcomponent you can find your reports in the same areas. We will look at some of these in the next section. Once you

have identified a report, you may find that the same report is able to satisfy a number of different report requirements by manipulation of the report selection criteria.

▶ **Report Painter report**
Report Painter is used to deliver many tabular style management reports in terms of producing financial statements. We will look at Report Painter in some detail at the end of this chapter.

▶ **SAP Query**
SAP Query lets you run queries on SAP Tables to return data. Before you start looking at queries, however, look at the numerous standard reports in the system, which are based on the same tables and thus should be able to return the same type of data for you.

▶ **ABAP report**
ABAP/4 is the programming language used to code SAP software and can also be used to produce custom reports. ABAP reports are the most powerful in terms of what the report can do. The downside of ABAP reports is that they cannot be created or changed by configuration or by users. Therefore, if you need to make changes in the future, you will need a programmer to make the changes. If you use ABAP reports, write them flexibly and adaptable to the possible changes in the business.

▶ **Data warehouse**
Many organizations look to a data warehouse solution to run alongside their SAP system to take reporting out of the system. SAP's own data warehousing tool is referred to as SAP NetWeaver Business Intelligence (BI).

Any data warehouse solution will be restricted in terms of what it can do, and most tend to be able to produce tabular style reports. The detail is still within SAP ERP ECC, so you may not be able to get all of your reporting requirements from your data warehouse solution. One benefit of using a data warehouse is that it reduces the load on your SAP ERP ECC system, as users who only run reports don't use up processing power doing so. The downside is that sometimes your data warehouse solution will only be updated overnight, so you may have data that is a day old.

▶ **Out of Scope**
The final category you may need is for reports that are no longer required. Be sure to also collect the reason for this classification to ensure that you have an audit trail.

12.3   Common Reporting Requirements

In this section, we look at the common reporting requirements that may arise in a typical organization. This is intended to provide guidance and is not a complete list of SAP reports. We will classify reports as operational reports (which are needed on a day-to-day basis) and management reports (which are run periodically and do not go into detail).

Dynamic Selections

The design of most SAP standard reports is to provide the maximum amount of flexibility. Often, a standard report can be used to satisfy different reporting requirements by manipulating the selection criteria.

In most standard SAP reports, you can use the **Dynamic Selections** button to bring in additional selection characteristics. For instance, you may want to run a GL line item report, but only want to see a specific document type. For this you can use the standard GL line item report and use the **Dynamic Selections** button to restrict the report to a particular document type. Think about what you can include and what you can exclude to make a report work in different ways. Figure 12.1 is an example of a new GL report (FAGLL03). It shows the improvement in functionality available to you, that is, the ability to report by additional dimensions that are available as a result of the new GL.

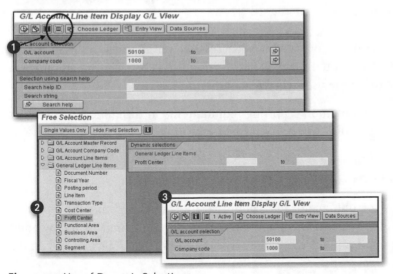

Figure 12.1 Use of Dynamic Selections

Report Variants

When you make selections on reports, some may involve a lot of work, especially if you are saving dynamic selections or ranges of values. In such situations, use the **Variant** option, shown in Figure 12.2, which allows you to save the selection criteria for later use. This is of great benefit if you want to enable different users to run the same report with similar selection criteria.

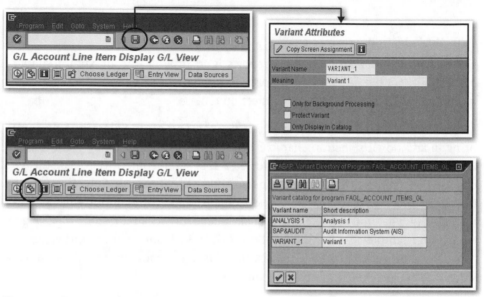

Figure 12.2 Creating and Using Report Variants

Once a variant is defined, you can make it accessible for all users in the system. If you are concerned about too many variants being used, you can search for them by variant name or by the user who created them.

We will now look at common reporting requirements in different areas, such as accounts payable, accounts receivable, asset accounting, and so on.

12.3.1 Accounts Payable

Common reporting requirements in accounts payable revolve around the reporting of invoices due for payment. This information is important from a cash flow point of view, as each vendor invoice contains payment terms that determine when the invoice is due for payment.

For example, you may receive a phone call from a vendor asking about an invoice that has not been paid yet. For such a scenario, the simple approach is to run a vendor line item report that shows all the vendor items. From this report you can select additional fields that you want to see in the report, which makes this report very flexible for answering queries from vendors.

Also, as part of period end reporting you may want to produce a list of vendor balances (as part of your reconciliation of the vendor reconciliation account). The standard SAP reports let you produce these balances.

Figure 12.3 shows the SAP Easy Access Menu path and the available **accounts payable** reports, (along with the transaction codes for these reports), which you may find useful.

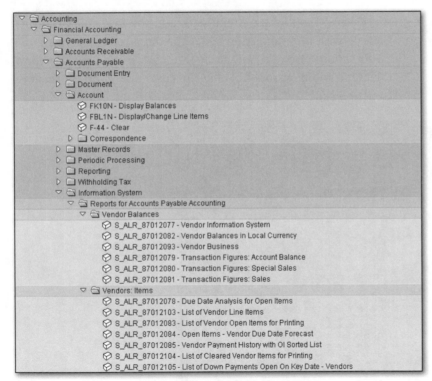

Figure 12.3 Useful Reports in the Accounts Payable Area

12.3.2 Accounts Receivable

Common reporting requirements in accounts receivable revolve around the reporting of unpaid customer items. This is more of an internal requirement than an external requirement, and the most flexible report is the customer line item report. This should be the first report you turn to when dealing with customer queries.

In addition, you should use the dunning program to generate dunning letters (see Chapter 6, Section 6.8.3), which provides you with some analysis of what customer items are outstanding.

For period end reporting, you may want to produce some customer balance statistics for monitoring purposes, and SAP does provide a number of balances reports for you to run.

Figure 12.4 shows the SAP Easy Access Menu path and the available **accounts payable** reports, (along with the transaction codes for these reports), which you may find useful. You should also take a look at the (customer) analysis report (Transaction FD11), as it combines a number of useful customer report dimensions into the same transaction code.

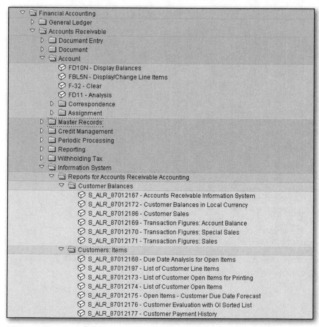

Figure 12.4 Useful Reports in the Accounts Receivable Area

12.3.3 Asset Accounting

The main report users run in Asset Accounting is the Asset Explorer, which provides analysis for a particular asset. This was introduced as part of Chapter 7 already.

In addition, you should consider the Asset History Sheet, which is a very detailed asset register. This does not need to be run for your entire organization and can be run for asset class or even an individual asset.

In Figure 12.5 we show where to find the common Asset Reports in the SAP Easy Access Menu. You will see that there are a number of very good asset reports available to here to deliver your business requirements.

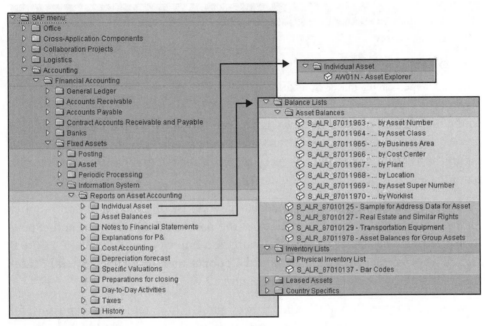

Figure 12.5 Useful Reports in the Asset Accounting Area

12.3.4 General Ledger

Within finance, operational reporting requirements usually involve the checking and confirmation of balances on accounts. This may be just the GL account or a combination of the GL account with a cost center or profit center. With a new GL implementation, SAP has combined all of these into the GL, which means the former GL line items report has been vastly improved.

If you activate the new GL, you will need to use the new reports, as the information is now stored in different tables (see Chapter 4, Section 4.1.3). Table 12.2 shows the transaction codes for the **Display GL Balances** and **Display GL Line Items** reports in the classic GL and the new GL.

Report	Classic GL	New GL
Display GL Balances	FS10	FAGLB03
Display GL Line Items	FBL3n	FAGLL03

Table 12.2 Reports in the Classic GL and New GL

In the reports available in the new GL, you can add selection parameters based on profit center and segment, neither of which were available before (see example in Figure 12.1). This is indicated on every report in the GL that has the word *new*, in parentheses, after its name (see Figure 12.6).

In terms of producing monthly financial statements, the most common requirements are the production of variations of the profit and loss, income and expenditure, and balance sheet reports. These are also improved with SAP ERP ECC 6.0 and can be accessed from the **Standard Reports** menu under **Financial Statement/Cash Flow** option, as shown in Figure 12.6.

Most accountants will find the GL balances and GL line item reports most useful for their day-to-day analysis and reconciliation work. Experienced users will also bring in the additional fields to their reports for advanced functionality.

In addition to these standard reports, you may want to create your own versions of reports to focus on something specifically important to your own business. To do this, you use the Report Painter tool. In the next section, we will go through an example of how to set up a simple report you may want to include as part of your monthly analysis in the next section.

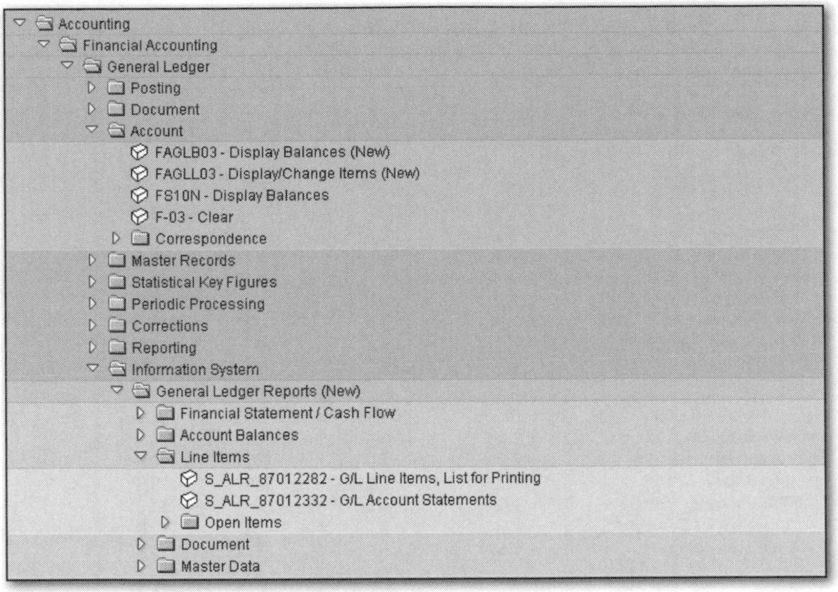

Figure 12.6 Examples of New GL Reports

12.4 Creating Basic Management Accounting Reports with Report Painter

In this section, we will explain the use of Report Painter, which you can access from the application side of the system using the path **SAP Menu • Information Systems • Ad Hoc Reports • Report Painter • Report • Create**, or you can use Transaction code grr1.

Report Painter can provide tabular style reports based on combinations of characteristics and dimensions that are common to most accounting reporting requirements. Figure 12.7 explains this graphically. It is important to be clear that this is the only format Report Painter works in and that it cannot provide any line item analysis; it can only return a value based on the criteria you specify.

Current Period 3 Fiscal Year 2008 Company Code 1000	**Monthly Results Schedule**			
	Period Actual	Period Plan	Variance	% Variance
Domestic Sales	11,092	12,000	-908	-7.6
International Sales	6,701	6,000	701	11.7
Misc Income	2,101	1,800	301	16.7
Total Income	**19,894**	**19,800**	**94**	**0.5**
Direct Labour	1,510	1,500	10	0.7
Materials	4,810	4,350	460	10.6
Other Sales & Distrib Cos	812	620	192	31.0
Total Direct Costs	**7,132**	**6,470**	**662**	**10.2**
Administration Costs	781	800	-19	-2.4
Marketing Costs	1,092	1,100	-8	-0.7
Warehouse Costs	1,390	1,520	-130	-8.6
Indirect Labour	481	160	321	200.6
Misc Operating Costs	332	275	57	20.7
Other Support Services Cc	120	120	0	0.0
Total Indirect Costs	**4,196**	**3,975**	**221**	**5.6**
Result	**8,566**	**9,355**	**-789**	**-8.4**

Figure 12.7 Example of a Monthly Financial Statement

In this section, while not going into a detailed explanation of all of the components of Report Painter (or Report Writer, which is its more powerful companion), we will guide you through the different steps you need to complete to create a report in your system similar to the one shown in Figure 12.7. You should be able to adapt these steps to the specific configuration of your own system to make the report useful to you.

12.4.1 Decide on the Report Type

First, you should be clear on the report you want to create. If you have followed the steps in the chapter so far, you will be able to select a report from your reporting suite definition and already know the dimensions and characteristics involved.

For our example, we have a clear idea of what our report looks like in our legacy system and we have obtained a printout of it, as shown in Figure 12.8.

DEPARTMENTAL COST ANALYSIS SCHEDULE

| **COST CENTRE** | 1000 | **Period** | 1 - 3 |
| US North Marketing | | **Fiscal Year** | 2008 |

REPORT RUN BY : NARIF   11:27:01   07/12/08

	Actual	Plan	Variance	% Variance
Direct Labour	2,100	2,100	0	0.0%
Materials	10,720	10,000	720	7.2%
Misc Sales Costs	1,120	1,250	-130	-10.4%
Distribution Costs	460	300	160	53.3%
Total Direct Costs	**14,400**	**13,650**	**750**	**5.5%**
Warehouse Costs	1,200	1,200	0	0.0%
Marketing Costs	1,490	1,000	490	49.0%
Indirect Labour	706	250	456	182.4%
Support Services Cost	1,700	1,700	0	0.0%
Total Indirect Costs	**5,096**	**4,150**	**946**	**22.8%**
TOTAL DEPARTMENTAL COSTS	**19,496**	**17,800**	**1,696**	**9.5%**

Figure 12.8 Example Report: Departmental Cost Schedule

We will now create a report from the new GL library (0L) and call the report Z-CCTR1, as shown in Figure 12.9. From the **Create Report** screen, select **Library** and specify a report name. Next, click on **Create**.

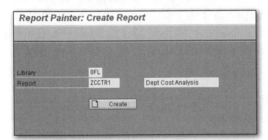

Figure 12.9 Create New Report

Each Report Painter report has four components that need to be defined:

▶ Rows

▶ Columns

▶ General data selection

▶ Report group

The first three are defined within the report, and the fourth is defined outside of the report. The general data selection represents items that are common to the entire report and not specific to either the rows or the columns. For instance, in our example, the report is run for a cost center, so this is general to the report and should be included in the general data selection.

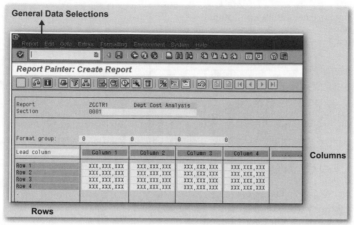

Figure 12.10 Components of a Report Painter Report

Thinking back to the simple format that we want to report by (see Table 12.1 earlier), the characteristics were (1) GL accounts and (2) cost center, which need to be included in the report. The dimensions were (3) actuals, (5) budgets, (6) period, and (7) fiscal year. All of these must be included in our report definition, so it is important to be clear on where they should appear. Figure 12.11 shows where we will define each of these in order to return the reporting data that we are looking for.

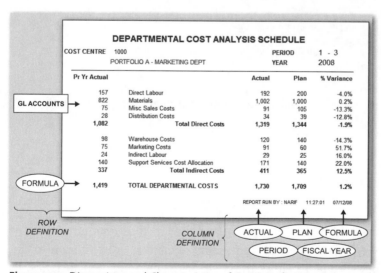

Figure 12.11 Dimensions and Characteristics of Our Sample Report

We now go through the steps that you should follow to define your report.

12.4.2 Define a Row

To define the first row, you need to double-click on **Row 1**, shown earlier in Figure 12.10. This brings up the screen shown in Figure 12.12 where you define the characteristics for this row. For our requirements, we only want to define GL account in the row.

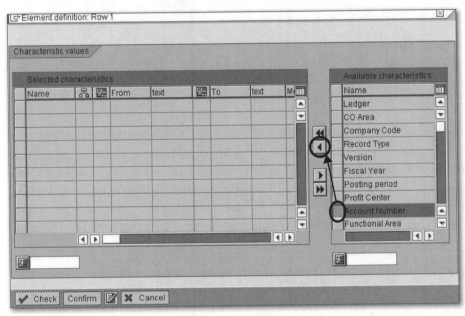

Figure 12.12 Adding Characteristics

It is possible to combine characteristics, which will return combined results. For instance, you may choose to combine the GL account with an account assignment object (cost center or profit center), which will provide the combined analysis on each line.

Having selected the characteristics, you need to assign values to them. You can define a value in the report (which we refer to as *hard coding* a value) or allow the user to define the value. For hard coding values, you can select values in the **From** and **To** cells. You can also select a hierarchy or group, as shown in Figure 12.13, if you have set these up as part of your master data.

By selecting a hierarchy or group, you add flexibility to your report, so that when you change the values in the hierarchy or group, the report is automatically updated.

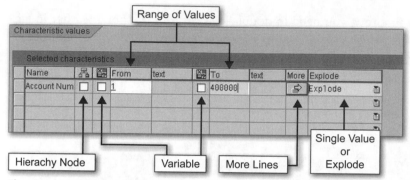

Figure 12.13 Additional Controls of Characteristics definition

The common thing to do is to use a variable, which makes this field a selection criteria for the user to define when they run the report. Many variables are defined in the system that you can use. A variable forms part of the report selection criteria and allows the user to define this value for this characteristic or dimension in the report. Variables are available for use in rows, columns, and general data selection. Selecting a variable makes your report flexible to be used for a number of different reports.

In a simple scenario, you may define a single value or a range of values. You can also combine a number of GL accounts in the same reporting line. Enter the value of the first GL account and then click on the **More** button on the same line. This will open up additional lines for you below the current line.

The next option you have for the row is whether to return a **Single Value** or **Explode** the line. If you have assigned multiple GL codes to the row, then the default setting of **Single Value** will return a single line for your report. If you select **Explode**, the report will return a line per GL account. Which option you select depends on the type of report you want to produce. In our scenario, as shown in

Figure 12.13, we selected **Explode**, as we want to see the breakdown of all the lines. If you have combined characteristics, you may choose to explode only one of the characteristics.

Once you have completed the definition of the row, click on the **Check** button, shown in Figure 12.14, to confirm the values. The final step for this row is to add the description, which is what the user sees when the report data is returned. This process is called text maintenance and is also shown in Figure 12.14.

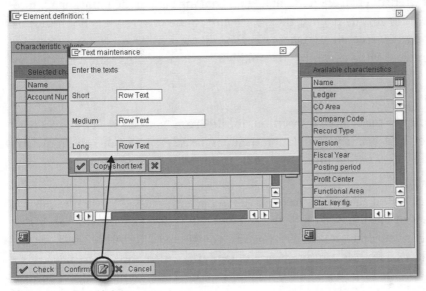

Figure 12.14 Text Maintenance

This completes the definition of a normal row. This same approach should be followed to create any additional rows that are needed for your report. The only variation to this is the definition of a formula row, which we will look at later in this chapter.

12.4.3 Define a Column

We will now look at the steps involved in defining a column. To start, you need to double-click on **Column 1**, shown earlier in Figure 12.10. The **Select element type** dialog box displays, as shown in Figure 12.15, where you should select **Key figure with characteristics**. You may select **Predefined key figure** when you are familiar with the settings behind it.

Figure 12.15 Creating a New Element

The definition of a column is very similar to the definition of a row in that you select characteristics that are relevant to you. Looking back at the reporting requirements, we have already defined the GL account in the rows, so it is not necessary to include the GL account anywhere else. For our first column, we want to return actual numbers, which requires the following characteristics, shown in Figure 12.16:

▸ **Record Type**
This indicates the type of transaction. In the **From** column, select **1** for actuals and **2** for budgets. If your solution includes assessments or distributions, you should decide whether these need to be included as part of this selection.

▸ **Version**
This is an object that needs to be included because the SAP system requires a definition of version (see Chapter 8, section 8.4.1). For actuals, you can define the default version **0** and for plan records; you should select the correct version that is needed for this column. Please note that it is also possible to make this a variable, so the user can define which version he wants to see in the report.

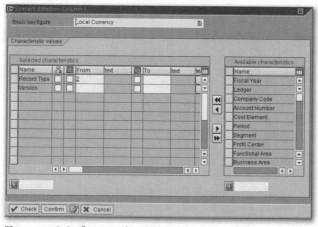

Figure 12.16 Definition of a Column

You then also need to defined the column texts as you did earlier for the row text to complete the definition of this column. The same approach should be adopted for the other columns, ensuring that you select the appropriate record type.

12.4.4 Define Formula Rows and Columns

Once you have defined more than one row (or column), when you define an additional row (or column) you have the option of defining a formula, as shown in Figure 12.17.

Figure 12.17 Defining a Formula Element

Two types of formulas are required in this report. For our example, we have a simple subtraction of values, which can be achieved easily. Double-click on the row where you want to add the row formula, and then select the **Formula** option. You are now shown a screen that includes all the rows you defined, and also a calculator pad, as shown in Figure 12.18. To subtract (or add) columns, you need to define a formula based on these values, by clicking on the column **ID** and then the subtract (or add) button and then clicking on the row **ID** to which you want to add it. Click on the checkmark button to save your formula.

Figure 12.18 Defining a Simple Formula

Like with other rows, enter a text description to explain the objective of the row. This completes your formula row.

For column variances, you can apply the same rule to determine the actual variance, by defining a formula that subtracts the actual less the budget.

For the variance percentage, you need to define a formula that calculates the variance. This is shown in the example in Figure 12.19.

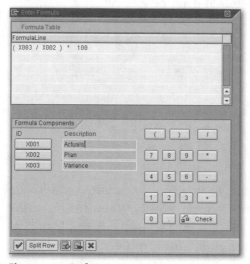

Figure 12.19 Defining a Logical Formula

The same rules that apply to columns apply to formulas and rows. Please note that you can create any complicated formula for which you can create a logic statement based on information within the report.

Having defined the rows and columns, you can define the dimensions and characteristics that apply to the entire report.

12.4.5 Define your General Data Selection

We now move on to the general data selection, which is where we define the settings that are common to the entire report. The items that are missing so far, as shown in Figure 12.20, are:

▸ **Ledger**
We define this as **0L**, in line with the completed new GL configuration (see

Chapter 4). In a multiledger scenario, you may choose to make this a variable and allow users to select for which ledger they want to run the report.

▶ **Fiscal Year**
For fiscal year, we will select a variable so the user can define for what Fiscal year they run the report.

▶ **Period**
For the posting period, we will select a variable. Because we want users to be able to run reports for a range of posting periods, we should define variables for both **From Period** and **To Period**.

For certain objects such as cost Center, profit center, and GL accounts, if you select a **From** and **To** variable, the system automatically lets you enter a master data group as well. Therefore, you can run the report for a range of cost centers or a cost center group that you have defined as part of your overall hierarchy.

The remaining object is **Cost Center**, for which we will also define a single variable, as the report is run for a single cost center at a time. You may choose to define a **From** and **To** variable and run the report for a range of cost centers.

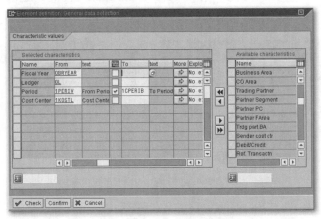

Figure 12.20 Defining Your General Data Selections

This completes the definition of all of our components within the report. We are now at the stage where you can make cosmetic changes to the report to make it more presentable for your users. We will now look at the report layout.

12.4.6 Report Layout

Within the report layout, you can define important settings that influence the report's appearance.

Change Report Layout

From the menu options, select **Formatting • Report Layout**. This opens up the screen where you can change the layout of the report. We now consider some of the more common options available to you on a variety of tabs. The first tab is the **Page/control** tab, discussed in Table 12.3.

Page/Control tab	
Field name	**Description**
Page Size	Lets you restrict the size of your page

Table 12.3 Page/Control Tab Settings

Next, we'll look at the **Rows** tab, shown in Figure 12.21. The main sections and their descriptions are shown in Table 12.4.

Rows tab	
Section name	**Description**
Summation interval	Once the report is run, the system allows you to summarize the level of detail you want. In the **Summation interval** section, you define the summation levels. You may choose to adjust this once you are familiar with the detail of your report.
Totals item	If your rows contain many values (e.g., in our rows, we selected ranges of GL accounts) and you selected the **Explode** option, then **Totals item** lets you specify how the total of those lines appears.
Treatment of zero rows	Your report may include a number of characteristics, and this option allows you to control the way in which you treat the lines that have no values to return.

Table 12.4 Rows Tab Settings

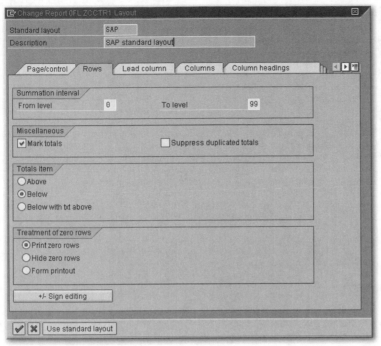

Figure 12.21 Change Report Layout: Rows Tab

On the **Lead column** tab, shown in Figure 12.22, you can configure the sections and fields as explained in Table 12.5.

Lead column tab	
Section/Field name	**Description**
Contents	Here you can define what information is displayed in the lead column.
(Lead column) **Width**	Controls the width of your lead column.
(Lead column) **Position**	Allows you to move the lead column "along the page." The default is Position 1. If you choose Position 2, the lead column will appear as the second column in the report, with column 1 coming before it. This can be a nice layout touch for your report.

Table 12.5 Lead Column Tab Settings

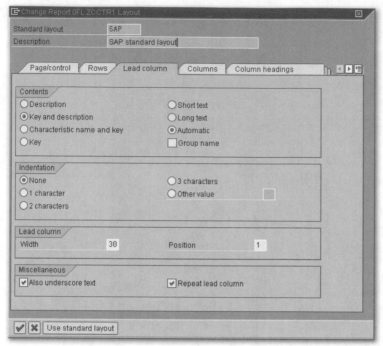

Figure 12.22 Change Report Layout: Lead Column Tab

On the Language-dependent tab, shown in Figure 12.23, you can configure the sections as explained in Table 12.6.

Language-dependent tab	
Field/Section name	**Description**
Decimal display	Here you define how to display the decimal point. You may decide to use the **User Parameters** option, as this is most flexible.
Debit/credit sign (+/-)	Here you define how debits and credits appear on the report. This should be consistent with your organization's general reporting rules to ensure that figures are commonly understood.

Table 12.6 Language-Dependent Tab Settings

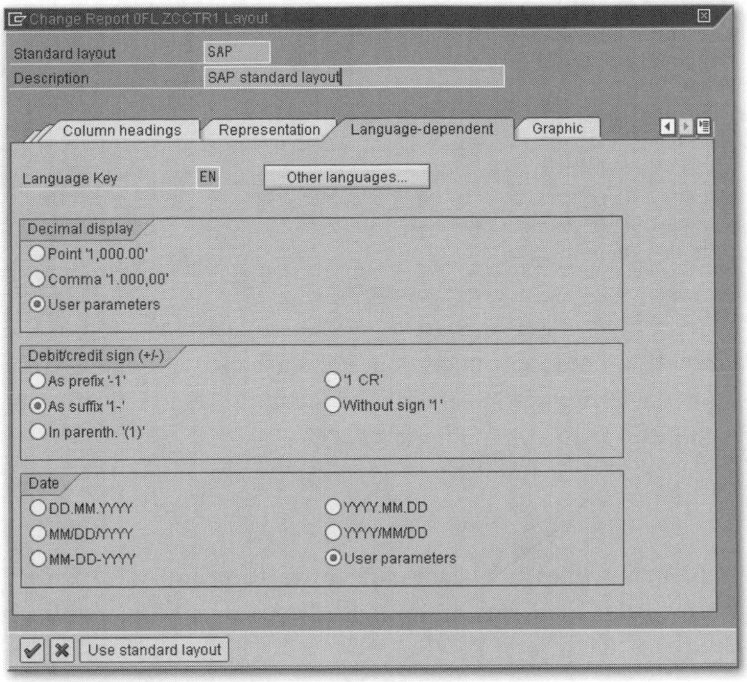

Figure 12.23 Change Report Layout: Language-Dependent Tab

Decimal Places

Decimal places are best defined within the control of the rows and columns. This is accessed through the same menu option **Formatting • Row** (or **Column**).

12.4.7 Other Report Layout Formatting

In this section we will look at some other report layout formatting options, including using flexible dimensions within a report, adding rows, using underlining and colors for emphasis, and using report texts.

Flexible Dimensions within the Report

The characteristics and dimensions allocated to the general data selection criteria can be configured as flexible dimensions within the report using the icon shown in Figure 12.24. If you had selected more than one cost center in this example, then after running the report, you could navigate between each individual cost center in the report.

Figure 12.24 Activating Flexible Dimensions in Your Report

A good example of this is if you have a multiledger scenario and want to run the same report to produce different reporting output. For such a situation, make the dimension **Ledger** a Variable in your general data selections. Then activate it in your report in the same way as shown in Figure 12.23.

Additional Rows

You may want to add blank lines between some rows to group information together. You do this by selecting the menu option **Edit • Rows • Insert blank row**.

Emphasize your Rows with Colors and Underlines

You can define colors for rows to ensure that they stand out. Using this function in combination with adding blank lines makes your report layout more presentable. To do so, you need to first select a row to which you want to apply the format. Then from the top menu options select **Formatting • Row**. This displays the **Row Formatting** screen shown in Figure 12.25.

Figure 12.25 Emphasize Your Row with Color and Underlines

Here you can choose to add an **Overscore** or **Underscore** to a row, or both, and you can add colors to the row. Click on the checkmark button to make your selections.

Report Texts

You can also add text to a report, in different locations, including a title page, header, footer, end page, and text for export. These are all accessed from the menu option, **Extras • Report Texts**. For our report, we only want to create a report header, but the same logic used for the header can be applied to the other locations to define standard text.

From the header option, you enter plain text, selection parameters, or general variables. For our example report, shown earlier in Figure 12.8, you need to first type the information shown in Figure 12.26 into the header, laid out as you would like to see it on your report.

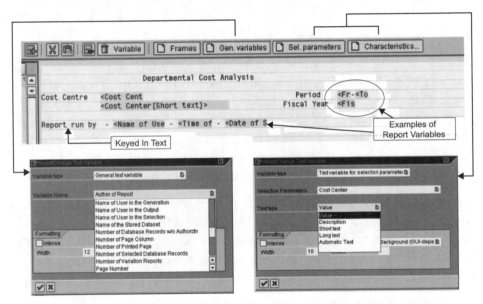

Figure 12.26 Adding Report Header Text

Then you assign the selection parameters that relate to the header. To do so, click on **Sel. Parameters**, and this will display the parameters available to you. This list will correspond to the characteristics and dimensions we defined as variables in our report. You have the option of returning the actual value (e.g., Cost Center

= 1000) or the text associated with the value (e.g., Cost Center = US Marketing North).

In our example, we want to include both of these, so we first insert the variable for the cost center value, and then below that we insert the variable for the cost center text. On the other side of the page, include the selection parameters for period and fiscal year in the same way as you did for cost center.

We also want to include in the header information about the person who ran the report. This information comes from the general variables report. We are specifically looking for the "selection" information, so you should select the time, date, and user involved in the report selection, because this refers to the point at which the report selection criteria were entered and the report run.

This completes the header, and you can save your configuration and exit. The same approach can be used for creating other report texts. Next, we will look at assigning a report group.

12.4.8 Assign Report Group

The final component of the report is the report group, which is required to run the report. A *report group* holds information related to the report that allows you to generate and execute it. The other important information contained in the report group are the drill-down features of the report that allow you to break down the numbers to show the line items from which they were created. Generation of a report happens when a component of the report is changed—either the report itself, a hierarchy within it, or the information held in the report group.

You can define the report group from within the report or from the **Change Report Group** (Transaction code gr52) option, which we will look at later. To define a report group from within the report, once you have configured all of your elements within the report, select the menu option **Environment • Assign Report Group**. You will be taken to the screen shown in Figure 12.27.

> **Note**
>
> You should define a convention of what names you will give to your reports and their report groups.

Figure 12.27 Assign Report Group to Report

If you enter a report group that does not already exist, the system will create it for you from this screen. You can have more than one report within the same report group, so if you have reports that are similar, you can enter them into the same report group. When you run this report group, the system will run the data for all reports within the report group, so it may take longer to run. Click on the **Execute** button to run the report.

Next, before we talk about report selection criteria, let us look changing report group options.

12.4.9 Change Report Group

Once you have created a report group, you maintain its settings using the path **SAP Easy Access Menu • Information System • Ad hoc reports • Report Painter • Report Writer • Report Group,** or you can use Transaction code gr52. This brings up the screen shown in Figure 12.28. Any changes made to the report or the report group require a regeneration of the report group. The system will do this automatically if you do not do it manually.

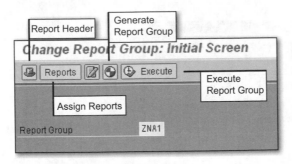

Figure 12.28 Editing the Report Group

Inside the report group, we first look at the **Change Report Group: Header** screen, shown in Figure 12.29. In this screen, you specify a **Description** for the report group, and also assign the **Report/report interface**. These interfaces are the drill-downs attached to this report group.

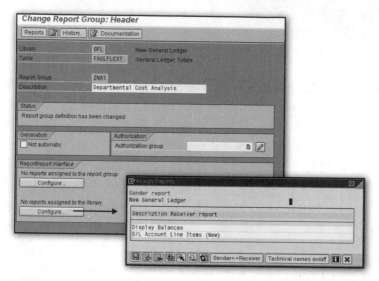

Figure 12.29 Change Report Group: Header

A drill-down is best demonstrated when you run the report. In the example shown in Figure 12.30, you can see that there is an amount of 400,469. If you want to know the breakdown of this value, you can double-click on the value, and any drill-downs (report/report interfaces) assigned to the report or the report group become active.

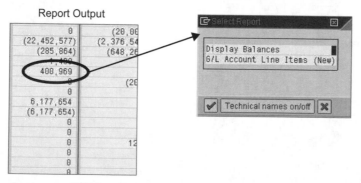

Figure 12.30 Drill-Down Function within Report Painter Reports

We defined the report/report interfaces in the header, as previously shown in Figure 12.29. You can select SAP transactions, programs, or other Report Painter reports. The usual drill-downs are:

▶ **Display Balances**—FAGLB03

▶ **GL Account Line Items (new)**—FAGLL03

This concludes the creation of a sample report. You should now be in a position to create this report, as well as create additional reports to meet your own requirements.

12.5   Summary

The objective of this chapter was to discuss the common reporting tools available to you to deliver your organization's reporting requirements. We covered the following areas:

▶ The processes you should adopt to gather reporting requirements and align them to reporting solutions

▶ How standard reports can deliver benefit

▶ The improvements to reporting as a result of the new GL

▶ The process of creating a management report with Report Painter

▶ The scope of this chapter should provide you with a good overview of the reporting options available address the numerous reporting requirements often put forward by the user community.

About the Authors

Naeem Arif is an experienced SAP Consultant, having started his SAP career in 1995 on version 3.0h. He has been involved in the successful delivery of more than 12 projects across the full SAP ERP Financials landscape, working for some of the largest SAP consultancies in the world.

Sheikh Tauseef is a highly-experienced SAP consultant with a track record of delivering quality SAP ERP Financials implementation projects across North America, Europe and Pakistan. During his career, Tauseef, who is a Chartered Accountant, has worked for global consultancies and brings an international perspective to the book.

Index

P

Y

year end
definition, 415

Z

ZDI, 244
Zero-balancing, 127, 146
document splitting, 147

Gain unique and practical insights to U.S. tax issues from an SAP perspective

Learn about tax withholding and reporting, record retention, federal income tax integration, tax-related master data, and more

359 pp., 2007, 69,95 Euro / US$ 69.95
ISBN 978-1-59229-155-7

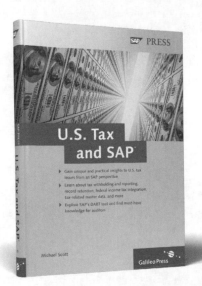

U.S. Tax and SAP

www.sap-press.com

Michael Scott

U.S. Tax and SAP

If you have an SAP implementation and have been frustrated by complex US taxation issues, you've come to the right place for answers. In the post-Sarbanes-Oxley era, this book is the pre-eminent resource that combines US tax knowledge with SAP system knowledge. Based on ECC 6.0, this engaging reference guide written in an engaging conversational style—provides practical information, examples, and tips, to help answer your taxation problems. If you are part of an SAP implementation team, you'll learn about tax requirements and the techniques needed to solve tax-related problems. If you are in the tax group you'll understand what can and cannot be done to solve tax issues, while gaining a detailed understanding of SAP's DART tool. In addition, interested IRS and financial auditors can also learn about the DART tool, and discover the tax solutions and controls offered by SAP.